AF684397

Contributions to Finance and Accounting

The book series 'Contributions to Finance and Accounting' features the latest research from research areas like financial management, investment, capital markets, financial institutions, FinTech and financial innovation, accounting methods and standards, reporting, and corporate governance, among others. Books published in this series are primarily monographs and edited volumes that present new research results, both theoretical and empirical, on a clearly defined topic. All books are published in print and digital formats and disseminated globally. This book series is indexed in Scopus.

Dirk Broeders • Aerdt Houben • Matteo Bonetti
Editors

Central Bank Capital in Turbulent Times

The Risk Management Dimension of Novel Monetary Policy Instruments

Springer

Editors
Dirk Broeders
European Central Bank
Frankfurt, Germany

Aerdt Houben
De Nederlandsche Bank
Amsterdam, The Netherlands

Matteo Bonetti
De Nederlandsche Bank
Amsterdam, The Netherlands

ISSN 2730-6038 ISSN 2730-6046 (electronic)
Contributions to Finance and Accounting
ISBN 978-3-031-73548-6 ISBN 978-3-031-73549-3 (eBook)
https://doi.org/10.1007/978-3-031-73549-3

This work was supported by De Nederlandsche Bank.

© The Editor(s) (if applicable) and The Author(s) 2025. This book is an open access publication.

Open Access This book is licensed under the terms of the Creative Commons Attribution 4.0 International License (http://creativecommons.org/licenses/by/4.0/), which permits use, sharing, adaptation, distribution and reproduction in any medium or format, as long as you give appropriate credit to the original author(s) and the source, provide a link to the Creative Commons license and indicate if changes were made.
The images or other third party material in this book are included in the book's Creative Commons license, unless indicated otherwise in a credit line to the material. If material is not included in the book's Creative Commons license and your intended use is not permitted by statutory regulation or exceeds the permitted use, you will need to obtain permission directly from the copyright holder.
The use of general descriptive names, registered names, trademarks, service marks, etc. in this publication does not imply, even in the absence of a specific statement, that such names are exempt from the relevant protective laws and regulations and therefore free for general use.
The publisher, the authors and the editors are safe to assume that the advice and information in this book are believed to be true and accurate at the date of publication. Neither the publisher nor the authors or the editors give a warranty, expressed or implied, with respect to the material contained herein or for any errors or omissions that may have been made. The publisher remains neutral with regard to jurisdictional claims in published maps and institutional affiliations.

This Springer imprint is published by the registered company Springer Nature Switzerland AG
The registered company address is: Gewerbestrasse 11, 6330 Cham, Switzerland

If disposing of this product, please recycle the paper.

Foreword

Central banks globally are navigating unprecedented challenges, grappling with significant financial losses and uncertainties that test their resilience. At the heart of these challenges lies central bank capital, which serves to absorb shocks confronting monetary systems. The workshop titled "Central Bank Capital in Turbulent Times," held in Amsterdam on April 11 and 12, 2024, gathered leading experts to discuss these issues, share insights, and propose innovative strategies for the future of central bank capital. This book compiles the exceptional contributions presented during the event.

Central bank capital often carries an air of mystique. On the one hand, it plays a secondary role in supporting a central bank's objectives, because a central bank cannot default if it has the authority to issue legal tender. Indeed, as long as the present discounted value of future revenues—seigniorage—exceeds expected costs and losses, a central bank remains in a viable financial position. In this respect, central banks differ fundamentally from commercial banks. Moreover, a central bank typically has the implicit backing of its shareholder, the government, as a systemically crucial national institution.

On the other hand, adequate central bank capital adds to the credibility, independence, and effectiveness of monetary policy implementation. Specifically, capital is a primary tool for absorbing losses from monetary policy actions, safeguarding the central bank's room for maneuver when such losses emerge. This raises questions about optimal capital levels, particularly when central bank risk taking changes. Over the past decade, quantitative easing has reshaped central bank balance sheets, creating a significant mismatch between long-duration investments and short-duration funding. While quantitative easing has evolved into a conventional monetary policy tool at the effective lower bound, higher interest rates have more recently exposed central banks to the increased attendant risks and losses. Thus, central banks must critically evaluate their capital levels from a forward-looking perspective and design policies that reflect these realities. More risk necessitates more capital to bolster resilience in future crises.

Ultimately, central bank capital is public money that could serve other societal purposes, and negative capital constitutes a public liability. Hence, transparency on central bank finances should also be a guiding principle. Central banks must be prepared to discuss their monetary policy decisions openly, explaining how these decisions fulfill their mandate and impact the real economy and public finances. They should also be transparent about how their decisions affect their balance sheets and capital, highlighting their crucial role in risk absorption during crises.

While mandates vary across jurisdictions, central banks can learn from each other, sharing best practices and establishing common principles for accounting, risk management, and capital adequacy. Such principles could ensure regular evaluations and adjustments of capital levels to maintain resilience, absorb unexpected losses, adapt to evolving risks, and effectively fulfill their mandates under changing economic conditions.

This book assists central banks in establishing robust capital policies to address the challenges they face. This includes safeguarding their profitability, creating additional buffers during periods when risks rise, and developing frameworks that enable operations during times of reduced capital. Continuous dialogue with key stakeholders and the public is essential to account for the use of public resources. Adequate central bank capital is in the end crucial for maintaining trust in money and in financial stability.

Governor of De Nederlandsche Bank, Klaas Knot
Chair of the Financial Stability Board
Amsterdam, The Netherlands

Acknowledgments

This book is based on the proceedings of the workshop "Central Bank Capital in Turbulent Times," held at hotel The Grand in Amsterdam, the Netherlands, on April 11 and 12, 2024. The contributions in this book are written in a personal capacity, and the views expressed are those of the authors. These views do not necessarily reflect those of the organizations with which the authors are affiliated. The responsibility for the content of each chapter lies entirely with the individual authors.

The editors would like to extend their heartfelt gratitude to all the contributors to this book and to the participants of the workshop. Special thanks go to De Nederlandsche Bank for its financial support. We are particularly indebted to the following individuals for their guidance and assistance in organizing the workshop: Janine Bond, Kees Bouter, Katja Deinema, Daniel Dimitrov, Silvia Caserta, Renske Heijs van Veen, Linda Hovenier, Kobe van Itterbeeck, Klaas Knot, Fernando Monar, Bastiaan Postma, Corina Ruhe, Olaf Sleijpen, Jan Smit, and Paul Wessels.

Introduction to Central Bank Capital in Turbulent Times

Central banks play a crucial role in the global financial system, acting as the backbone of monetary policy and economic stability. Their ability to implement monetary policies, maintain financial stability, and manage crises is fundamentally linked to their capital adequacy. The importance of central bank capital has grown in recent years due to a combination of unprecedented economic challenges, evolving financial stability concerns, and emerging external risks such as climate change and loss of biodiversity. This volume aims to provide a comprehensive analysis of central bank capital across three main dimensions: its theoretical and practical importance, its role amid changing policy environments, and the implications of external environmental changes.

In recent years, central banks around the world have faced unprecedented challenges that have tested their resilience and adaptability. The Global Financial Crisis of 2008, followed by the prolonged period of unconventional monetary policies, the economic disruptions caused by the COVID-19 pandemic, and the unjustified war in Ukraine have all impacted central bank balance sheets. Large-scale asset purchases, commonly known as Quantitative Easing (QE), and other unconventional monetary policies such as long-term lending operations have expanded central bank balance sheets to levels never seen before. As interest rates rise and economic conditions shift, these bloated balance sheets have started to generate substantial losses, posing new challenges for central bank capital adequacy.

At the same time, the financial landscape is evolving with the advent of digital currencies and advancements in financial technology. Central banks are exploring the potential issuance of central bank digital currency (CBDC), which could transform the way money is used and managed. The implications of such digital currencies on central bank balance sheets, profitability, and risk management are not yet fully understood, adding another layer of complexity to the capital adequacy discussion.

Moreover, the growing recognition of climate change and environmental risks has brought new dimensions to the responsibilities of central banks. As stewards of financial stability, central banks are considering how climate-related risks can impact the financial system and their own balance sheets. The transition to a low-carbon economy poses both risks and opportunities, requiring central banks to adapt their policies and frameworks to support sustainable finance while maintaining their core mandates.

The Structure of This Book

This book is structured into three parts to provide a comprehensive analysis of contemporary thinking about central bank capital.

Part I: The Importance of Central Bank Capital

Part I focuses on the fundamental importance of central bank capital, exploring its role from both theoretical and practical perspectives. It examines historical instances of central banks operating with negative equity, the determinants of central banks' financial performance, and the fiscal implications of central bank losses. This section provides a deep dive into how central banks have navigated financial challenges in the past and the lessons that can be applied today.

Willem Buiter's chapter, "Central Bank Capital Adequacy: the Simple Analytics and Complex Politics," sets the stage by examining the significant operating and balance sheet losses many central banks have faced since 2022. Buiter highlights the unique nature of irredeemable central bank money, which functions as a liability only in name, and discusses how central banks like the Fed and the ECB have managed these losses on their balance sheets. He points out that central banks can technically avoid insolvency by increasing the present discounted value of seigniorage but notes that this strategy may compromise their monetary policy and financial stability mandates, potentially necessitating recapitalization by the Treasury, thereby threatening their independence.

In "Central Bank Capital and Trust in Money: Lessons from History for the Digital Age," Sarah Bell, Jon Frost, Boris Hofmann, Damiano Sandri, and Hyun Song Shin adopt a historical perspective, demonstrating that central banks have operated successfully even with negative equity. They argue that a negative equity position does not inherently undermine trust in money, but cautionary tales from the Bank of Amsterdam in the 1700s and emerging market crises in the late twentieth century underscore the need for adequate fiscal backing. They emphasize that private holders' portfolio decisions are pivotal and that there are critical tipping points where trust in traditional forms of money can erode in favor of alternatives.

Igor Goncharov, Zoltán Novotny-Farkas, and Carmine Pizzo's chapter, "Accounting Policies, Distribution Rules and the Financial Performance of Central Banks," provides an empirical analysis of 148 central banks over the period from 2010 to 2022. They document a notable deterioration in central banks' capital buffers and profitability, particularly in 2022, driven by economic factors such as inflation and increased balance sheet size. They find that financial reporting choices aimed at transparency, such as adopting IFRS and fair value reporting, have led to greater volatility in central bank profits and a higher incidence of losses and capital shortfalls. Their findings highlight potential threats to central bank financial independence and suggest possible reporting options to mitigate these issues.

Stephen G. Cecchetti and Jens Hilscher, in "Fiscal Consequences of Central Bank Losses," analyze the fiscal ramifications of central bank losses resulting from the large-scale asset purchases post-Global Financial Crisis and during the pandemic. They argue that these losses, which vary significantly across central banks, are a by-product of quantitative easing policies and need to be assessed against the benefits these policies provided. They also highlight that losses differ qualitatively depending on whether the central bank chooses to buy domestic or foreign assets, thus resulting in transfers either within or between countries. Their empirical analysis reveals a marked variation in losses as a percentage of GDP across different central banks.

The final chapter in this part, "Central Bank Capital and Shareholder Relationship" by Matteo Bonetti, Dirk Broeders, Damiaan Chen, and Daniel Dimitrov, explores the financial risks assumed by central banks through monetary policy operations. They propose an option pricing framework to examine the risk-sharing mechanism between central banks and their shareholders that follows from dividend and recapitalization policies. They emphasize the importance of a balanced equilibrium approach to maintain central bank independence and credibility. They also analyze potential risk-shifting implications of the capital policy via monetary policy that are present in the dividend and recapitalization agreements with the shareholders.

Part II: Central Bank Capital and Changes in the Policy Environment

Part II shifts the focus to the changing policy environment and how it affects central bank capital. It discusses the consequences of last-resort policies during crises and the evolving perspectives on quantitative easing. Further it examines the impact of digital currencies on central bank profitability and risk management. This section highlights the dynamic nature of central bank operations and the need for adaptable capital policies to ensure long-term stability and independence.

Kathryn Dominguez, in "Consequences of Last-Resort Policy for Central Bank Balance Sheets," examines the impact of pandemic-era last-resort policies on central bank balance sheets. She provides a comparative analysis of expanded asset holdings and subsequent balance sheet reductions, finding that markets have generally taken a benign view of central bank losses resulting from extraordinary interventions. Her analysis suggests that these policies have not impaired central banks' ability to achieve their monetary policy and financial stability objectives.

"New Perspectives on Quantitative Easing and Central Bank Capital Policies" by Tobias Adrian, Christopher Erceg, Marcin Kolasa, Jesper Lindé, Roger McLeod, Romain Veyrune, and Pawel Zabczyk, revisits the role of QE in light of recent high inflation. They argue that QE should be assessed based on its macroeconomic benefits rather than central bank profits or losses. Using an open economy DSGE model, they show that QE can significantly boost output and inflation during deep recessions, despite central bank losses, and advocate a forward-looking approach to profit allocation policies to protect central bank autonomy.

David Vestin, Anders Vredin, and Magnus Åhl, in "Central Bank Capital and Independence: A Quantitative Case Study," focus on the Swedish Riksbank's experiences in their discussion of the importance of central bank profitability and capital buffers. They present a method for estimating the probability of recapitalization and highlight the challenges posed by financial market volatility and legislative frameworks, suggesting that current conditions lead to a high likelihood of future recapitalizations.

Ulrich Bindseil, Marco Marrazzo, and Stephan Sauer, in their chapter "The Impact of Central Bank Digital Currency on Central Bank Profitability, Risk Taking and Capital," analyze the potential implications of issuing central bank digital currency (CBDC). They argue that while CBDC may increase the central bank balance sheet size, its impact on profitability and risk depends significantly on its design and adoption. They use scenario analyses to highlight key drivers and conclude that well-established risk management frameworks can mitigate the financial risks associated with CBDC.

Part III: Central Bank Capital and Changes in the External Environment

Part III addresses the external changes and emerging risks that central banks must consider. It explores the implications of climate change and environmental risks on central bank capital, emphasizing the need for proactive and resilient approaches to manage these challenges. This section underscores the importance of integrating sustainability into central bank policies and the potential for collaboration with other stakeholders to promote a smooth transition to a low-carbon economy.

Dirk Schoenmaker, in "Impact of Transitions on the Financial Stability and LOLR Roles of Central Banks," argues that central banks should consider transition risks as endogenous and implement macroprudential limits on carbon exposures to facilitate a smooth transition to a low-carbon economy. He emphasizes that effective macroprudential policies can minimize climate-induced financial instability and reduce the need for last-resort assistance to carbon-heavy banks, which could otherwise prompt substantial central bank losses.

In "Through the Lens of Legal Mandate: Central Bank Capital in a Time of Climate Crisis," Megan Bowman and Anat Keller examine how central banks can use "soft" capital to address climate and nature-related risks within their legal mandates. They argue that central banks need to be resilient and sustainable internally to effectively meet climate challenges, and they advocate for the development of "regulatory ecosystems for sustainable finance" to promote cooperation and facilitate the net zero transition.

In these three parts, this volume provides a holistic view of central bank capital, integrating theoretical insights, empirical evidence, and practical considerations in the context of evolving monetary policies and external environmental challenges. This comprehensive analysis is crucial for understanding the complex dynamics of central bank capital and its critical role in maintaining financial and economic stability.

The Outlook for Central Bank Capital

This volume provides a comprehensive understanding of central bank capital, emphasizing its pivotal role in the financial system and the challenges and opportunities it presents. By analyzing historical experiences, evolving policies, and emerging risks, it offers valuable insights for monetary policymakers, risk managers, and researchers about the future of central bank capital. Four main lessons emerge from this exploration:

One, central bank capital is not merely a static financial buffer but a dynamic and resilient component. Historical case studies, such as central banks operating with negative equity, demonstrate that trust and mandate fulfillment can persist even under financial strain. Recent events, like the Global Financial Crisis and the COVID-19 pandemic, show how central banks have managed significant balance sheet expansions and operating losses. This resilience underscores the importance of flexible and robust capital management strategies that adapt to changing economic conditions without compromising core functions and independence. While central bank capital is not a necessary or sufficient condition for trust in money, this book also shows that its value is influenced by the solidity of public accounts, institutional frameworks, and private portfolio decisions. The use of money is subject to tipping points below which trust in the currency erodes.

Two, changes in monetary and financial stability policies profoundly affect central bank capital. The exploration of tools like QE, CBDCs, and last-resort policies highlights their influence on the financial health and risk profiles of central banks. While QE has provided crucial economic stimulus during crises, it has also led to significant balance sheet losses in the aftermath, raising questions about long-term implications. Similarly, the potential introduction of CBDCs presents both opportunities and risks, impacting balance sheet dynamics and profitability. This lesson emphasizes the need for continuous reassessment and updating of capital policies to manage financial impacts effectively and maintain operational independence and credibility.

Three, central banks must integrate emerging risks, such as those related to climate change and nature loss, into their capital management frameworks. The radical uncertainty surrounding climate change increases risks, necessitating forward-looking capital frameworks. Risk managers can exploit scenario analyses to account for the impact of extreme adverse conditions on capital. As the global financial system recognizes the material risks posed by climate change, central banks must also adapt by incorporating these risks into their financial stability and monetary policy frameworks. This includes managing transition risks as endogenous, developing measures to comprehend and mitigate physical risks, and exploiting "soft" capital forms like organizational cultural capital to contribute to a sustainable economy. Central banks can play a proactive role in facilitating a smooth transition to a low-carbon economy, thereby mitigating potential financial instabilities and ensuring resilient capital frameworks in the face of long-term environmental challenges.

Four, transparency about the benefits of monetary policy and the potential implications for central bank capital is essential to maintain credibility and effectiveness. Central banks worldwide are facing challenges with a structural decline in profitability alongside an increase in balance sheet size and associated risks, highlighting the growing importance of central bank capital. This capital should be considered in a broad context, incorporating a comprehensive cost–benefit analysis of central bank operations that accounts for their overall economic impact, including benefits like stable prices, recession avoidance, and reduced public sector interest payments. Transparency is also related to the relationship between accounting methods and central bank capital, requiring a balance between loss absorption speed and balance sheet volatility.

These lessons collectively offer a detailed understanding of the multifaceted role that central bank capital plays in the pursuit of their mandates and in their adaptation to both internal policy changes and external environmental shifts. They highlight the importance of historical resilience, the need for adaptable policies in a changing financial landscape, the forward-looking integration of environmental risks, and the critical importance of transparency in relation to trust.

Dirk Broeders
Aerdt Houben
Matteo Bonetti

Contents

Part I The Importance of Central Bank Capital

Central Bank Capital Adequacy: The Simple Analytics and Complex Politics 3
Willem H. Buiter

Central Bank Capital and Trust in Money: Lessons from History for the Digital Age 45
Sarah Bell, Jon Frost, Boris Hofmann, Damiano Sandri, and Hyun Song Shin

Accounting Policies, Distribution Rules, and the Financial Performance of Central Banks 61
Igor Goncharov, Zoltán Novotny-Farkas, and Carmine Pizzo

Fiscal Consequences of Central Bank Losses 95
Stephen G. Cecchetti and Jens Hilscher

Central Bank Capital and Shareholder Relationship 125
Matteo Bonetti, Dirk Broeders, Damiaan Chen, and Daniel Dimitrov

Part II Central Bank Capital and Changes in the Policy Environment

Consequences of Last-Resort Policy for Central Bank Balance Sheets 167
Kathryn M. E. Dominguez

New Perspectives on Quantitative Easing and Central Bank Capital Policies 187
Tobias Adrian, Christopher Erceg, Marcin Kolasa, Jesper Lindé, Roger McLeod, Romain Veyrune, and Pawel Zabczyk

Central Bank Capital and Independence: A Quantitative Case Study 215
David Vestin, Anders Vredin, and Magnus Åhl

The Impact of Central Bank Digital Currency on Central Bank Profitability, Risk Taking and Capital 249
Ulrich Bindseil, Marco Marrazzo, and Stephan Sauer

Part III Central Bank Capital and Changes in the External Environment

Impact of Transitions on the Financial Stability and LOLR Roles of Central Banks 275
Dirk Schoenmaker

Through the Lens of Legal Mandate: Central Bank Capital in a Time of Climate Crisis 295
Megan Bowman and Anat Keller

Index 315

Contributors

Tobias Adrian International Monetary Fund, Washington, DC, USA

Magnus Åhl National Institute of Economic Research, Stockholm, Sweden

Sarah Bell Bank for International Settlements, Basel, Switzerland

Ulrich Bindseil European Central Bank, Frankfurt, Germany

Matteo Bonetti De Nederlandsche Bank, Amsterdam, The Netherlands

Megan Bowman King's College, London, UK

Dirk Broeders European Central Bank, Frankfurt, Germany

Willem H. Buiter Maverecon LLC, New York, NY, USA

Stephen G. Cecchetti Brandeis International Business School, Waltham, MA, USA

Damiaan Chen De Nederlandsche Bank, Amsterdam, The Netherlands

Daniel Dimitrov De Nederlandsche Bank, Amsterdam, The Netherlands

Kathryn M. E. Dominguez University of Michigan, Ann Arbor, MI, USA

Christopher Erceg International Monetary Fund, Washington, DC, USA

Jon Frost Bank for International Settlements, Basel, Switzerland

Igor Goncharov Lancaster University Management School, Lancaster, UK

Jens Hilscher University of California, Davis, CA, USA

Boris Hofmann Bank for International Settlements, Basel, Switzerland

Anat Keller King's College, London, UK

Marcin Kolasa International Monetary Fund, Washington, DC, USA

Jesper Lindé International Monetary Fund, Washington, DC, USA

Marco Marrazzo European Central Bank, Frankfurt, Germany

Roger McLeod International Monetary Fund, Washington, DC, USA

Zoltán Novotny-Farkas Vienna University of Economics and Business, Vienna, Austria

Carmine Pizzo Lancaster University Management School, Lancaster, UK

Damiano Sandri Bank for International Settlements, Basel, Switzerland

Stephan Sauer European Central Bank, Frankfurt, Germany

Dirk Schoenmaker Rotterdam School of Management, Erasmus University, Rotterdam, The Netherlands

Hyun Song Shin Bank for International Settlements, Basel, Switzerland

David Vestin Sveriges Riksbank, Stockholm, Sweden

Romain Veyrune International Monetary Fund, Washington, DC, USA

Anders Vredin Sveriges Riksbank, Stockholm, Sweden

Pawel Zabczyk International Monetary Fund, Washington, DC, USA

List of Figures

Central Bank Capital and Trust in Money: Lessons from History for the Digital Age

Fig. 1 Evolution of central bank equity.. 48
Fig. 2 Central bank finances: balance sheet and the drivers of equity............ 49
Fig. 3 No association between central bank equity and future inflation......... 51
Fig. 4 Examples of large and persistent negative central bank equity levels.. 52
Fig. 5 After Bank of Amsterdam equity turned negative, the agio collapsed.. 54
Fig. 6 Fiscal origins of high inflation.. 56
Fig. 7 Exchange rate pass-through.. 57

Accounting Policies, Distribution Rules, and the Financial Performance of Central Banks

Fig. 1 Trends in central banks' profitability. 69
Fig. 2 Trends in central banks' equity. 71
Fig. 3 Central bank earnings (ROA) and currency peg. 91

Fiscal Consequences of Central Bank Losses

Fig. 1 Total assets of the Federal Reserve and Eurosystem Jan 2006 to Mar 2024, weekly. 96
Fig. 2 Bank of England Asset Purchase Facility Net Profits and Losses, 2013 to 2071. 112
Fig. 3 Bank of England Asset Purchase Facility Net Losses with and without sales, 2024 to 2031. 113
Fig. 4 Federal Reserve Transfers to the US Treasury, 1994 to 2030. 115
Fig. 5 Swiss National Bank Net Income 2005 to 2023, percent of GDP. 118
Fig. 6 Eurosystem Profit and Loss, 2000 to 2031, percent of GDP. 121

Central Bank Capital and Shareholder Relationship

Fig. 1 Central bank equity payoff at maturity 135
Fig. 2 Equity value as a function of asset value. 136
Fig. 3 Indifference curves in terms of policy parameters κ_Π and κ_C 139
Fig. 4 Constraints and feasible combinations of policy parameters. 143
Fig. 5 Stackelberg solutions. 146
Fig. 6 Option and equity value as a function of risk. 149
Fig. 7 Indifference curves. 151
Fig. 8 Feasible region. 152
Fig. 9 Stackelberg equilibrium solution. 153
Fig. 10 Stackelberg equilibrium (CB chooses first). 154
Fig. 11 The inverses option value functions. 160

Consequences of Last-Resort Policy for Central Bank Balance Sheets

Fig. 1 Currency values against the dollar. 172
Fig. 2 Central Bank total assets (Trillions of US$). 178

New Perspectives on Quantitative Easing and Central Bank Capital Policies

Fig. 1 Ex ante: deep liquidity trap. 199
Fig. 2 Ex post: deep liquidity trap. 200
Fig. 3 Ex ante: shallow liquidity trap. 201
Fig. 4 Ex post: shallow liquidity trap with forward guidance commitment. 203
Fig. 5 Distributions of Central Bank Profits to the Government (average over 2019–2022). 207

Central Bank Capital and Independence: A Quantitative Case Study

Fig. 1 The Riksbank's equity and total capital. 221
Fig. 2 The Riksbank's annual profits and transfers to the government budget. 222
Fig. 3 Assumptions for baseline and sensitivity scenarios. 238
Fig. 4 Equity development in baseline and sensitivity scenarios. 239
Fig. 5 Near-term probability of recapitalization as a function of capital injection in 2024 242

The Impact of Central Bank Digital Currency on Central Bank Profitability, Risk Taking and Capital

Fig. 1 Flow chart of CBDC issuance process. 255
Fig. 2 Financial accounts representation of CBDC 256
Fig. 3 Stylised central bank balance sheet and related remuneration. 258

Impact of Transitions on the Financial Stability and LOLR Roles of Central Banks

Fig. 1 The x-curve of transition dynamics. 278
Fig. 2 Transition to electric driving....279
Fig. 3 Carbon emissions pathways and financial stability....287

Through the Lens of Legal Mandate: Central Bank Capital in a Time of Climate Crisis

Fig. 1 Diagram of central bank's powers and legitimacy....310

List of Tables

Central Bank Capital Adequacy: The Simple Analytics and Complex Politics

Table 1 Central Bank Conventional Balance Sheet 12
Table 2 Central Bank Comprehensive Balance Sheet 15
Table 3 Alternative but Equivalent Central Bank Comprehensive Balance Sheet 16
Table 4 Treasury Conventional Balance Sheet 17
Table 5 Treasury Comprehensive Balance Sheet 19
Table 6 State Conventional Balance Sheet 19
Table 7 State Comprehensive Balance Sheet 21

Accounting Policies, Distribution Rules, and the Financial Performance of Central Banks

Table 1 Central banks' use of accounting frameworks and accounting policies 66
Table 2 Descriptive statistics 70
Table 3 Central bank financial performance and accounting policies 73
Table 4 Factors associated with central bank financial performance: accounting rules and economic factors 75
Table 5 Central bank financial performance and accounting policies 79
Table 6 The impact of dividend distribution rules 83

Fiscal Consequences of Central Bank Losses

Table 1 Stylized balanced sheets 102
Table 2 Consolidated balance sheet of the public sector 103
Table 3 Consolidated balance sheet of the private sector 104
Table 4 Stylized Balance Sheet of the Domestic Central Bank in an Open Economy 117
Table 5 Stylized Central Bank Balance Sheets in a Two-Country Monetary Union 119

Central Bank Capital and Shareholder Relationship

Table 1 Central bank's accounting (Marked-to-Market) balance sheet............131
Table 2 Central bank's balance sheet including the implicit options 134
Table 3 Stackelberg equilibrium combinations 147
Table 4 Different central banks' capital policies at the end of 2022 157
Table 5 Baseline model calibration...159

Consequences of Last-Resort Policy for Central Bank Balance Sheets

Table 1 Central Bank sovereign bond asset-purchase Announcements during the pandemic...170
Table 2 First announcements by central banks of enhanced LOLR during the pandemic...173
Table 3 Central Bank announcements of non-sovereign asset-purchase programs during the pandemic................................175
Table 4 Central Bank QE and QT announcements and balance sheet changes...179
Table 5 Central Bank accounting and distribution rules................................181
Table 6 Announcements of post-pandemic Central Bank losses....................182
Table 7 Annual Federal Reserve Balance Sheet Gains and Losses (billions)....183

Central Bank Capital and Independence: A Quantitative Case Study

Table 1 The Riksbank's balance sheet..225
Table 2 Variables included in the BVAR model..236
Table 3 Baseline assumptions in model-based simulations...........................237
Table 4 Recapitalization and dividend probabilities in the near term. 242
Table 5 Recapitalization probability and dividend size in the longer term, 2027–2059. 243

The Impact of Central Bank Digital Currency on Central Bank Profitability, Risk Taking and Capital

Table 1 Balance sheet and profitability impact for three digital euro demand scenarios (billion euros)..263

Impact of Transitions on the Financial Stability and LOLR Roles of Central Banks

Table 1 Micro versus macro perspective...281

Part I
The Importance of Central Bank Capital

Central Bank Capital Adequacy: The Simple Analytics and Complex Politics

Willem H. Buiter

Abstract Many central banks have incurred significant operating losses since 2022. With assets priced at fair value, many central banks have also incurred unprecedented balance sheet losses and have deeply negative equity. Fortunately, irredeemable central bank money is a liability in name only. The Fed and the ECB record losses that would bring equity below some threshold as a positive asset or negative liability on their conventional balance sheets. This *deferred asset* is a misleading version of an implicit liability in their comprehensive balance sheet or intertemporal budget constraint—the present discounted value (PDV) of net remittances to the national Treasury. A central bank without significant foreign-currency liabilities can avoid insolvency by increasing the PDV of seigniorage. If this threatens its inflation or financial stability mandates, its solvency and effective pursuit of these mandates may require indemnification of its losses or recapitalization by the Treasury. This may pose a threat to its independence.

Keywords Capital adequacy · Central bank · Central bank capital · Deferred asset

1 Introduction

Central banks are financial entities with a balance sheet and a profit and loss account. No matter how well managed they are, central banks can and do incur significant operating losses and material revaluation losses on loans and investments. An

I would like to thank Anne Sibert and Ebrahim Rahbari for helpful discussions and comments. The organizers of the workshop and the other participants provided many useful insights. Special thanks are due to Dirk Broeders whose helpful questions and suggestions greatly facilitated the editing and revision of my chapter.

W. H. Buiter (✉)
Maverecon LLC, New York, NY, USA

© The Author(s) 2025

D. Broeders et al. (eds.), *Central Bank Capital in Turbulent Times*,
Contributions to Finance and Accounting,
https://doi.org/10.1007/978-3-031-73549-3_1

example involves the operating losses and mark-to-market losses faced by many advanced economy (AE) central banks since 2022. Many of them acquired large quantities of long-duration fixed interest rate financial instruments at very low yields during the quantitative easing (QE) episodes since the Great Financial Crisis (GFC) of 2007–09, and when engaged as sovereign bond purchaser of first resort, lender of last resort (LOLR), and market maker of last resort (MMLR) during the financial upheaval and recession that followed the onset of the Covid-19 pandemic. The interest rate risk was largely unhedged. The material AE monetary tightening (rate hikes and asset purchases tapering followed by quantitative tightening (QT)) that started at the end of 2021 has caused large declines in net interest income. In many cases this turned negative. The associated significant increases in longer-maturity yields caused large mark-to-market losses on central bank holdings of long-duration fixed-rate securities and loans.[1] In addition to market risk (interest rate risk, exchange rate risk, and stock market risk in the case of the Hong Kong Monetary Authority (HKMA), the Bank of Japan (BoJ), and the Swiss National Bank (SNB)), many AE central banks now have considerable exposure to private sector credit risk and other forms of counterparty risk.

Central banks often hold significant amounts of debt issued by their own sovereign. Sovereign debt default is a material risk when the public debt burden is high relative to the government's fiscal capacity, and the debt is not denominated in a nation's own currency, as is the case for many emerging markets and developing economies (EMDEs). When a nation is part of a currency union, the national government does not have ultimate control over the central bank's asset purchases, seigniorage revenue, and remittances to its national Treasury. This makes sovereign debt default a non-trivial risk for some euro area member states, now that public debt-to-GDP ratios are often near peacetime highs, many member states run structural primary deficits, the era of near-zero or even negative neutral real interest rates may well be over, and sustainable growth rates of real GDP will likely remain modest.

Since end-2021, interest rates on reserve balances (deposits held with the central bank by commercial banks) have risen sharply in most AEs other than Japan.[2] As of February 22, 2024, they stood at 5.40% in the USA, 4.00% in the euro area, and 5.25% in the UK. On December 1, 2021, they were 0.15% in the USA, −0.50% in

[1] A more recent example with a favorable outcome for the central bank's balance sheet and bottom line are the Bank of England's (BoE's) emergency long-dated gilt purchases from September 28, 2022, till October 14, 2022. The purpose (which was successful) was to rescue pension funds engaged in liability-driven investment (LDI) that found themselves on the wrong side of a sharp increase in long-dated gilt yields following the fiscal extravaganza proposed on September 23, 2022 by the (short-lived) administration of Liz Truss. In this case, the BoE exited the £19.3 billion purchases under the emergency program within 3 months and at a profit because of a rise in government bond prices.

[2] The BoJ raised the target range for its uncollateralized overnight call rate from −0.10-0% to 0-0.10% on March 19, 2024. It also ended its yield curve control policy, which had capped the 10-year JGB yield at 1.00%. Purchases of ETFs and J-REITs were discontinued. This was the BoJ's first rate hike since 2007.

the euro area and 0.10% in the UK. Net interest expense of the European Central Bank (ECB) was €7.2 billion in 2023.[3] Net interest income had been €0.9 billion in 2022 and €1.6 billion in 2021. De Grauwe and Ji (2023) estimated in September 2023 that the Eurosystem would be paying €136 billion in interest on €3.6 trillion of reserves in 2023; the Federal Reserve System (Fed) would pay $162 billion in interest on $3.1 trillion of reserves, and the Bank of England (BoE) would pay £39 billion in interest on £909 billion of reserves. Since policy rates in all three central banks have gone up by 25 basis points from the July 2023 levels assumed by De Grauwe and Li, the 2023 interest payments are likely to have been even higher. On October 27, 2022, the ECB reduced the remuneration of minimum reserves from the rate on the main refinancing operations (MRO) to the deposit facility rate (DFR). The ECB decided on July 27, 2023 that minimum required reserves would be remunerated at 0%, which lowered Eurosystem central bank losses (the DFR was 3.50% at the time). The full DFR continues to be paid on excess reserves held in the deposit facility.[4] On March 13 the ECB announced that the spread between the MRO rate and the DFR would be reduced in September 2024 from 50 bps to 15 bps, which will have a negative impact on the Eurosystem's net interest income.

In addition to changes in long-term interest rates, a potentially important source of market risk for central banks is their exposure to foreign currency-denominated assets and liabilities. Examples of significant losses on foreign securities include the Czech National Bank (CNB) and the SNB, to be discussed further in Sect. 5.

Insolvency for central banks must mean *equitable insolvency*—failure to pay contractual, legal obligations as they fall due—rather than balance sheet insolvency or negative conventional equity, capital, or net worth—the face value of legally enforceable contractual liabilities exceeding the fair value of legally enforceable contractual assets.[5] There are two reasons why negative net worth on the conventional central bank balance sheet need not imply equitable insolvency.

The first reason is the fact that one key liability of the central bank—central bank fiat money—is a liability in name only. It can be created at effectively zero marginal cost. Central bank currency (notes and (sometimes) coins) is irredeemable: it has no redemption date or maturity period and promises to pay nothing forever. Central bank currency is surely viewed as an asset by its holder, but X amount of central bank currency is only a claim by the holder on the central bank for X amount of central bank currency. It is therefore not, in any meaningful sense, a liability of the

[3] See Annual Accounts 2023 (europa.eu).

[4] Euro area banks are required to hold a minimum of 1% of certain liabilities (mainly customers' deposits) as reserves at their national central bank. Average reserve requirements for the Reserve maintenance period that started 2023–12–20 and ended 2024–01–30 were €162.3 billion, see Minimum reserves (europa.eu). With the DFR at 4.00%, the Eurosystem saved itself €6.5 billion by having a zero interest rate on minimum required reserves rather than the DFR paid on excess reserves held in the deposit facility. Current account holdings in excess of the minimum required are remunerated at the lower of the DFR rate and 0%.

[5] Equitable insolvency is also known as "cash flow insolvency" or the failure to pass the "ability to pay test". See Buiter (2008).

central bank. I believe the same holds for central bank fiat money in the form of checkable deposits (required and excess reserves) with the central bank. These can be created at effectively zero marginal cost. There is no redemption date or maturity period. The interest rate is set by the central bank, and any interest is paid in central bank fiat money.

Central bank fiat money is therefore more akin to a perpetuity issued by the central bank that either promises to pay nothing forever or promises to pay an interest rate set by the central bank, with interest paid in central bank fiat money. The central bank's non-monetary, domestic-currency-denominated liabilities are redeemable—albeit only in central bank money. Only if the central bank is willing and able to create the necessary central bank money to service its non-monetary domestic currency-denominated liabilities, can default on these liabilities be ruled out. I believe most central banks are willing and able to do so. Insolvency concerns regarding the central bank should therefore focus on the non-monetary liabilities of the central bank that are not denominated in (and cannot be serviced with) central bank currency. This includes the foreign-currency-denominated, gold-denominated, and other deliverable commodity-denominated liabilities of the central bank. One would expect historical central bank defaults—which are few and far between—to be the result of foreign-currency-denominated, gold-denominated, or other deliverable commodity-denominated liabilities, combined with the absence of a beneficial owner with sufficiently deep foreign currency, gold, or deliverable commodity pockets. An example is the Reserve Bank of Zimbabwe, which in February 2010 failed to redeem as scheduled bonds it had issued to mining companies in lieu of cash payments for gold deposited with the central bank by the mining companies.[6]

The second reason why negative conventional net worth need not imply equitable insolvency for the central bank is the omission from the conventional balance sheet of potentially very large "implicit" assets and liabilities. The conventional balance sheet only contains legally enforceable, contractual revenue and expenditure claims—what I call *explicit* assets and liabilities. The central bank—and the Treasury—have significant non-contractual, not legally enforceable sources of revenue and expenditure. These implicit assets and liabilities must be added to the conventional balance sheet, yielding the comprehensive balance sheet (or intertemporal budget constraint (IBC)) of the central bank, the Treasury, and the consolidated State. Equitable insolvency occurs if net worth on the comprehensive balance sheet is negative.

The good news is that the ability of AE central banks to pursue their financial stability and price stability (or dual) mandates, avoid equitable insolvency, and maintain their operational independence does not appear to have been materially

[6] See Reserve Bank of Zimbabwe Defaults on Redemption of Bonds Issued to Gold Firms (voazimbabwe.com). It is possible that the Banco Central de Bolivia (BCB) assumed part of the unpaid liabilities of three state banks (issued during the 1970s and 1980s), effectively and *de jure*. In 1989 this debt amounted to around USD 194 million (see Kehoe et al. (2019)). The BCB could and did issue US dollar-denominated debt. The widespread Bolivian sovereign debt default in 1986 may have included foreign currency-denominated debt owed by the BCB.

impacted, thus far, by the recent episodes of large losses and negative conventional equity. The bad news is that realized central bank losses could become large enough to threaten some central banks with equitable insolvency unless there is either a bailout by the beneficial owner(s), or central bank monetary issuance on a scale that threatens its price stability (or dual) mandate or the financial stability mandate.

As noted, negative (conventional) equity does not mean that the central bank is *equitably* insolvent, i.e., that it will default on its legal, contractual financial obligations—its *explicit* liabilities. Nor does negative (conventional) equity mean that it will necessarily be unable to effectively pursue its mandates. Conversely, a central bank can have positive conventional equity yet be in deep longer-term *equitable* insolvency trouble, or (if it takes the necessary measures to avoid equitable insolvency) may be unable to pursue its price stability or dual mandate and its financial stability mandate effectively in anything but the very short run. Large future net remittances to the Treasury could produce such a configuration. Non-negative conventional equity is therefore neither necessary nor sufficient for a central bank to be a going concern financially and for it to be able to pursue its mandates effectively in the medium and long-term. There is no alternative to a quantitative forward-looking analysis of the IBC or comprehensive balance sheet of the central bank, presented and contrasted with the conventional balance sheet in Sect. 3. Section 4 looks at the political economy issues raised by large central bank losses and possible deeply negative conventional equity. If equitable insolvency is a serious threat, either the present discounted value (PDV) of current and future seigniorage will have to be increased or the PDV of current and future remittances to the beneficial owner of the central bank—the Treasury or Ministry of Finance of the central government (henceforth the Treasury)—will have to be reduced. With sufficiently large losses—losses that threaten to create negative equity on the comprehensive balance sheet—the political choice, if equitable insolvency is to be avoided, is between higher inflation and higher taxes or lower public spending. Section 5 looks at some recent examples of central bank losses and negative conventional equity. It addresses three capital adequacy issues for central banks. First, central banks (notably the Fed and the ECB) need to stop the deferred asset gibberish. They must be honest about potentially deeply negative conventional equity or net worth. Second, central banks need to recognize and report all unrealized capital losses (and gains) on their balance sheet (and on all off-balance sheet assets). There must be a timely determination of what past unrealized losses (and gains) imply for likely future realized capital losses (and gains). Third, there needs to be a clear and explicit profit-and-loss sharing agreement and recapitalization arrangement with the beneficial owner(s) of the central bank. For the ECB this would be the 20 national central banks of the euro area, and through them, their 20 national Treasuries. The at-times bizarre (partly or wholly private), formal ownership structure of some central banks (the central banks of Belgium, Greece, Italy, Japan, South Africa, Switzerland, Turkey, and the 12 Federal Reserve Banks of the USA (see Rossouw, 2016)) does not change the economic and political reality that the *de facto* beneficial owner of the central bank is always the national Treasury or Ministry of Finance.

The conclusion is that the implications of large losses and negative conventional equity for a central bank's ability to pursue its price stability (or dual) mandate and its financial stability mandate, effectively and sustainably, depend on the answer to the following question. Are the current and projected future seigniorage issuance, policy rates, and asset purchases required to ensure equitable solvency of the central bank consistent with its price stability mandate (or dual mandate) and its financial stability mandate only if there is, now or in the future, one or more positive net financial transfers from the fiscal authority to the central bank? If the answer to the question is affirmative, this is most likely because, without net transfers from the Treasury to the central bank, the seigniorage issuance of the central bank necessary to avoid equitable insolvency will exceed the level consistent with price stability. In that case, not only must current and/or future remittances from the central bank to its beneficial owner be reduced, but there will also be one or more future positive net transfers from the Treasury to the central bank, or recapitalizations of the central bank by the Treasury. The PDV of all current and future net transfers from the central bank to the fiscal authority could even become negative. The key political economy issue is whether the Treasury is willing and able to contemplate higher future tax revenues and/or lower future public spending to make up for the lower (possibly negative) PDV of remittances from the central bank to the Treasury required for the effective pursuit of price stability.

2 How Do Central Banks Report Operating Losses and Unrealized Asset Revaluations?

Some central banks use fair value accounting (also known as market value accounting or mark to market) and report changes in the market value of the securities, loans, and other investments in their balance sheet and income statement (the profit and loss account). Examples include the SNB, the Reserve Bank of Australia (RBA), and the CNB. Many central banks, including the Fed, the ECB, the BoE, and the BoJ, do not use mark-to-market accounting in their main balance sheet accounts for their held-to-maturity (HTM) assets. Instead, some form of historical cost accounting is used—typically amortized cost (subject to impairment). It is not uncommon for assets that would be classified as available-for-sale (AFS) if held by private entities to be effectively treated as HTM, with unrealized capital gains and losses not showing up as other comprehensive income (OCI) in the comprehensive income account, nor as accumulated other comprehensive income (AOCI) on the balance sheet as part of owners' equity. Any market losses (or gains) are unrealized and don't flow through to the central bank's (comprehensive) income statement or to the balance sheet until the assets are sold or mature.[7]

[7] The Fed publishes the capital gains and losses on its SOMA holdings (the overwhelming majority of its assets and liabilities) in the Federal Reserve Banks Combined Quarterly Financial Report

I believe that all assets owned by the central bank (even the HTM securities) should be reported in the central bank's official balance sheet at fair value rather than at amortized cost (or historical cost). At the very least, all AFS securities (using the normal GAAP or IFRS definitions of available-for-sale) should be reported at market value, and any unrealized gains or losses on these instruments should appear as OCI in the comprehensive income statement and as AOCI in the equity section of the balance sheet.

As noted, many central banks have incurred operating losses, including since 2022 the Fed, the BoE, the ECB, and many of the national central banks (NCBs) of the Eurosystem (including, for 2022 and 2023, the Bundesbank and De Nederlandsche Bank (DNB)), the RBA and the SNB. For 2023, the Fed reported its largest annual operating loss ever of $114.3 billion.[8] For 2022, net income was $58.8 billion. It had been $107.9 billion in 2021. Rather than reducing its capital below a threshold level, the Fed cumulates its recognized losses (once its capital (or equity) hits a threshold level) into a positive "deferred asset"—or a negative liability.[9] The ECB, which for 2023 reported its first loss since 2004, resorts to the same accounting sleight of hand; the "Loss for the year" (€1.3 billion in 2023) is reported as a positive asset on its balance sheet.[10] We will discuss this deferred asset accounting gimmick in Sect. 5. Belhocine et al. (2023) project (in their baseline scenario) losses in 2023 and 2024 for the Eurosystem as a whole, and five years of losses for the Bundesbank. Of the five NCBs for which individual projections were made (Bundesbank, Banque de France, Banca d'Italia, Banco de España, and DNB) only the Banca d'Italia is projected to avoid annual losses.

For the limited set of assets that the ECB values at market prices on its balance sheet (foreign reserves, including gold, securities, and financial instruments, but not any securities held for monetary policy purposes), unrealized gains and losses are treated asymmetrically.[11] "Unrealized gains are not recognized as income in the profit and loss account but are recorded directly under the liability item

(see Federal Reserve Banks Combined Quarterly Financial Report (Unaudited)—September 30, 2023), separately from the Combined statements of conditions, Combined statements of operations and Combined statements of changes in capital. In these three Combined statements, Treasury securities, federal agency and GSE MBS, and GSE debt securities are reported at amortized cost (Table 3). Domestic SOMA portfolio holdings are reported both at Amortized costs and at Fair value. The difference between the two, Cumulative unrealized gains (losses), net is also reported. It was −$1301.9 bn on September 30, 2023.

[8] See Federal Reserve Board—Federal Reserve Board announces preliminary financial information for the Federal Reserve Banks' income and expenses in 2023.

[9] "When Reserve Bank income is not sufficient to cover interest expense, realized losses, operating and other expenses, a deferred asset is created". ... "The deferred asset reflects the amount by which earnings failed to cover expenses and, as a result, the amount of future earnings that must be withheld as a result. Put differently, if a Reserve Bank were to incur an overall loss, its capital would not fall, rather it would suspend remitting to the Treasury until such time as it had returned to positive earnings and had earned back any losses to date." Carpenter et al. (2013). P. 13.

[10] The same treatment of recognized losses had been adopted in 2004 and 2003.

[11] See FAQs on the ECB's Annual Accounts (europa.eu).

'Revaluation accounts' Unrealized gains are therefore not part of the ECB's result for the year, and consequently also not part the distributable profit." Unrealized losses are recorded in the profit and loss account if they exceed the previous revaluation gains recorded in the corresponding revaluation account. Other central banks follow similar asymmetric valuation rules. This asymmetric treatment of unrealized revaluation gains and losses is justified with the "prudence principle". It looks deeply distortionary to me—a systematic understatement of central bank profits.

Mark-to-market losses on the balance sheet of the BoE's Asset Purchase Facility Fund Limited (the BEAPFF), which has held the assets acquired through QE and all other monetary policy operations since 2009, were estimated at £191.1 billion as of February 28, 2023.[12] The total value (at initial purchase price) of the assets of the Asset Purchase Facility (APF) in 2023 Q1 was £824.2 billion. The Office for Budget Responsibility in March 2023 estimated the mark-to-market loss on the gilts held in the APF at £165 billion.[13]

As noted, several central banks have reported negative equity, including the central banks of Chile, Slovakia, the Czech Republic, Israel, Mexico, and Australia (see Bell et al., 2023). The Bundesbank and DNB avoided negative equity for 2023, despite three consecutive years of losses for the Bundesbank and two for DNB. Many more central banks would have significant negative equity if all assets were marked to market. This includes the Fed in 2022 and 2023, the ECB in 2022, and the BoE in 2022 and 2023, as discussed in Sect. 5, and almost surely also the Bundesbank and DNB. Central bank remittances to the Treasury generally reflect the net income (or profit) reported in their financial accounts. Reported net income depends on the accounting treatment of unrealized capital gains and losses.

3 From the Conventional Balance Sheet to the Comprehensive Balance Sheet

In this section, we derive the conditions that must be satisfied for a central bank to avoid equitable insolvency. We construct the comprehensive balance sheet or IBC of the central bank. The central bank is equitably solvent if and only if its comprehensive net worth is non-negative. We start with the conventional balance sheet and the budget constraint of a stylized central bank. The conventional balance sheet contains only what we call *explicit* assets and liabilities. These are contractual assets and liabilities—legal entitlements or obligations. Loans, securities, and mortgages are examples. *Implicit* assets and liabilities do not represent formal,

[12] See Bank of England Asset Purchase Facility Fund Limited Annual Report and Accounts 1 March 2022–28 February 2023

[13] See The fiscal impact of quantitative easing and quantitative tightening—Office for Budget Responsibility (obr.uk).

contractual commitments—legal entitlements or obligations. This includes statutory entitlements and obligations. An implicit asset is the PDV of an expected future non-contractual income or revenue stream. For the general government, the PDV of future tax revenues is an example. For a central bank, the PDV of future seigniorage revenues is a key implicit asset, see Del Negro and Sims (2015). An implicit liability is the PDV of an expected future non-contractual stream of expenditures or outlays. For the general government, the PDV of future social security benefits is an example. A central bank implicit liability would be the PDV of future non-interest payments to the private sector (helicopter money drops if monetized) or the PDV of future transfer payment (remittances) to its beneficial owner. The distinction between statutory obligations (obligations that don't arise from a formal legal contract but are imposed by law) and contractual obligations can at times get fuzzy—public sector defined benefit pensions are an example. The key point is that the comprehensive balance sheet includes the PDV of all future revenue and expenditure streams, that is, it includes all explicit and implicit assets and liabilities.

3.1 The Accounts of the Central Bank

We start with the conventional balance sheet of the central bank. On the liability side of the conventional balance sheet the central bank has monetary liabilities, with nominal value M and non-monetary liabilities, with nominal value N. Monetary liabilities include currency (notes and (sometimes) coins) in circulation and commercial banks' required and excess reserves held with the central bank. Central bank digital currencies (CBDCs) are (or will be) part of the monetary base. The average interest rate on the outstanding stock of central bank money is i^M. Non-monetary liabilities (e.g., bonds issued by the central bank) earn an interest rate i^N. On the asset side of the conventional balance sheet of the central bank we have gold and foreign exchange reserves, R^* in foreign currency, loans to the public, with nominal value L, short (zero duration) nominal government debt, with nominal value B^{cb}, and government consols, of which a quantity $B^{l,\, cb}$ is held by the central bank. For simplicity, I omit the physical assets (other than gold), mainly real estate, owned by most central banks. I also do not explicitly include foreign-currency-denominated liabilities, as this can be handled by allowing R^* to be negative. The foreign exchange rate (domestic currency price of foreign currency) is denoted with e, the foreign interest rate is i^*, the interest rate on loans is i^L, the interest rate on short (instantaneous) government debt is i, and consols (or perpetuities) have a coupon $\gamma > 0$ and a price P^l. Conventional (financial) net worth, capital or equity is denoted W^{cb} in nominal terms. For simplicity, I adopt a continuous time, deterministic framework in the following.

Table 1 Central Bank Conventional Balance Sheet

Assets	Liabilities and Conventional Net Worth
eR^*	M
B^{cb}	N
$P^l B^{l,cb}$	
L	
	W^{cb}

Assuming efficient financial markets, the rates of return on short bonds and consols must be equalized, i.e. $\frac{\gamma}{P^l(t)} + \frac{\dot{P}^l(t)}{P^l(t)} = i(t)$.[14] The price of the consol is then given by:

$$P^l(t) = \lim_{v \to \infty} \left(\gamma \int_t^v e^{-\int_t^s i(u)du} ds \right)$$

$$= \frac{\gamma}{i},$$

if i is (expected to be) constant.

Higher expected future short-term interest rates (and associated higher interest rates on long-duration bonds, including consols) will depress the mark-to-market or fair value of long-duration debt instruments. Table 1 includes the two sources of mark-to-market losses on conventional explicit assets that have impacted many AE central banks since the start of the post-Covid rate hiking cycle. The first is a decline in the market price of domestic-currency-denominated debt instruments, captured in Table 1 by a decline in the price of consols, P^l, driven by an increase in current and future expected policy yields, i. This befell both the USA and the UK in 2022 and 2023, as well as Australia, the euro area, Japan, New Zealand, and Sweden (see Bell et al., 2023). The second is a reduction in the domestic currency value of the stock of foreign-currency-denominated assets, captured in Table 1 by a decrease in e—an appreciation of the domestic currency. This befell both Switzerland and the Czech Republic in 2022. Higher interest expenses contributed to operating losses for many central banks, including the Bundesbank, DNB, the BoE, the ECB, and the NCBs of the Eurosystem, and the Fed in the second half of 2022 and in 2023.

The flow budget constraint (really the budget identity) of the central bank is given in Eq. (1); C^{cb} is the non-interest current expenditure of the central bank (the cost of running the organization), T^{cb} is the net non-interest payments (remittances) made

[14] Here and in the following a dot above a variable denotes its instantaneous rate of change over time.

by the central bank to the Treasury, and H is the net non-interest payments made by the central bank to the private sector.

$$\begin{aligned}&\dot{M}+\dot{N}-\dot{B}^{cb}-P^{l}\dot{B}^{l,cb}-\dot{L}-e\dot{R}^{*}\\&\equiv C^{cb}+T^{cb}+H+i^{M}M+i^{N}N-iB^{cb}-\gamma B^{l,cb}-i^{L}L-i^{*}eR^{*}.\end{aligned} \tag{1}$$

We can rewrite Eq. (1) as the equation of motion for the value of the conventional *non-monetary* net liabilities of the central bank:

$$\begin{aligned}\frac{d}{dt}\left(N-B^{cb}-P^{l}B^{l,cb}-L-eR^{*}\right)&\equiv i(t)\left(N-B^{cb}-P^{l}B^{l,cb}-L-eR^{*}\right)\\&+C^{cb}+T^{cb}+H-\left(\dot{M}-i^{M}M\right)-Z^{cb}.\end{aligned} \tag{2}$$

where

$$\begin{aligned}Z^{cb}=\left(i-i^{N}\right)N-\left(i-\left(\frac{\gamma}{P^{l}}+\frac{\dot{P}^{l}}{P^{l}}\right)\right)P^{l}B^{l,cb}\\-\left(i-i^{L}\right)L-\left(i-\frac{\dot{e}}{e}-i^{*}\right)R^{*}\end{aligned} \tag{3}$$

The term Z^{cb} is the implicit "tax" levied by the central bank on its conventional assets and non-monetary liabilities when the (instantaneous) rate of return on its explicit assets exceeds the short interest rate on the public debt used in the PDV calculations, or when the (instantaneous) rate of return on its non-monetary explicit liabilities is below the short interest rate on the public debt. Z^{cb} can be positive or negative.

We can integrate Eq. (2) forward in time to obtain the following intertemporal budget identity:

$$\begin{aligned}&N(t)-B^{cb}(t)-P^{l}(t)B^{l,cb}(t)-L(t)-e(t)R^{*}(t)\\&\equiv\int_{t}^{\infty}e^{-\int_{t}^{s}i(u)du}\left(\dot{M}(s)-i^{M}(s)M(s)-C^{cb}(s)-T^{cb}(s)-H(s)+Z^{cb}(s)\right)ds\\&+\lim_{v\to\infty}e^{-\int_{t}^{v}i(u)du}\left(N(v)-B^{cb}(v)-P^{l}(v)B^{l,cb}(v)-L(v)-e(v)R^{*}(v)\right).\end{aligned} \tag{4}$$

We turn the intertemporal budget identity into an intertemporal budget *constraint* by imposing the no Ponzi finance condition or solvency constraint that the PDV of the central bank's *non-monetary* net explicit liabilities must be non-positive in the infinitely distant long run (Reis, 2015):

$$\lim_{v\to\infty} e^{-\int_t^v i(u)du}\left(N(v)-B^{cb}(v)-P^l(v)B^{l,cb}(v)-L(v)-e(v)R^*(v)\right)\leq 0. \tag{5}$$

The specification of the solvency constraint in terms of the PDV of the central bank's net *non-monetary* explicit liabilities reflects our assumption that central bank money is a liability in name only.

The IBC of the central bank is given in Eq. (6):

$$\begin{aligned} &N(t)-B^{cb}(t)-P^l(t)B^{l,cb}(t)-L(t)-e(t)R^*(t)\\ &\quad\leq\int_t^\infty e^{-\int_t^s i(u)du}\left(\dot{M}(s)-i^M(s)M(s)+Z^{cb}(s)-C^{cb}(s)-T^{cb}(s)-H(s)\right)ds. \end{aligned} \tag{6}$$

The intertemporal seigniorage identity (see Buiter, 2007, 2021) is given in Eq. (7):

$$\begin{aligned} &\lim_{v\to\infty}\int_t^v e^{-\int_t^s i(u)du}\left(\dot{M}(s)-i^M(s)M(s)\right)ds+M(t)\\ &\quad=\lim_{v\to\infty}\int_t^v e^{-\int_t^s i(u)du}\left(\left[i(s)-i^M(s)\right]M(s)\right)ds+\lim_{v\to\infty}e^{-\int_t^v i(u)du}M(v). \end{aligned} \tag{7}$$

Two familiar measures of flow seigniorage income are $\dot{M}(s)-i^M(s)M(s)$ (Seigniorage 1) and $[i(s)-i^M(s)]M(s)$ (Seigniorage 2). Through the application of integration by parts (or through brute force in the discrete-time version of the intertemporal seigniorage identity (see Buiter, 2007, 2021), it can be shown that the PDV of all current and future Seigniorage 1 plus the value of the initial stock of central bank money equals the PDV of all current and future Seigniorage 2 plus the PDV of the terminal stock of central bank money, i.e., Eq. (7).

Using Eq. (7), the IBC of the central bank in Eq. (6) can be written equivalently as in Eq. (8):

$$\begin{aligned} &M(t)+N(t)-B^{cb}(t)-P^l(t)B^{l,cb}(t)-L(t)-e(t)R^*(t)\leq e^{-\int_t^\infty i(u)du}M(\infty)\\ &\quad+\int_t^\infty e^{-\int_t^s i(u)du}\left(\left[i(s)-i^M(s)\right]M(s)+Z^{cb}(s)-C^{cb}(s)-T^{cb}(s)-H(s)\right)ds. \end{aligned} \tag{8}$$

Note that because central bank money is irredeemable (it is a liability in name only), there is no presumption that the PDV of the terminal stock of central

Table 2 Central Bank Comprehensive Balance Sheet

Assets	Liabilities and Comprehensive Net Worth
$e(t)R^*(t)$	$N(t)$
$B^{cb}(t)$	$V_t(\{C^{cb}, i\})$
$P^l(t)B^{l,\,cb}(t)$	$V_t(\{T^{cb}, i\})$
$L(t)$	$V_t(\{H, i\})$
$V_t\left(\{\dot{M} - i^M M, i\}\right)$	
$V_t(\{Z^{cb}, i\})$	
	$\hat{W}^{cb}(t)$

bank money, $\lim_{\nu\to\infty} e^{-\int_t^{\nu} i(u)du} M(\nu)$, should be equal to zero. Let $V_t(\{x, i\})$ denote the integral (sum) of the PDVs of all current and future values of x, when the instantaneous discount rate is i, that is, $V_t(\{x, i\}) = \lim_{\nu\to\infty} \int_t^{\nu} e^{-\int_t^{s} i(u)du} x(s)ds$. We can rewrite the substance of the IBC of the central bank in Eq. (6) as the central bank's comprehensive balance sheet, shown in Table 2. Comprehensive net worth (or comprehensive capital or equity) of the central bank is denoted $\hat{W}^{cb}$.

Central bank equitable solvency requires that $\hat{W}^{cb} \geq 0$. Comparing Tables 1 and 2, we see that the comprehensive balance sheet omits one conventional explicit liability (the stock of central bank money) M, and adds two implicit assets and three implicit liabilities. The implicit assets are the PDV of current and future Seigniorage 1, $V_t\left(\{\dot{M} - i^M M, i\}\right)$ and the PDV of current and future discount rate corrections, $V_t(\{Z^{cb}, i\})$. The implicit liabilities are the PDV of primary current expenditures $V_t(\{C^{cb}, i\})$, the PDV of non-interest payments (remittances) to the Treasury $V_t(\{T^{cb}, i\})$, and the PDV of non-interest payments to the private sector $V_t(\{H, i\})$.

Rate of return corrections (Z^{cb}) are present because the interest rate on (short) government debt is used to discount all future primary (non-interest) revenues and expenditures. This interest rate may differ from the interest rate (rate of return) on the central bank's other conventional (explicit) assets and liabilities. For instance, if i^N, the interest rate on non-monetary liabilities is below i, the interest rate on short government bonds used in the present value calculations, Z^{cb} will be boosted. If $\frac{\gamma}{P^l(t)} + \frac{\dot{P}^l(t)}{P^l(t)}$, the rate of return on consols (coupon rate plus capital gains), is below i, the interest rate on short government bonds, Z^{cb}, will be lowered. Note that Z^{cb} and $V_t(\{Z^{cb}, i\})$ can be negative. The same holds for $V_t(\{T^{cb}, i\})$ if the Treasury is committed to compensate the central bank for (some of) its losses or if it is committed to recapitalize the central bank should its conventional net worth fall below some threshold level.

Using Eq. (8) we can obtain the following alternative but equivalent comprehensive balance sheet of the central bank given in Table 3.

Table 3 Alternative but Equivalent Central Bank Comprehensive Balance Sheet

Assets	Liabilities and Comprehensive Net Worth
$e(t)R^*(t)$	$M(t)$
$B^{cb}(t)$	$N(t)$
$P^l(t)B^{l,\,cb}(t)$	$V_t(\{C^{cb}, i\})$
$L(t)$	$V_t(\{T^{cb}, i\})$
$V_t\left(\{[i - i^M]\, M, i\}\right) + \lim_{\nu\to\infty} e^{-\int_t^\nu i(u)du} M(\nu)$	$V_t(\{H, i\})$
$V_t(\{Z^{cb}, i\})$	
	$\hat{W}^{cb}(t)$

From Tables 1 and 2 we can establish the following relationship between conventional financial net worth and comprehensive net worth:

$$W^{cb} = eR^* + B^{cb} + P^l B^{l,cb} + L - M - N \tag{9a}$$

$$\begin{aligned}\hat{W}^{cb} &= eR^* + B^{cb} + P^l B^{l,cb} + L - N + V_t\left(\left\{\dot{M} - i^M M, i\right\}\right) \\ &\quad + V_t\left(\left\{Z^{cb}, i\right\}\right) - V_t\left(\left\{C^{cb}, i\right\}\right) - V_t\left(\left\{T^{cb}, i\right\}\right) - V_t\left(\{H, i\}\right),\end{aligned} \tag{9b}$$

$$\begin{aligned}\hat{W}^{cb}(t) &= W^{cb}(t) + V_t\left(\left\{\dot{M} - i^M M, i\right\}\right) + M(t) + V_t\left(\left\{Z^{cb}, i\right\}\right) \\ &\quad - V_t\left(\left\{C^{cb}, i\right\}\right) - V_t\left(\left\{T^{cb}, i\right\}\right) - V_t\left(\{H, i\}\right).\end{aligned} \tag{10}$$

Conventional net worth can be negative when comprehensive net worth is non-negative (the central bank is equitably solvent) and vice versa—conventional net worth can be non-negative when comprehensive net worth is negative (the central bank is equitably insolvent).

From Tables 1 and 3, we can obtain the following equivalent relationship between conventional net worth and comprehensive net worth:

$$\begin{aligned}\hat{W}^{cb}(t) &= W^{cb} + V_t\left(\left\{\left(i - i^M\right) M, i\right\}\right) + \lim_{\nu\to\infty} e^{-\int_t^\nu i(u)du} M(\nu) \\ &\quad + V_t\left(\left\{Z^{cb}, i\right\}\right) - V_t\left(\left\{C^{cb}, i\right\}\right) - V_t\left(\left\{T^{cb}, i\right\}\right) - V_t\left(\{H, i\}\right).\end{aligned} \tag{11}$$

Note that Eq. (11) can also be obtained by applying the intertemporal seigniorage identity of Eqs. (7–10). The implicit seigniorage asset can either be written as $V_t\left(\left\{\dot{M} - i^M M, i\right\}\right) + M(t)$ or as $V_t\left(\left\{\left(i - i^M\right) M, i\right\}\right) + \lim_{\nu\to\infty} e^{-\int_t^\nu i(u)du} M(\nu)$.

Table 4 Treasury Conventional Balance Sheet

Assets	Liabilities and Conventional Net Worth
$P^K K$	$B^p + B^{cb}$
	$P^l[B^{l,p} + B^{l,cb}]$
	W^g

Comprehensive net worth is conventional net worth plus the implicit assets and minus the implicit liabilities.

3.2 *The Treasury Accounts*

We now introduce the conventional and comprehensive balance sheets of the Treasury—the beneficial owner of the central bank. The following additional notation is used: B^p is the stock of short-duration government debt held by the public (outside the central bank); $B^{l,p}$ is the stock of consols held by the public; K is the stock of physical capital owned by the government; P^K is the price of a unit of physical capital; ϱ is the nominal return on a unit of capital and δ the depreciation rate of capital; C^g is primary current government expenditure and T^p is tax revenues paid by the public.

The conventional balance sheet of the Treasury is given in Table 4. Treasury conventional (financial) net worth is denoted W^g.

The flow budget constraint of the Treasury is given in Eq. (12).

$$\begin{aligned} \dot{B}^p + \dot{B}^{cb} + P^l\left(\dot{B}^{l,p} + \dot{B}^{l,cb}\right) - P^K\dot{K} &\equiv C^g - T^p - T^{cb} + i\left(B^p + B^{cb}\right) \\ &+ \gamma\left(B^{l,p} + B^{l,cb}\right) - \left(\varrho - \delta P^K\right)K. \end{aligned} \tag{12}$$

We can rewrite this as

$$\begin{aligned} &\frac{d}{dt}\left(B^p + B^{cb} + P^l\left[B^{l,p} + B^{l,cb}\right] - P^K K\right) \\ &\equiv i\left(B^p + B^{cb} + P^l\left[B^{l,p} + B^{l,cb}\right] - P^K K\right) + C^g - T^p - T^{cb} - Z^g, \end{aligned} \tag{13}$$

where

$$Z^g = \left(i - \left[\frac{\gamma}{P^l(t)} + \frac{\dot{P}^l(t)}{P^l(t)}\right]\right) P^l\left(B^{l,p} + B^{l,cb}\right) \\ - \left(i - \left[\frac{\varrho}{P^K} - \delta + \frac{\dot{P}^K}{P^K}\right]\right) P^K K. \tag{14}$$

Integrating Eq. (13) forward in time we obtain:

$$B^p(t) + B^{cb}(t) + P^l(t)\left[B^{l,p}(t) + B^{l,cb}(t)\right] - P^K(t)K(t)$$

$$\equiv \int_t^{\infty} e^{-\int_t^s i(u)du}\left(T^p(s) + T^{cb}(s) + Z^g(s) - C^g(s)\right) ds \\ + \lim_{v\to\infty} e^{-\int_t^v i(u)du}\left(B^p(v) + B^{cb}(v) + P^l(v)\left[B^{l,p}(v) + B^{l,cb}(v)\right] - P^K(v)K(v)\right).$$

We impose the no Ponzi finance condition or solvency constraint that the PDV of the Treasury's net conventional (or explicit) liabilities must be non-positive in the infinitely distant long run[15]:

$$\lim_{v\to\infty} e^{-\int_t^v i(u)du}\left(B^p(v) + B^{cb}(v) + P^l(v)\left[B^{l,p}(v) + B^{l,cb}(v)\right] \\ - P^K(v)K(v)\right) \leq 0.$$

This results in the IBC of the Treasury:

$$B^p(t) + B^{cb}(t) + P^l(t)\left[B^{l,p}(t) + B^{l,cb}(t)\right] - P^K(t)K(t) \\ \leq \int_t^{\infty} e^{-\int_t^s i(u)du}\left(T^p(s) + T^{cb}(s) + Z^g(s) - C^g(s)\right) ds. \tag{15}$$

Using the same notational conventions as in Tables 2 and 3, we can present the comprehensive balance sheet of the Treasury as in Table 5. Comprehensive Treasury net worth is denoted $\hat{W}^g$.

[15] Note that the Treasury on its own does not have any monetary liabilities.

Table 5 Treasury Comprehensive Balance Sheet

Assets	Liabilities and Comprehensive Net Worth
$P^K K$	$B^p + B^{cb}$
$V_t(\{T^p, i\})$	$P^l[B^{l,p} + B^{l,cb}]$
$V_t(\{T^{cb}, i\})$	$V_t(\{C^g, i\})$
$V_t(\{Z^g, i\})$	
	$\hat{W}^g$

Table 6 State Conventional Balance Sheet

Assets	Liabilities and Conventional Net Worth
eR^*	M
L	N
$P^K K$	B^p
	$P^l B^{l,p}$
	W^s

The Treasury is equitably solvent if and only if comprehensive net worth is non-negative: $\hat{W}^g \geq 0$. From Tables 4 and 5 it follows that

$$W^g = P^K K - \left(B^p + B^{cb} + P^l \left[B^{l,p} + B^{l,cb}\right]\right), \tag{16a}$$

$$\begin{aligned} \hat{W}^g = {} & P^K K - \left(B^p + B^{cb} + P^l \left[B^{l,p} + B^{l,cb}\right]\right) + V_t\left(\{T^p, i\}\right) \\ & + V_t\left(\left\{T^{cb}, i\right\}\right) + V_t\left(\{Z^g, i\}\right) - V_t\left(\{C^g, i\}\right), \end{aligned} \tag{16b}$$

$$\hat{W}^g = W^g + V_t\left(\{T^p, i\}\right) + V_t\left(\left\{T^{cb}, i\right\}\right) + V_t\left(\{Z^g, i\}\right) - V_t\left(\{C^g, i\}\right). \tag{17}$$

3.3 *The Consolidated Accounts of the Treasury and the Central Bank*

Because the Treasury is the beneficial owner of the central bank it makes sense to consolidate their accounts. The conventional balance sheet of the State—the consolidated Treasury and central bank—is given in Table 6. The conventional financial net worth of the State is denoted as W^S. Note that $W^s = W^{cb} + W^g$.

The flow budget constraint of the State is given in Eq. (18):

$$\begin{aligned} & \dot{M} + \dot{N} + \dot{B}^p + P^l \dot{B}^{l,p} - \dot{L} - e\dot{R}^* - P^K \dot{K} \equiv C^{cb} + C^g + H - T^p \\ & + iB^p + \gamma B^{l,p} + i^M M + i^N N - i^L L - i^* eR^* - \left(\varrho - \delta P^K\right) K. \end{aligned} \tag{18}$$

We can rewrite this as Eq. (19):

$$\begin{aligned}&\frac{d}{dt}\left(N + B^{p} + P^{l}B^{l,p} - L - eR^{*} - P^{K}K\right)\\&\quad\equiv i\left(N + B^{p} + P^{l}B^{l,p} - L - eR^{*} - P^{K}K\right)\\&\quad+ C^{cb} + C^{g} + H - T^{p} - Z^{cb} - Z^{g} - \left(\dot{M} - i^{M}M\right).\end{aligned} \tag{19}$$

We can integrate Eq. (19) forward in time to obtain Eq. (20):

$$\begin{aligned}&N(t) + B^{p}(t) + P^{l}(t)B^{l,p}(t) - L(t) - e(t)R^{*}(t) - P^{K}(t)K(t) \equiv \int_{t}^{\infty} e^{-\int_{t}^{s} i(u)du}\\&\times\left(T^{p}(s) - C^{cb}(s) - C^{g}(s) - H(s) + Z^{cb}(s) + Z^{g}(s) + \dot{M}(s) - i^{M}(s)M(s)\right)ds\\&+ \lim_{v\to\infty} e^{-\int_{t}^{v} i(u)du}\left(N(v) + B^{p}(v) + P^{l}(v)B^{l,p}(v) - L(v)\right.\\&\left.-e(v)R^{*}(v) - P^{K}(v)K(v)\right).\end{aligned} \tag{20}$$

We next impose the equitable solvency constraint or no indefinite Ponzi-finance condition, that the PDV of the terminal net *non-monetary* debt of the State cannot be positive:

$$\begin{aligned}&\lim_{v\to\infty} e^{-\int_{t}^{v} i(u)du}\left(N(v) + B^{p}(v) + P^{l}(v)B^{l,p}(v)\right.\\&\left.-L(v) - e(v)R^{*}(v) - P^{K}(v)K(v)\right) \le 0.\end{aligned} \tag{21}$$

Note that for the consolidated State we maintain the assumption that central bank money is a liability in name only, although it is an undoubted asset to the holder. This produces the IBC of the State in Eq. (22):

$$\begin{aligned}&N(t) + B^{p}(t) + P^{l}(t)B^{l,p}(t) - L(t) - e(t)R^{*}(t) - P^{K}(t)K(t)\\&\le \int_{t}^{\infty} e^{-\int_{t}^{s} i(u)du}\left(T^{p}(s) - C^{cb}(s) - C^{g}(s) - H(s) + Z^{cb}(s) + Z^{g}(s)\right.\\&\left.+ \dot{M}(s) - i^{M}(s)M(s)\right)ds.\end{aligned} \tag{22}$$

Table 7 State Comprehensive Balance Sheet

Assets	Liabilities and Comprehensive Net Worth
eR^*	N
L	B^p
$P^K K$	$P^l B^{l,p}$
$V_t\left(\left\{\dot{M} - i^M M, i\right\}\right)$	$V_t(\{C^{cb}, i\})$
$V_t(\{T^p, i\})$	$V_t(\{C^g, i\})$
$V_t(\{Z^{cb}, i\})$	$V_t(\{H, i\})$
$V_t(\{Z^g, i\})$	
	$\hat{W}^s$

Using the intertemporal seigniorage identity in Eq. (7), the IBC of the State can equivalently be written as in Eq. (23):

$$\begin{aligned} & M(t) - e^{-\int_t^\infty i(u)du} M(\infty) + N(t) + B^p(t) + P^l(t)B^{l,p}(t) - L(t) - e(t)R^*(t) \\ & - P^K(t)K(t) \leq \int_t^\infty e^{-\int_t^s i(u)du} \Big(T^p(s) - C^{cb}(s) - C^g(s) - H(s) \\ & + Z^{cb}(s) + Z^g(s) + \left[1 - i^M(s)\right] M(s)\Big)\, ds. \end{aligned} \tag{23}$$

Table 7 gives the comprehensive balance sheet of the State. Comprehensive net worth of the State is denoted W^s.

The State is equitably solvent if and only if $\hat{W}^s \geq 0$. From Tables 6 and 7 it follows that

$$\begin{aligned} \hat{W}^s(t) = & W^s(t) + V_t\left(\left\{\dot{M} - i^M M, i\right\}\right) + M(t) + V_t\left(\left\{T^p, i\right\}\right) \\ & + V_t\left(\left\{Z^{cb}, i\right\}\right) + V_t\left(\left\{Z^g, i\right\}\right) \\ & - V_t\left(\left\{C^{cb}, i\right\}\right) - V_t\left(\left\{C^g, i\right\}\right) - V_t\left(\left\{H, i\right\}\right). \end{aligned} \tag{24}$$

Applying the intertemporal seigniorage identity of Eqs. (7) to (24), we obtain the equivalent relationship between comprehensive and conventional net worth:

$$\begin{aligned} \hat{W}^s(t) = & W^s(t) + V_t\left(\left\{\left(i - i^M\right) M, i\right\}\right) + e^{-\int_t^\infty i(u)du} M(\infty) \\ & + V_t\left(\left\{T^p, i\right\}\right) + V_t\left(\left\{Z^{cb}, i\right\}\right) + V_t\left(\left\{Z^g, i\right\}\right) \\ & - V_t\left(\left\{C^{cb}, i\right\}\right) - V_t\left(\left\{C^g, i\right\}\right) - V_t\left(\left\{H, i\right\}\right). \end{aligned} \tag{25}$$

Note that $\hat{W}^s = \hat{W}^{cb} + \hat{W}^g$.

4 Seigniorage vs. Central Bank Remittances to the Treasury

Does a large loss or negative conventional net worth impede a central bank from effectively pursuing its objectives? The objectives of the central bank are financial stability and either price stability or a dual mandate like the Fed's maximum employment and stable prices. The instruments of the central bank are one or more short-term nominal interest rates, its selection of eligible collateral and the haircuts on the collateral, yield curve control, and the size and composition of its portfolio, which notably includes its monetary liabilities—which are liabilities in name only.[16] The exchange rate can be treated as an instrument, although, in the absence of effective capital controls, setting or targeting the exchange rate constrains the control of the central bank over the size and composition of its balance sheet and over its policy rates.

Does a large central bank loss or negative conventional net worth constrain the setting of the policy rate(s) and the size and composition of its portfolio? Only if it threatens the equitable solvency of the central bank and if the only way to maintain or restore equitable solvency is the issuance of central bank money on a scale that threatens either financial stability or price stability (or the dual mandate).[17] The relevant constraint on the central bank's ability to avoid equitable insolvency is the non-negativity of its comprehensive net worth, $\hat{W}^{cb} \geq 0$. From Eq. (10) (or Eq. 11), $\hat{W}^{cb} \geq 0$ can be translated into a constraint on the minimal size of conventional net worth, W^{cb}, provided estimates of all the implicit assets and liabilities can be constructed. The empirical estimation of the implicit assets and liabilities is bound to be complex and time-consuming. Their value depends, among other things, on future monetary policy $V_t\left(\left\{\dot{M} - i^M M, i\right\}\right)$, future values of the policy rates and asset purchases (or sales) and on the responses by economic agents to past, current, and future monetary policy (through the other interest rates in $V_t(\{Z^{cb}, i\})$).

Consider the comprehensive balance sheet of the central bank in Table 2. At any given time, t, the outstanding stocks of explicit assets and liabilities, $R^*(t)$, $B^{cb}(t)$, $B^{l,\,cb}(t)$, $L(t)$, and $N(t)$, are given by history. For simplicity, I assume in the following that the monetary authority takes the two asset prices $e(t)$ and $P^l(t)$ as given. I also take as given the PDV of current and future discount rate corrections, $V_t(\{Z^{cb}, i\})$, and the PDV of the cost of running the central bank, $V_t(\{C^{cb}, i\})$. Last, I also assume that the central bank can neither engage in remittances to the private sector nor impose taxes on the private sector, so $V_t(\{H, i\}) = 0$. This means that the outstanding stock of monetary liabilities, $M(t)$, given by history, the central bank

[16] Many central banks set multiple separate but closely related short-term rates for deposits, regular lending operations and emergency lending operations. The ECB, for instance, sets the overnight interest rate on the deposit facility, the one-week interest rate on the (collateralized) main refinancing operations and the interest rate on the (collateralized) overnight marginal lending facility.

[17] The inflationary impact of additional central bank monetization can be moderated by raising reserve requirements and/or higher policy rates.

implicit asset $V_t\left(\left\{\dot{M} - i^M M, i\right\}\right)$, the PDV of current and future net seigniorage revenue, and the central bank implicit liability $V_t(\{T^{cb}, i\})$, the PDV of current and future net remittances from the central bank to the Treasury, are the key determinants of equitable (in)solvency of the central bank. Note that the rules governing net remittances from the central bank to the Treasury are not a central bank choice variable but the outcome of a political decision-making process in which the central bank is but one of the players—and generally not the most influential one (see Bonetti et al. (2024)).

Many central banks have a rule for remittances that sets remittances in any given period equal to the larger of zero and some measure of profits in that period, if conventional net worth is above some threshold level. If conventional net worth is at or below the threshold level, remittances are zero. Such a rule clearly cannot handle large losses or deeply negative equity, which call for negative remittances from the central bank to the Treasury or a recapitalization of the central bank by the Treasury. The fact that current-period unrealized capital gains and losses are often not adequately allowed for in the definition of current-period profits does not help either.

From Eqs. (9a)–(10) it follows that if conventional net worth is negative ($W^{cb}(t) < 0$), equitable solvency can still be ensured in two ways. First, the outstanding stock of central bank money is a liability in name only. Second, even if $W^{cb} + M$ is seriously negative, the central bank can ensure equitable solvency ($\hat{W}^{cb}(t) \geq 0$) if there is either a sufficiently large value for the PDV of seigniorage or a sufficiently small (and possibly negative) value for the PDV of its remittances to the Treasury. Given the PDV of remittances to the Treasury, the PDV of seigniorage required to ensure equitable solvency may be so large that the current and future monetary issuance it implies is inconsistent with the price stability mandate (dual mandate) or the financial stability mandate of the central bank. This could be remedied by an appropriate reduction in the PDV of the remittances to the Treasury. The problem is that remittances to the Treasury, especially when they become negative, are not under the control of the central bank. The Treasury certainly controls the values of T^{cb} when these values are negative. It may also be able to influence, constrain, (co)determine, or even control the magnitude of positive values of T^{cb}. Substantive central bank operational independence may be restricted when it is not in control of the net remittances to the Treasury or when there is no BoE-style (or Sveriges Riksbank-style) recapitalization agreement between the Treasury and the central bank.

The comprehensive balance sheet of the Treasury, given in Table 5, shows why a reduction in central bank remittances, $V_t(\{T^{cb}, i\})$, can be politically and economically costly. If the Treasury is to avoid a worsening of its equitable solvency condition, it either must reduce the PDV of current and future primary current public expenditures, $V_t(\{C^g, i\})$, or boost the PDV of current and future tax revenues, $V_t(\{T^p, i\})$.

The comprehensive balance sheet of the consolidated State, which eliminates the remittances because they are an intra-public sector transfer of resources, makes clear what the true monetary and fiscal dilemma is. Consider the comprehensive balance sheet of the State in Table 7 and Eq. (24) (or equivalently Eq. 25). A threat to the equitable solvency of the consolidated State can be addressed in one of two ways: either by boosting the PDV of current and future seigniorage, $V_t\left(\left\{\dot{M} - i^M M, i\right\}\right)$, or by some combination of a lower PDV of current and public expenditures, $V_t(\{C^g, i\})$ and a higher PDV of current and future taxes, $V_t(\{T^p, i\})$. In a functional polity, at least one of these options will be preferred to a sovereign default.[18] The U.S. Congress has flirted repeatedly with "accidental" sovereign default by failing to raise the federal debt ceiling until the very last minute, a phenomenon suggestive of federal political dysfunctionality.[19]

5 Some Recent Central Bank Losses, Negative Equity, Remittances, and Recapitalizations

In this section, we consider the profits and losses in the income accounts and on the balance sheets of seven AE central banks. We try to assess whether any large losses that occurred may have adversely impacted central bank operational independence and the central bank's ability to pursue its mandates (especially price stability).

5.1 *The Czech National Bank*

The CNB records its assets at fair value and is completely open about its repeated negative equity. It reported a loss of CZK 412 billion (US$ 19 billion, around 6.1% of Czech annual GDP) in 2022 and negative (conventional) equity of CZK 481 billion at the end of 2022, mostly as a result of foreign currency positions.[20] The CNB had negative (conventional) equity from 1998 until 2013, when it entered an asymmetric exchange rate commitment with the euro, and again every year following the exit from the exchange rate commitment in 2017 until 2023 (see Franta et al., 2022; Galuščák & Branislav, 2023).[21]

For 2023 the CNB reported a preliminary profit of CZK 55 billion, implying continuing negative (conventional) equity at the end of 2023 of around CZK 426

[18] The central bank is considered part of the sovereign.

[19] According to the U.S. Department of the Treasury "Since 1960, Congress has acted 78 separate times to permanently raise, temporarily extend, or revise the definition of the debt limit ...". While this is good news—Congress does the right thing when all else fails—it can also be a source of concern: opportunities to get it catastrophically wrong arise frequently. See Financial Markets, Financial Institutions, and Fiscal Service | U.S. Department of the Treasury.

[20] See annual report Czech National Bank.

[21] See Czech National Bank (2023), page 35. It was an asymmetric commitment to maintain the Czech koruna exchange rate with the euro at or above 27 korunas per euro.

billion.[22] With banknotes and coins in circulation of CZK 709 billion at the end of 2023, and Liabilities to banks operating on domestic market of CZK 2556 billion, it is clear that the non-monetary explicit liabilities of the CNB are less than its explicit assets—its net-of-money conventional equity is materially positive at around CZK 2839 billion at the end of 2023.[23]

The CNB objected in May 2010 to the ECB's view, expressed in its Convergence Report, that negative capital may adversely affect a central bank's ability to perform its tasks. As noted, it has had negative equity for most of the past 25 years. Most of its assets are foreign-currency-denominated. International reserves, including gold, were around 98% of the CNB's assets at the end of 2022. If the central bank has credibility and the Czech koruna rises in value, the value of its foreign-currency-denominated assets falls. In addition, deposits of domestic financial intermediaries were 64% of the CNB's liabilities at the end of 2022. High policy rates and a stronger external value of the currency hurt net operating income, asset values, and equity.

The Czech National Bank does not have a recapitalization or negative remittances agreement with the Czech Treasury. *"The CNB is not a part of the public budgets of the Czech Republic. On the contrary, it is strictly separated from them by law and covers its operating expenses from its own revenues by law. The CNB is not funded by taxes and so its expenses are not covered by taxpayers."*[24] There have been no negative remittances from the CNB to the Czech Treasury or recapitalizations of the CNB by the Czech Treasury. The CNB does pay any surplus profit to the Czech Treasury.[25] All of the CZK 55 billion profit for the year 2023 was retained to boost the still negative equity.

Is there any convincing evidence that the CNB was unwilling to raise the policy rate further (or to keep it higher for longer) because of its negative impact on central bank equity and net operating income? A comparison with the ECB suggests that this has not been the case.[26]

The YoY CPI inflation rate in the Czech Republic was 3.7% in February 2020, it peaked at 18.0% in September 2022 and fell to 6.9% in December 2023 and to 2.0% in March 2024, ticking up to 2.9% in April 2024. Core CPI inflation in December 2023 was 4.4%, 2.8% in March 2024, and 3.5% in April 2024. The headline HICP inflation rate was 3.1% in April 2024. The CNB has a 2% inflation target (like the

---

[22] See Performance—Czech National Bank (cnb.cz).

[23] See Oracle Interactive Dashboards—BISTAT (cnb.cz).

[24] See Performance—Czech National Bank (cnb.cz).

[25] "The generated profit is allocated to its reserve fund and to other funds created from this profit, and for other uses within the Bank's budget. Any remaining profit is transferred by the CNB to the state budget" (from Czech National Bank (2023)).

[26] I assume that the ECB, although slow to raise the policy rates during the post-Covid inflation episode, was not influenced in its management of the policy rates and the size and composition of its balance sheet by concerns about losses and negative equity. The decision to cut the interest rate it paid on required reserves and subsequently to set it at zero was clearly motivated by concerns about losses and negative equity.

ECB), and its policy rate (the two-week repo rate) was cut by 25 bps from its post-Covid high to 6.75% in December 2023 and by three further 50 bps cuts to 5.25% in May 2024. In April 2024, the ECB kept its MRO rate at the post-Covid high (set in September 2023) of 4.50%, with euro area annual headline HICP inflation in March 2024 and in April 2024 at 2.4%, and core inflation 2.9% in March 2024 and 2.7% in April 2024. The euro area's annual HICP inflation rate in February 2020 was 1.6%, and euro area inflation peaked at 10.6% in November 2022. The ECB started its post-Covid rate hikes late—in July 2022. The CNB had started its rate hikes in June 2021. The CNB's latest move to rate cutting may well be too soon and too aggressive.

While the post-Covid record of the CNB does not support the view that operating losses and negative conventional equity have interfered with the effective pursuit of its inflation objective, there remains a risk that the CNB could suffer further losses of a magnitude that threaten its equitable solvency unless it engages in current and future monetary issuance of a magnitude that is inconsistent with the inflation target. A UK-style or Swedish-style recapitalization agreement with the Czech Ministry of Finance would be desirable to address that eventuality.

5.2 *The Swiss National Bank*

The SNB posted an annual loss of CHF 132.5 billion (US$143 billion) in 2022, the largest loss in its 115-year history, equal to around 17% of Swiss annual GDP that year.[27] The SNB (like the CNB) marks to market all its assets. It reflects any change in the market value of its portfolio in its income statement and balance sheet. The drivers of the 2022 loss were falling stock and fixed-income markets and a strengthening of the Swiss franc. It made a loss of CHF 131 billion on its foreign currency positions. In 2021 there had been a profit of CHF 26.3 billion. Despite the massive loss in 2022, the equity of the SNB remained positive at CHF 65.8 billion at the end of 2022, down from CHF 204.2 billion at the end of 2021. For 2023, the SNB posted an annual loss of around CHF 3 billion, bringing its equity capital at the end of 2023 down to around CHF 63 billion.[28] The SNB cut its main policy rate by 25 bps from its post-Covid peak of 1.75% to 1.50% in March 2024, where it remained in May 2024. This should boost net operating income and, by weakening the Swiss Franc, raise asset values. Swiss headline CPI inflation following Covid peaked at 3.5% YoY in August 2022 and was back at 1.4% in April 2024 with core inflation at 1.2%. There is no evidence that operational independence or anti-inflationary policy effectiveness were adversely impacted by the massive losses in 2022.

[27] See Annual result of the Swiss National Bank for 2022 (snb.ch).

[28] See Annual loss and negative distribution reserve of the Swiss National Bank preclude profit distribution (snb.ch).

At the end of 2022, banknotes in circulation were CHF 82 billion and sight deposits of domestic banks CHF 467 billion. The net-of-money (conventional) equity of the SNB remains large and equitable insolvency is unlikely to pose a problem. The National Bank Act (NBA) provides the statutory framework for the SNB and its activities, including the distribution of its net profits between its private shareholders and its beneficial owners—the Swiss Cantons and the Confederate government. There is no obligation for the Confederation and the Cantons to compensate the SNB for excessive losses or to recapitalize it should its (conventional) equity fall below some threshold level. It would make sense to adopt a UK-style or Swedish-style recapitalization arrangement.

5.3 *The Sveriges Riksbank*

The new Sveriges Riksbank Act (effective as of January 1, 2023) sets an upper limit (called the target level) and a lower limit (called the base level, equal to two-thirds of the target level) on the Riksbank's equity.[29] It also specifies the conditions under which the equity is so small (below one-third of the target level) that the Riksbank must apply for a capital injection from the Swedish Parliament.[30] In the annual accounts, the Riksbank's gold, foreign exchange, and (domestic and foreign) bond holdings are valued at current market prices (Nordström and Vredin, 2022). Like the ECB, the Riksbank does not record in the profit and loss account any unrealized gains on a financial instrument that it values at current market prices. Such unrealized gains are entered on the balance sheet into the revaluation account for that financial instrument. Unrealized losses on a financial instrument during a year are entered into that year's profit and loss account if they exceed the accumulated unrealized gains on the revaluation account for that financial instrument at the end of the year—another example of the asymmetric, supposedly prudence principle-driven treatment of unrealized gains and losses. The Riksbank reported a financial loss in 2022 of SEK 81 billion (driven by a large reduction in the value of its bond holdings as interest rates rose sharply), large enough to result in negative reported equity of SEK 2 billion at the end of 2022. A capital injection from the Swedish parliament was legally required during the 2023 financial year. The Riksbank reported a profit of SEK 16 billion for 2023. No transfer of profits to the Treasury will be made for 2023, because even with the full retention of the 2023 profits by the Riksbank, its conventional equity does not reach the target level for equity pursuant to the Sveriges Riksbank Act. There is no evidence that the loss and the negative conventional equity have adversely affected the Riksbank's ability to

[29] See The Sveriges Riksbank Act 2022_1568.

[30] The normal capital injection would restore equity to the base level. Depending on the magnitude of unrealized gains or losses on the balance sheet, the maximum capital injection would restore capital to the target level and the minimum capital injection could be zero.

pursue its mandates—low and stable inflation and financial stability. With banknotes and coins in circulation worth SEK 58 billion at the end of 2013 and other monetary liabilities of SEK 247 billion, the Riksbank's conventional net-of-money equity is over SEK 300 billion.

The Riksbank on 8 May 2024 cut its policy interest rate by 25 bps to 3.75%. Its post-Covid policy interest rate had peaked at 4.00% as set on September 27, 2023. It remains to be seen whether such an early start to rate cuts is consistent with bringing inflation down sustainably to the 2% target. The official inflation target variable is the CPIF (the consumer price index with a fixed interest rate), whose inflation rate had come down to 2.3% in April 2024. CPIF inflation ex energy was 2.9% in April 2024, with HICP inflation at 2.4%, CPI inflation at 3.9%, and core CPI inflation at 2.9%. Whatever happens in the future, the recapitalization arrangement with the Swedish parliament is no doubt sufficient to ensure that the monetary issuance necessary to prevent equitable insolvency will not prevent the Riksbank from engaging in the effective pursuit of its inflation target or of its financial stability mandate.

5.4 *The Bank of England*

On April 28, 2023, the BoE estimated that its QE and QT programs would likely generate a total (realized) financial loss, starting with their inception in 2009, of around 100 billion pounds sterling by 2033 (cumulative realized profits had peaked in September 2022 at £124 billion).[31] These estimates depend on the future path of market interest rates and therefore are highly uncertain. A House of Commons Report, published on February 7, 2024, refers to estimates of the total cumulative lifetime (since 2009) net present value of QE and QT cashflows ranging from −£50 billion to −£130 billion.[32] The most recent Bank of England report on its Asset Purchase Facility (APF), published on February 6, 2024, contains estimates of the net cumulative lifetime NPV of APF cashflows of −£50 billion and −£80 billion.[33]

The BoE has both an APF profit and loss sharing agreement and recapitalization and income sharing agreement with HM Treasury. The profit and loss sharing agreement handles the realized profits and losses of its Asset Purchase Facility, which conducts all QE and QT operations and other asset purchases and sales conducted to implement the BoE's monetary policy. It currently accounts for around 80% of the BoE's assets. On April 28, 2023, the BoE estimated that its quantitative easing (QE) and quantitative tightening (QT) programs, initiated in 2009, would likely generate a total lifetime (realized) financial loss of around 100 billion pounds

[31] See Asset Purchase Facility Quarterly Report—2023 Q1 | Bank of England.

[32] See Quantitative Tightening (parliament.uk).

[33] See Asset Purchase Facility Quarterly Report—2023 Q4 | Bank of England.

sterling by 2033.[34] Any realized losses incurred by the BEAPFF are compensated by HM Treasury and any realized profits are transferred to HM Treasury. Cumulative total transfers from the BEAPFF to HM Treasury peaked at £123.8 bn in September 2022. The direction of the quarterly net transfers has reversed since then, with HM Treasury transferring £5 billion to the BEAPFF between October 2022 and January 2023 (see Bank of England (2023)). During 2023 around £38 billion was transferred from HM Treasury to the BoE.[35]

In addition, the BoE has a clear framework for capital and income sharing with HM Treasury (see HM Treasury (2018)). It specifies a Target (currently £3.5 billion), a Floor (£0.5 billion), and a Ceiling (£5.5 billion) for the loss-absorbing capital of the BoE.[36] If actual loss-absorbing capital is above the Ceiling, 100% of net profits are paid as dividends to the Treasury. Above the Target but below the Ceiling, 50% of net profits are paid as dividends to the Treasury. Below the Target but above the Floor, the BoE retains 100% of net profits. Below the Floor, the BoE receives a capital injection from the Treasury to return its capital to the Target. The three capital thresholds are supposed to be calculated using a forward-looking, scenario-based approach to assess potential losses in a set of severe but plausible events, for the types of operations that are backed by the BoE's capital, and for the types of operations for which the BoE can request an indemnity from the Treasury. The Governors and Court of the BoE approve these scenarios, but they are not in the public domain.

Note that since BoE sterling notes in circulation on March 13, 2024 were £87 billion and sterling reserve balance liabilities were £795 billion, the BoE's net-of-money conventional equity was around £885 billion, which should be a reasonable buffer against equitable insolvency. The one weakness of the BoE's recapitalization agreement with HM Treasury is that it is a Memorandum of Understanding rather than an arrangement based on law—requiring legislative approval for any amendments. While the BoE was late in responding to the post-Covid inflation surge in December 2021 (albeit ahead of the Fed (in March 2022) and the ECB (in July 2022)), I would attribute this to forecast errors rather than to a loss of independence. The same applies to the failure to raise the Bank Rate above 5.25% even though CPI inflation YoY was still 3.2% in March 2024, with core CPI inflation at 4.2%. Because of the profit and loss sharing and recapitalization agreements with HM Treasury, fear of insolvency can never have been an issue.

[34] See Asset Purchase Facility Quarterly Report—2023 Q1 | Bank of England.

[35] See Asset Purchase Facility Quarterly Report—2023 Q4 | Bank of England.

[36] Loss-absorbing capital is the BoE's total conventional capital less any capital components that cannot absorb losses, such as intangible assets, net pension scheme assets (net of deferred tax), illiquid investments, and property revaluation reserves. The BoE received its first capital injection from HM Treasury (£1.2 billion) in March 2019. See Bank of England (2020). For the year ended 28 February 2021, the BoE's loss-absorbing capital was again just below the £3.5 billion Target, at £3475 million. For the year ended February 2022 it was £3280 million. For the year ended February 2023 it was £3394 million.

5.5 *The Bank of Japan*

The Bank of Japan (BoJ) is at material risk of very significant mark-to-market losses now that it has ended (on March 19, 2024) more than seven years of yield curve control (YCC) that started in September 2016 when the overnight rate was set at −0.10%, where it stayed until March 19, 2024, when it was raised to a range from 0 to 0.1%. In December 2022, the cap on the 10-year yield on Japanese government bonds (JGBs) was raised from 0.25 to 0.50%. In July 2023, the cap was raised to 1.00%. On October 31, 2023, the BoJ announced that the 1 percent ceiling on 10-year yields would be regarded as a "reference". It would no longer strictly cap 10-year JGB yields at 1.00% by open-ended fixed-rate purchase operations. Even after the official end of YCC, the BoJ stated that "In case of a rapid rise in long-term interest rates, it will make nimble responses by, for example, increasing the amount of JGB purchases and conducting fixed-rate purchase operations of JGBs ...".[37] This still looks like YCC-lite. There is also a sustainability question mark behind a policy that attempts to prevent serious losses on a very large stock of long-duration, fixed-interest debt by purchasing more of such debt. The BoJ owned 53% of outstanding JGBs (excluding Treasury bills) as of the end of September 2023, worth ¥587 trillion at book value, close to 100% of GDP (which was ¥591 trillion in 2023), much of it fixed rate and long duration. Unrealized losses on the BoJ's holdings of JGBs were about 8.8 trillion yen (US$68.4 billion) at the end of 2022, mostly as a result of the BoJ raising the 10-year yield cap on December 20, 2022.[38] Much larger losses are likely now that YCC has ended. So far, the increase in the 10-year JGB yield has been modest. It peaked at 0.98% on November 1, 2023, but stood at 0.93% on May 16, 2024. On March 31, 2023, the capital base of the BoJ was ¥11.9 trillion.[39] As of March 12, 2024, Banknotes stood at ¥121 trillion and Current deposits at ¥530 trillion. The net-of-money conventional equity of the BoJ is therefore around ¥663 trillion, which suggests that equitable insolvency is unlikely to become an issue, even if the valuation of the BoJ's holdings of long-duration fixed-rate debt instruments takes a serious beating in the years to come. The Bank of Japan does not have a formal recapitalization agreement with the Japanese government. Given the magnitude of the possible losses the case for such an agreement could not be stronger.

Japan's YoY CPI inflation rate peaked at 4.30% in January 2023. In March 2024, the month that the BoJ raised is policy rate (by 10 bps) for the first time since 2007, CPI inflation was down to 2.7%; excluding fresh food, the inflation rate was 2.60% and excluding both food and energy it was 2.9%. It is possible that fear of massive

[37] See changes in the monetary framework BoJ.

[38] See BOJ's unrealized losses on JGB holdings grow to 68.4bn Nikkei Asia. The book value of the BoJ's holdings of JGBs at the end of December 2022 was ¥564.1 trillion, while their market value was ¥555,2 trillion.

[39] This is the sum of paid-in Capital (negligible at ¥100 million), Reserves (¥3.5 trillion), and Provisions (¥8.3 trillion).

losses on its JGB portfolio account has prevented the BoJ from raising the policy rate earlier and to a higher level and ending YCC sooner.

5.6 *The Fed*

The Fed has three capital adequacy issues: (1) the deferred asset fudge; (2) no recapitalization agreement with the U.S. Treasury; and (3) large mark-to-market losses. We consider these in turn.

5.6.1 The Fed's Deferred Asset Fudge

When the Fed incurs losses that would reduce its capital below some threshold level, it creates a "deferred asset" (Buiter, 2023). The Federal Reserve Act requires the Reserve Banks to remit excess earnings to the U.S. Treasury after providing for operating costs, payments of dividends, and any amount necessary to maintain surplus.[40] During a period when earnings are not sufficient to provide for those costs, a deferred asset is recorded. The deferred asset is the amount of future net earnings the Reserve Banks will need to realize before their remittances to the U.S. Treasury resume."[41] As of December 31, 2023, the deferred asset increase since the start of the year was $116.4 billion. The deferred asset was zero until year-end 2021. It was first recorded at a positive value in Q3, 2022. It had reached $16.6 bn end the end of 2022, so by the end of 2023 the deferred asset was $133.0 billion. The deferred asset is sometimes included in the Fed's accounts as a positive asset (in the Federal Reserve Banks Combined Quarterly Financial Report where it is referred to as "Deferred asset—remittances to the Treasury"); $105.9 billion is the figure for September 30, 2023.[42] Sometimes it is included in the Fed's accounts as a negative liability (in the Consolidated Statement of Condition of All Federal Reserve Banks); −$157.4 billion is the Fed's May 15, 2024 figure for "Other liabilities and accrued dividends".[43]

[40] See Federal Reserve Board—Federal Reserve Board announces Reserve Bank income and expense data and transfers to the Treasury for 2022.

[41] The use of the "deferred asset" may have been motivated by an incorrect analogy with the deferred assets private companies can have on their balance sheet. Such assets represent expenditures that have been made but will only be recognized as expenses on future financial statements. An example is the deferred tax asset commonly used in corporate accounting. A deferred tax asset results from an overpayment or advance payment of taxes. The deferred tax asset is eventually returned to the company as tax relief, if the cumulative value of future taxes is equal to or larger than the deferred tax asset.

[42] See Federal Reserve Banks Combined Quarterly Financial Report (Unaudited)—September 30, 2023.

[43] See Federal Reserve Balance Sheet: Factors Affecting Reserve Balances—H.4.1—July 18, 2024. Minus $157.4 billion is the figure in Table 5, Consolidated Statement of Condition of All

If this is proper accounting, why not have every privately owned company include losses that would take the firm's capital below some threshold level as a deferred asset (or a negative liability) on its balance sheet? After all, the privately owned company is obliged to remit excess earnings to its shareholders after providing for operating costs, debt service, and any amount necessary to maintain surplus. The corporate deferred asset is the amount of future net earnings the company will need to realize before its payment of dividends to its shareholders resumes. This is dangerous nonsense. Why not add as a (positive) liability the value (or PDV) of the future profits the Fed will have to pay to the Treasury because the Fed's capital exceeds the threshold level? The Fed's net worth would always be at the threshold level.

The statement that "The deferred asset is the amount of future net earnings the Reserve Banks will need to realize before their remittances to the U.S. Treasury resume" ignores two contingencies. The first (and less likely) contingency is that the Reserve Banks cannot, under any circumstances, realize sufficient future net earnings to resume remittances to the Treasury. From Eq. (6) and Table 2, without material foreign currency liabilities, equitable insolvency can happen only if there is a cap on the growth rate of central bank money. Equitable insolvency can be avoided if the growth rate of central bank money can be kept sufficiently far above the own interest rate on central bank money. It is an open question whether the growth rate of the demand for central bank money can always be kept far enough above the own interest rate on central bank money. The second contingency is that the Reserve Banks can realize sufficient future net earnings only by issuing seigniorage and setting the policy rate in a manner that is inconsistent with the price stability (or dual) mandate and/or with the financial stability mandate.

The Fed rules out these two contingencies about the deferred asset: "Negative net income, and the corresponding creation of a deferred asset, do not affect the Federal Reserve's ability to conduct monetary policy or meet its financial obligations." In terms of the central bank's comprehensive balance sheet in Table 2, I interpret this as meaning that Fed losses, no matter how large, do not have two prima facie possible consequences. First, they never affect current and future seigniorage, $V_t\left(\left\{\dot{M} - i^M M, i\right\}\right)$, current and future Fed policy interest rates, and the size and composition of its balance sheet in ways that weaken the Fed's ability to conduct monetary policy. Second, they do not threaten the Fed's equitable solvency; $\hat{W}^{cb} \geq 0$ remains satisfied and the Fed remains able to meet its financial obligations. These consequences can be ruled out only if the Fed can freely choose the PDV of current and future net remittances to the Treasury, $V_t(\{T^{cb}, i\})$, which in the case of the USA is a dubious assumption were this to involve negative remittances from the Fed to the U.S. Treasury or Fed recapitalization by the U.S. Treasury.

Federal Reserve Banks (continued) for "Other liabilities and accrued dividends", which includes the liability for earnings remittances due to the U.S. Treasury. Table 6, Statement of Condition of Each Federal Reserve Bank, May 15, 2024 (continued) has a figure of −\$168.9 billion for "Earnings remittances due to the U.S. Treasury".

5.6.2 No Recapitalization Agreement with the U.S. Treasury

Effectively what the Fed does (and the ECB too) is create an incomplete comprehensive balance sheet that adds part of $V_t(\{T^{cb}, i\})$ to the liability side of the conventional balance sheet, but omits the rest of $V_t(\{T^{cb}, i\})$ and the other implicit assets and liabilities that are part of the comprehensive balance sheet, notably the PDV of current and future seigniorage, $V_t\left(\left\{\dot{M} - i^M M, i\right\}\right)$.[44] It then effectively assumes that $V_t(\{T^{cb}, i\})$ is a choice variable of the Fed, which reduces its value, in any period, by the amount of that period's reported loss, if that loss would take Fed net worth below some threshold level, currently just below \$43 billion.[45]

In terms of Eqs. (1) and (2), any current cash loss that would reduce Fed net worth below some threshold level is offset by a reduction in current and/or future T^{cb}, net transfer payments from the central bank to the Treasury. In terms of Eqs. (10) or (11) and Tables 2 or 3, any losses that would otherwise threaten to drive conventional (or comprehensive) net worth below some threshold level are neutralized by a matching reduction in the PDV of net transfer payments from the central bank to the Treasury, $V_t(\{T^{cb}, i\})$. This could, if the losses are large and persistent enough, result in a sequence of negative values of T^{cb} or even a negative value of $V_t(\{T^{cb}, i\})$. Unlike the UK or Sweden, the USA has no explicit formal agreement (let alone a law) that the Treasury must recapitalize the central bank should the central bank's capital fall below some threshold level. While there are (capped) U.S. Treasury guarantees (through equity investments) for some of the special emergency funding facilities created by the Fed following the outbreak of the Covid pandemic, there also is nothing comparable to HM Treasury's compensation of the Bank of England for losses on its QE, QT (and other monetary policy operations) conducted through the BEAPFF.

Section 7 of the Federal Reserve Act only deals with the "Dividends and Surplus Funds of Reserve Banks". There is no provision for a net transfer of funds from the U.S. Treasury to the Fed should the Fed incur excessive losses on its monetary policy operations or for the recapitalization of the Fed by the U.S. Treasury should the Fed's equity fall below some threshold level. The bizarre ownership structure of the Federal Reserve System does not help.[46]

The simplest way of describing the "deferred asset" practice is that the Fed sets some floor for $\hat{W}^{cb}$ (or for W^{cb}) and chooses the value of $V_t\left(\left\{\dot{M} - i^M M, i\right\}\right)$ to be consistent with its price stability (or dual) mandate and its financial stability

[44] The PDV of central bank primary current expenditures, $V_t(\{C^{cb}, i\})$ is also omitted.

[45] This is the sum of paid-in capital (\$35.945 billion as of September 30, 2023, and \$6.785 billion of surplus. The Federal Reserve Act requires that the aggregate Federal Reserve Bank surplus not exceed a cap of \$6.825 billion.

[46] The Board of Governors is an independent federal government agency, and the 12 regional Federal Reserve Banks are set up formally like private corporations. Member banks own stock in the Federal Reserve Banks and earn legally required dividends—at a maximum rate of interest of 6%. The so-called stock is effectively a fixed interest rate perpetual debenture that is junior to all other creditors.

mandate. It then adjusts $V_t(\{T^{cb}, i\})$ to make sure the floor for $\hat{W}^{cb}$ (or W^{cb}) is met. As noted, this could require negative values of T^{cb} in some periods or even a negative value for $V_t(\{T^{cb}, i\})$. Such Treasury behavior is far from self-evident. If the implicit "deferred asset" assumption is invalid, realized losses may call instead for recourse to additional current and future seigniorage (a larger value of $V_t\left(\left\{\dot{M} - i^M M, i\right\}\right)$ if equitable insolvency of the Fed is to be avoided. The amount of monetization required to ensure the absence of equitable insolvency may be inconsistent with price stability or financial stability if the financial loss is large enough. This possibility is not recognized by the Fed.

5.6.3 Large Mark-to-Market Losses

The recapitalization issue matters because the Fed's operating losses and realized valuation losses since September 2022 (which created a \$133.0 billion deferred asset at the end of 2023) are dwarfed by the Fed's unrealized losses on its investments, driven by the increase in long-term interest rates and the Fed's large holdings of mostly long-duration fixed-rate securities. The size of the Fed's balance sheet in the week from December 31, 2007 was \$922 billion.[47] In the week from December 30, 2019 it was \$4174 billion. It peaked at \$8965 billion in the week from April 11, 2022. As of the week from March 18, 2024, it was \$7514 billion. During the Covid pandemic, from January 2020 till April 2022, the Fed bought approximately \$4764 billion worth of public and private securities. During the nine months ended September 30, 2022, the increase in cumulative unrealized losses on the Fed's SOMA holdings was \$1253 billion.[48] The change in the cumulative unrealized gains (losses) is not reported in the Combined statements of operations. Realized losses were a mere \$226 million. For the nine months ended September 30, 2023, realized losses were \$56 million, but there was a further \$222 billion increase in cumulative unrealized losses, which reached \$1301.9 billion. As of September 2023, with mark-to-market accounting for assets, and subtracting the \$105.9 billion deferred asset, the reported Total Reserve Bank capital of \$42.7 billion turns into a fair-value-and-no-deferred-assets Total Reserve Bank capital of −\$1365.1 billion. With Federal Reserve notes outstanding of \$2272.4 billion and deposits of depository institutions of \$3066.6 billion, the net-of-money conventional equity of the Fed, at \$3973.9 billion, does not suggest any need for equitable insolvency concerns, even if all the unrealized losses on the balance sheet were to become realized losses overnight. Only a quantitative implementation of the Fed's comprehensive balance sheet can determine whether, if the unrealized losses were to become realized losses, and if no U.S. Treasury financial support for the Fed were forthcoming, the current and future seigniorage issuance required to avoid equitable insolvency would be consistent

[47] See Federal Reserve Board—Recent balance sheet trends.

[48] See Federal Reserve Banks Combined Quarterly Financial Report (Unaudited)—September 30, 2023.

with the Fed's maximum employment and stable prices mandate and the financial stability mandate.

Headline CPI inflation was 3.4% YoY in April 2024, with core inflation at 3.6%. The Fed appears to have underestimated the persistence of post-Covid inflation. As with the UK, I do not believe that fear of even larger balance sheet losses or loss of operational independence can account for the late and insufficient raising of the policy rate. It is possible that the decision in May 2024 to slow down the pace of QT was partly motivated by a desire not to realize losses, in addition to concerns about commercial bank demand for reserves with the Fed.

5.7 The European Central Bank and the Eurosystem

How does the ECB manage operating losses and possible negative equity? The ECB in 2022 made an operating loss of €1.6 billion which was covered by the release of that same amount from the provision for financial risks, which stood at €6.6 billion after the release. The reported profit for the year 2022 was therefore zero. For 2023, the ECB reported a €1.3 billion loss. This was after the release of the remaining €6.6 billion balance from the provision of financial risk.[49] The main driver of the increased operating loss of €7.9 billion was the increase in the ECB's net interest expense to €7.2 billion in 2023 from a net interest income of €900 million in 2022. The €1.3 billion reported loss for 2023 is carried forward on the ECB's balance sheet as a positive asset, the Loss for the year, "to be offset against future profits"—the ECB's version of the deferred asset fudge, which was also used in 2004 and 2003, the previous years with reported losses. Like the Fed, the ECB omits mentioning that such future profits may never materialize or may do so only if (1) the ECB engages in monetary issuance of a magnitude that is incompatible with its price stability mandate or its financial stability mandate, or (2) if the ECB is the beneficiary of a recapitalization (or other net transfer of funds or indemnity) by its shareholders—the euro area's 20 national central banks and, ultimately, their beneficial owners—the 20 national fiscal authorities of the euro area member states.[50] The balance sheet of the consolidated Eurosystem does not

[49] Provisions went down from €6636 million at the end of 2022 to €67 million at the end of 2023. See Annual Accounts 2023 (europa.eu).

[50] I take it as a given that every central bank has a financial stability mandate, even if this is not explicitly spelled out in legislation. The 2010 Dodd-Frank Wall Street Reform and Consumer Protection Act contains the latest specification of the financial stability role of the Fed. The ECB asserts that "Financial stability is a precondition for price stability and vice versa" (ECB (2021)). There is a reference to financial stability in the TFEU, Article 125, section 5: "The ESCB shall contribute to the smooth conduct of policies pursued by the competent authorities relating to the prudential supervision of credit institutions and the stability of the financial system". See EUR-Lex—12016E127—EN—EUR-Lex (europa.eu).

contain a "'Loss for the year" asset category. It is possible that "Loss for the year' is included in "Other assets" of the Eurosystem.

In its Annual Accounts 2023, the ECB reports its net equity, which consists of its "capital, any amounts held in the provision for financial risks and the general reserve fund, the revaluation accounts, any accumulated losses from previous years and any profit/loss for the year".[51] Net equity was €44.5 billion at the end of 2023, down from €51.6 billion at the end of 2022. Unrealized gains (losses) on gold and foreign exchange and on some securities are recorded on the liability side of the balance sheet under the item Revaluation accounts.[52] Unrealized gains (losses) on most securities (including those held for monetary policy purposes) are excluded and therefore do not show up either on the balance sheet or in the profit and loss account—they are treated as HTM securities.[53] The notes to the ECB's financial statements contain the market values of securities held for monetary policy purposes.[54] At the end of 2023, securities held by the ECB under the SMP, APP, and PEPP were worth €425.3 billion at amortized cost and €385.5 billion at market value. The difference, €39.8 billion, still leaves the ECB, at the end of 2023, with positive net equity of €4.7 billion when assets are valued at market prices.[55] Even if the deferred asset (Loss for the year) is deducted, net equity at fair value would be €3.4 billion. At the end of 2022, securities held for monetary policy purposes were worth €457.3 billion at amortized cost and €398.0 billion at market value. This means negative net equity at market value for the ECB of €7.7 billion at the end of 2022, assuming there were no unrealized gains or losses on the assets excluded from these calculations (mainly Intra-Eurosystem claims and Other assets).

If the operating loss were to exceed the ECB's *financial resources* (its "... capital, the amounts held in the provision for financial risks and the general reserve fund, the revaluation accounts and any profit for the year"), the Governing Council can make a claim against the Eurosystem's monetary income of the relevant financial year. Monetary income is the net income derived from assets held against monetary liabilities (mainly banknotes in circulation and bank deposits with the central bank). Unrealized capital gains or losses on assets held against monetary liabilities are not reflected in the monetary income statement. Net equity exceeds

[51] See Annual Accounts 2023 (europa.eu).

[52] "... gold, foreign exchange and financial instruments (other than securities classified as held-to-maturity, non-marketable securities and securities held for monetary policy purposes) are revalued at market rates and prices" (ECB (2023)). Securities classified as held-to-maturity are valued at amortized cost (subject to impairment). The same applies to non-marketable securities.

[53] "... all securities currently held by the Eurosystem for monetary policy purposes (under the Securities Markets Program, the asset purchase program and the pandemic emergency purchase program) are accounted for at amortized cost subject to impairment based on monetary policy considerations". See FAQs on the ECB's Annual Accounts (europa.eu).

[54] See Annual Accounts 2023 (europa.eu).

[55] This assumes that there were no capital gains or losses on Intra-Eurosystem claims (€125.4 billion at the end of 2023) or on Other assets (€34.7 billion), or that these asset categories are valued in the balance sheet at fair value rather than at amortized cost.

financial resources by the sum of any accumulated losses from past periods and any loss in this period. I assume that "... any profit/loss for the year" in the ECB's definition of net equity means that a reported loss in the current year *increases* net equity by the amount of the loss. I also assume that "any accumulated losses from previous years" in the definition of net equity means any accumulated losses from previous years that have not been recouped out of subsequent profits. If this is correct, net equity exceeds financial resources by an amount equal to the value of what the Fed calls the deferred asset—the amount of future profits that must be earned before the central bank can resume its remittances to its shareholders or beneficial owner(s).

Net equity information was provided in the ECB's Annual Accounts 2023 for the years 2019 to 2023, but financial resources were not mentioned. Information on financial resources was provided in the ECB's Annual Accounts 2022 for the years 2018 to 2022, but net equity was not mentioned. The numbers for net equity are the same as for financial resources in the overlap years from 2019 to 2022. This makes sense if "any accumulated losses from previous years" refers to accumulated past reported losses that have not (yet) been netted out against subsequent profits. There had not been any ECB-reported losses between 2004 and 2023 and it is likely that the accumulated reported losses in 2004 would have been "paid down" by positive profits between 2004 and 2019.

As noted, on December 31, 2022, the ECB's net equity totaled €51.6 billion (of which €8.9 billion was paid-up capital), with a balance sheet size of €698.9 billion. ECB net equity and financial resources were €1.8 billion higher than in 2021 because of (i) the boost to the revaluation accounts as a result of the appreciation of the U.S. dollar against the euro and the rise in the market price of gold and (ii) an increase in the paid-up capital because of the accession of Croatia. As of December 31, 2023, net equity was €44.5 billion, with a balance sheet size of €674.5 billion. The revaluation accounts again increased in value in 2023. It is ironic that the limited set of assets that the ECB does mark to market (and that are included in the revaluation accounts) had positive revaluations in 2022 and in 2023.

What happens if the losses in a year exceed the sum of the ECB's financial resources and the monetary income of the Eurosystem for that year? Note that the monetary income of the consolidated Eurosystem was likely negative in 2022 and 2023 (see Belhocine et al., 2023). To avoid equitable insolvency, the ECB either must boost its monetary liabilities (seigniorage) or increase its paid-up capital. As regards seigniorage, although both the ECB and the NCBs of the euro area countries are legally entitled to issue euro banknotes, the ECB has never issued physical currency (notes and coins) itself and does not handle cash in any way. The €125.4 billion worth of banknotes in circulation on the balance sheet of the ECB at the end of 2023 represent its attributed 8% share of the €1567.7 billion worth of banknotes circulated by the 20 NCBs of the Eurosystem. The banknotes are backed by ECB claims on the NCBs, which bear the MRO interest rate. The ECB does not hold other monetary liabilities (required or excess reserves). Any decision to allow the ECB to increase its monetary liabilities at its discretion would have to be taken by the ECB Governing Council. I consider discretionary money creation by the ECB to be not impossible, but highly unlikely.

The ECB's paid-up capital is provided by the Eurosystem NCBs. The ECB can decide to increase its paid-up capital (or make further calls for foreign reserve assets from the Eurosystem NCBs) within the limits and according to the conditions set by the EU Council. The original subscribed capital was €5 billion. Subscribed capital at the end of 2023 is €10.8 billion of which €8.9 billion is paid-up capital. Even if the EU Council were to agree on an increase in the subscribed and paid-up capital, the Eurosystem NCBs that would have to provide the additional capital might not be able to afford it unless they themselves can boost their financial resources either by increasing their monetary liabilities or by being recapitalized by their beneficial owners—their respective national Treasuries.

The size of the consolidated balance sheet of the Eurosystem (the ECB and the 20 euro area NCBs) was €6935 billion at the end of 2023, down from €7951 billion at the end of 2022 and from €8564 billion at the end of 2021.[56] For 2023, capital and reserves were reported to be €120 billion, the same as in 2022 and a small increase over €113 billion at the end of 2021. Revaluation accounts were €635 billion at the end of 2023, an increase of €47 billion over the €588 billion at the end of 2022, which itself represented an increase of €33 billion over 2021. Here too, the assets included in the Revaluation accounts are likely to be unrepresentative of the total asset portfolio. Significant unrealized capital losses on long-duration securities held in the monetary policy portfolio—and therefore not included in the Revaluation accounts—would undoubtedly depress the market value of total assets significantly below the value given in the balance sheet and would result in negative equity if all assets were carried at fair value. Eurosystem cumulative capital gains (losses), realized and unrealized, from 2022 Q1 till 2023 Q3 were -€879 billion.[57] Unrealized capital losses are even larger—as noted, the Revaluation accounts for 2022 and 2023 showed a two-year net gain of €80 billion. Belhocine et al. (2023) estimate that, assuming the QE book remains static in its size and composition as of year-end 2021, valuation losses (relative to the valuation at end-2021) would be €758 billion at the end of 2022 and €1015 billion at the end of 2023.

The Consolidated Eurosystem financial resources available for absorbing losses would be €999 billion at the end of 2022 and €1106 billion at the end of 2023, if we add all Other liabilities to the sum of Capital and reserves, General provisions, and Revaluation accounts. Other liabilities were €291 bn at the end of 2022 and €261bn at the end of 2023, so if none of the Other liabilities are loss-absorbing, consolidated Eurosystem financial resources available for absorbing losses would be €708 billion at the end of 2022 and €845 billion at the end of 2023.

While data on the consolidated balance sheet of the Eurosystem are readily available, I have been unable to find Informative data on the profit and loss account

[56] See Consolidated balance sheet of the Eurosystem as at 31 December 2023 (europa.eu).

[57] See https://data.ecb.europa.eu/ and enter QSA.Q.N.I9.W0.S121.S1.N.A.K.F3.T._Z.XDC._T.S.V.N._T. The asset revaluation series is called "Changes in positions other than transactions".

of the consolidated Eurosystem.[58] Belhocine et al. (2023) project the net income of the Eurosystem over a ten-year horizon, and find that losses, while large, will be temporary and recoupable. They can be managed without capital contributions or indemnities from the national fiscal authorities. That is important, because some of the euro area member states have overly indebted and fiscally fragile governments that may not have the fiscal and financial resources to indemnify or recapitalize their NCBs. No sovereign default was considered as a possible source of central bank losses in Belhocine et al. (2023).

The bottom line is that the Eurosystem's financial resources would be hit hard if the current unrealized losses of around €1 trillion were to turn into realized losses over the ten-year horizon considered by Belhocine et al. (2023). They would be hit even harder if the coming decade were to see one or more significant sovereign defaults in the euro area. But with €1553 billion in currency in circulation and €3399 billion in the Current accounts and Deposit facility as of May 10, 2024, the net-of-money conventional equity is large, and equitable insolvency is not a material risk. A quantified comprehensive balance sheet for the Eurosystem is an essential input into any meaningful numerical analysis of the inflation risk posed by massive Eurosystem losses in the absence of substantial financial support for the Eurosystem by the euro area fiscal authorities.

Without going into the details of the losses and possible negative equity of the 20 individual euro area NCBs, I note that during 2023, the Bundesbank suffered a "Loss for the year" of €2.4 billion, following a loss of €172 million in 2022 and a loss of €seven million in 2021. Distributable profit was zero in all three years. The operating loss in 2023 was €21.6 billion. The zero distributable profit was achieved after the release of €19.2 billion of provisions for general risks and a further €2.4 billion withdrawal from the reserves. The Financial Times reported on June 26, 2023, that the German Federal Audit Office (Bundesrechnungshof) had warned that the Bundesbank may require a bailout from the German federal government (its sole owner) due to losses incurred through its participation in the Eurosystem's bond-buying scheme.[59] Many other euro area central banks are likely to have suffered losses and negative equity (most definitely if all assets are recorded at fair value). DNB in 2022 recorded its first annual loss since 1931. In 2023 its loss was almost €3.5 billion, with further losses expected for 2024. For 2023, just over €2.3 billion was released from the provision for financial risks and just over €1.1 billion was charged to capital and reserves. DNB recognizes that "In an extreme case, a capital contribution from the Dutch State may be necessary" (DNB, 2022), a

[58] It would be helpful to have more information about some of the entries in the consolidated balance sheet. For instance, I would like to know whether "Other assets", worth €394 billion at the end of 2023, includes "Loss for the year" – which does not appear separately as an asset on the consolidated balance sheet of the Eurosystem (but does appear separately as an asset on the ECB's balance sheet). I also would like to know what is included in "Other liabilities", worth €262 billion at the end of 2023; specifically, whether it contains any loss absorbing items akin to provisions or reserves.

[59] See Bundesbank may need recapitalisation to cover bond-buying losses (ft.com).

possibility recognized on July 4, 2022 by the Dutch Ministry of Finance in its annual information letter to the Dutch House of Representatives about DNB's financial risks—the Dutch State is DNB's sole shareholder.[60]

5.8 Does a Central Bank Financial Rescue by the Treasury Undermine Central Bank Independence?

Threats to the operational independence of AE central banks are likely to be more common and more severe in the years and decades to come than in any peacetime period since the 1950s. We are at risk of fiscal unsustainability leading to peacetime fiscal dominance in some AEs—a phenomenon historically associated with dysfunctional EMDEs. The reasons are the massive and unprecedented peacetime build-up of public debt since the GFC and the recent marked increase in cyclically adjusted primary public sector deficits as a share of GDP. Dealing effectively with this unprecedented peacetime public debt burden is likely to be complicated by political resistance to meaningful cuts in public spending or increases in taxes. Indeed, we are likely to see growing pressure to materially boost public spending. The drivers are the rising cost of health care for aging populations, the need to invest in climate change and biodiversity, and significantly higher defense spending. Add to that a likely materially positive neutral real interest rate, and slow growth of potential output. Slow growth will be driven by demographics, deglobalization, and climate change, notwithstanding the total-factor-productivity-growth-boosting potential of AI. The pressure on AE central banks to purchase sovereign debt and to boost remittances to the government (even if this requires price stability threatening seigniorage) may be hard to resist.

If a central bank gets indemnified or recapitalized by the fiscal authority, this may undermine the central bank's operational independence if the central bank and the fiscal authority have conflicting objectives and if the Treasury makes recapitalization contingent on the central bank acting in a (from the central bank's perspective) suboptimal manner. This may impact its monetary policy role as well as its financial stability roles as LOLR, MMLR, and microprudential and macroprudential supervisor and regulator. The good news is that it is hard to find examples of AE central banks after 1946 compromising their mandates when faced with the choice between equitable insolvency risk and excessive recourse to seigniorage. I believe that this reflects the fact that there have been few, if any, post-1946 instances of AE central banks facing serious equitable insolvency risk. There is no evidence that, when faced with material insolvency risk, central banks were able to resist political pressure for excessive monetization of government debt or excessive remittances to the Treasury. The bad news is that fiscal dominance can be imposed even if there is

[60] See https://www.tweedekamer.nl/kamerstukken/brieven_regering/detail?id=2022Z13993&did=2022D28898

no central bank insolvency risk. We are likely to soon experience unprecedentedly intense and persistent reaching for fiscal dominance in AEs by increasingly over-indebted and fiscally constrained governments. The risk of loss of central bank operational independence is minimized if there is an explicit and clear profit and loss sharing and recapitalization agreement between the central bank and the Treasury. Ideally, this would be part of a robust legal framework establishing the operationally independent central bank and governing its modus operandi. It is key to have widespread and deep political support for central bank operational independence as a necessary institutional precondition for lasting price stability.

6 Conclusions

The conventional balance sheet of the central bank is quite uninformative about the financial resources it has at its disposal to avoid equitable insolvency and about its ability to pursue its financial stability mandate and its price stability or dual mandate. Quantitative analysis of the comprehensive balance sheet—the intertemporal budget constraint—of the central bank and the consolidated State is essential. Equitable insolvency of the central bank occurs when the sum of the implicit liabilities and the face value of explicit liabilities exceeds the sum of the implicit assets and the fair value of the explicit assets—i.e., when comprehensive net worth is negative. The comprehensive balance sheet recognizes the fact that central bank fiat money is irredeemable and therefore a liability in name only. The key implicit asset of the central bank is the present discounted value of current and future seigniorage. A key implicit liability is the present discounted value of current and future net transfer payments (remittances) to the central bank's beneficial owner—the national Treasury. Equitable insolvency for a central bank is possible when the central bank has significant foreign-currency-denominated or deliverable commodity-denominated liabilities. It is also possible that, without recapitalization by the Treasury (or an international organization like the IMF or World Bank), the amount of monetary issuance required to avoid equitable insolvency is inconsistent with the pursuit of the central bank's price stability and financial stability mandates. As far as I can tell, this has not been a material issue for any AE central bank since the German hyperinflation of 1922–23 and Hungary's hyperinflation of 1945–46. It has been an issue for quite a few EMDEs. Argentina is a repeated example. In the most recent episode, with a YoY inflation rate of 143% in October 2023, Argentina elected, in November 2023, Javier Milei as president. During his election campaign, Milei favored abolishing Argentina's central bank and adopting the US dollar as the national currency—a proposition he has distanced himself from since the election. It would have been a non-starter in any case. The net US dollar holdings of the Argentine government and central bank are so small (and the ability of the Argentine government to borrow additional US dollars is so restricted) that the exchange rate of the Argentine peso for the US dollar would have been extremely weak on conversion. Even complete dollarization is a credible commitment to avoid excessive future recourse to seigniorage only for the duration of the abolition of the central bank. Any future president could resurrect the national central bank and create a new Argentine peso.

It is possible for central bank conventional net worth to be negative while comprehensive net worth is positive (the central bank can meet all its contractual financial obligations) and the central bank achieves its price stability and financial stability mandates. We have recently seen many examples of this and would see many more if all assets were marked to market. Conversely, equitable insolvency is possible in the medium and long run because comprehensive net worth is negative even when conventional net worth is positive. It is time for central banks and national Treasuries to produce complete comprehensive balance sheets, including that of the consolidated general government and central bank. Only with these comprehensive balance sheets can the monetary and fiscal authorities determine whether the current and prospective future monetary and fiscal policies are in the "region of stability"—whether politically feasible and sustainable fiscal and monetary policies are consistent with the maintenance of financial stability and macroeconomic stability—stable prices and full employment (see BIS, 2023). It is an open question whether the AE public debt explosions since the GFC and especially since the Covid-19 crisis, and the massive expansions of AE central banks' balance sheets, will be compatible with a sustainable return to inflation rates of two percent in the years to come. If the neutral real interest rate is persistently and significantly higher than between the GFC and early 2022 and if higher real GDP growth does not come to the rescue, many AEs will be faced with a painful choice between material fiscal tightening and price stability—an Argentina-lite dilemma. It is true that in the long run, if the economy is not at the effective lower bound, and with inflation expectations fully adjusted, the real seigniorage revenue that can be extracted is limited (Buiter, 2021). In the short run—the time frame that matters politically—the siren call of higher seigniorage revenue rather than higher taxes or lower public spending will be hard to resist.

References

Bank for International Settlements (BIS). (2023). *BIS Annual Economic Report 2023*, 25 June 2023. https://www.bis.org/publ/arpdf/ar2023e2.pdf

Bank of England. (2020). *Annual Report and Accounts*, 1 March 2019–29 February 2020. https://www.bankofengland.co.uk/-/media/boe/files/annual-report/2020/boe-2020.pdf

Bank of England. (2023). *Bank of England Asset Purchase Facility Fund Limited Annual Reports and Accounts*, 1 March 2022–28 February 2023. https://www.bankofengland.co.uk/-/media/boe/files/asset-purchase-facility/2023/afp-annual-report-2023.pdf

Belhocine, N., Bhatia, A. V., & Frie, J. (2023). Raising rates with a large balance sheet: The Eurosystem's net income and its fiscal implications. *IMF Working Paper*, WP/23/145, 7 July 2023. https://www.imf.org/en/Publications/WP/Issues/2023/07/07/Raising-Rates-with-a-Large-Balance-Sheet-The-Eurosystems-Net-Income-and-its-Fiscal-535549

Bell, S., Chui, M., Gomes, T., Mosser-Boehm, P., & Tejada, A. P. (2023). Why are central banks reporting losses? Does it matter? *BIS Bulletin* No 68, 7 February 2023. https://www.bis.org/publ/bisbull68.pdf

Bonetti, M., Broeders, D., Chen, D., & Dimitrov, D. (2024). *Central Bank Capital and Shareholder Relationship*. Working Papers, 809, De Nederlandsche Bank.

Buiter, W. H. (2007). "Seigniorage", *Economics*, the Open-Access, Open-Assessment E-Journal, ISSN 1864-6042, Kiel Institute for the World Economy (IfW), Kiel, Vol. 1, Iss. 2007–10, pp. 1–49, https://doi.org/10.5018/economics-ejournal.ja.2007-10

Buiter, W. H. (2008). *Can Central Banks Go Broke?*. Centre for Economic Policy Research Policy Insight No. 24, May 2008.

Buiter, W. H. (2021). *Central Banks as Fiscal Players; The Drivers of Fiscal and Monetary Policy Space*. Frederico Caffè Lectures, Cambridge University Press.

Buiter, W. H. (2023). Is the Fed's Negative Capital a Problem?. *Project Syndicate*, September 28. https://www.project-syndicate.org/commentary/federal-reserve-negative-capital-future-implications-by-willem-h-buiter-2023-09

Carpenter, S., Ihrig, J., Klee, E., Quinn, D., & Boote, A. (2013). *The Federal Reserve's Balance Sheet and Earnings: A primer and projections*. Finance and Economics Discussion Series Divisions of Research & Statistics and Monetary Affairs Federal Reserve Board, Washington, DC, January 2013. https://www.federalreserve.gov/pubs/feds/2013/201301/index.html

Czech National Bank. (2023). *Annual Report of the Czech National Bank 2022*. https://www.cnb.cz/export/sites/cnb/en/about_cnb/.galleries/performance/annual_reports/download/vz_2022_en.pdf. May 30, 2023.

De Grauwe, P., & Ji, Y. (2023). *Central banks can fight inflation without massive handouts to banks*, OMFIF, 5 September 2023. https://www.omfif.org/2023/09/central-banks-can-fight-inflation-without-massive-handouts-to-banks/

Del Negro, M., & Sims, C. A. (2015). When does a central bank's balance sheet require fiscal support. *Journal of Monetary Economics*, *73*, July 2015, 1–19.

DNB. (2022). *"Letter regarding DNB's capital position"* – September 20. https://www.dnb.nl/en/general-news/nieuwsberichten-2022/dnb-foresees-deterioration-of-capital-position/

ECB. (2021). The role of financial stability in the ECB's monetary policy strategy. *Financial Stability Review*, November 2021. https://www.ecb.europa.eu/press/financial-stability-publications/fsr/focus/2021/html/ecb.fsrbox202111_08~d3131413c2.en.html

ECB. (2023). Commentary on the consolidated balance sheet of the Eurosystem as at 31 December 2022. *Annual Report*. https://www.ecb.europa.eu/pub/annual/balance/html/ecb.eurosystembalancesheet202306_c"mmentary~786c61e933.en.html

Franta, M., Holub, T., & Saxa, B. (2022). Exiting from and exchange rate floor in a small open economy: Balance sheet implications of the Czech National Bank's exchange rate commitment. *International Journal of Central Banking*, issue 74, June 22, 51–105. https://www.ijcb.org/journal/ijcb22q2a2.pdf.

Galuščák, K., & Branislav, S. (2023). Central bank losses will eventually turn into profits. *OMFIF Insights*, 24 August 2023. https://www.omfif.org/2023/08/central-bank-losses-will-eventually-turn-into-profits/

HM Treasury. (2018). *Financial relationship between HM Treasury and the Bank of England: Memorandum of understanding*, June. https://www.bankofengland.co.uk/-/media/boe/files/memoranda-of-understanding/financial-relationship-between-hmt-and-the-boe-memorandum-of-understanding.pdf

Kehoe, T. J., Machicado, C. G., & Peres-Cajías, J. (2019). *The Monetary and Fiscal History of Bolivia, 1960–2017*. National Bureau of Economic Research Working Paper, 25523, February. https://www.nber.org/system/files/working_papers/w25523/w25523.pdf.Staff Report 579, Federal Reserve Bank of Minneapolis. February 2019.

Nordström, A., & Vredin, A. (2022). *Does central bank equity matter for monetary policy*. Sveriges Riksbank Staff Memo, December https://www.riksbank.se/globalassets/media/rapporter/staff-memo/engelska/2022/does-central-bank-equity-matter-for-monetary-policy.pdf

Reis, R. (2015). *Different types of central bank insolvency and the central role of seigniorage.* NBER Working Paper 21226, May. https://www.nber.org/papers/w21226

Rossouw, J. (2016). Private shareholding: An analysis of an eclectic group of central banks. *South African Journal of Economic and Management Sciences, 19*(1). Pretoria; https://doi.org/10.4102/sajems.v19i1.1329

Open Access This chapter is licensed under the terms of the Creative Commons Attribution 4.0 International License (http://creativecommons.org/licenses/by/4.0/), which permits use, sharing, adaptation, distribution and reproduction in any medium or format, as long as you give appropriate credit to the original author(s) and the source, provide a link to the Creative Commons license and indicate if changes were made.

The images or other third party material in this chapter are included in the chapter's Creative Commons license, unless indicated otherwise in a credit line to the material. If material is not included in the chapter's Creative Commons license and your intended use is not permitted by statutory regulation or exceeds the permitted use, you will need to obtain permission directly from the copyright holder.

Central Bank Capital and Trust in Money: Lessons from History for the Digital Age

Sarah Bell, Jon Frost, Boris Hofmann, Damiano Sandri, and Hyun Song Shin

Abstract Historically, central banks have at times operated successfully with negative equity. This indicates that a negative equity position of the central bank can be fully consistent with preserving trust in money. In addition, there is no evidence of any systematic relationship between the equity position of central banks and their ability to meet their monetary policy objectives. However, the case of the Bank of Amsterdam in the late 1700s, and the emerging market crises of the 1980s and 1990s, provide cautionary tales on the importance of fiscal backing in upholding trust in money. The pivotal economic determinant behind the trust in money is the portfolio decision of private holders of central bank money. In particular, there are potential "tipping points" when they abandon existing forms of money in favor of alternatives.

Keywords Central banking · Central bank solvency · Fiscal sustainability · Money · Trust

1 Introduction

Central banks are unlike private financial entities in that they are public institutions that pursue public policy objectives. Their aim is not the pursuit of profits. Any profits or losses are the result of policy actions in pursuit of their policy mandate.

The views expressed here are those of the authors and do not necessarily reflect those of the Bank for International Settlements (BIS). We thank Dirk Broeders, Michael Chui, Alison Arnot, and Bernardus Doornik for comments, and Cecilia Franco, Olivier Sirello, Albert Pierres Tejada, and Jai Yoon for helpful data and research support.

S. Bell · J. Frost · B. Hofmann · D. Sandri · H. S. Shin (✉)
Bank for International Settlements, Basel, Switzerland
e-mail: Sarah.Bell@bis.org; Jon.Frost@bis.org; Boris.Hofmann@bis.org; Damiano.Sandri@bis.org; Hyunsong.Shin@bis.org

© The Author(s) 2025

D. Broeders et al. (eds.), *Central Bank Capital in Turbulent Times*,
Contributions to Finance and Accounting,
https://doi.org/10.1007/978-3-031-73549-3_2

In particular, because central banks are issuers of fiat money, their liabilities are unlike the debt liabilities of private sector entities that are subject to repayment or redemption. Therefore, the standard tests of solvency—of having positive equity—do not apply in the same way to central banks. They can operate with negative equity, and many have done so in recent decades. The key question addressed in this paper is whether (and how much) central bank capital matters in preserving the trust in money. This question has gained more attention recently as central banks have raised policy rates to combat inflation, resulting in valuation losses on their longer-duration assets and a higher cost of remuneration on reserve balances.

The short answer (to be developed further below) is that a strong capital position is neither necessary nor sufficient for preserving trust in money. A strong capital position of the central bank in the conventional accounting sense is not an absolute prerequisite for preserving trust in money. This is evidenced by central banks that have operated effectively with negative equity. Still, these central banks have all benefited from support by fiscal authorities with sustainable debt levels. Conversely, there have been instances where trust in money eroded due to concerns about fiscal sustainability, despite central banks having positive capital. This suggests that the sustainability of public finances plays a critical role.

Instead of the central bank's capital position, our paper highlights the importance of a related set of issues as key for the preservation of trust in money. The pivotal economic mechanism that we highlight is the portfolio decision of private holders of central bank money. When private holders have access to alternative forms of money and other financial claims, fiat money needs to command unquestioned trust on the part of the private holders. While network effects will preserve support from private financial entities, erosion of trust could shift the economy closer to potential "tipping points" when holders abandon domestic money in favor of alternatives, whether they are metal coins in the 1700s or other reserve fiat currencies or crypto stablecoins in the modern era. It is in this context of the portfolio choice of private holders of central bank money that the capital position of the central bank enters into the analysis. This is because a weak or negative equity position of the central bank will have a bearing on how the tipping point of the switch to an alternative currency is determined. The outward symptom of such a tipping point would be the sudden collapse of the exchange rate during a currency crisis. The collapse of the currency can be seen as the point where there is a sudden loss of trust in money.

Before addressing these fundamental issues, we begin with an overview of the empirical evidence behind central bank capital and policy effectiveness. As we show below, there is little evidence from the major advanced and emerging market economies (EMEs) of any systematic relationship between the size of the equity buffer of a central bank and subsequent inflation. This finding holds even when comparing central banks with positive equity with those with negative equity. The key is the unquestioned trust in money secured by a credible central bank (Carstens, 2024).

While there is no one-for-one relationship between the equity level of the central bank and strength of the trust in money, it is illuminating to examine historical cases where the fiat money system came under sufficient stresses that trust in money broke down. We examine one such case—the demise of the Bank of Amsterdam in the late 1700s, arguably an early proto-central bank that issued fiat currency as book entries used for the settlement of wholesale payments.

The example of the Bank of Amsterdam as discussed by Bolt et~al. (2024) highlights how the portfolio choice of private holders of central bank money is the key economic determinant of the trust in money. The capital position of the central bank enters into the analysis especially when the central bank lacks credible fiscal support. In this case, a weak or negative equity position of the central bank influences the tipping point for the switch to an alternative currency. We return with a more detailed discussion of these issues below.

This paper adds to a growing literature on the role of central bank capital (see e.g., Stella, 1997, 2002; Bindseil et~al., 2004; Cúrdia & Woodford, 2011; Archer & Moser-Boehm, 2013; Del Negro & Sims, 2015; Hall & Reis, 2015; Reis, 2015; Nordström & Vredin, 2022; Wessels & Broeders, 2022). It also addresses the role of fiscal-monetary interactions for monetary stability (Sims, 1994; Buiter, 2020; Cochrane, 2023).

The paper is organized as follows. Section 2 opens with an overview of the evolution of central bank equity in recent decades and examines the empirical association between central bank capital and monetary stability. Section 3 gives a cautionary tale from monetary history, describing the downfall of the Bank of Amsterdam. Section 4 discusses how the mechanisms outlined in the loss of trust in money can play out in emerging market currency crises. Section 5 concludes by discussing some lessons for the digital age.

2 Central Bank Capital and Economic Outcomes

We begin with an overview of the evolution of central banks' equity in recent decades and its association with inflation and other macroeconomic outcomes. To measure central banks' equity, we rely on data from the International Monetary Fund (IMF) International Financial Statistics. Specifically, we use "Shares and Other Equity"of the central bank, as provided in line 17a.[1] We normalize equity by the size of central bank assets. The equity-to-asset ratio provides an indication of the central bank's ability to absorb losses that may materialize from a decline in asset values.

Figure 1a shows the median level of central bank equity in percent of assets across an unbalanced panel of 47 countries since the 1950s. The country selection is based on data availability.[2] The level of central bank equity has varied considerably

[1] See https://data.imf.org/?sk=4c514d48-b6ba-49ed-8ab9-52b0c1a0179b

[2] The country sample comprises Argentina, Australia, Austria, Belgium, Brazil, Canada, Chile, China, Croatia, Czechia, Denmark, Estonia, Finland, France, Germany, Greece, Hong Kong, Hungary, India, Indonesia, Ireland, Israel, Italy, Japan, Latvia, Lithuania, Luxembourg, Malaysia,

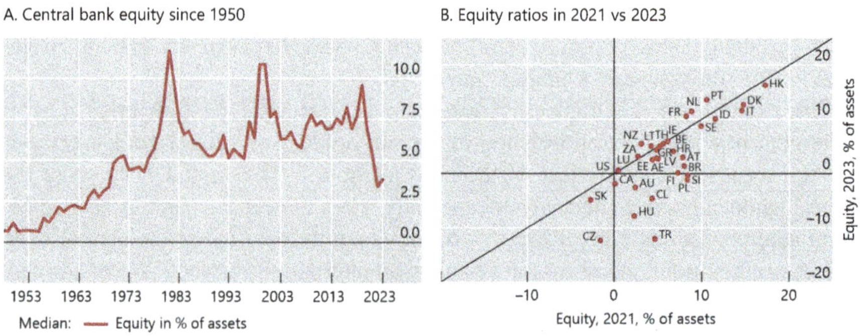

Fig. 1 Evolution of central bank equity. Sources: IMF; national data; BIS

over time. Starting from about 1% in the early 1950s, central bank equity followed an upward trend until 1980, reaching over 10% of assets. Equity levels then hovered around 5–10% until the post-pandemic inflation surge.

Over the past two years, the median equity ratio has fallen substantially. Figure 1b shows that the decline has been common across most countries, with equity levels in 2023 generally lower than those in 2021. This mainly reflects the impact of the post-pandemic monetary policy tightening that was required to curb inflationary pressures. Rising interest rates reduced profits or even led to losses, especially for those central banks that engaged in large asset purchase programs after the Great Financial Crisis (GFC) and during the Covid-19 pandemic. These purchases were funded mainly through interest-bearing commercial bank reserves. When central banks increased interest rates to curb inflation, net interest income declined because a large portion of their liabilities were linked to policy rates. Asset valuations also came under pressure with rising bond yields. This put further strain on the profitability of central banks that recognize market value in calculating net profits. Reflecting these dynamics, a number of central banks have reported losses. In many of these cases, losses are sizeable and may result in negative equity (Bell et~al., 2023).[3]

The balance sheet of a typical central bank comprises foreign and domestic currency securities on the asset side. These are funded largely by banknotes in circulation and commercial bank reserves on the liability side (Fig. 2a). Specific variations in balance sheets depend on the responsibilities of a given central bank. For example, foreign assets may be held for a variety of purposes, including foreign exchange (FX) intervention, the need to meet foreign currency debt obligations,

Mexico, the Netherlands, New Zealand, Norway, Peru, Philippines, Poland, Portugal, Slovakia, Slovenia, South Africa, South Korea, Spain, Sweden, Switzerland, Thailand, Türkiye, the United Arab Emirates, and the United States.

[3] See Cecchetti and Hilscher (2024) for an analysis of recent central bank losses in the wake of large-scale asset purchases.

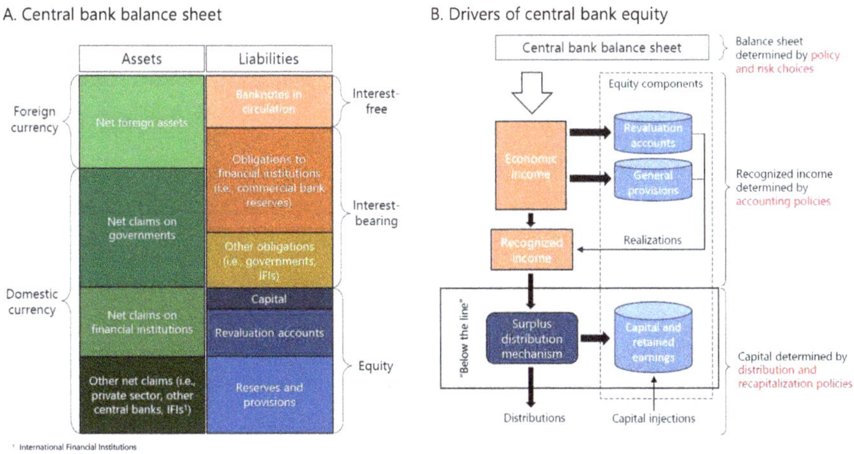

Fig. 2 Central bank finances: balance sheet and the drivers of equity. Sources: Authors, based on Archer and Moser-Boehm (2013)

and the need to cover trade balances. FX reserves are also a prerequisite for a central bank's ability to intervene to offset domestic currency depreciation. In some countries, the central bank acts as the banker for the government. Other central banks hold assets or liabilities to support operations that provide or reduce commercial bank reserves (Rule, 2015).

The financial strength of a central bank is determined by a combination of interacting factors, chiefly the structure of the balance sheet, the policies that determine recognition of income, and the rules that determine whether and how much income is retained or distributed (Fig. 2b). Traditionally a central bank's primary source of income is seigniorage, the net income earned on assets funded through currency issuance (a non-interest-bearing liability). For many central banks, and especially those in EMEs and small open economies, exchange rate translation gains and losses normally dominate profit and loss (P&L) movements. Conversely, for other central banks, variations in P&L primarily reflect changes in net interest income or asset valuation adjustments. Different accounting approaches, e.g., fair value, historic cost, or an asymmetric approach,[4] affect the size and volatility of net income from asset valuations in the short term, although the results wash out over the long term. From there, income recognition and distribution rules determine the size of buffers held against losses. These rules vary considerably across central banks (Bell et~al., 2023).

As public institutions with policy mandates, central banks typically transfer their excess profits to the fiscal authority. In principle, a central bank at one end of the

[4] The Eurosystem's asymmetric approach for central banks recognizes unrealized gains in asset values accounted for at fair value in revaluation accounts, but it recognizes losses directly in the profit and loss, after the revaluation account for this specific asset is fully depleted.

spectrum must remit all excess profits. At the other end of the spectrum, a central bank may be allowed to retain all of its earnings. In practice, most central banks fall in the middle of these two extremes. Many hold equity positions, i.e., capital plus retained earnings and other buffers in the form of provisions and reserves.

Approaches to distributing excess profits can be either rule-based or discretionary. They can be driven by targets for capital or components thereof and can have additional provisions that apply under specific circumstances. Approaches can be summarized in four types (Archer & Moser-Boehm, 2013):

1. Those that allow for general risk provisions (in addition to any revaluation buffers).
2. Those that provide for smoothing mechanisms.
3. Those that include equity protection mechanisms contingent on targets, e.g., with a rule that losses have to be compensated before distribution starts again or reaches a target equity level.
4. Those that place a cap on annual distributions.

Poorly designed surplus distribution arrangements, e.g., those that monetize unrealized gains by distributing them to the fiscal authority, can exacerbate decapitalization, impede rebuilding of equity, and even risk interfering with policy objectives if the government takes advantage of the opportunity of recapitalization to influence policy (Ueda, 2003). By contrast, those that are based on realized profits and losses and that have mechanisms for automatic recapitalization (with full fiscal backing) neutralize the impact of financial outcomes. A fully automated and credible rule for recapitalization of the central bank in case of losses can be regarded as a substitute for positive equity (Bindseil et~al., 2004).[5]

Unlike commercial banks, central banks do not seek profits; they cannot be insolvent in the conventional sense, as they can, in principle, issue more currency to meet their domestic currency obligations; and they face no regulatory capital minima precisely because of their unique purpose. Accordingly, they are backed (indirectly) by taxpayers. Even without explicit fiscal backing, insolvency of a central bank would be possible only if the reduction in equity were to exceed the net present value of future seigniorage income.

Did fluctuations in equity levels in the past correlate with changes in inflation rates? And, more specifically, did declines in equity levels foreshadow stronger inflationary pressures? To examine the relationship between central bank equity and subsequent inflation, we estimate the following panel regressions:

$$\pi_{i,t+h} = \alpha_i + \beta e_{i,t} + \gamma_t + \varepsilon_{i,t+h} \tag{1}$$

The dependent variable $\pi_{i,\,t+h}$ is the annual inflation rate $h \geq 1$ year in the future for country i. The regressor $e_{i,\,t}$ is the central bank's equity in percent of

[5] See Long and Fisher (2024) for a survey of central bank profit distribution and recapitalization arrangements across jurisdictions.

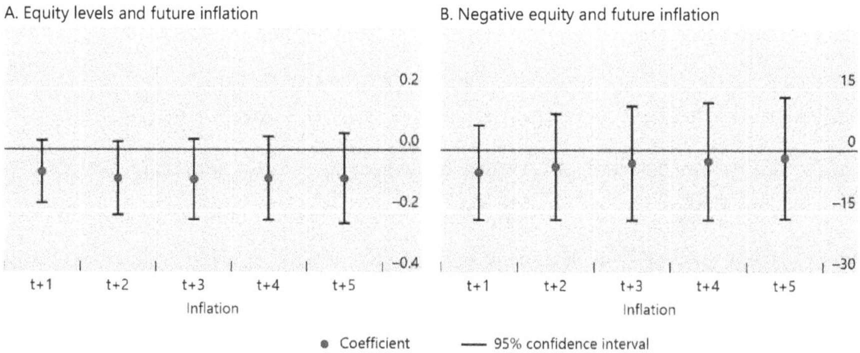

Panel A shows the relationship between central bank equity in percent of assets and future inflation, from one to five years ahead. Panel B shows the relationship between a negative central bank equity dummy and future inflation, from one to five years ahead. The regression sample includes 47 countries from 1950 to 2023. Data are at annual frequency.

Fig. 3 No association between central bank equity and future inflation. Sources: IMF; national data; BIS

assets. The regression includes country-fixed effects α_i to control for time-invariant country characteristics that may affect inflation as well as time-fixed effects γ_t to capture inflationary pressures arising from global shocks (e.g., commodity prices). As illustrated in Fig. 3a, we do not find evidence of a statistically significant relationship between equity levels and subsequent inflation outturns. These results are obtained after capping inflation rates at 200% to ensure that the regression estimates are not distorted by a few hyperinflation episodes. However, the point estimates remain statistically insignificant even without capping the inflation rates or when controlling for lagged inflation in the regression specification.

A possible conjecture is that equity levels may not matter for inflation when they are positive, but they could jeopardize price stability when they are negative.[6] To test for this hypothesis, we estimate an alternative version of Eq. (1) where $e_{i,t}$ is a dummy that takes the value of 1 to identify periods of negative central bank equity. As shown in Fig. 3b, we still do not detect a statistically significant association with future inflation.

Additional evidence that negative central bank equity does not inherently compromise inflation stability is provided by the experience of several central banks that successfully operated with negative equity for extended periods. Chile, Czechia, and Israel are well-known examples of such cases. As Fig. 4 illustrates, central banks in these countries have faced persistent phases of negative equity, at times exceeding 20% of assets, and equity was still negative as of the latest available observation. Yet inflation rates have remained far lower than in past decades and are falling again as of the latest available observation, as central banks pursued credible inflation-targeting mandates in a context of relatively sound fiscal positions.

[6] In this vein, Goncharov et~al. (2023) find that central banks are more likely to report slightly positive than slightly negative profits, particularly when political pressure is greater.

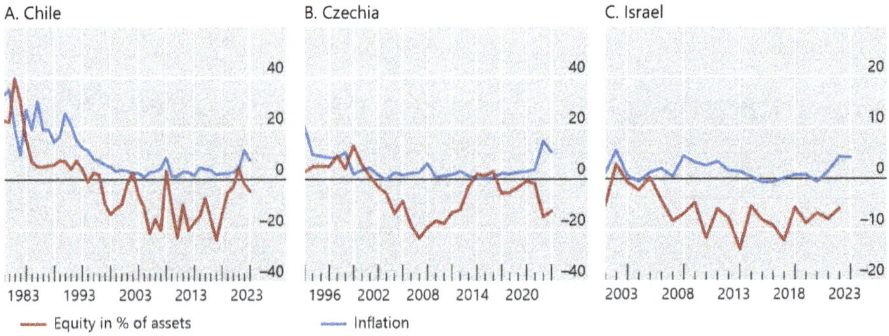

Fig. 4 Examples of large and persistent negative central bank equity levels. Sources: IMF; national data; BIS

3 A Cautionary Tale from History: The Bank of Amsterdam

These recent experiences underscore that, when solid institutional foundations are in place, negative or low central bank equity does not interfere with the ability of central banks to fulfill their mandate. Yet, this does not imply that there are no limits. If we go back somewhat further in history, we find a striking example of the limits of trust in fiat money.

Indeed, the Bank of Amsterdam provides a particularly vivid cautionary tale on the role of central bank capital—and what happens when it is depleted against the background of weak public finances. The Bank was founded in 1609 as a public deposit bank owned by the municipality of Amsterdam (see Bolt et~al., 2024; Shin & Schnabel, 2004). Its initial mandate was to "*check . . . the confusion of coin, and to be of use to all persons who are in need of any kind of coin in business*". From the outset, it accepted silver and gold coins in deposit, assessing their quality and validity, and provided payment services. The Bank of Amsterdam subsequently operated for over 200 years and increasingly took on the role of a proto-central bank. It issued a fiat currency—the Bank guilder—that was used in international trade and wholesale payments and is sometimes considered the first global reserve currency (Quinn & Roberds, 2016). The relatively simple structure of the Bank allows us to see the underlying economics more clearly.

At its core, the Bank of Amsterdam functioned as a wholesale payment system. Merchants held deposits at the Bank, denominated in Bank guilders. Bank guilders traded at a premium (agio) to metal coins, which was usually around 5%. The agio indicated how much clients were willing to pay for the convenience and security of holding Bank guilders over (nominally equivalent) guilder coins and thus represented an indicator of trust in the fiat currency. When merchants wanted to make a payment, the Bank transferred funds between merchants' accounts using simple entries in a paper ledger. In addition to this system for wholesale payments, individuals could make retail payments by going to so-called cashiers, who issued receipts that could be used as money in daily transactions.

The Bank was able to grow and become successful due to the trust in its stability, sound finances, and backing by the municipality of Amsterdam. Bank guilders were backed by holdings of silver and gold coins, and implicitly by Amsterdam city authorities. On numerous instances during its history, the Bank was able to continue functioning even through difficult circumstances. For instance, in 1672 (the "year of disaster", when the Netherlands was invaded and a severe economic crisis ensued), depositors demanded their funds from the Bank. Voltaire (1751) recounted the decision by the city authorities to open the vaults to public view. This demonstrated not only that the metal coins were still there, but also that they had been in the vault ever since the fire at the city hall decades earlier—the visitors could see coins with burn marks. Episodes like these built trust that Adam Smith (1776) would later refer to, in describing the Bank as follows:

> At Amsterdam, however, no point of faith is better established than that for every guilder, circulated as bank money, there is a correspondent guilder in gold or silver to be found in the treasure of the bank. The city is guarantee that it should be so. The bank is under the direction of the four reigning burgomasters who are changed every year. Each new set of burgomasters visits the treasure, compares it with the books, receives it upon oath, and delivers it over, with the same awful solemnity, to the set which succeeds; and in that sober and religious country oaths are not yet disregarded.

Yet soon after Smith's praise, trust in the Bank started to erode. In 1780, the Fourth Anglo-Dutch War broke out. This led to naval confrontations with the English in waters around the world. It also affected the ships and activity of the other great institution of the time—the Dutch East India Company (VOC). Throughout its history, the Bank had engaged in limited lending to the VOC, often on a seasonal basis, to allow for settlement liquidity in the period between ships' departure and their return with goods and fresh coin. Such lending had always occurred in secret, but it had been an important part of the Bank's operation and ability to support international trade. But starting in 1782, the Bank lent increasingly large amounts to the VOC, until such lending made up the majority of the Bank's assets. And when the VOC lost ships and was unable to repay the loans, trust in the Bank and the Bank guilder started to erode. As Bank equity turned negative (Fig. 5a), the agio fell below 5%. By 1790, it fell even below 0% (Fig. 5b).

The city authorities made limited attempts to recapitalize the Bank, but the funds were soon redirected to the city coffers and the Bank remained policy insolvent. If the city authorities had successfully recapitalized the Bank, it may have survived.[7] But in retrospect, the fiscal capacity of the city at the time was far too limited to support a global institution like the Bank; the lack of credible fiscal backing was a handicap that would have been hard to overcome. In the absence of sufficient fiscal support, trust in Bank guilders broke down. In 1795, as French revolutionary armies conquered Amsterdam, they made the full extent of the Bank's losses public, and

[7] If it had, the Bank would have likely transformed over time into a modern central bank, and the Netherlands would today have the oldest central bank in the world. That honour instead goes to Sveriges Riksbank, which was founded in 1668, modelled on Stockholms Banco, which was in turn modelled on the Bank of Amsterdam.

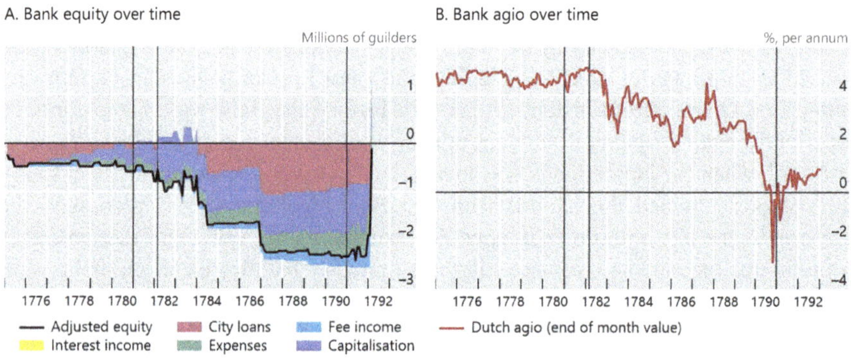

The three vertical lines refer to specific events in the downfall of the Bank: 1780 – outbreak of the Fourth Anglo-Dutch War; 1782 – Bank steadily ramps up lending; 1790 – agio turns negative.

Fig. 5 After Bank of Amsterdam equity turned negative, the agio collapsed. Source: Bolt et~al. (2024), Quinn and Roberds (2016), van Dillen (1934); authors' calculations

the agio fell to −30%. The Bank continued as a weakened institution for another 25 years. The lack of a trusted monetary unit of account had real economic costs, with income per capita falling over this period. The Bank guilder lost its role as an international reserve currency, and the center of global commerce moved to London.

In the model of Bolt et~al. (2024), the value of bank money to users (i.e., the deposits issued by the Bank of Amsterdam) depends on its value in settlement of wholesale trade transactions, and therefore on the volume of trade and the general buoyancy of the economy. In the face of a negative shock to the economy that reduces the value to users, there is reduced demand for bank money. The network effects in the use of bank money further amplify the decline in the value to users of holding bank money. Other things equal, the excess supply of bank money would put downward pressure on the exchange rate (the "agio").

In principle, the Bank of Amsterdam could respond to the negative shock by reducing the money supply to restore the agio to the desired level. It could do so by selling local coins in the daily open market and debiting the accounts of the buyers, thereby reducing the money supply. However, in the presence of illiquid loans on the balance sheet, there is a hard limit to the reduction in the money stock. The hard limit binds more as losses mount and negative equity eats into the asset value of the Bank. Once the Bank has sold all the liquid assets (the coins), it has only illiquid assets (the loans). The sales needed to stabilize the agio cannot go further, as there is no more capacity for a reduction in the deposits. Bolt et~al. (2024) solve for the tipping point where negative equity and asset illiquidity render fiat money worthless.

Two key features stand out from Bolt et~al. (2024), which resonate even for debates of today.

First, while the network effects of fiat money allow monetary regimes to persist for quite some time, there are limits to how resilient such arrangements can be. Being able to issue fiat money gives the central bank considerable latitude to leverage up its balance sheet without loss of confidence in the value of money. Yet the Bank of Amsterdam's failure is a vivid lesson in how a central bank that loses public trust can push its luck too far. When it reaches the tipping point, it fails.

Second, the tipping point comes closer when central bank equity becomes more negative and when economic fundamentals are weaker. Crucially, the Bank of Amsterdam did not receive fiscal support from a sovereign with (adequate) power to tax. The ultimate backing for the value of money is the fiscal sustainability of the consolidated public sector, consisting of the central bank and fiscal authorities (Sims, 1994; Cúrdia & Woodford, 2011; Reis, 2015). In this sense, fiat currencies need backing, and modern central banks need credible fiscal support from the government that flows from the sustainability of public finances.

The credibility of fiat money may be at risk if holders of fiat money doubt the willingness of the fiscal authority to recapitalize the central bank in times of need. The loss of confidence manifests itself in a switch in the portfolio of monetary instruments used in the economy. The loss of trust results in a coordinated switch away from Bank money to metal coins. In a modern context, such a shock could occur through dollarization, as we have seen in the case of many emerging market economies, or potentially through "cryptoization", where the portfolio decision in the money system tilts toward modern digital assets such as cryptocurrencies or private stablecoins.

4 Cautionary Tales from Emerging Markets

The experiences of many EMEs in the second half of the twentieth century provide another cautionary tale. These underscore the key role of fiscal sustainability for the preservation of trust in money, and of the exchange rate as a key catalyst in this relationship.

Across major EMEs, there is a positive correlation between average nominal government debt growth and average inflation over the past four decades (Fig. 6a). The correlation is especially strong in Latin America, which experienced very high debt growth and hyperinflation over this period. By and large, EMEs in Asia and advanced economies exhibit correlations that are much lower. The correlation between government debt growth and inflation is mirrored in the close correlation between debt growth and base money growth, reflecting monetary accommodation of fiscal trends, i.e., fiscal dominance (Fig. 6b).

The experience of Latin American EMEs in the 1980s and early 1990s shows how unsustainable fiscal developments, accommodated through the money printing press, lead to a progressive loss of price stability (Fig. 6c). Government financing through the central bank was trending higher over this period, accompanied by rising inflation. At the same time, central bank equity declined significantly. This indicates the strains that fiscal crises place on central banks as they are called upon to provide financial support to the government in the run-up and during the crisis, incurring losses in the process. These observations are consistent with formal

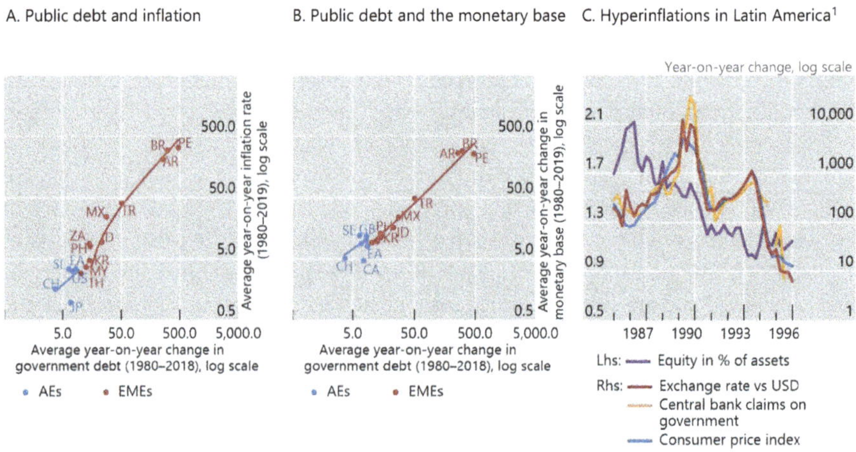

[1] Simple average across AR, BR, MX and PE.

Sources: Reinhart and Rogoff (2011); IMF, *Historical Public Debt Database* and *International Financial Statistics*; Datastream; Global Financial Data; national data; authors' calculations.

Fig. 6 Fiscal origins of high inflation. Sources: Reinhart and Rogoff (2011); IMF, *Historical Public Debt Database* and *International Financial Statistics*; Datastream; Global Financial Data; national data; authors' calculations

evidence showing that the extent of deficit monetization was the key driving force behind most of the high inflation or hyperinflation experiences in Latin American economies (Sargent et~al., 2009; Ramos-Francia et~al., 2018).

These past episodes of emerging market crises show that the exchange rate plays a key role in the process. The unfolding of unsustainable fiscal-monetary interactions was associated with a massive depreciation of the currency (Fig. 6c). The exchange rate depreciated along with rising inflation rates, with exchange rate movements predating jumps in inflation.

The role of the exchange rate highlights the portfolio choice of private entities who have access to central bank money as well as to alternatives. A sudden depreciation of the domestic currency can be seen as a sign that the portfolio choice of such entities has reached the tipping point whereby they sell the domestic currency in favor of the alternative.

Effectively, the trust in domestic money comes under strain, and a surge in inflation is the symptom of this strain. As a consequence, exchange rate pass-through is higher during currency crisis periods. In Latin America, the pass-through of exchange rate changes to future inflation was persistently near one in the 1980s and early 1990s, when these countries experienced large depreciations (Fig. 7a). Only since the beginning of the 2000s has pass-through fallen significantly. In emerging Asia, pass-through has for most of the past two decades been lower than in Latin American countries (Fig. 7b). But also there, the Asian crisis of 1997 triggered a temporary significant rise in pass-through.

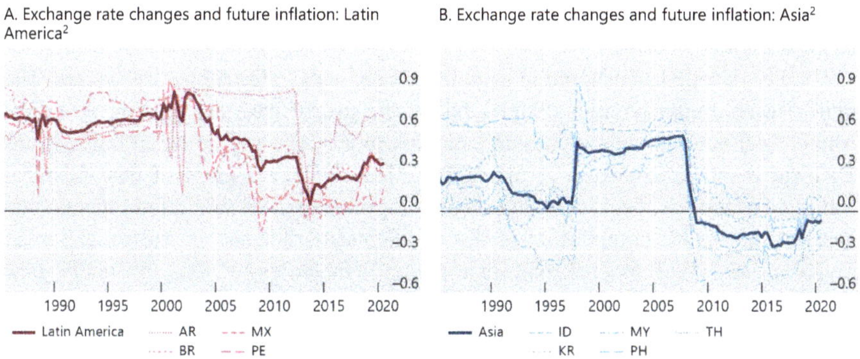

[1] Correlation coefficient on a 10-year rolling window. [2] Simple average across individual countries within the panels. Correlation between the changes in the local exchange rate vis-à-vis the US dollar and the one-quarter-forward inflation rate, where the level of the exchange rate is positive when the local currency is deprecating vis-à-vis the US dollar.

Fig. 7 Exchange rate pass-through. Sources: IMF *International Financial Statistics*; Global Financial Data; national data; authors' calculations

Note that in many cases where inflation surged, central banks have continued to hold positive equity. It is not the central bank's capital position that has driven trust. Rather, it is the portfolio choice of private holders of fiat money, who know that an unsustainable fiscal position puts the sustainability of the consolidated public sector—the government and the central bank—in danger. Domestic holders can move to alternative forms of money, in particular the US dollar. It is in this context that trust in money can be endangered.

5 Concluding Remarks

Central banks are unlike private financial entities in that central banks are public institutions that pursue public policy objectives. The standard test of solvency—having positive equity—does not apply in the same way to central banks. Instead, we have focused on the trust in money as the key issue and asked whether (and how much) central bank capital matters in preserving the trust in money.

The short answer is that a strong capital position is neither necessary nor sufficient for preserving trust in money. Nevertheless, central bank capital matters for the trust in money. This is because the pivotal economic mechanism highlighted in this paper is the portfolio decision of private holders of central bank money. While network effects will preserve support from private financial entities, erosion of trust could shift the economy closer to potential tipping points when holders abandon domestic money in favor of alternatives, whether they are metal coins in the 1700s or other reserve fiat currencies or cryptocurrencies and stablecoins in the modern era. A weak or negative equity position of the central bank will have a bearing on how the tipping point of the switch to an alternative currency is determined. The outward symptom of such a tipping point would be the sudden collapse of the exchange rate during a currency crisis.

The last decade has ushered in a number of changes to the monetary system. The rapid rise of digital payments and a fall in the use of cash are leading to a shift from central bank money to commercial bank money in daily financial transactions (Di Iorio et~al., 2024; Auer et~al., 2022). Meanwhile, the entry of new financial technology (fintech) firms and large technology companies (big techs) means that there are non-bank competitors in the payments market and in the provision of private money (such as electronic or e-money) (Feyen et~al., 2021). Finally, new digital currencies, e.g., cryptocurrencies and stablecoins, are being promoted as an alternative to central bank fiat currencies and commercial bank money—even if their use as money in practice is quite limited (BIS, 2022).

Since the Covid-19 pandemic, further changes are afoot. The global inflationary shock and rapid rise in interest rates led to large-scale losses on long-term bond portfolios—including those held on central bank balance sheets. Central banks in a number of jurisdictions had losses (Bell et~al., 2023). Meanwhile, for some jurisdictions, the falling use of cash may erode seigniorage and thus central bank income in the years ahead. This may require central banks to consider alternative sources of income. They could shift to fees, increase reliance on reserve requirements, or revise recapitalization arrangements with the government. (Of course, if central banks choose to issue central bank digital currencies (CBDCs) that do not pay interest, and these are widely adopted, this could offer a source of income that is similar to seigniorage from cash today.)

In this context, it would be tempting to think that the economics of central bank money may change in the coming years. Yet we argue that the form that money takes (whether physical cash, physical ledger entries, or digital formats) matters little for the underlying economics. And losses by several major central banks do not change the longer-term economic forces determining trust in fiat money. Indeed, the economics remain the same. In particular, the timeless principle of the need for sound public finances underpinning monetary stability is as relevant today as it was in the eighteenth, nineteenth, or twentieth centuries.

Going forward, independent central banks with clear mandates, and solid fiscal backing, remain the best bet for a stable monetary system.

References

Archer, D., & Moser-Boehm, P. (2013). Central bank finances. *BIS Working Papers*, no 71, April.

Auer, R., Cornelli, G., & Frost, J. (2022). The pandemic, cash and retail payment behaviour: Insights from the future of payments database. *BIS Working Papers*, no 1055, December.

Bank for International Settlements (BIS). (2022). The future monetary system. *Annual Economic Report 2022*, Chapter III, June, pp 75–115.

Bell, S., Chui, M., Gomes, T., Moser-Boehm, P., & Pierres Tejada, A. (2023). Why are central banks reporting losses? Does it matter? *BIS Bulletin*, no 68, February.

Bindseil, U., Manzanares, A., & Weller, B. (2004). The role of central bank capital revisited. ECB *Working Paper Series*, no 392, September.

Bolt, W., Frost, J., Shin, H. S., & Wierts, P. (2024). The Bank of Amsterdam and the limits of fiat money. *Journal of Political Economy, 132*(12), 3919–3941.

Buiter, W. (2020). *Central banks as fiscal players: The drivers of fiscal and monetary policy space*. Cambridge University Press.

Carstens, A. (2024). Trust and macroeconomic stability: A virtuous circle, *lecture at the Center for Financial Studies*. Goethe University, Frankfurt, 18 March.

Cecchetti, S., & Hilscher, J. (2024). Fiscal consequences of central bank losses. *NBER Working Papers*, no 32478, May.

Cochrane, J. (2023). *The fiscal theory of the price level*. Princeton University Press.

Cúrdia, V., & Woodford, M. (2011). The central-bank balance sheet as an instrument of monetary Policy. *Journal of Monetary Economics, 58*(1), 54–79.

de Voltaire, M. (1751). *Le siècle de Louis XIV*, translated by T Francklin and T Smolett (1779), *The works of M. de Voltaire*, chapter 10, London: S Crowder and Co.

Del Negro, M., & Sims, C. (2015). When does a central bank's balance sheet require fiscal support? *Journal of Monetary Economics, 73*(July), 1–19.

Di Iorio, A., Kosse, A., & Szemere, M. (2024). Tap, click and pay: How digital payments seize the day. *CPMI Briefs*, no 3, February.

Feyen, E., Frost, J., Gambacorta, L., Natarajan, H., & Sall, M. (2021). Fintech and the digital transformation of financial services: Implications for market structure and public policy. *BIS Papers*, no 117, July.

Goncharov, I., Ioannidou, V., & Schmalz, M. C. (2023). (Why) do central banks care about their profits? *Journal of Finance, 78*(5), 2991–3045.

Hall, R., & Reis, R. (2015). Maintaining central-bank financial stability under new-style central banking. *NBER Working Papers*, no 21173, July.

Long, J., & Fisher, P. (2024). Central bank profit distribution and recapitalisation. *Bank of England Staff Working Paper*, no 1069, April.

Nordström, A., & Vredin, A. (2022). Does central bank equity matter for monetary policy?, Sveriges Riksbank *Staff Memo*, December.

Quinn, W., & Roberds, W. (2016). Death of a reserve currency. *International Journal of Central Banking, 12*(4), 63–103.

Ramos-Francia, M., García-Verdú, S., & Sánchez-Martínez, M. (2018). *Inflation dynamics under fiscal deficit regime switching in Mexico*. Banco de México Working Papers, no 2018-21.

Reinhart, C., & Rogoff, K. (2011). From financial crash to debt crisis. *American Economic Review, 101*(5), 1676–1706.

Reis, R. (2015). Different types of central bank insolvency and the central role of seigniorage. *NBER Working Papers*, no 21226, May.

Rule, G. (2015). *Understanding the central bank balance sheet*. Bank of England Centre for Central Banking Studies.

Sargent, T. J., Williams, N., & Zha, T. (2009). The conquest of South American inflation. *Journal of Political Economy, 117*(2), 211–256.

Shin, H. S., & Schnabel, I. (2004). Liquidity and contagion: The crisis of 1763. *Journal of the European Economic Association, 2*(6), 929–968.

Sims, C. (1994). A simple model for study of the determination of the price level and the interaction of monetary and fiscal policy. *Economic Theory, 4*(3), 381–399.

Smith, A. (1776). *An inquiry into the nature and causes of the wealth of nations*. McMaster University Archive for the History of Economic Thought.

Stella, P. (1997). Do central banks need capital?. *IMF Working Papers*, no 97/083, July.

Stella, P. (2002). Central bank financial strength, transparency, and policy credibility. *IMF Working Papers*, no 02/137, August.

Ueda, K. (2003). The role of capital for central banks, speech at the Fall Meeting of the Japan Society of Monetary Economics, 25 October.
Wessels, P., & Broeders, D. (2022). On the capitalisation of central banks. *De Nederlandsche Bank Occasional Studies*, *20*(4).

Open Access This chapter is licensed under the terms of the Creative Commons Attribution 4.0 International License (http://creativecommons.org/licenses/by/4.0/), which permits use, sharing, adaptation, distribution and reproduction in any medium or format, as long as you give appropriate credit to the original author(s) and the source, provide a link to the Creative Commons license and indicate if changes were made.

The images or other third party material in this chapter are included in the chapter's Creative Commons license, unless indicated otherwise in a credit line to the material. If material is not included in the chapter's Creative Commons license and your intended use is not permitted by statutory regulation or exceeds the permitted use, you will need to obtain permission directly from the copyright holder.

Accounting Policies, Distribution Rules, and the Financial Performance of Central Banks

Igor Goncharov, Zoltán Novotny-Farkas, and Carmine Pizzo

Abstract This paper provides comprehensive evidence on the financial performance of 148 central banks and its determinants over the period of 2010–2022. We observe a deterioration in central banks' capital buffers (i.e., equity) and profitability over our sample period, with the year 2022 seeing the largest percentage of central banks reporting losses (40%). While this deterioration in financial performance reflects the outcome of economic factors such as inflation and increased balance sheet size, we show that central banks' financial reporting choices and distribution rules also play a substantial role. Specifically, we find that financial reporting choices that aim to increase central bank transparency by allowing economic signals to be reflected in financial statements in an unbiased and timely manner (e.g., adoption of IFRS and fair value reporting) are associated with higher volatility of central bank profits and a higher likelihood of central bank losses and capital shortfalls. In turn, discretionary accounting policies, such as general risk provisions, can help central banks smooth their performance, but they have been less effective in reducing the likelihood of adverse performance in recent years. We further find that central banks build stronger capital buffers when distribution rules allow central banks to decide on the level of dividends or facilitate intertemporal dividend smoothing, but there is no evidence that equity targets reduce the likelihood of capital shortfalls. Because economic factors that increase the likelihood of losses and negative equity (e.g., inflation, bloated balance sheets) will likely persist in the coming years, our findings highlight potential issues with central bank (financial) independence. The paper ends by discussing reporting options central banks might take to mitigate these effects.

I. Goncharov (✉) · C. Pizzo
Lancaster University Management School, Lancaster, UK
e-mail: i.goncharov@lancaster.ac.uk; c.pizzo@lancaster.ac.uk

Z. Novotny-Farkas
Vienna University of Economics and Business, Vienna, Austria
e-mail: zoltan.novotny-farkas@wu.ac.at

© The Author(s) 2025

D. Broeders et al. (eds.), *Central Bank Capital in Turbulent Times*,
Contributions to Finance and Accounting,
https://doi.org/10.1007/978-3-031-73549-3_3

Keywords Central bank accounting · Central bank profitability · Monetary stability

1 Introduction

Central banks are exposed to risks, which affect their periodic financial performance and equity. Recent rises in interest rates and associated drops in market values of assets have a strong impact on central bank financials. The central bank literature has long debated whether central banks must be well capitalized and have a healthy balance sheet structure (e.g., Stella, 1997, 2008; Archer & Moser-Boehm, 2013; Nordström & Vredin, 2022; Wessels & Broeders, 2022; Bell et al., 2023). As the balance sheet equation that equates assets to equity and liabilities also holds for central banks, any declines in asset values must be covered by either decreases in equity or increases in liabilities (e.g., currency in circulation) that would allow a central bank to continue running its operations (e.g., Reis, 2013; Hall & Reis, 2015).

Theoretically, it is often argued that negative equity should not pose an issue for central banks that are able to generate seigniorage profits when inflation picks up and interest rates rise. However, this argument ignores the institutional implications of both central bank earnings and equity. Importantly, accounting earnings form the basis of central banks' distributions to the government. In case of large losses or negative equity, the government may be concerned about the implications of missing central bank dividends or the need to recapitalize a central bank. In addition, the public may misperceive poor financial performance for the poor execution of the monetary policy, damaging the transmission mechanism for policy (Archer & Moser-Boehm, 2013). To avoid these public or political pressures, Goncharov et al. (2023) find that central banks take actions to avoid losses.

Central banks' actions to avoid losses such as managing earnings through discretionary accounting choices pose unique risks of their own, including the loss of accountability and credibility (central banks' main asset), or sending signals that contradict central bank monetary policy statements. Furthermore, when reporting pressure is high and reporting agents run out of pure accounting options (e.g., tapping into general risk provisions), prior literature argues they may resort to using non-accounting or real decisions to report desirable performance figures (e.g., Graham et al., 2005). In the case of central banks, such real decisions may include the choice of macroeconomic parameters such as the interest rate or the value of a foreign currency peg (Goncharov et al., 2023).

Motivated by the (perceived) importance of financial performance of central banks, this paper reviews trends in central bank financial performance over the last decade, focusing on both periodic financial performance measures (profitability, losses) and central bank capital (i.e., equity). We begin our analysis by examining economic factors that may systematically affect central bank financial performance. For example, we consider inflation, balance sheet size, and economic growth. Furthermore, because prevailing accounting rules determine what items are recognized on the face of financial statements and how they are measured, this paper examines the impact of major accounting rules for central bank earnings and equity. Specifically, we focus on both accounting frameworks (e.g., International Financial Reporting Standards or IFRS, Eurozone accounting rules) and specific accounting policies that are expected to have important implications for central bank financial performance, the volatility of earnings, and the likelihood of reporting adverse financial results, i.e., losses and negative equity.

In terms of specific accounting policies, we consider the financial statement effects of reporting fair value and foreign currency revaluations in the income statement. Unlike historical (amortized) cost, fair value reporting is expected to reflect economic signals in financial statements in an unbiased and timely manner, but its introduction can substantially increase the volatility of earnings and equity (Barth et al., 1995; Hodder et al., 2006). We also consider general risk provisions that are banned under IFRS because of their discretionary nature, but they can help central banks smooth out fluctuations of their financial performance measures and dividend distributions to the treasury. Finally, we investigate the role of various central bank dividend distribution rules on central bank equity and the likelihood of incurring negative equity.

Using the information on 148 central banks over years 2010–2022, we find that central banks experience a large decline in profitability with a sizeable share of loss-making observations (23%) during our sample period that includes a spike in inflation and substantial interest rate increases after the height of the COVID-19 pandemic. This resulted in a marked decline in the equity-to-assets ratio for central banks in developed and Eurozone countries from over 10% in 2010 to less than 5% in 2022. We find that the year 2022 was possibly the worst year on record for central bank financial performance with the highest share of central banks reporting a loss (40%) and negative equity (13%). The results of our regression analyses show that this poor financial performance is (partly) explained by larger balance sheets that expose central banks to new types of risks (e.g., interest rate risk, market price risk) and higher inflation, which led to rising interest rates that caused increases in central bank interest expenses and (un)realized losses due to declines of asset values, especially for central banks that apply IFRS and fair value reporting.

Further exploring the role of accounting rules, we find that most central banks now use IFRS and over half of central banks record fair value revaluations of some of their financial assets and foreign currency revaluations in the income statement. The use of IFRS and fair value reporting has increased over time (Goncharov & Novotny-Farkas, 2024). In turn, because IFRS does not allow general risk provisions, such provisions are mostly used by central banks that apply local GAAP (i.e., accounting rules used by local firms and commercial banks) or those using central-bank-specific accounting frameworks (e.g., Eurozone rules).[1] We find these accounting choices have economically large associations with the likelihood

[1] Goncharov and Novotny-Farkas (2024) find that central banks often deviate from IFRS requirements, and some central banks using IFRS report general risk provisions.

of incurring losses and negative equity. For example, while recognizing foreign exchange revaluations in income is associated with a 55% (96%) higher probability of incurring losses (negative equity), the use of general risk provisions is associated with a 73% (88%) lower likelihood of losses (negative equity). We find that this result is attributable to substantially higher (lower) volatility of central bank earnings under fair value revaluations in the income statement (when using general risk provisions) and holds after accounting for differences in macroeconomic conditions and past performance.

Unlike accounting rules, distribution rules seem to have a less pronounced relationship with central bank financial performance. This result may explain why some central banks effectively achieve their preferred dividend policy by changing accounting rules rather than seemingly less flexible distribution rules. Indeed, we find that accounting changes that have important implications for central bank earnings and dividends are more common during our sample period than changes in distribution rules.[2] Expectedly, we find a higher equity-to-assets ratio and a lower incidence of negative equity when central banks have more discretion in determining the distribution, can draw on external resources when needed or smooth the dividend distribution. In turn, government discretion in setting dividends and any form of mandatory dividends are associated with a lower equity-to-assets ratio and a higher incidence of negative equity. Somewhat surprisingly, we find mixed results for distribution rules that rely on equity targets, perhaps because they are inappropriately configured or set equity targets that provide insufficient buffers against the high losses that some central banks incurred during our sample period.

We conclude the paper by discussing the implications of our results. Because central banks face similar reporting pressures as firms do,[3] we argue that the literature on corporate reporting can be helpful in both understanding how central banks can (and do) respond to reporting pressures, and what implications such behavior may have for central bank independence and the role of central bank financial reporting as a communication device. Although we use the literature on corporate reporting, we caution against "mechanically" comparing or equating central bank performance to that of profit-oriented firms or commercial banks. Specifically, in the case of central banks, while financial losses may provide useful signals of performance, one should not per se view financial losses as evidence of poor monetary policy performance, as such (mis)perception could alter the behavior of central banks in important and unintended ways. To mitigate this risk, central banks must educate their stakeholders to avoid the misinterpretation of their accounting numbers.

---

[2] For example, we find that 14% of central banks in our sample switched their accounting framework (e.g., switched from local GAAP to IFRS), and 21% of central banks made changes to their accounting policy on the measurement or recognition of fair value revaluations during our sample period. However, we find none of central banks introduced changes to four distribution rules, and only 11% of central banks made some changes to at least one of the other six distribution rules that we consider in our analysis.

[3] We report some anecdotes in Sect. 5; see also Goncharov et al. (2023).

This paper adds to the scarce empirical literature on central bank finances. While previous studies mostly provide case-based evidence on financial performance of a handful of large central banks or discuss expected rather than actual performance (e.g., Christensen et al., 2015; Hall & Reis, 2015), we add to Goncharov and Novotny-Farkas (2024) and Goncharov et al. (2023) by providing large-scale empirical evidence on central bank financial performance and the effects of financial reporting choices. We also add to Archer and Moser-Boehm (2013) by systematically analyzing the implications of distribution rules for central bank capital.

2 Sample, Accounting Frameworks and Central Bank Accounting Choices

To provide a comprehensive overview of recent trends in central bank financial performance and their determinants, we use a sample of 148 central banks with available financial statements data on S&P Capital IQ for the period 2010–2022.[4] Using the data from Goncharov and Novotny-Farkas (2024), we identify central banks' accounting frameworks and their key accounting policies from the notes to the financial statements, auditor reports, and other published sources. We were able to retrieve accounting frameworks and key accounting policies for 138 central banks and 1735 central-bank-year observations. The data on central bank dividend distribution rules is based on our coding of central banks' charters obtained from the IMF's Central Bank Legislation Database (CBLD).

Unlike firms, central banks enjoy substantial discretion in choosing accounting frameworks, i.e., the set of rules detailing how to recognize, measure, and report transactions in financial statements. For instance, some central banks adopt IFRS, while others develop their own accounting standards to suit their reporting needs. In this respect, transparent accounting frameworks (e.g., IFRS) can improve central banks' accountability by providing more comparable information and timely incorporation of economic signals into financial statements.

We find that central banks adopt three types of accounting frameworks: (1) IFRS (e.g., Bank of England, Reserve Bank of Australia), (2) local GAAP (e.g.,

[4] S&P Capital IQ provides as-reported information on main financial statement positions. While using these data allows us to analyse a comprehensive sample of central banks, the reported figures may not fully reveal the extent of central bank losses when central banks report losses intransparently as discussed in Sect. 6. For example, some central banks may report accumulated losses outside of equity and provide little information on the balance sheet to help identify any accumulated losses. Specifically, the National Bank of Slovakia reported accumulated losses under other assets and provided detailed information on the magnitude of accumulated losses only in the footnotes to the financial statements. Such reporting practices complicate the comparative analysis of central bank financial statements. As we use as-reported figures in our tests, we acknowledge that the actual extent of central bank (equity) losses may be higher if financial statements were recast to provide more comparable figures.

Table 1 Central banks' use of accounting frameworks and accounting policies

Central bank accounting frameworks	*N*	%
IFRS	969	55.82
GAAP	257	14.80
CB-Specific	509	29.32
Total	1735	100
Central bank accounting policies		
FX_P&L	862	58.88
FV_P&L	840	58.13
GRP	389	24.80

This table reports descriptive statistics for central banks' accounting frameworks and policies. *IFRS* is an indicator taking the value of one for central-bank-years using IFRS, and zero otherwise. *GAAP* is an indicator taking the value of one for central-bank-years using local GAAP, and zero otherwise. *CB-specific* is an indicator taking the value of one for central-bank-years using a central-bank-specific accounting framework, and zero otherwise. *FX_P&L* is an indicator taking the value of one for central-bank-years recognizing foreign exchange revaluations in the income statement, and zero otherwise. *FV_P&L* is an indicator taking the value of one for central-bank-years measuring financial assets at fair value and recognizing the revaluation difference in the income statement, and zero otherwise. *GRP* is an indicator taking the value of one for central-bank-years reporting general risk provisions, and zero otherwise

Swiss National Bank, Bank of Japan), and (3) central-bank-specific accounting frameworks (e.g., the U.S. Federal Reserve, hereafter the Fed, and European Central Bank, hereafter the ECB). Goncharov and Novotny-Farkas (2024) show that over the past decades the share of central banks adopting IFRS has significantly increased. During our sample period, 56% of central banks report under IFRS (Table 1). Conversely, the share of central banks using local GAAP (i.e., non-IFRS accounting frameworks that apply for commercial banks or firms in the country where a central bank is located) has decreased. While about a third of central banks use a central-bank-specific framework, only 15% use local GAAP.

However, due to little external enforcement, central banks also enjoy substantial discretion in *which* accounting policies they apply. For instance, some central banks using IFRS might deviate from some IFRS requirements, such as fair value recognition rules (Goncharov & Novotny-Farkas, 2024).[5] Thus, we also examine the use of three specific accounting policies that significantly affect central banks' financial performance, that is: (1) the recognition of foreign exchange revaluations in the

[5] The most common deviations from IFRS are disregarding the requirement that foreign exchange and fair value revaluations are ought to be reported in the income statement (Goncharov & Novotny-Farkas, 2024).

income statement (*FX_P&L*), (2) the recognition of financial assets revaluations in the income statement (*FV_P&L*), and (3) the use of general risk provisions (*GRP*). While recognizing fair value and foreign exchange revaluations in the income statement improves transparency and decreases the possibility that financial statement users miss or misinterpret relevant information (Hirst & Hopkins, 1998), it also exposes central banks' profits to changes in market conditions, such as changes in interest and exchange rates.[6] Although general risk provisions are banned under IFRS because of their highly discretionary nature and the concern that firm managers may use this discretion opportunistically (e.g., to increase bonuses), they are a valid tool for central banks to absorb future losses and smooth the earnings and dividend stream to the government.

Table 1 reports descriptive statistics for key accounting policies and finds that 59% of central banks recognize foreign currency revaluations in the income statement and/or report financial assets at fair value with asset revaluations recognized in income, but only 25% of central banks use general risk provisions. However, as in Goncharov and Novotny-Farkas (2024), we find that the use of fair value reporting and general risk provisions significantly differs across accounting frameworks (untabulated). In line with the assumption that IFRS adoption fosters accounting transparency (Armstrong et al., 2010), we find that most IFRS adopters record fair value and foreign currency revaluations in the income statement. Conversely, most central banks applying a central-bank-specific framework use general risk provisions. We expect these differences to have important implications for the magnitude and the volatility of central bank profits, the likelihood of a central bank reporting losses and capital shortfalls, especially when distribution rules are not taking these accounting differences into account (e.g., by requiring the distribution of unrealized fair value gains).

3 Trends in Central Bank Profitability and Equity

We begin our analysis by examining trends in central bank financial performance using two complementary metrics: profitability and equity. These measures are connected as lower profitability and accounting losses increase the probability of depleting equity and reporting capital shortfalls. Furthermore, examining equity in addition to examining profitability is important because some accounting gains and losses are reported directly in equity, bypassing the income statement (e.g., revaluations of available-for-sale securities under IFRS).

Unlike commercial firms, central banks do not aim to maximize profits (Stella, 2008; Archer & Moser-Boehm, 2013). However, central banks' distribution rules

[6] For instance, due to the appreciation of the Swiss Franc, the Swiss National Bank recognized a substantial exchange rate loss (26 billion CHF) in the income statement for 2015. Due to these exchange rate losses, the SNB reported an accounting loss of 23 billion CHF in that year.

require their profits to be transferred to their governments as dividends, significantly contributing to government budgets. Besides, previous literature in economics often focuses on central bank equity. Although central banks cannot go bankrupt, negative equity indicates that a central bank is unable to cover some of its outstanding liabilities with its assets and may require recapitalization by the government (de Haan & Eijffinger, 2016), compromising central bank independence (Bernanke, 2010; Goncharov & Novotny-Farkas, 2024).

Figure 1 shows the state of central banks' profitability during our sample period. Panel A plots the histogram of return on assets or ROA (i.e., the ratio of central bank profits to total assets) following Goncharov et al. (2023), but for our more recent sample period. The average (median) central bank in our sample has an ROA of about 1% (0.5%) (see Table 2). We find a high propensity of central banks to report small positive profits (first interval of the histogram to the right of zero) over small losses (first interval to the left of zero). Goncharov et al. (2023) attribute this discontinuity in the distribution of profits around zero to central bank loss avoidance behavior.

Panel B of Fig. 1 shows trends in ROA and reveals that although central banks in developing countries have, on average, a higher ROA than central banks in developed countries, all central banks experience a large decline in profitability over recent years. These substantial declines may explain why we observe a sizeable share of loss-making observations (23%) during our sample period, which includes a spike in inflation and substantial interest rate increases after the height of the COVID-19 pandemic (see Table 2). Indeed, Panel C of Fig. 2 shows that 40% of central banks globally reported a loss in 2022. Comparing these statistics to the earlier period (1992–2014) from Goncharov et al. (2023) reveals that 2022 is the worst year on record since the early 1990s.[7] Although central banks in developing countries generally report losses more frequently than central banks in developed countries, the increase in the share of loss-making central banks in 2022 is more pronounced for developed than developing countries. As a result, the median ROA of central banks in developed countries has dropped to 0 in 2022. Despite low profitability, very few Eurozone central banks report a loss during our sample period, possibly due to the use of accounting discretion.[8] However, because of both large

[7] Prior to 1990s many central banks were not reporting financial statements or the income statement. The previous peak was observed in 2004 with 24% of central banks reporting a loss. However, note that this paper and Goncharov et al. (2023) rely on different databases, i.e., S&P Capital IQ here versus BvD Bankscope, and there are differences in the coverage of central banks between the two datasets, which complicate the timeseries comparisons of descriptive statistics. At the time of writing this paper, only 106 central banks have released their income statement for 2022 and were covered by S&P Capital IQ.

[8] Our review of central bank financial statements revealed that central banks use general risk provisions to avoid losses. For example, in 2022, the ECB has released general risk provisions in the amount equal to ECB's loss before provisions. As a result, the ECB reported a profit of 0 for 2022, narrowly avoiding a loss. However, Eurozone central banks have substantially depleted their general risk provisions that were built up during the period of low interest rates and relatively high profitability.

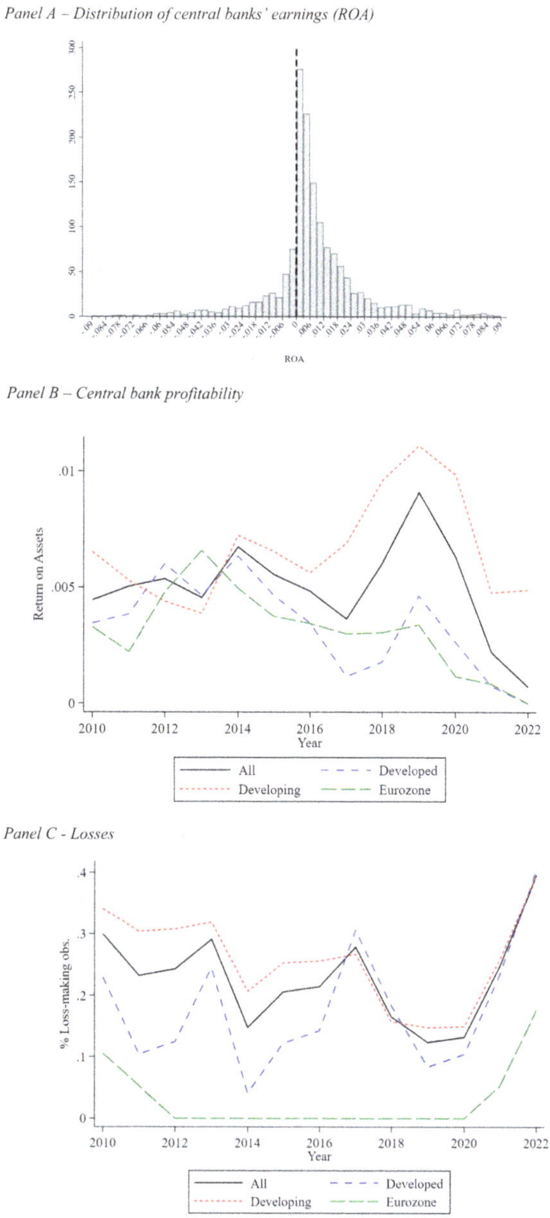

Fig. 1 Trends in central banks' profitability. Notes: This figure reports the evolution of central bank profitability over our sample period (2010–2022). *Panel A* plots the distribution of central banks' return on assets (*ROA*), where ROA is defined as earnings divided by average total assets. The distribution of *ROA* is trimmed at [−0.09; 0.09]. The dotted vertical line shows when *ROA* equals zero. The number of observations falling into each bin is reported on the vertical axis. *Panel **B*** plots the annual median *ROA*, separately for developed, developing, and Eurozone countries. *Panel **C*** plots the percentage of loss-making central banks (*Loss*), separately for developed, developing, and Eurozone countries

Table 2 Descriptive statistics

	N	Mean	St. Dev	Min	p25	p50	p75	Max
ROA	1622	0.009	0.037	−0.657	0.000	0.005	0.016	0.319
Neg. Equity	1805	0.092	0.289	0.000	0.000	0.000	0.000	1.000
Loss	1743	0.229	0.421	0.000	0.000	0.000	0.000	1.000
σ(ROA)	1517	0.016	0.029	0.000	0.002	0.006	0.020	0.387
Equity/Assets	1816	0.081	0.128	−0.864	0.024	0.069	0.138	0.801
Assets ($)	1784	21.252	4.177	9.094	18.244	21.135	24.378	33.185
IFRS	1735	0.559	0.497	0.000	0.000	1.000	1.000	1.000
GAAP	1735	0.148	0.355	0.000	0.000	0.000	0.000	1.000
CB-specific	1736	0.294	0.456	0.000	0.000	0.000	1.000	1.000
FX_P&L	1464	0.589	0.492	0.000	0.000	1.000	1.000	1.000
FV_P&L	1445	0.581	0.494	0.000	0.000	1.000	1.000	1.000
GRP	1569	0.248	0.432	0.000	0.000	0.000	0.000	1.000
GDP Growth	1898	0.029	0.058	−0.542	0.013	0.031	0.051	0.868
Recession	1898	0.163	0.369	0.000	0.000	0.000	0.000	1.000
Δ Exchange Rate	1656	0.060	0.244	−0.271	−0.003	0.007	0.072	5.867
Inflation	1848	0.058	0.196	−0.026	0.014	0.031	0.060	5.572
Developed	1911	0.333	0.472	0.000	0.000	0.000	1.000	1.000

This table reports summary statistics for the variables used in the empirical analysis. *ROA* is computed as central bank earnings over average total assets. *Neg. Equity* is an indicator taking the value of one for all central-bank-years with negative equity, and zero otherwise. *Loss* is an indicator taking the value of one for all central-bank-years with losses (i.e., ROA < 0), and zero otherwise. *σ(ROA)* is the three-year standard deviation of *ROA*. *Equity/Assets* is the ratio of central bank equity to total assets. *Assets ($)* is the natural logarithm of total assets in thousands, converted in current US dollars. *IFRS* is an indicator taking the value of one for central-bank-years using IFRS, and zero otherwise. *GAAP* is an indicator taking the value of one for central-bank-years using local GAAP, and zero otherwise. *CB-specific* is an indicator taking the value of one for central-bank-years using a central-bank-specific accounting framework, and zero otherwise. *FX_P&L* is an indicator taking the value of one for central-bank-years recognizing foreign exchange revaluations in the income statement, and zero otherwise. *FV_P&L* is an indicator taking the value of one for central-bank-years measuring financial assets at fair value and recognizing the revaluation difference in the income statement, and zero otherwise. *GRP* is an indicator taking the value of one for central-bank-years reporting general risk provisions, and zero otherwise. *GDP Growth* is the percentage change in real GDP, measured in 2015 US dollars. *Recession* is an indicator for central-bank-years with negative GDP growth, and zero otherwise. *Δ Exchange Rate* is change in the exchange rate of the local currency against the US Dollar. *Inflation* is the country rate of consumer price inflation. *Developed* is an indicator for developed economies based on the United Nations classification

losses following recent interest rate increases and running out of accounting options that Eurozone central banks can use for avoiding losses (De Nederlandsche Bank, 2022), we observe an increase in the share of loss-making Eurozone banks in 2022.[9]

[9] For example, the Deutsche Bundesbank released all of its general risk provisions (€19 billion) in 2023, but still incurred a net loss of over €2 billion.

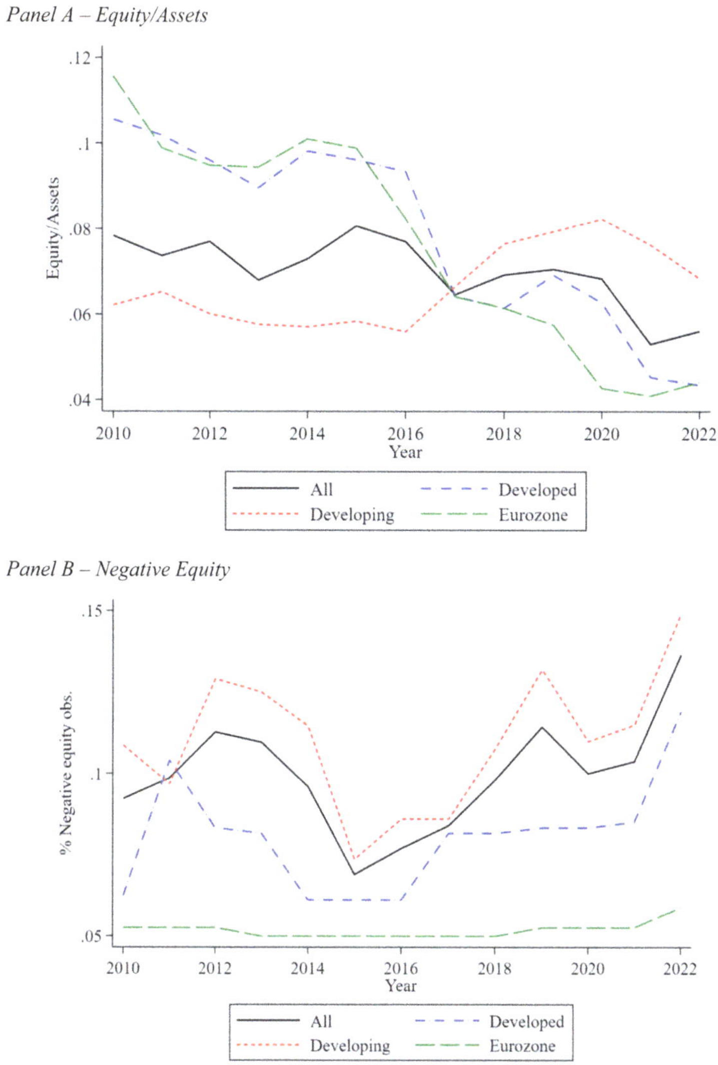

Fig. 2 Trends in central banks' equity. Notes: This figure reports the evolution of central bank capital over our sample period (2010–2022). *Panel* ***A*** plots the annual median equity-to-assets ratio (*Equity/Assets*), separately for developed, developing, and Eurozone countries. *Panel* ***B*** plots the annual percentage of central banks reporting negative equity (*Neg. Equity*), separately for developed, developing, and Eurozone countries. For this figure, we recast the financial statements of the National Bank of Slovakia to reveal its negative capital (i.e. calculated the difference between reported equity position and the component of other assets attributable to accumulated losses). Note that the total number of observations in each group (e.g., Eurozone) varies over time due to data availability in S&P Capital IQ

The increased frequency of losses, especially in recent years, might reduce capital buffers, raising concerns about central banks' financial strength (Goncharov & Novotny-Farkas, 2024). Thus, Fig. 2 examines the evolution of central bank capital buffers during our sample period. We observe a marked decline in the equity-to-assets ratio for central banks in developed and Eurozone countries from over 10% in 2010 to less than 5% in 2022. Despite their high average equity-to-assets ratio, central banks in developing countries report negative equity more often than their counterparts from developed countries.[10] Overall, the reduction in capital buffers and the increased frequency of losses in recent years suggest that discretionary accounting policies, such as general risk provisions, have been less effective in shielding central banks from adverse outcomes. Indeed, the year 2022 has the highest share of central banks reporting negative equity (13%) since the early 1990s (Panel B of Fig. 2).

So far, our graphical evidence shows two seemingly contradictory findings. On the one hand, central banks in developing countries are, on average, more profitable and better capitalized than central banks in developed or Eurozone countries. On the other hand, central banks in developing countries report losses and negative equity more often than other central banks. However, the analysis thus far ignores the critical role of central banks' accounting policies. For example, central banks might use general risk provisions to smooth reported income when interest rates rise and asset values decline. In this respect, some accounting policies can reduce the likelihood of reporting losses and negative equity, especially during turbulent times. Thus, we provide some preliminary evidence on the role of accounting policies on central banks' financial performance.

In Table 3, we report univariate comparisons of the average profitability (*ROA*), profit variability ($\sigma(ROA)$), likelihood of reporting losses (*Loss*), and negative equity (*Neg. Equity*) for central banks that recognize foreign exchange (*FX_P&L*) or fair value (*FV_P&L*) revaluations in income or report general risk provisions (*GRP*). We find that central banks adopting more transparent accounting policies, such as recognizing fair value or foreign exchange revaluations in income, have, on average, higher profit variability. This higher profit variability significantly increases the likelihood of central bank losses and capital shortfalls. For example, recognizing foreign exchange revaluations in income is associated with a 55% (=[0.256–0.165]/0.165) and 96% higher probability of incurring losses and negative equity, respectively. Conversely, the use of general risk provisions helps central banks to smooth their performance and is associated with a reduced likelihood of losses (negative equity) by 73% (88%).

[10] We observe only two central banks in developed economies (the National Bank of the Republic of Belarus and the Bank of Israel) consistently operating with negative equity during our sample period. Furthermore, recasting the financial statements of the National Bank of Slovakia (i.e., calculating the difference between reported equity position and the component of other assets attributable to accumulated losses) reveals that the bank had negative capital during our sample period.

Table 3 Central bank financial performance and accounting policies

	FX_P&L			*FV_P&L*			*GRP*		
	0	1	*p*-value	0	1	*p*-value	0	1	*p*-value
ROA	0.004	0.013	<0.001	0.005	0.126	<0.001	0.009	0.006	0.102
Loss	0.165	0.256	<0.001	0.158	0.262	<0.001	0.283	0.077	<0.001
Neg. Equity	0.055	0.108	<0.001	0.063	0.109	0.003	0.121	0.015	<0.001
$\sigma(ROA)$	0.005	0.025	<0.001	0.008	0.235	<0.001	0.021	0.006	<0.001

This table reports univariate tests for the differences in the means of *ROA*, $\sigma(ROA)$, *Loss*, and *Neg. Equity* by accounting policy. *ROA* is computed as central bank profit over average total assets. *Loss* is an indicator taking the value of one for all central-bank-years with losses (i.e., ROA < 0), and zero otherwise. *Neg. Equity* is an indicator taking the value of one for all central-bank-years with negative equity, and zero otherwise. $\sigma(ROA)$ is the three-year standard deviation of *ROA*. *FX_P&L* is an indicator taking the value of one for central-bank-years recognizing foreign exchange revaluations in the income statement, and zero otherwise. *FV_P&L* is an indicator taking the value of one for central-bank-years measuring financial assets at fair value and recognizing the revaluation difference in the income statement, and zero otherwise. *GRP* is an indicator taking the value of one for central-bank-years reporting general risk provisions, and zero otherwise

4 Factors Associated with Central Bank Financial Performance

In this section, we formally investigate factors associated with central bank profitability and financial strength. To do so, we estimate the following OLS specification:

$$\begin{aligned} \mathrm{Y_{i,t}} = {} & \beta_0 + \beta_1 \text{ Accounting rules}_{\mathrm{i,t}} + \beta_2 \text{ Distribution rules}_{\mathrm{i,t}} \\ & + \beta_3 \text{Economic factors}_{\mathrm{i,t}} + \alpha_{\mathrm{t}} + \varepsilon_{\mathrm{i,t}} \end{aligned} \tag{1}$$

where *Y* is one of our measures of central bank financial position and performance: (1) return on assets (*ROA*), defined as profit over average total assets; (2) the three-year standard deviation of *ROA* (σROA); (3) an indicator for loss-making observations (*Loss*); and (4) an indicator for observations with negative equity (*Neg. Equity*). We use three sets of independent variables that capture central bank accounting frameworks or their accounting policies, distribution rules, and economic factors.

We begin our analysis by considering the economic drivers of central bank financial performance. Although previous literature discusses why some central banks incurred negative equity and newspapers often report on cases of extraordinary central bank performance (e.g., Stella, 2005; Archer & Moser-Boehm, 2013), prior literature provides little guidance on what factors systematically drive central bank financial results. Furthermore, the relationship between macroeconomic factors and central bank financial results can be context- or time-specific. For example, an economic crisis may lead to a large write-off of marketable securities held at fair value on a central bank's balance sheet, but also increase the value of foreign currency assets and lead to large revaluation gains in case of the devaluation of local currency, because foreign currency holdings are denominated in local currency on a central bank's balance sheet. Thus, we explore the role of different economic factors such as the level (*Developed*) and the rate of economic development (*GDP Growth*), the impact of economic recessions (*Recession*), currency exchange rate fluctuations (*Δ Exchange Rate*), and inflation (*Inflation*). All macroeconomic variables come from the World Development Indicators except for currency exchange rates against the US dollar, which we obtain from the Bank of International Settlements.

We also consider recent expansions of central bank balance sheets due to quantitative easing (QE) or perusing a certain exchange rate regime by including the lagged natural logarithm of total assets (*Assets ($)*). While significant expansions of central bank balance sheets during the Global Financial Crisis allowed central banks to generate large profits in its aftermath and make large distributions to the government, bloated balance sheets expose central banks to various risks (e.g., interest-rate risk, foreign exchange risk, credit risk). Some of these risks have materialized when the inflation and interest rates increased in recent years: While the interest income on these assets remained largely flat or did not increase much, central banks have incurred larger interest rate expenses by paying larger interest on reserves of commercial banks (Kjellberg & Åhl, 2022). Furthermore, higher interest rates lead to lower discounted values of assets held at fair value. Central banks that do not mark assets to their market values realize fair value losses when they sell assets that were purchased during times of low interest rates (and low inflation). An interesting empirical question is whether any increases in profitability due to larger balance sheets outweigh the accounting losses due to balance sheet expansion (e.g., because of asset write-offs or negative interest margins) over the 2010–2022 period.

Finally, to account for persistent trends in central bank financial performance, we are interested in the relationship between lagged central bank's financial position (*Equity/Assets*) and current central bank performance. All our estimations include year fixed effects (α_t) and cluster standard errors at the central bank level.[11]

Table 4 reports the results. We find that higher inflation is negatively related to our measure of central bank accounting profitability (*ROA*) and positively associated with the volatility of central bank performance (σROA). A one percentage point increase in inflation reduces central bank ROA by 0.03 percentage points (columns 1 to 3). This result is most likely explained by higher interest rates—central banks' response to rising inflation—that significantly increase interest rate expenses and lead to a number of central banks reporting losses or narrowly avoiding losses. Indeed, we find that higher inflation increases the probability of reporting accounting losses (*Loss*) and our results for the relationship between accounting

[11] We assign all Eurozone central banks to the same cluster because Eurozone central banks jointly make decisions that affect their balance sheets.

Table 4 Factors associated with central bank financial performance: accounting rules and economic factors

	(1)	(2)	(3)	(4)	(5)	(6)	(7)	(8)	(9)	(10)	(11)	(12)
	$ROA_{i,t}$			$\sigma(ROA)_{i,t\text{-}2:t}$			$Loss_{i,t}$			$Neg.\ Equity_{i,t}$		
$IFRS_{i,t}$		0.008**			0.015***			0.034			−0.024	
		(0.003)			(0.003)			(0.052)			(0.042)	
$CB\text{-}specific_{i,t}$			−0.006*			−0.015***			−0.123*			−0.038
			(0.003)			(0.003)			(0.063)			(0.056)
$GDP\ Growth_{i,t}$	0.001	−0.001	0.003	−0.016	−0.019	−0.009	−0.401	−0.410*	−0.363	0.133	0.143	0.149
	(0.030)	(0.030)	(0.029)	(0.020)	(0.018)	(0.019)	(0.242)	(0.246)	(0.249)	(0.155)	(0.219)	(0.213)
$Recession_{i,t}$	−0.004	−0.003	−0.003	0.005	0.006	0.005	−0.017	−0.024	−0.027	0.036	0.033	0.033
	(0.006)	(0.007)	(0.007)	(0.007)	(0.007)	(0.007)	(0.050)	(0.051)	(0.051)	(0.030)	(0.032)	(0.032)
$\Delta\ Exchange\ Rate_{i,t}$	0.026**	0.027**	0.027**	−0.003	−0.001	−0.001	−0.161	−0.144	−0.125	−0.089**	−0.096**	−0.085**
	(0.012)	(0.012)	(0.012)	(0.006)	(0.006)	(0.007)	(0.130)	(0.131)	(0.121)	(0.039)	(0.043)	(0.038)
$Inflation_{i,t}$	−0.029***	−0.029***	−0.029***	0.016***	0.014***	0.012**	0.268*	0.246	0.216	0.265***	0.285***	0.271***
	(0.009)	(0.009)	(0.009)	(0.005)	(0.004)	(0.005)	(0.161)	(0.155)	(0.141)	(0.057)	(0.064)	(0.061)
$Developed_{i}$	−0.004*	−0.001	−0.002	−0.008*	−0.002	−0.001	−0.057	−0.046	−0.005	−0.037	−0.048	−0.018
	(0.002)	(0.003)	(0.003)	(0.004)	(0.003)	(0.003)	(0.057)	(0.054)	(0.052)	(0.037)	(0.044)	(0.052)
$Assets\ (\$)_{i,t\text{-}1}$	0.000	0.000	0.000	0.000	0.000	0.000	0.012**	0.012**	0.012**	0.007**	0.007*	0.007*
	(0.000)	(0.000)	(0.000)	(0.000)	(0.000)	(0.000)	(0.005)	(0.005)	(0.005)	(0.003)	(0.004)	(0.004)
$Equity/Assets_{i,t\text{-}1}$	0.070***	0.066***	0.071***	−0.010	−0.018	−0.007	−0.714***	−0.697***	−0.652***	−1.246***	−1.318***	−1.324***
	(0.012)	(0.012)	(0.012)	(0.022)	(0.022)	(0.022)	(0.175)	(0.175)	(0.167)	(0.275)	(0.296)	(0.296)

(continued)

Table 4 (continued)

	(1)	(2)	(3)	(4)	(5)	(6)	(7)	(8)	(9)	(10)	(11)	(12)
	$ROA_{i,t}$			$\sigma(ROA)_{i,t\text{-}2:t}$			$Loss_{i,t}$			$Neg.\ Equity_{i,t}$		
Constant	0.002	−0.002	0.004	0.008	−0.000	0.012	0.049	0.025	0.073	0.039	0.058	0.052
	(0.007)	(0.008)	(0.008)	(0.009)	(0.008)	(0.009)	(0.105)	(0.112)	(0.106)	(0.069)	(0.076)	(0.075)
Fixed Effects	Year	Year	Year	Year	Year	Year	Year	Year	Year	Year	Year	Year
Observations	1524	1432	1433	1393	1310	1311	1509	1417	1418	1555	1456	1457
Adjusted R-squared	0.081	0.089	0.086	0.038	0.095	0.091	0.092	0.096	0.108	0.311	0.334	0.336

This table reports OLS coefficients for Eq. (1). *ROA* is computed as central bank profit over average total assets. *σ(ROA)* is the three-year standard deviation of ROA. *Loss* is an indicator taking the value of one for all central-bank-years with losses (i.e., ROA < 0), and zero otherwise. *Neg. Equity* is an indicator taking the value of one for all central-bank-years with negative equity, and zero otherwise. *IFRS* is an indicator taking the value of one for central-bank-years using IFRS, and zero otherwise. *CB-specific* is an indicator taking the value of one for central-bank-years using a central-bank-specific accounting framework, and zero otherwise. *GDP Growth* is the percentage change in real GDP, measured in 2015 US dollars. *Recession* is an indicator for central-bank-years with negative GDP growth, and zero otherwise. *Δ Exchange Rate* is change in the exchange rate of the local currency against the US Dollar. *Inflation* is the country rate of consumer price inflation. *Developed* is an indicator for developed economies based on the United Nations classification. *Assets ($)* is the natural logarithm of total assets in thousands, converted in current US dollars. *Equity/Assets* is the ratio of central bank equity to total assets. Standard errors (in parentheses) are clustered by central bank. We assign all Eurozone central banks to the same cluster. All estimations include year fixed effects. ***, **, and * indicate statistical significance at the 1%, 5%, and 10% levels, respectively

profitability and inflation are more pronounced for the period of 2021–2022 when central banks started raising interest rates.[12]

This result highlights an important difference between the definition of central bank income commonly used in the economics literature and the definition used by IFRS, and other accounting frameworks applied by central banks. When a central bank issues currency, it records the face value of the currency in circulation as a liability and the cost of printing money as an expense (KPMG, 2012). Because monetary seigniorage is defined as the net change in base money deflated by consumer price level, the economic income of the central bank increases with inflation (Reis, 2015). However, because currency in circulation is held at its nominal value on central banks' balance sheets, increases in inflation do not have income-increasing effects on central banks' accounting profitability.[13]

Expectedly, because the depreciation (appreciation) of the local currency leads to significant unrealized foreign exchange gains (losses), we find a positive relationship between central bank profitability (*ROA*) and local currency depreciation (*Δ Exchange Rate*). We also find that currency depreciations (appreciations) reduce (increase) the likelihood of incurring negative equity (*Neg. Equity*).

The statistically weak results for some economic factors may be explained by the strong tendency of central banks to manage their earnings and smooth their performance figures (e.g., by using general risk provisions). For example, some of the central banks set aside general risk provisions for future increases in interest rates, effectively reallocating higher future expenses due to interest rate increases to earlier periods when these central banks were exposed to stable conditions and reported higher profits (e.g., the Deutsche Bundesbank).

We find that larger balance sheets (proxied by *Assets ($)*) increase the likelihood of central bank losses and negative equity. For example, a one standard deviation increase in the logarithm of total assets *Assets ($)* (4.177) increases the probability of losses by 5.1 percentage points or 22% of the unconditional mean. However, the net average effect of *Assets ($)* on profitability over 2010–2022 is very close to zero and central banks are yet to realize most of the losses due to recent interest rate increases.[14]

---

[12] Specifically, we estimated Eq. (1) by interacting *Inflation* with an indicator variable taking the value of one for years 2021–2022, and zero otherwise. Due to space constraints, we do not tabulate these results, but they are available from the authors upon request.

[13] Using a sample of central banks from the period that largely precedes our analysis (i.e., 1992–2014), Goncharov et al. (2023) find no significant association between inflation and accounting profitability. However, they find central banks that face reporting pressures may delay raising interest rates when inflation takes up because such interest rate increases have income-decreasing effects and may lead to losses. To support this conclusion, the authors show that interest rates are lower and the inflation is higher for central banks that report small positive profits (more likely to be affected by reporting pressures) than those that report small losses (less likely to be affected by reporting pressures).

[14] We obtain similar results when estimating Eq. (1) separately using observations from the Eurozone or from central banks implementing QE (i.e., the Fed, Swiss National Bank, Bank of Japan, Bank of England, and Sveriges Riksbank).

It is important to note that during the sample period central banks with QE have transferred significant amounts of money to the government after incurring high profits for many years. For example, the Fed has reported a combined profit of 1.08 trillion US dollars over 2010–2022 and transferred over a trillion US dollars in dividends to the Treasury over the same period. These transfers did not allow the central banks to build sufficient (equity) reserves during the period of relatively stable economic conditions. Furthermore, the majority of central banks do not have an arrangement with their government that would allow them to automatically recoup losses and recapitalize when they fully recognize losses due to higher interest rates. This increases concerns for central bank independence. Even when dividend distribution rules allow for automatic recapitalization in case of losses, Goncharov et al. (2023) find that central banks face reporting pressures and may as a result not act fully independently.

Finally, we find that central bank performance tends to be persistent as central banks with better financial position (*Equity/Assets*) tend to report higher future profitability, incur less losses, and are thus less likely to incur negative equity.

We next examine whether our results for different accounting frameworks and policies hold after accounting for differences in economic circumstances among central banks. We find that IFRS adopters have higher profitability and profit variability than other central banks, on average (columns 1 to 6 of Table 4). Conversely, central-bank-specific frameworks are associated with lower profit variability, possibly because they allow the use of discretionary general risk provisions to smooth reported income. Furthermore, we also observe a negative, albeit statistically weak, relationship between central-bank-specific frameworks and the level of profits or the likelihood of central bank losses.

Further, consistent with our univariate results, Table 5 reports that recognizing foreign exchange and fair value revaluations in income is strongly related to the volatility of reported profits. This higher profit volatility explains why *FX_P&L* and *FV_P&L* are simultaneously associated with higher levels of profitability and the likelihood of reporting losses. Recognizing general risk provisions is negatively associated with the volatility of reported profits and the likelihood of central bank losses or negative equity.

Overall, our evidence suggests that central banks face a trade-off in adopting more market-based accounting frameworks (e.g., IFRS) and policies (e.g., foreign exchange or fair value revaluations in the income statement). On the one hand, market-based accounting frameworks and policies allow financial statements to reflect economic signals in an unbiased and timely manner. For example, when interest rates rise, market-based accounting frameworks allow central banks to report securities at their current value and transparently recognize the resulting (large) losses on financial statements. On the other hand, by increasing the likelihood of reporting losses and negative equity, these accounting frameworks and policies may lead to public pressure, trigger negotiations about central bank dividends and recapitalization, and thus endanger central banks' independence (Goncharov & Novotny-Farkas, 2024).

Table 5 Central bank financial performance and accounting policies

	(1)	(2)	(3)	(4)	(5)	(6)	(7)	(8)	(9)	(10)	(11)	(12)
	$ROA_{i,t}$			$\sigma(ROA)_{i,t-2:t}$			$Loss_{i,t}$			$Neg.\ Equity_{i,t}$		
$FX\_P\&L_{i,t}$	0.005*			0.018***			0.076*			0.060*		
	(0.003)			(0.003)			(0.044)			(0.033)		
$FV\_P\&L_{i,t}$		0.005*			0.012***			0.087*			0.052	
		(0.003)			(0.003)			(0.045)			(0.035)	
$GRP_{i,t}$			−0.002			−0.011***			−0.178***			−0.074**
			(0.002)			(0.003)			(0.040)			(0.032)
$GDP\ Growth_{i,t}$	0.005	−0.001	0.001	−0.005	−0.005	−0.014	−0.431*	−0.411	−0.362*	0.212	0.250	0.205
	(0.031)	(0.031)	(0.031)	(0.018)	(0.018)	(0.018)	(0.257)	(0.261)	(0.216)	(0.231)	(0.230)	(0.230)
$Recession_{i,t}$	−0.001	−0.004	−0.004	0.010	0.009	0.007	−0.014	−0.008	0.003	0.038	0.032	0.047
	(0.008)	(0.007)	(0.007)	(0.008)	(0.008)	(0.007)	(0.054)	(0.056)	(0.054)	(0.035)	(0.035)	(0.037)
$\Delta\ Exchange\ Rate_{i,t}$	0.043**	0.049**	0.025**	−0.001	0.005	−0.006	−0.389***	−0.363***	−0.180	−0.143**	−0.110*	−0.109**
	(0.021)	(0.021)	(0.011)	(0.014)	(0.009)	(0.006)	(0.108)	(0.126)	(0.143)	(0.060)	(0.057)	(0.048)
$Inflation_{i,t}$	−0.035*	−0.040**	−0.027***	0.024*	0.017*	0.018***	0.362***	0.328***	0.277*	0.281***	0.248***	0.299***
	(0.019)	(0.018)	(0.009)	(0.014)	(0.009)	(0.006)	(0.102)	(0.113)	(0.164)	(0.051)	(0.044)	(0.072)
$Developed_i$	−0.005	−0.005	−0.005	−0.006**	−0.007*	−0.006*	−0.029	−0.017	0.009	−0.024	−0.023	−0.007
	(0.003)	(0.003)	(0.003)	(0.003)	(0.004)	(0.004)	(0.050)	(0.052)	(0.042)	(0.036)	(0.039)	(0.042)
$Assets\ (\$)_{i,t-1}$	−0.000	0.000	0.000	0.000	0.000	0.000	0.012**	0.011**	0.010**	0.007**	0.007*	0.007*
	(0.000)	(0.000)	(0.000)	(0.000)	(0.000)	(0.000)	(0.006)	(0.005)	(0.005)	(0.004)	(0.004)	(0.004)
$Equity/Assets_{i,t-1}$	0.063***	0.069***	0.071***	−0.018	−0.019	−0.011	−0.515***	−0.621***	−0.582***	−1.225***	−1.267***	−1.280***
	(0.015)	(0.014)	(0.013)	(0.026)	(0.025)	(0.023)	(0.161)	(0.172)	(0.162)	(0.342)	(0.321)	(0.305)

(continued)

Table 5 (continued)

	(1)	(2)	(3)	(4)	(5)	(6)	(7)	(8)	(9)	(10)	(11)	(12)
	$ROA_{i,t}$			$\sigma(ROA)_{i,t-2:t}$			$Loss_{i,t}$			$Neg.\ Equity_{i,t}$		
Constant	0.004	0.002	0.005	0.004	0.007	0.015	−0.018	0.008	0.100	−0.011	0.007	0.051
	(0.009)	(0.009)	(0.008)	(0.009)	(0.010)	(0.010)	(0.115)	(0.119)	(0.104)	(0.073)	(0.077)	(0.073)
Fixed Effects	Year	Year	Year	Year	Year	Year	Year	Year	Year	Year	Year	Year
Observations	1246	1238	1320	1150	1145	1213	1234	1225	1307	1248	1245	1332
Adjusted R-squared	0.076	0.094	0.079	0.154	0.102	0.069	0.085	0.095	0.110	0.274	0.300	0.325

This table reports OLS coefficients for Eq. (1). *ROA* is computed as central bank profit over average total assets. $\sigma(ROA)$ is the three-year standard deviation of ROA. *Loss* is an indicator taking the value of one for all central-bank-years with losses (i.e., ROA < 0), and zero otherwise. *Neg. Equity* is an indicator taking the value of one for all central-bank-years with negative equity, and zero otherwise. *FX_P&L* is an indicator taking the value of one for central-bank-years recognizing foreign exchange revaluations in the income statement, and zero otherwise. *FV_P&L* is an indicator taking the value of one for central-bank-years measuring financial assets at fair value and recognizing the revaluation difference in the income statement, and zero otherwise. *GRP* is an indicator taking the value of one for central-bank-years reporting general risk provisions, and zero otherwise. *GDP Growth* is the percentage change in real GDP, measured in 2015 US dollars. *Recession* is an indicator for central-bank-years with negative GDP growth, and zero otherwise. Δ *Exchange Rate* is change in the exchange rate of the local currency against the US Dollar. *Inflation* is the country rate of consumer price inflation. *Developed* is an indicator for developed economies based on the United Nations classification. *Assets ($)* is the natural logarithm of total assets in thousands, converted in current US dollars. *Equity/Assets* is the ratio of central bank equity to total assets. Standard errors (in parentheses) are clustered by central bank. We assign all Eurozone central banks to the same cluster. All estimations include year fixed effects. ***, **, and * indicate statistical significance at the 1%, 5%, and 10% levels, respectively

5 Dividend Distribution Rules

Dividend distribution rules play an important role for central banks' financial performance. In this section, we examine the relationship between central banks' financial performance, accounting rules, and distribution rules. Because most dividend rules require that central banks distribute their profits to the government, high dividend distributions can deplete central banks' capital and impact central bank independence (Archer & Moser-Boehm, 2013). To prevent this, carefully designed dividend distribution rules may allow central banks some flexibility in deciding on the amount of dividends, take the level of central bank equity into account when determining dividends, facilitate the automatic recapitalization of central banks in case of (capital) losses or allow central banks to smooth their dividend payments over time (Hall & Reis, 2015). In this respect, dividend distribution rules and accounting policies are two complementary drivers of central banks' financial strength (i.e., equity). On the one hand, dividend distribution rules allocate income between distributable and retained income. On the other hand, accounting policies determine the level of accounting income used for dividend distribution. For instance, general risk provisions can smooth dividend distribution by smoothing accounting income.[15]

Central banks' dividend distribution rules exhibit vast heterogeneity. Some dividend distributions are based on explicit rules, while others allow discretionary decisions by central banks, their shareholders (the government), or both parties. Further, dividend distribution rules can simultaneously include several features, such as equity targets, dividend smoothing arrangements, and the ability to draw on external capital (i.e., a negative dividend) in case of certain events. In our analysis, we rely on the classification of dividend distribution rules in Archer and Moser-Boehm (2013) and broadly classify central banks' dividend distribution rules based on two features: (1) which party makes the dividend decisions (*Central Bank*, *Government*, and *Joint*), and (2) how the dividend amount is set (*External Resource*, *Equity Target*, *Distribution Smoothing*, *Earnings Retention*, *Promised Distribution*, *Mandatory Distribution*, and *Exclude FX_FV*). In general, dividend distribution rules involving non-trivial equity targets, retaining (part of) the surplus, or providing central banks with greater discretion can help central banks improve their financial position (Archer & Moser-Boehm, 2013). However, because central banks have some discretion in implementing dividend distribution rules or might deviate from

[15] Anecdotal evidence suggests that central banks have greater discretion in changing accounting rules than distribution rules. For instance, the Fed reports accumulated losses as a deferred asset. The underlying assumption is that these losses reduce future transfers to the Treasury before reserves are rebuilt. This accounting policy provides two benefits. First, it avoids the possibility of ever reporting negative equity. Second, it ensures that the Fed does not pay dividends until accumulated losses are fully covered (Archer & Moser-Boehm, 2013).

these rules under government pressure and pay higher dividends, such effects might not be observable in practice.[16]

Table 6 examines the relationship between our dividend distribution rules and central banks' financial strength, proxied by the likelihood of reporting negative equity (*Neg. Equity*) and the equity-to-assets ratio (*Equity/Assets*). In Columns (1) and (5), we report the results for all central banks, while in Columns (2)–(4) and (6)–(8) we examine the relationship for each accounting framework separately. We find that dividend decisions made by governments (*Government*) are associated with lower equity buffers, especially for central banks with central-bank-specific frameworks. Importantly, governments' dividend decisions are a major determinant of negative equity for central banks with central-bank-specific frameworks. Conversely, when central banks have discretion on dividend decisions (*Central Bank*), the equity buffer is higher for central banks adopting local GAAP, and there is a significant reduction in the probability of reporting negative equity for all central banks and most accounting frameworks. We also observe that joint dividend decisions (*Joint*) increase the equity-to-assets ratio, but this effect is mainly concentrated among IFRS adopters.

Furthermore, we do not find a significant positive association between dividend distribution rules featuring equity targets (*Equity Target*) and central banks' equity-to-assets ratio. Indeed, we find that equity targets help increase equity buffers only for central banks reporting under local GAAP. A possible explanation for these results is that the dividend distribution rule might set a low equity target. Moreover, we observe a positive relationship between distribution smoothing mechanisms (*Distribution Smoothing*) and equity buffers. Expectedly, allowing central banks to draw additional capital resources (*External Resource*) increases equity buffers under most frameworks, but it does not insure against reporting negative equity. Finally, the resulting equity buffer is lower when central banks have a promised (*Promised Distribution*) or mandated dividend distribution (*Mandatory Distribution*) such as a dividend equaling a fixed percent of paid-in capital or a certain fixed amount of currency per share.

Overall, these results suggest that financial strength is higher (lower) when central banks (governments) have more discretion in determining the dividend amount. Besides, the ability to draw external resources (*External Resource*) when needed and to smooth the dividend distribution (*Distribution Smoothing*) is associated

[16] For example, the Swiss National Bank faced following demands after reporting accounting losses: "I'm not going to assume from a first-half loss that there won't be a year-end dividend... Until now, we are maintaining our long-term view of a 1 billion franc dividend at year-end." (*Reuters*, July 31, 2015). Governments can also raid central bank reserves regardless of the prevailing dividend distribution rules. For example, "[i]n the U.S., Congress grabbed $19 billion from a Federal Reserve capital surplus account in December to help fund infrastructure projects, a move Fed Chairwoman Janet Yellen said impinged on the central bank's independence" (*Wall Street Journal*, May 8, 2016). In turn, central banks can be exposed to political pressures, negatively impacting their independence, despite automatic recapitalization rules if a central bank has to go cap-in-hand to the government.

Table 6 The impact of dividend distribution rules

	(1)	(2)	(3)	(4)	(5)	(6)	(7)	(8)
	Neg. Equity$_{i,t}$				*Equity/Assets*$_{i,t}$			
	All	IFRS	GAAP	CB-specific	All	IFRS	GAAP	CB-specific
Dividend decision:								
Central bank$_{i,t}$	−0.106***	−0.068**	−0.216	−0.155*	0.003	0.003	0.036*	−0.007**
	(0.032)	(0.032)	(0.208)	(0.082)	(0.002)	(0.004)	(0.019)	(0.003)
Government$_{i,t}$	0.090	0.111	−0.210	0.611***	−0.006*	−0.001	−0.006	−0.009*
	(0.170)	(0.116)	(0.135)	(0.204)	(0.003)	(0.004)	(0.011)	(0.005)
Joint$_{i,t}$	0.051	0.087	0.063	−0.022	0.007***	0.011***	0.006	0.000
	(0.048)	(0.074)	(0.154)	(0.036)	(0.002)	(0.003)	(0.014)	(0.003)
Dividend amount:								
External Resource$_{i,t}$	−0.027	0.008	−0.216	0.150	0.005**	0.006**	0.056*	−0.005
	(0.051)	(0.046)	(0.262)	(0.140)	(0.002)	(0.003)	(0.028)	(0.006)
Equity Target$_{i,t}$	0.077	0.041	0.172	0.099	−0.003	−0.006*	0.037*	−0.003
	(0.051)	(0.055)	(0.176)	(0.079)	(0.003)	(0.003)	(0.021)	(0.004)
Distribution Smoothing$_{i,t}$	−0.001		−0.248	0.022	0.010**		0.006	−0.005
	(0.073)		(0.155)	(0.141)	(0.005)		(0.012)	(0.011)
Earnings Retention$_{i,t}$	0.014	0.084	−0.174	0.002	−0.000	−0.001	0.019	0.005
	(0.044)	(0.082)	(0.163)	(0.031)	(0.002)	(0.003)	(0.015)	(0.003)
Promised Distribution$_{i,t}$	−0.194			−0.144	−0.085***			−0.103*
	(0.125)			(0.226)	(0.026)			(0.058)
Mandatory Distribution$_{i,t}$	0.046	−0.033		0.021	−0.007*	−0.010		0.008
	(0.064)	(0.087)		(0.152)	(0.004)	(0.007)		(0.007)
Exclude FX_FV$_{i,t}$	0.074	0.042	0.008	−0.191	0.001	0.004	−0.017	−0.002
	(0.048)	(0.042)	(0.147)	(0.144)	(0.002)	(0.003)	(0.017)	(0.006)

(continued)

Table 6 (continued)

	(1)	(2)	(3)	(4)	(5)	(6)	(7)	(8)
Controls:								
GDP Growth$_{i,t}$	0.296	0.166	4.459***	0.454	0.025	0.044	−0.446***	0.081
	(0.281)	(0.358)	(1.078)	(0.438)	(0.038)	(0.048)	(0.156)	(0.065)
Recession$_{i,t}$	0.017	−0.045	0.275**	−0.028	0.009**	0.009*	−0.019	0.011**
	(0.042)	(0.045)	(0.114)	(0.030)	(0.003)	(0.006)	(0.017)	(0.005)
	Neg. Equity$_{i,t}$				*Equity/Assets*$_{i,t}$			
Δ Exchange Rate$_{i,t}$	0.031	−0.021	−0.077	0.037	0.090***	0.122***	−0.036	0.098
	(0.121)	(0.143)	(0.440)	(0.183)	(0.027)	(0.025)	(0.094)	(0.058)
Inflation$_{i,t}$	0.404	0.321	0.654	1.211	−0.199***	−0.243***	−0.097	0.038
	(0.375)	(0.346)	(0.955)	(0.754)	(0.041)	(0.041)	(0.093)	(0.076)
Developed$_{i}$	−0.043	−0.065	0.081	−0.220*	−0.006***	−0.009**	0.019	0.004
	(0.044)	(0.057)	(0.165)	(0.107)	(0.002)	(0.003)	(0.011)	(0.005)
*Assets ($)*$_{i,t-1}$	0.006	0.004	−0.005	−0.013	0.001**	0.001***	0.003	0.000
	(0.005)	(0.006)	(0.019)	(0.012)	(0.000)	(0.000)	(0.002)	(0.001)
Equity/Assets$_{i,t-1}$	−1.371***	−0.756*	−1.834***	−1.053	0.953***	0.956***	0.886***	0.862***
	(0.401)	(0.380)	(0.426)	(0.780)	(0.016)	(0.018)	(0.040)	(0.035)
Constant	−0.001	−0.037	0.224	0.490	−0.008	−0.019**	−0.102*	−0.009
	(0.116)	(0.162)	(0.669)	(0.336)	(0.007)	(0.009)	(0.059)	(0.017)
Fixed effects	Year	Year	Year	Year	Year	Year	Year	Year
Observations	1054	575	136	336	1054	575	136	336
Adjusted R-squared	0.333	0.148	0.676	0.539	0.918	0.922	0.910	0.860

This table reports OLS coefficients for Eq. (1). *Neg. Equity* is an indicator taking the value of one for all central-bank-years with negative equity, and zero otherwise. *Equity/Assets* is the ratio of central bank equity to total assets. *IFRS* is an indicator taking the value of one for central-bank-years using IFRS, and zero otherwise. *GAAP* is an indicator taking the value of one for central-bank-years using local GAAP, and zero otherwise. *CB-specific* is an indicator taking the value of one for central-bank-years using a central-bank-specific accounting framework, and zero otherwise. *Central Bank* is an indicator taking the value of one when a central bank has discretion over earnings distribution, and zero otherwise. *Government* is an indicator taking the value of one when the government controls the earnings distribution, and zero otherwise. *Joint* is an indicator taking the value of one for central-bank-years where the central banks and the government jointly decide on the earnings distribution, and zero otherwise. *External Resource* is an indicator taking the value of one for central-bank-years having the possibility to draw additional resources (i.e., a negative dividend) from governments or governmental agencies to enhance their financial strength, and zero otherwise. *Equity Target* is an indicator taking the value of one for central-bank-years with capital targets or target-like mechanisms that can adjust dividend distribution to enhance financial strength, and zero otherwise. *Distribution Smoothing* is an indicator taking the value of one for central-bank-years whose dividend distribution is adjusted based on past performance, and zero otherwise. *Earnings Retention* is an indicator taking the value of one for central-bank-years retaining a fixed part of their earnings as surplus to enhance their financial strength, and zero otherwise. *Promised Distribution* is an indicator taking the value of one for central-bank-years with a promised or standardized earnings distribution with limited conditionality, and zero otherwise. *Mandatory Distribution* is an indicator taking the value of one for central-bank-years with a mandatory and unconditional earnings distribution, and zero otherwise. *Exclude FX_FV* is an indicator taking the value of one for central-bank-years that exclude from the calculation of distributable earnings the (unrealized) revaluations gains or losses on financial assets or foreign exchange, and zero otherwise. *GDP Growth* is the percentage change in real GDP, measured in 2015 US dollars. *Recession* is an indicator for central-bank-years with negative GDP growth, and zero otherwise. *Δ Exchange Rate* is change in the exchange rate of the local currency against the US Dollar. *Inflation* is the country rate of consumer price inflation. *Developed* is an indicator for developed economies based on the United Nations classification. *Assets ($)* is the natural logarithm of total assets in thousands, converted in current US dollars. Missing coefficients are due to a lack of variation of a given variable in a subsample. Standard errors (in parentheses) are clustered by central bank. We assign all Eurozone central banks to the same cluster. All estimations include year fixed effects. ***, **, and * indicate statistical significance at the 1%, 5%, and 10% levels, respectively

with improved central banks' financial strength. However, we acknowledge that the decision to adopt specific dividend distribution policies is not random. For instance, central banks with greater equity buffers might adopt specific dividend rules to afford larger distributions. Thus, we refrain from drawing a causal interpretation of the effect of central banks' dividend distribution rules on central banks' financial position. However, our descriptive results are informative about patterns of financial performance associated with specific dividend distribution rules.

6 Discussion of the Results and Policy Implications

Our analysis shows that central banks often use accounting rules such as IFRS that aim to increase central bank transparency by reflecting economic signals in financial statements in an unbiased and timely manner, but also expose central banks to greater earnings volatility and increase the likelihood of losses and negative equity. In turn, discretionary accounting policies, such as general risk provisions, can help central banks smooth their performance. However, using provisions for avoiding losses and negative equity depends on a central bank's ability to build them during periods of high performance. Furthermore, such provisions are quickly depleted when central banks face large losses as has been the case after recent increases in interest rates. Prevailing dividend distribution rules can further deteriorate central bank equity if they do not allow central banks to retain a large surplus that can be used for covering losses in the future. Because central banks require sufficient capital buffers to act (financially) independently and economic factors that increase the likelihood of losses and negative equity will likely persist in the coming years, our analysis points to potential challenges for central bank independence and the effectiveness of their monetary policies.

Central bank financial reporting is often inappropriately compared to firm financial reporting, and central bank governors often face similar reactions to their reported figures as firm managers do. For example, after the Swiss National Bank (SNB) announced "an eye-popping net loss" of 30 billion CHF for the first quarter of 2015 due to the revaluation of its foreign currency holdings, a news article quoting a participant of the SNB's shareholders meeting noted that "shortly before the announcement… 'the directors looked very stressed.'" (*AEI* 2015). Because central banks often use same financial reporting standards as firms do, capital market participants can better understand central banks' financial position and performance, but they are also tempted to both use the metrics commonly applied in firm financial analysis and valuation, and interpret central bank performance the same way as the performance of profit-maximizing firms.

There is substantial evidence that capital market participants scrutinize central bank financial statements, looking for information that is relevant for understanding central bank monetary policy (e.g., asset maturities, foreign currency reserves), but also for information that is not directly related to central bank monetary policy such as central bank earnings, accounting policies, and accounting assumptions used for measuring central bank assets and liabilities (Goncharov & Novotny-Farkas, 2024; Goncharov et al., 2023).[17] As firm managers are (rightfully) blamed for poor performance figures and (unexpected) losses as a result of their strategic decisions and operating policies, the public may misperceive central bank losses as a sign of failed monetary policies (Archer & Moser-Boehm, 2013). By reporting on central bank "profit warnings" and the likelihood of a central bank "going bust" alongside stories on performance figures of publicly quoted firms and commercial banks, news media may amplify these effects. Therefore, insights from the accounting literature that examines accounting and real actions (i.e., those affecting cash flows) of reporting agents that face various reporting pressures (e.g., Kanodia & Sapra, 2016) could be helpful for understanding what central banks are expected to do when facing reporting pressures, what are the consequences of their actions, and what are the possible remedies if certain consequences are deemed undesirable.

Accountability is crucial for firms because it fosters transparency and trust among stakeholders, which can lead to lower costs of capital and improved firm performance (e.g., Leuz & Verrecchia, 2000; Kanodia & Sapra, 2016). By holding firms accountable for their actions and financial reporting, users of firm financial statements can make more informed decisions, reducing information asymmetry and ultimately enhancing market efficiency. More transparent accounting can help central banks achieve greater accountability to its different stakeholders. However, accounting must provide a sufficient degree of discretion to account for unforeseen circumstances and to allow reporting agents to signal private information (e.g., building provisions to signal future defaults). This signaling role of accounting information could be detrimental for central banks if the world of "Fed watchers" reads too much into accounting policy changes or misperceives them as signals of changing monetary policies.

A large literature in accounting and corporate finance shows that—when facing reporting pressures (e.g., to report profits rather than losses or meat and beat other performance benchmarks)—firms manage their earnings to achieve desirable performance results. Corporate managers do so even when taking myopic actions to boost firm performance is harmful in the long term (Jensen, 1986; Stein, 1989; Graham et al., 2005). While most of those manipulations remain undetected (Zakolyukina, 2018), the discoveries of accounting irregularities lead to very large capital market penalties and the loss of trust in corporate reporting (Dechow et al.,

[17] For example, Bank of America Merrill Lynch analysts questioned an unusual new accounting policy when the Fed switched from reporting accumulated losses in equity to reporting them as a deferred asset, noting that "Fed's accounting changes present a further challenge to government credibility, which in turn could contribute to underperformance of the long end of the Treasury curve" (*Financial Times*, January 20, 2011). Furthermore, analysts used footnote disclosures of net pension liabilities from the Fed's financial statements to gauge long-term performance of certain asset classes. Specifically, an analyst inferred from the Fed's disclosures that its "pension fund allocation appears to reflect the Fed's caution about the reflation trade: it seems to underweight assets". However, there were no reasons to believe these changes reflected the opinion of the Fed's staff economists about which assets will outperform (see "The Federal Reserve's pension fund isn't trying to tell you anything" in *Financial Times*, March 30, 2017).

1996; Graham et al., 2008; Giannetti & Wang, 2016). Goncharov et al. (2023) argue and show that central banks are exposed to similar reporting pressures because they face political pressure (especially when reporting to politicians with extreme, left or right, views), public scrutiny over reported figures (e.g., because of the requirement to hold press conferences upon the release of financial statements or issue profit warnings), governments' budgetary pressures (e.g., related to central bank dividend payments), and other reporting pressures that result from issues with de facto central bank independence. The authors demonstrate that central banks have greater flexibility in their reporting than firms do, and that reporting pressures are significant enough to shape the distribution of central bank earnings (especially around a zero-profit threshold). Because financial reporting pressures are likely to persist, how do central banks mitigate these pressures or their effect on their behavior?

Disclosing information on central bank assets used for monetary policy purposes (such as QE assets or foreign currency reserves) does not require the publication of full financial statements. Central banks may thus choose not to report full financial statements or significantly redact their disclosures. The former is likely impossible in the environment of high accountability of all government institutions and because financial statements that follow international accounting norms are required by the IMF and safeguards assessments.[18] However, the Bank of England reported prior to 2015 an IFRS income statement that deviated from IFRS presentation and disclosure requirements and showed only information on earnings before and after tax. Such disclosure practices afford less transparency and may unduly fixate market participants' attention on bottom-line earnings without understanding the context of this figure (Sloan, 1996). If regulators are primarily concerned about the efficiency of central bank operations and their governance, central banks can separately disclose their operating expenses (similar to income statements of the Board of Governors of the Federal Reserve System).

As an alternative, central banks can implement accounting rules that provide more control over financials (see Goncharov & Novotny-Farkas, 2024). For example, general risk provisions are banned by IFRS due to their lack of transparency, but this accounting policy significantly reduces the volatility of profits and the likelihood of losses. Indeed, Goncharov et al. (2023) show that using provisions is one of the main tools for central bank earnings management and that central banks enjoy high discretion in determining the values of these provisions. For example, some central banks use unusually round general risk provisions (i.e., compare provisions of €400,000,000.00 to reporting of other income and expenses, e.g., €626,073,422.88). The ECB chose in 2022 to release provisions in the amount (1.6 billion) that matches losses before provisions (−1.6 billion), thus reporting net earnings for 2022 that were exactly zero and narrowly avoiding a loss. In turn,

[18] One of the few exceptions is the Central Bank of the Republic of China (Taiwan). We were able to find only information on the central bank's balance sheet with no supporting footnote disclosures in English.

recording fair value revaluations in profit or loss does not allow a central bank to tailor its profits if assets are marked-to-market.[19]

While using accounting discretion can help central banks achieve desirable profit and equity targets and to deflect the (undue) attention to central bank performance figures, uncommon and highly discretionary accounting policies can adversely affect public perceptions. The press and market participants scrutinize accounting assumptions and question cases when monetary policies do not align with accounting policies. To illustrate, we provide a case of reading signals in the Deutsche Bundesbank's decision to increase provisions and its projections of future interest rates in the Eurozone: "After setting aside €1.9 billion for 'general risk provisions' and deducting interest expenditure to the tune of €1 billion, [the Deutsche Bundesbank] announced it would transfer €1.9 billion to the German Federal Treasury... 'The continuation of the asset purchases has driven up the Bank's interest rate risk,' President Weidmann said in the report. In 2016, the German central bank made such provisions for the first time as it expected 'very low interest income' from the ECB's asset purchases and the income generated from negative rates in deposits to turn 'quickly' into expenditure if interest rates pick up" (*Deutsche Welle*, February 27, 2018). "With its increased risk provisions, the Bundesbank also contradicts the [ECB's] interest rate policy. Many observers of European monetary policy no longer expect the ECB's interest rate to rise this year and next, due to the economic downturn. Weidmann also did not respond to multiple requests at the press conference to reveal the specific interest rate path. However, he made it clear that... higher interest rates [are] still the baseline scenario of the Bundesbank" (authors' translation from German, *Die Welt*, February 28, 2018).

While central banks may choose to measure assets at their fair values in their financial statements, they have a choice of whether to recognize fair value revaluations in the financial statements (i.e., on the face of the balance sheet and/or in the income statement) or to disclose them (only) in the footnotes to the financial statements. The accounting literature finds that markets respond differently to disclosed than recognized amounts (e.g., Aboody, 1996; Ahmed et al., 2006; Müller et al., 2015; Michels, 2017). Morris and Shin (2007) extend this logic to central banks' reporting. Indeed, these arguments clearly apply for the case of the Fed, where little notice was given to huge unrealized losses in Q3 2018 that were disclosed in the notes but were not recognized because the Fed reports assets on the balance sheet at their amortized (historical) cost. Recognizing these unrealized losses would have wiped out the Fed's equity. Such disclosures can help meet the

[19] Standard setters (e.g., IASB and FASB) differentiate between fair values using only observable market prices (i.e., Level 1 fair values), and those relying on some unobservable data (i.e., Level 2 fair values when market values of similar assets are available, or Level 3 fair values when relying on mark-to-model estimates). Preparers have high discretion in estimating Level 2 and Level 3 fair values (e.g., predictions of future cash flows, discount rate assumptions) and the literature finds that firms and financial institutions often manipulate such valuations (e.g., Huizinga & Laeven, 2012; Hanley et al., 2018; Black et al., 2022; Gad et al., 2023).

accountability demands, while preventing possible negative impacts of recognition on both market perceptions and (importantly) dividends.

Other examples of disclosures that apparently aim to deflect market participants' undue attention to central bank performance figures include "mislabeling" the amounts. For example, the Fed can avoid reporting negative equity by reporting accumulated losses—a component of equity—elsewhere on the balance sheet (e.g., as a deferred asset similar to how accumulated losses were reported by private firms in some countries, or as a negative liability).[20] There are also recent examples of central bank disclosures that refer to other line items than net income in the announcements of central bank annual results. For example, despite releasing general risk provisions, the Deutsche Bundesbank incurred a net loss for 2022, but referred in its press release announcing its annual results only to the amount of income after the utilization of profits (i.e., after transfers from or to equity reserves) as the "distributable profit" for the year 2022, without mentioning the net loss for the period in a deviation to its previous reporting practice.[21] While net income was negative (−€172 million), the figure after the utilization of profits was exactly zero. Following this announcement, some media broadcasted that "Bundesbank reports zero loss for 2022" (*Bloomberg*, March 1, 2023). The accounting literature suggests that disclosure processing costs (i.e., costs of monitoring for, acquiring, and analyzing firm disclosures) affect investor information choices, trades, and equity market outcomes, especially when dealing with unsophisticated investors (e.g., Blankespoor et al., 2020).

Because accounting earnings consist of cash flows (e.g., gains or losses on sale of securities) and accounting adjustments called accruals (e.g., accrued interest, unrealized gains or losses), central banks can either use accounting or real decisions to achieve desirable earnings and equity figures. Evidence from the firm setting indicates that firms usually prefer managing accruals to managing cash flows for target beating, as it is less costly to change accounting records than decisions affecting actual cash receipts or cash expenses (Roychowdhury, 2006). For example, cutting discretionary R&D expenses to meet a profit target may be critical for firms' future market position. However, some studies find that perceptions matter, and the risk of auditors or regulators uncovering such accrual manipulations may change the perceived costs and shift the focus toward cash manipulation, which cannot be easily distinguished from regular operating decisions (Graham et al., 2005; Roychowdhury, 2006). Similarly, central banks face the risk of "being accused of accounting shenanigans" when they use unusual accounting policies that can diminish their credibility (*Reuters*, January 21, 2011). Importantly, accruals only reallocate income over time and accounting choices that move earnings in one direction usually revert within 4 years, moving earnings in the opposite direction

[20] Recognizing accumulated losses as an asset is not possible under IFRS (or US GAAP) because an asset is an economic resource controlled by an entity that has the potential to produce economic benefits (e.g., cash inflows).

[21] See https://www.bundesbank.de/en/tasks/topics/annual-report-2022-904442

(Dechow & Dichev, 2002; Baber et al., 2011). Thus, past accounting decisions constrain central banks' ability to change earnings in the current period. For example, this is the case when a central bank has used up all its general risk provisions that were built up in previous years.

Real decisions that increase central bank earnings include (a) increases in fees that a central bank charges for its services or an imposition of new fees; (b) generating income from other sources (e.g., trading securities for gain maximization); and (c) changes in monetary policy decisions that affect earnings. We discuss the latter two possibilities as they represent, in our view, major risks of exposing central banks to high reporting pressures, especially when they run out of accounting or accrual options. Central banks now hold a larger share of stocks and corporate bonds directly or through funds. For example, *Bloomberg* (March 13, 2024) estimates that the Bank of Japan holds the equivalent of about 7% of the Japanese stock market through ETFs. Trading these shares for pure gain maximization would raise questions about the fit of this activity with the main goals of a central bank, the use of sensitive information for gain trading, and possible disruption of the market from such trades.

Alternatively, there is a possibility that high reporting pressures may affect (on the margin) the decisions of central banks about monetary policy parameters. For example, Goncharov et al. (2023) discuss the possibility that (some) central banks may be less aggressive in raising interest rates because higher interest rates lead to higher interest expenses and the devaluation of assets held at fair value, thus lowering income. The authors find that central banks that avoid losses and face higher reporting pressures have lower interest rates and higher inflation than central banks that face no or little such pressures. These results provide suggestive evidence that central banks' profit considerations may impair the effectiveness of monetary policy.

Extending this evidence, we note that large foreign currency holdings shape the distribution of central bank profits, making it less possible for central banks to control their profits and equity in case of large swings in exchange rates as the case of SNB demonstrates. Using the data and borrowing the methods from Goncharov et al. (2023), we contrast the central banks that have a currency peg to those using floating rates. Panel A of Fig. 3 shows that the distribution of ROA for central banks that have a floating exchange rate exhibits a less pronounced discontinuity around zero than the general population of central banks in Fig. 1. However, central banks may have some control over when and how they set a currency peg. Panel B of Fig. 3 shows results for central banks that maintain a peg (but may set a different exchange rate over time), and Panel C for those that introduce a peg. The discontinuity is more pronounced in these cases and Panel C exhibits a dip right before zero, suggesting the peg value may be calibrated to avoid small losses. Similar "kinks" in the earnings distribution were reported using firm data and attributed to firms managing their earnings and avoiding losses using both accrual and cash flow decisions (Burgstahler & Dichev, 1997). While there are several possible explanations for this association, interpreting this result as evidence of (some) central banks using a peg regime to manage earnings and to avoid losses indicates the presence of externalities of

Panel A – Central banks without a peg

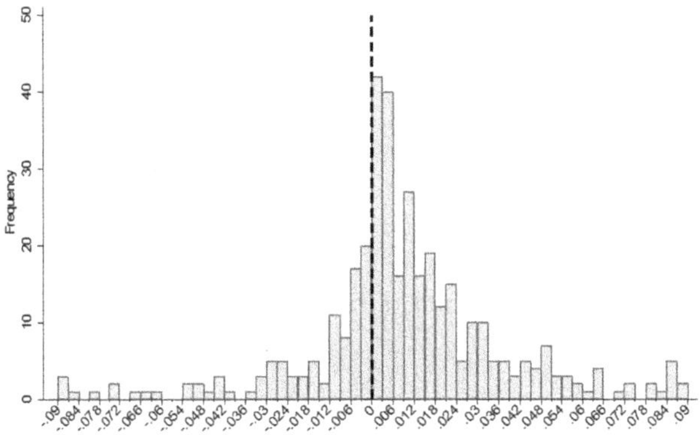

Panel B – Central banks maintaining a peg

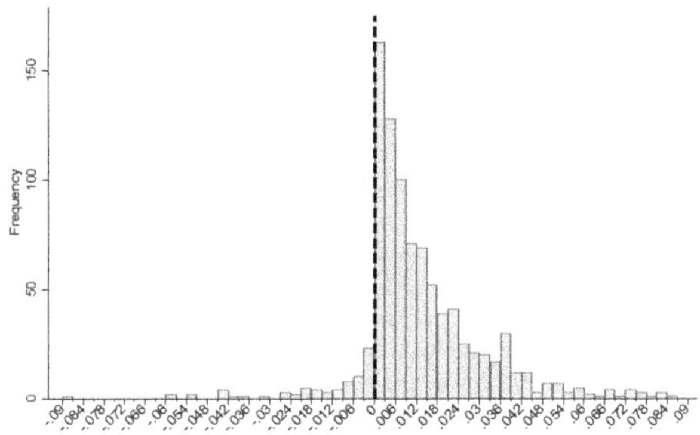

Panel C – Central banks introducing a peg

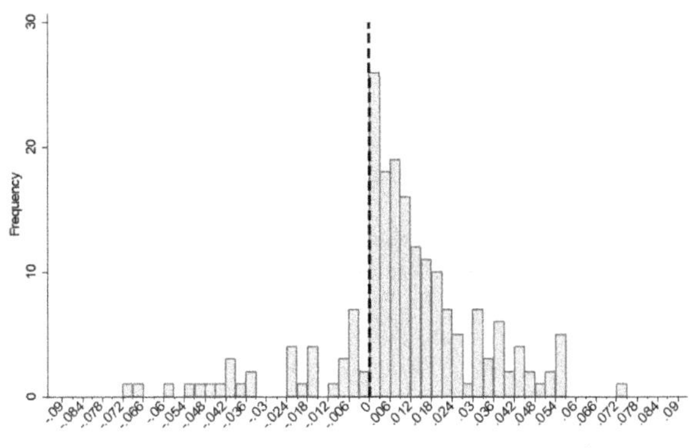

Fig. 3 Central bank earnings (ROA) and currency peg. Notes: This figure plots the distribution of central bank profits over years 1992–2014 ($N = 2591$) for countries without an exchange rate peg during the sample period (*Panel **A***), for observations with an exchange rate peg (*Panel **B***) or those introducing an exchange rate peg in a given year (*Panel **C***). The distribution of ROA is trimmed at [−0.09; 0.09]. The dotted vertical line shows when ROA equals zero. The number of observations falling into each bin is reported on the vertical axis

reporting pressures, especially if central banks cannot change accounting policies or run out of pure accounting options.

Finally, when deciding on accounting rules, their interrelation with dividend distribution rules and their impact on dividend distributions must be considered (Goncharov & Novotny-Farkas, 2024). Accounting rules provide more flexibility when making decisions about dividend transfers even when central banks have rigid dividend distribution rules. It seems that many central banks have sufficient flexibility in choosing how they determine their (distributable) income, but they do not have high flexibility in changing dividend distribution rules that are subject to negotiations with the government and rarely change based on our observations and data.

References

Aboody, D. (1996). Recognition versus disclosure in the oil and gas industry. *Journal of Accounting Research, 34*, 21–32.

Ahmed, A. S., Emre, K., & Lobo, G. J. (2006). Does recognition versus disclosure matter? Evidence from value-relevance of banks' recognized and disclosed derivative financial instruments. *The Accounting Review, 81*(3), 567–588.

Archer, D., & Moser-Boehm, P. (2013). *Central bank finances*. BIS Papers 71.

Armstrong, C. S., Barth, M. E., Jagolinzer, A. D., & Riedl, E. J. (2010). Market reaction to the adoption of IFRS in Europe. *The Accounting Review, 85*(1), 31–61.

Baber, W. R., Kang, S.-H., & Li, Y. (2011). Modeling discretionary accrual reversal and the balance sheet as an earnings management constraint. *The Accounting Review, 86*(4), 1189–1212.

Barth, M. E., Landsman, W. R., & Wahlen, J. M. (1995). Fair value accounting: Effects on banks' earnings volatility, regulatory capital, and value of contractual cash flows. *Journal of Banking and Finance, 19*(3–4), 577–605.

Bell, S., Chui, M., Gomes, T., Moser-Boehm, P., & Pierres Tejada, A. (2023). *Why are central banks reporting losses? Does it matter?* BIS Bulletin 68.

Bernanke, B. (2010). *Central bank independence, transparency, and accountability*. Speech at the Institute for Monetary and Economic Studies International Conference, Bank of Japan, Tokyo, 25 May 2010.

Black, J., Chen, J. Z., & Cussatt, M. (2022). Managerial discretion and the comparability of fair value estimates. *Journal of Accounting and Public Policy, 41*(1), 106878.

Blankespoor, E., deHaan, E., & Marinovic, I. (2020). Disclosure processing costs, investors' information choice, and equity market outcomes: A review. *Journal of Accounting and Economics, 70*(2), 101344.

Burgstahler, D., & Dichev, I. (1997). Earnings management to avoid earnings decreases and losses. *Journal of Accounting and Economics, 24*(1), 99–126.

Christensen, J. H. E., Lopez, J. A., & Rudebusch, G. D. (2015). A probability-based stress test of Federal Reserve assets and income. *Journal of Monetary Economics, 73*, 26–43.

de Haan, J., & Eijffinger, S. (2016). *The politics of central bank independence*. DNB Working Paper 59.

De Nederlandsche Bank. (2022). *DNB's capital position, letter to the Ministry of Finance*. 9 september 2022. https://www.dnb.nl/media/p4igu5fc/letter-regarding-dnb-s-capital-position-september-2022.pdf. Accessed 10 February 2024.

Dechow, P. M., & Dichev, I. D. (2002). The quality of accruals and earnings: The role of accrual estimation errors. *The Accounting Review, 77*(4), 35.

Dechow, P. M., Sloan, R. G., & Sweeney, A. P. (1996). Causes and consequences of earnings manipulation: An analysis of firm subject to enforcement actions by the SEC. *Contemporary Accounting Research, 13*(1), 1–36.

Gad, M., Goncharov, I., & Müller, M. A. (2023). *Reporting quality and organizational form choice: Evidence from open-end and closed-end firms*. SSRN Working Paper 4568358.

Giannetti, M., & Wang, T. Y. (2016). Corporate scandals and household stock market participation. *The Journal of Finance, 71*(6), 2591–2636.

Goncharov, I., Ioannidou, V., & Schmalz, M. C. (2023). (Why) do central banks care about their profits? *Journal of Finance, 78*(5), 2991–3045.

Goncharov, I., & Novotny-Farkas, Z. (2024). *Central bank independence and accounting choice*. SSRN Working Paper 3330830.

Graham, J. R., Harvey, C. R., & Rajgopal, S. (2005). The economic implications of corporate financial reporting. *Journal of Accounting and Economics, 40*(1–3), 3–73.

Graham, J. R., Li, S., & Qiu, J. (2008). Corporate misreporting and bank loan contracting. *Journal of Financial Economics, 89*(1), 44–61.

Hall, R. E., & Reis, R. (2015). *Maintaining central-bank financial stability under new-style central banking*. NBER Working Paper Series 21175.

Hanley, K. W., Jagolinzer, A. D., & Nikolova, S. (2018). Strategic estimation of asset fair values. *Journal of Accounting and Economics, 66*(1), 25–45.

Hirst, D. E., & Hopkins, P. E. (1998). Comprehensive income reporting and analysts' valuation judgments. *Journal of Accounting Research, 36*(3), 47–75.

Hodder, L. D., Hopkins, P. E., & Wahlen, J. M. (2006). Risk-relevance of fair-value income measures for commercial banks. *The Accounting Review, 81*(2), 337–375.

Huizinga, H., & Laeven, L. (2012). Bank valuation and accounting discretion during a financial crisis. *Journal of Financial Economics, 106*(3), 614–634.

Jensen, M. C. (1986). Agency cost of free cash flow, corporate finance, and the market for takeovers. *American Economic Review, 76*(2), 323–329.

Kanodia, C., & Sapra, H. (2016). A real effects perspective to accounting measurement and disclosure: Implications and insights for future research. *Journal of Accounting Research, 54*(2), 623–676.

Kjellberg, D., & Åhl, M. (2022). *The Riksbank's financial result and capital are affected by higher interest rates*. Sveriges Riksbank Economic Commentary No 8.

KPMG. (2012). *Current trends in central bank financial reporting practice*. KPMG's Central Bank Network Advisory Group.

Leuz, C., & Verrecchia, R. (2000). The economic consequences of increased disclosure. *Journal of Accounting Research, 38*(Supplement), 91–124.

Michels, J. (2017). Disclosure versus recognition: Inferences from subsequent events. *Journal of Accounting Research, 55*(1), 3–34.

Morris, S., & Shin, H. S. (2007). Optimal communication. *Journal of the European Economic Association, 5*(2–3), 594–602.

Müller, M. A., Riedl, E. J., & Sellhorn, T. (2015). Recognition versus disclosure of fair values. *The Accounting Review, 90*(6), 2411–2447.

Nordström, A., & Vredin, A. (2022). *Does central bank equity matter for monetary policy?* Sveriges Riksbank Staff Memo December 2022.

Reis, R. (2013). The mystique surrounding the central bank's balance sheet, applied to the European crisis. *American Economic Review, 103*(3), 135–140.

Reis, R. (2015). Comment on: "When does a central bank's balance sheet require fiscal support?" by Marco Del Negro and Christopher A. Sims. *Journal of Monetary Economics, 73*, 20–25.

Roychowdhury, S. (2006). Earnings management through real activities manipulation. *Journal of Accounting and Economics, 42*(3), 335–370.

Sloan, R. G. (1996). Do stock prices fully reflect information in accruals and cash flows about future earnings? *The Accounting Review, 71*(3), 289–315.

Stein, J. C. (1989). Efficient capital markets, inefficient firms: A model of myopic corporate behavior. *The Quarterly Journal of Economics, 104*(4), 655–669.

Stella, P. (1997). *Do central banks need capital?* IMF Working Paper No 97/83.
Stella, P. (2005). Central bank financial strength, transparency, and policy credibility. *IMF Staff Papers, 52*(2), 335–365.
Stella, P. (2008). *Central bank financial strength, policy constraints and inflation*. IMF Working Paper No 08/49.
Wessels, P., & Broeders, D. (2022). *On the capitalisation of central banks*. DNB Occasional Studies 20-04.
Zakolyukina, A. A. (2018). How common are intentional GAAP violations? Estimates from a dynamic model. *Journal of Accounting Research, 56*(1), 5–44.

Open Access This chapter is licensed under the terms of the Creative Commons Attribution 4.0 International License (http://creativecommons.org/licenses/by/4.0/), which permits use, sharing, adaptation, distribution and reproduction in any medium or format, as long as you give appropriate credit to the original author(s) and the source, provide a link to the Creative Commons license and indicate if changes were made.

The images or other third party material in this chapter are included in the chapter's Creative Commons license, unless indicated otherwise in a credit line to the material. If material is not included in the chapter's Creative Commons license and your intended use is not permitted by statutory regulation or exceeds the permitted use, you will need to obtain permission directly from the copyright holder.

Fiscal Consequences of Central Bank Losses

Stephen G. Cecchetti and Jens Hilscher

Abstract In response to the Global Financial Crisis, central banks engaged in large-scale asset purchases funded by the issuance of reserves. These "unconventional" policies continued during the pandemic, so that by 2022 central banks' balance sheets had grown up to ten-fold. As a result of rapidly increasing interest rates, these massive portfolios began producing substantial losses. We interpret these losses as fiscal policy consequences of quantitative easing and stress that they must be balanced against the prior benefits of implementing purchase policies. Importantly, losses differ qualitatively depending on whether the central bank chooses to buy domestic or foreign assets, thus resulting in transfers either within or between countries. Effects of losses may differ due to accounting rules (when losses are realized) and when the fiscal authority compensates for losses (the structure of indemnification agreements). Data from the Federal Reserve, the Eurosystem, and the Bank of England show that maximum annual losses are between 0.3 and 1.5% of GDP. By contrast, the Swiss National Bank is sustaining losses up to 17% of GDP.

Keywords Bank of England · Central bank balance sheet · Central bank capital · Central bank losses · Consolidated balance sheet · European Central Bank · Federal Reserve · Large-scale asset purchases · Monetary policy · Negative carry · Quantitative easing · Swiss National Bank

---

We thank Nazim Belhocine, Ashok Vir Bhatia, Jan Frie, Andrew Levin, Fergal Shortall, and Christina Paragon Skinner, for helping us with the data; Swarali Havaldar for research assistance; seminar participants at King's Business School, the London Business School, and UC Davis, as well as David Aikman, Ricardo Reis, Kim Schoenholtz, and Jeremy Stein for comments and discussions. All errors are our own.

S. G. Cecchetti (✉)
Brandeis International Business School, Waltham, MA, USA
e-mail: cecchett@brandeis.edu

J. Hilscher
University of California, Davis, CA, USA
e-mail: jhilscher@ucdavis.edu

© The Author(s) 2025

D. Broeders et al. (eds.), *Central Bank Capital in Turbulent Times*,
Contributions to Finance and Accounting,
https://doi.org/10.1007/978-3-031-73549-3_4

"As the sole issuer of euro-denominated central bank money, the euro system will always be able to generate additional liquidity as needed. So, by definition, it will neither go bankrupt nor run out of money. And in addition to that, any financial losses, should they occur, will not impair our ability to seek and maintain price stability." ECB President Christine Lagarde, Committee on Economic and Monetary Affairs Monetary Dialogue," 19 November 2020.[1]

"A negative equity does not affect the Riksbank's ability to conduct monetary policy in the short term." Sveriges Riksbank Governor Erik Thedéen, Riksdag Committee on Finance, 24 October 2023.[2]

1 Introduction

During and after the Global Financial Crisis of 2008–09, central banks around the world engaged in large-scale asset purchase programs significantly increasing the size of their balance sheets. Purchases continued during the pandemic in the early 2020s. This pattern is evident in Fig. 1 where we plot the consolidated assets of the Federal Reserve System and the Eurosystem.[3] In both of these cases, total assets peaked at nearly 10 times their level in 2008.

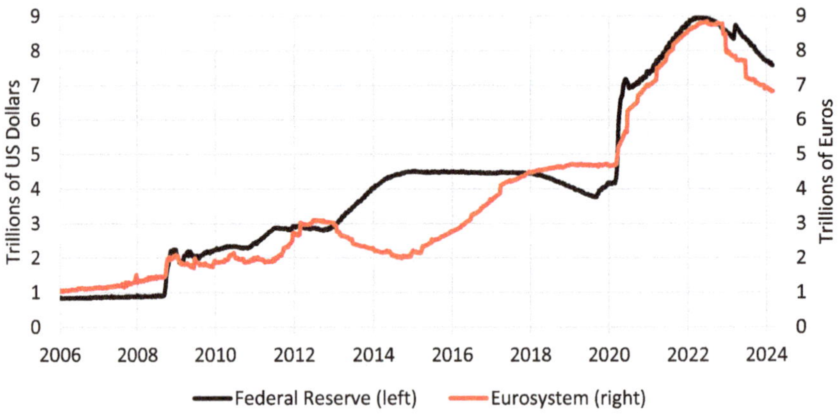

Fig. 1 Total assets of the Federal Reserve and Eurosystem Jan 2006 to Mar 2024, weekly. Source: FRED

---

[1] Dialogue available here: CRE_Monetary_Dialogue_19112020_EN.pdf (europa.eu).

[2] See Thedéen: The Riksbank needs to restore its capital https://www.riksbank.se/en-gb/press-and-published/speeches-and-presentations/2023/thedeen-the-riksbank-needs-to-restoreits- capital/#:~:text=When%20the%20value%20of%20the,policy%20in%20the%20short%20term. | Sveriges Riksbank.

[3] The Federal Reserve System's balance sheet consolidates the balance sheets for the 12 Federal Reserve banks while the Eurosystem's combines that of the European Central Bank and the (currently) 20 National Central Banks in the euro area.

Importantly, central banks purchased bonds when short- and long-term rates were low. So, when interest rates rose in 2022 and 2023, their holdings started to generate losses.[4] This sparked a debate both over whether it was prudent to amass these portfolios in the first place, and over whether the mounting losses would undermine the ability of central banks to meet their price stability objectives. Indeed, some observers argue that it is important to focus on both central bank capital and profitability, concepts that were previously of limited interest to researchers and policymakers. The idea seems to be that the valuation effects and implications for net interest margins—i.e., losses associated with large asset purchases—are of sufficient size to have welfare implications for society. In contrast, the above quotes suggest that central banks themselves are much less concerned. And, as both President Lagarde and Governor Thedéen indicate, the idea that they might "run out of money" seems novel.[5]

In this paper, we strive to provide a framework for understanding the medium- and long-run implications of the losses arising from central banks' large-scale asset purchases. Specifically, we suggest that they are best viewed as a form of fiscal policy.

To understand this conclusion, we start by showing how losses resulting from central bank policy are most easily understood if one consolidates the balance sheets of the central bank and the finance ministry. This change in accounting immediately clarifies how the ultimate economic effect of central banks' bond purchase programs and resulting potential losses arise from the fact that purchases change the maturity structure (and in some cases the gross quantity) of outstanding domestic sovereign debt.

When policymakers initially purchase the bonds, their objective is to reduce longer-term interest rates, compressing some combination of sovereign term spreads and risk premia on private sector bonds. If successful, these policies stimulate aggregate demand, stabilizing inflation, growth and employment, and the financial system. Ideally, this reduces the length and severity of recessions, thereby increasing aggregate welfare. To the extent that policies are enacted when term spreads are especially large, asset purchases also may generate large cash-flow gains from the fact that bond coupon payments exceed funding costs. However, as time passes and interest rates rise to their longer-run steady-state level, funding costs will rise and the central bank will begin to suffer losses. If interest rates even rise further, for example, due to policies designed to combat higher-than-expected inflation, these losses will increase. As a result, remittances from the central bank to the fiscal authority shrink. Depending on the structure of the indemnity agreement with the

[4] In their survey of pandemic-related policies in 40 jurisdictions, Cantú et al. (2021) catalogue 21 cases in which central banks purchased domestic government bonds and 13 in which they purchased private assets. The latter included the Federal Reserve, the Eurosystem, the Bank of Japan, the Bank of England, the Bank of Canada, and the Sveriges Riksbank.

[5] As we discuss shortly, we assume that central banks have fiscal support and do not consider the case where central bank actions could become inflationary due to large operational costs and no fiscal support.

finance ministry, as well as the accounting rules that are in place, central bank losses (negative payments) may trigger an explicit fiscal expenditure either immediately or at some time in the future. It is in this sense that central bank balance sheet policies have direct fiscal consequences.

Our main focus in this paper is to analyze how central banks' balance sheet policies can result in losses and transfers. First and foremost, these depend on what it is that the central bank chooses to purchase: domestic sovereign bonds, domestic private sector bonds, or securities issued by a foreign entity. We show that purchases of domestic sovereign bonds change the maturity structure of privately-held government debt, implying no direct ex ante transfer of wealth, though there may be transfers ex post. Similarly, purchasing private-sector bonds can create ex post transfers. But since owners of the bonds' issuing companies are domestic, this is a within-country transfer. In contrast, purchases of foreign securities, regardless of whether the issuer is a sovereign or private entity, may result in transfers to foreigners.

In addition, the central bank's governance structure and its specific policy objectives have implications. For example, an inflation-targeting central bank's jurisdiction may coincide with national boundaries, and asset purchases may be limited to primarily domestic securities. This describes the case of both the Federal Reserve and the Bank of England. Alternatively, a small open economy central bank targeting the exchange rate may purchase primarily foreign securities. As an example, consider the Swiss National Bank. Finally, as in the case of the Eurosystem, a monetary union with a set of national central banks and a common central bank at the center will have a set of rules regarding who holds which securities as well as how losses are distributed across member countries. We consider this case as well.

Before turning to a detailed analysis of the structure of central bank balance sheets and the implication of various types of losses, we should mention the issue of central bank solvency. As a technical matter, central banks have very little capital, so they are highly leveraged. For example, the Eurosystem as a whole has capital equal to €120 bn supporting total assets of €8.8 trillion in October 2022—a leverage ratio of roughly 75. Similarly, the Federal Reserve System has $43 billion of capital with peak assets of $9.0 trillion, implying leverage of over 200. As a result, even very modest losses can lead to technical insolvency.

Reis (2015) provides an excellent summary of the various ways in which a central bank can become insolvent. The bottom line is that failure to remain solvent in the absence of fiscal support will result in the central bank being forced to issue additional reserves to finance its liabilities, potentially putting price stability at risk.[6] Importantly, with the appropriate fiscal support, solvency will never be an issue. Buiter (2008) explains how recapitalization of a central bank is in essence a trivial

[6] Wessels and Broeders (2022b) also argue that solvency is essential if a central bank is to meet its policy objectives and retain credibility. They proceed to provide guidelines for determining the appropriate level of central bank capital.

transaction within the government in which the fiscal authority can simply exchange government bonds for central bank equity. As we will see below, this has no impact at all on the consolidated balance sheet of the government. But if one separates the two balance sheets, it does recapitalize the central bank. We also assume that the central bank will always have sufficient funds to run its operations and pursue its mandates. We thus exclude the possibility that the central bank may have to "fend for itself" and pay its own bills (salaries, rent, etc.). That is, we assume the appropriate level of support from a fiscal authority that is running a sustainable policy.

The form and timing of the fiscal support is important. There are two aspects that are relevant: when the central bank realizes losses and when the fiscal authority transfers funds to make the central bank whole again. If the central bank realizes losses when securities are sold or mature, then the timing of sales becomes relevant. This is the case for the Bank of England. At the same time, if the central bank uses fair value accounting, i.e., if the central bank uses mark-to-market valuation of its portfolio, then losses are generated as soon as interest rates increase. This is what the Sveriges Riksbank does. Turning to when these losses trigger payments from the fiscal authority, there are two possibilities. One is that losses are paid for as they arise (e.g., Bank of England), while the second is that payments are delayed in some way (Federal Reserve). As we discuss the cases of different central banks, we also consider the impact of these institutional differences.

We should also note the very legitimate view that insolvency could be a signal that politicians are treating the central bank as a source of funds. This obviously leads to concerns about fiscal dominance that could drive up sovereign risk premia and expected inflation.[7] However, these are rather curious concerns, especially given the relatively modest size of realized losses.

While we do not examine the benefits of central banks' large-scale asset purchases in any detail, it is important to balance them against the losses. Gagnon (2016) provides an overview of the literature studying the effects on quantitative easing (QE), citing "overwhelming evidence" that asset purchases eased financial conditions.[8] It is therefore likely that QE had a significant impact on aggregate demand, stabilizing growth and employment. This, in turn, generated direct fiscal benefits in the form of increased tax revenue. If the costs are in fact small, then they

[7] A number of papers discuss the relationship between the strength of central bank balance sheets and monetary policy, including inflation outcomes. These include Perera et al. (2013) who find that countries whose central banks have weak balance sheets experience higher inflation; Pinter (2018) who concludes that fiscal support is critical in determining the inflation outcome in these circumstances; Adler et al. (2016) who examine the impact of foreign exchange intervention on domestic monetary policy; Del Negro and Sims (2015) who discuss how losses can lead central banks to increase total government debt at a rate that is not sustainable, resulting in an explosive price path; and Nordström and Vredin (2022) and Wessels and Broeders (2022a) who both discuss the importance of having sufficient revenue to cover its operational costs if a central bank is to meet its monetary policy objectives.

[8] In contrast, in their extensive study of the impact of central bank balance sheet shrinkage (quantitative tightening) in seven jurisdictions, Du et al. (2024) conclude that the economic and financial impact is modest.

are most likely smaller than these benefits, even if the exact size of those benefits is uncertain.[9] Importantly, however, costs and benefits need to be compared from an ex-ante perspective and include the benefits that arose from the large portfolios prior to interest rate increases. That comparison is beyond the scope of our analysis. Instead, we take the realized losses as one indicator of costs, exploring their size and implications.

The remainder of this paper is organized as follows. In Sect. 2, we present balance sheets for all the various economic actors: central bank, fiscal authority, commercial banks, households, and nonfinancial firms. We then merge the fiscal authority and central bank balance sheets to describe the consolidated government balance sheet.

Using this balance sheet framework, in Sect. 3 we turn to the simple closed economy case and discuss the case where a central bank purchases solely domestic sovereign debt, as well the case where they also purchase private sector debt. We explain how purchases of long-term government bonds shorten the average maturity of outstanding government debt. The addition of more short-term liquid government bonds reduces the expected size of interest expenses but increases its variability.[10] Indeed, the realized path of interest rates resulted in higher interest costs. The impact on ex ante welfare derived from a change in the maturity structure depends on the relative importance of these two effects—the benefits of liquidity services relative to the deadweight loss from taxation.[11]

We next consider purchases of private sector debt in which the central bank exchanges risky long-term private bonds for overnight reserves. This transaction increases gross government debt and reduces its average maturity. Since the purchase of private sector debt is a simple intermediation transaction, it supplies liquid assets but creates duration risk for the public sector as well as exposing it to potential ex post losses in the event of a bond's default. In turn, this risk is compensated by the central bank receiving the associated credit spread of the debt. As with purchases of domestic sovereign debt, the net welfare effect is ambiguous.

We illustrate this analysis with a description of transfers to their respective fiscal authorities of the Bank of England and the Federal Reserve.[12] Both hold primarily domestic bonds. But the specific holdings, size and treatment of losses are different. First, the Bank of England holds almost exclusively UK gilts, while the Fed holds a mix of Treasuries and government-insured mortgage-backed securities (MBS). Second, the UK has indemnification rules which mean that any realized losses translate almost immediately into a fiscal expenditure. In the case of the Fed, the

---

[9] Greenlaw et al. (2018) summarize the extensive debate over the impact of the purchases during and in the aftermath of the 2007–08 financial crisis. For a comprehensive discussion of the impact of large-scale asset purchases during the COVID-19 pandemic, the experiences in 19 jurisdictions, see Committee on the Global Financial System (2023).

[10] See Greenwood et al. (2015b).

[11] For discussions of the costs of taxation, see Barro (1979), Lucas and Stokey (1983), Bohn (1990).

[12] For a comprehensive examination of how central banks and fiscal authorities handle transfers associated with profits and losses, see Chaboud and Leahy (2013).

losses simply postpone the date when transfers to the US Treasury will restart (they are currently on hold). Finally, the undiscounted sum of the Bank of England's losses appears to be larger than that of the Fed—7.87% versus 0.82% of nominal GDP—and could stretch out for decades as opposed to lasting for only a few years.

In Sect. 4 we turn to the open economy case where the central bank purchases foreign securities. Here, the transfers are between domestic residents and foreigners. Assuming that a country's government places different welfare weights on domestic and foreign residents, transfers are qualitatively different in terms of their welfare implications. We consider the case of the Swiss National Bank, which might be characterized as the central bank of a small open economy. In stark contrast to the Fed and the Bank of England, the size of central bank losses, which are mainly transfers to foreigners, is quite large, net income varying from +8% to −17% of GDP in a year.

Finally, in Sect. 5 we examine the case of a monetary union in which there is a common central bank as well as national central banks. This is the structure of the Eurosystem. The national Central Banks all have balance sheets and share both income and risk. The result is that there are transfers among countries that depend on the relative sizes and movements of interest rates. But those transfers appear to be small and the overall consolidated losses look to be even smaller than in the United States. Section 6 concludes.

2 Balance Sheets: Structure and Implications

The most straightforward way to understand the impact of central bank asset purchases is to see how they change various balance sheets. To do this, we start by presenting some stylized balance sheets for four sectors of a closed economy. These are the fiscal authority, the central bank, the private financial system, and private nonfinancial firms and households. Taken together, these provide a comprehensive summary of the wealth of an economy.

2.1 Public and Private Sector Balance Sheets

Table 1 provides four stylized balance sheets. For the time being, we ignore two potentially important financial exposures. First, some entities may own assets issued by foreign entities, possibly in foreign currency. For example, entities may hold foreign currency, referred to as reserves in the case of the central bank, or foreign assets, e.g., the holdings of a sovereign wealth fund. We introduce this in Sect. 4 below. Second, there may be off-balance sheet exposures in the form of contingent assets and liabilities, e.g., deposit insurance. Including these exposures can be done

Table 1 Stylized balanced sheets

A. Fiscal Authority

Assets	Liabilities
PV of Future Tax Revenue	Government Bonds
Account at Central Bank	Other Liabilities
Central Bank Net Worth	
Other Assets	
	Fiscal Net Worth

B. Central Bank

Assets	Liabilities
Government Bonds	Currency
Private Bonds	Commercial Bank Reserves
Loans to Banks	Fiscal Authority's Account
PV of Future Seigniorage	Other Liabilities
Other Assets	
	Central Bank Net Worth

C. Private Financial System

Assets	Liabilities
Commercial Bank Reserves	Public Customer Deposits
Government Bonds	Central Bank Borrowing
Private Bonds	Other Liabilities
Other Assets	
	Banking System Net Worth

D. Private Nonfinancial Firms and Households

Assets	Liabilities
Currency	PV of Future Tax Payments
Deposits at Commercial banks	PV of Future Seigniorage
Government Bonds	Private Bonds
Banking System Net Worth	Other Liabilities
Fiscal Net Worth	
Real Assets	Private Nonfin Net Worth

in principle, but since they are not needed for us to make our main points, we ignore them throughout.[13]

It is worth discussing each of these balance sheets very briefly. Starting with the fiscal authority, the main asset is the present value of future tax revenue. In addition, there is the account at the central bank; and, since they own the central bank, the central bank's net worth is an asset of the fiscal authority as well. Real assets owned by the government are reflected in "Other Assets." Turning to liabilities, the fiscal authority issues government bonds. Its liabilities include the present value of future social insurance payments (Social Security and Medicare in the United States), which we include in "Other Liabilities."

Panel B of Table 1 is a standard central bank balance sheet. The central bank owns government and private bonds, as well as making loans to banks. The present value (PV) of future seigniorage is also an asset. The central bank issues currency, reserve accounts, and provides an account to the fiscal authority.

Looking at the domestic financial system, again this is a standard balance sheet. Note that this is the balance sheet of the entire private financial system. So, in addition to banks, this includes insurance companies, pension funds, mutual funds, and other types of financial organizations.

Finally, we have the private nonfinancial sector balance sheet. Here, we are consolidating assets and liabilities within each of these sectors. For example, a household may make a loan to a firm or to another household. Furthermore, the firms are owned by the households.

[13] Off-balance sheet exposures generally shift risk among and within the various groups we consider. One of our goals is to improve our understanding of how central bank balance sheet actions change that allocation of risk, so we take as given the initial distribution and simply go on from there.

2.2 Consolidating the Public and Private Sector Balance Sheets

An important contribution of our paper is to examine the consequence of central bank policy from the perspective of the consolidated government balance sheet. We therefore now use the balance sheets in Table 1 to examine the consequences of consolidating the domestic fiscal authority (Table 1A) and the central bank (Table 1B) into what we will label the government's balance sheet. Table 2 presents the result.

Several implications of this consolidation are noteworthy. Looking at Table 2 we see that since three items are liabilities of one and assets of the other, they disappear. These are the fiscal authority's account at the central bank, the net worth of the central bank, and the domestic government bonds held at the central bank. In addition, the government bonds held by the central bank net out, so all that is left is government bonds held by the private sector—the combination of banks (and other financial institutions), firms, and households. This is an important point, and it is worth restating. Government bonds held by the central bank disappear from the public sector balance sheet. When this quantity changes, the government is simply lending more or less to itself. So, once we consolidate the fiscal authority and the central bank, the only bonds left are privately-held government bonds and the private sector bonds held by the public sector (a central bank asset).

This point is stronger than what is made by Barro (1974) when he noted the equivalence in present value between current and future taxation. In our case, a bond that is issued by one part of the government (fiscal authority) and then bought by another part of the government (central bank) does not enter the consolidated balance sheet. All future payments associated with such a bond appear as both assets and liabilities on the same balance sheet and therefore net out.

Turning to the private sector, consolidating the balance sheets of the financial and nonfinancial sector yields the balance sheet in Table 3. Note that the only private bonds (a liability) remaining are those held at the central bank.

Table 2 Consolidated balance sheet of the public sector

Assets	Liabilities
PV of Future Tax Revenue	Govt Bonds held by private sector
PV of Future Seigniorage	Currency
Private Bonds held by the Central Bank	Commercial Bank Reserves
Central Bank Loans to Banks	Other Liabilities
Other Assets	
	Fiscal Authority Net Worth

Table 3 Consolidated balance sheet of the private sector

Assets	Liabilities
Currency	PV of Future Tax Payments
Reserves	PV of Future Seigniorage
Government Bonds	Private Bonds held by the Central Bank
Fiscal Authority Net Worth	Central Bank Loans to Banks
Real Assets	
	Private Nonfinancial Net Worth

3 The Impact of Central Bank Purchases of Domestic Securities

Using the consolidated balance sheets from Sect. 2, we can examine two central bank actions: the purchase of a domestic government bond and the purchase of a private sector bond. Importantly, we use the framework to examine the implications of central bank losses. Since central bank actions affect seigniorage and the maturity structure of sovereign debt, we also discuss the optimal maturity structure of government debt and determinants of seigniorage revenue.

In the final part of this section, we examine two cases in which the central bank engages in primarily domestic bond purchases: The Bank of England and the Federal Reserve. We describe the size and the institutional treatment of the losses that are accruing. In the following sections, when discussing the open economy case, we consider the impact of asset purchases on the balance sheets of the Swiss National Bank and the Eurosystem.

3.1 Purchases of Domestic Sovereign Securities

When the central bank purchases a government bond in the secondary market, it changes the composition of government liabilities but not their level.[14] The standard case is that the central bank creates reserves to purchase long-term government bonds. The result is a shortening of the maturity structure of outstanding government liabilities leaving the total size unchanged.

The overall effect of a shortening of the maturity structure of government debt on cash flows is ambiguous. Longer-term bonds have, on average, higher interest costs due to the term spread. At the same time, fixed-rate long-term bonds have fixed funding costs, while short-maturity debt has variable funding cost. A shorter

[14] The central bank purchase of a government bond directly from the fiscal authority (in the primary market) creates new reserves, so it is the issuance of new government debt. That is, it increases the size of the public sector consolidated balance sheet, something that must be accompanied by an increase in the size of some asset, which could be either a real asset or a rise in the present value of future tax revenue.

maturity structure therefore results in more variable government debt funding costs. Since shortfalls have to be covered by higher taxes, and since costs of taxation likely increase more rapidly as the tax rate rises (the costs are convex), a shortening of the maturity structure may create a deadweight loss. At the same time, a shorter maturity structure may result in lower interest costs. This tradeoff was present prior to central bank asset purchases and one might assume the maturity structure was ex-ante optimal before the policy was enacted. In this case, large-scale asset purchases may have had a small expected cost associated with a move away from this optimum.

If the purchases also reduce the long-term interest rate (possibly by compressing the term premium), this might act as an offset to the deadweight loss from taxation. Importantly, however, this is only relevant for long-term bonds issued by the fiscal authority and sold to the private sector during the period over which large-scale asset purchases were being made. But such an action by the debt manager runs counter to the objectives of the central bank. Assuming some degree of coordination, the size of such issuance is likely to be small.[15] It is also possible to consider ex post costs of a shorter maturity structure. We discuss this below.

3.2 *Purchases of Domestic Private Securities*

When the central bank purchases a private bond, it changes the overall size of the consolidated government balance sheet, increasing both assets and liabilities.[16] Again, the central bank is creating reserves. But now it is using them to purchase private bonds. In essence, this transforms risky private sector debt into safe government debt. Importantly, since the private debt can be used to repay the reserves, *net* government debt does not increase and there is little if any need for additional future taxation. But again, there are consequences from the central bank financing long-term bonds by issuing short-term debt. In this case, there is a transfer of interest rate risk from private investors to future taxpayers. Rather than holding private fixed-rate debt, the private sector now holds variable-rate reserves.

If the long-term interest rates increase (as has been the case), it is the central bank that faces the risk of mark-to-market losses on the private bonds. The government (through the central bank) is compensated for this risk through the term spread. But that was likely low when the central bank bought the bonds. In addition, the purchase shifts risk of default on private debt from the private sector to the government. However, the fact that the central bank reaps the risk premium from the private

[15] See Greenwood et al. (2015a) for a discussion of this issue in the United States.

[16] As we note earlier, at least 13 central banks purchased private sector domestic assets during the pandemic. Quantities varied widely. For example, the Bank of Canada purchased only CA$218 million, while the Eurosystem purchased (and at this writing still holds) €344 billion.

bonds reduces the size of the loss (unless there are larger-than-expected defaults).[17] Furthermore, to the extent that there is a liquidity spread on private bonds, the government may be compensated for holding illiquid securities.

Taken together, it seems unlikely that the government faces more than a very modest ex ante expected cost from purchasing private sector debt. That said, the ex post losses accruing from interest rate increases—both the negative carry and the losses at maturity—are the same as those associated with the purchase of domestic sovereign bonds. In addition, there may be ex post costs that arise from private sector bonds defaulting at a higher-than-anticipated rate. The central bank balance sheets we consider either had very small holdings of private sector debt or were not hit by a lot of defaults, so we will not pursue this any further.

3.3 Central Bank Losses

We next consider the consequences of ex post central bank losses.[18] We can think of these losses as either declines in the value of the bonds the central bank holds or as negative cash flow. Valuation losses arise when interest rates rise, driving down the mark-to-market (or fair value) of both government and private bonds on the central bank's balance sheet. Cash flow losses come from two sources. The first is the negative net interest margin (or negative carry) and the second is the realized loss at maturity.

We first reiterate our earlier point about the consolidated government balance sheet. When the central bank uses reserves to purchase government bonds, losses from mark-to-market declines in the value of its government bond holdings do not appear on the consolidated balance sheet of the government. The losses of the central bank are the gains of the fiscal authority, so they are an internal government transfer. Using Table 1 as a guide, mark-to-market losses decrease central bank net worth as a result of the decline in the bond's value. But neither the holdings of government bonds by the central bank nor central bank net worth appear on the consolidated balance sheet (see Table 2).

However, the shortening of the maturity structure does have an effect. It shows up as negative carry. When the central bank purchased the government bonds, it replaced long-term bonds with reserves (which we think of having zero maturity). As a result, when the interest rate rises, the government's interest costs go up with it.

As we suggested earlier, in the absence of convex costs of taxation, these losses have no impact on welfare. What has changed is the overall interest cost of the

[17] When the central bank purchases private securities, it has to decide which ones to buy. As Cecchetti and Tucker (2021) discuss, this choice creates an opportunity to subsidize favored sectors. This is one reason that central banks were reluctant to purchase corporate bonds. This practice changed during the pandemic. See Buiter et al. (2023).

[18] For an in-depth discussion of central bank losses, see Archer and Moser-Boehm (2013).

debt relative to the no-large-scale-purchase counterfactual. There can, however, be distributional consequences to the extent that holders of debt and taxpayers are different. But if higher tax rates generate proportionally larger deadweight losses, then the shortening of the maturity structure of the government debt will reduce aggregate welfare. The reason is that the losses destabilize the tax rate needed to collect the revenue necessary to meeting the now variable interest payments on short-term debt. This reasoning does lead us to ask whether the impact of the central bank actions on the maturity structure of the government debt is good or bad—a question we return to shortly.[19]

The consequences of these losses are different for central bank holdings of private bonds. Here, both the valuation losses and the negative carry represent losses to the government (and gains to the private sector). Put slightly differently, when the central bank buys a bond issued by the private sector, it is as if they are making a loan to the issuing firm. The loan is funded by reserves. As the interest rate rises two things happen: the market value of the private domestic bond falls and the interest expense of the reserves rises. The first of these represents a loss in the net worth of the government and the second creates a net interest cost. Note that these two effects are not additive. Rather, they represent two ways of describing the same thing. The valuation loss is equal to the present value of the negative carry over the life of the bond plus the loss at maturity. Again, there may be distributional consequences. Relative to the no-purchase counterfactual, the government's net interest costs are higher. This reflects the fact that the private investors from whom the bonds were purchased are receiving higher interest rates on short-term deposits compared to the coupon payments on the bond.

To help understand the mechanics of these losses, consider a simple example where the central bank holds a 3% annual coupon bond with 10 years remaining to maturity. Assume that the bond has a face value of 100 and that the central bank accounts for the purchase at historical cost. If the yield to maturity (when purchased) is 2%, then the purchase price for this bond is 109. Now, assume that the interest rate rises to 4%, so the price of the bond falls to 91.9. Immediate sale of the bond generates a capital loss of $(109–91.9) = 17.1$. The alternative to selling the bond is to finance the purchase of 109 at the current interest rate (4%), receive the coupon payments (3%), and then receive 100 at maturity. This results in an annual loss of $(0.04) x (109)–3 = 4.36–3 = 1.36$, plus a realized loss at maturity of 109–100 = 9. The present value of these losses is the same as the loss that would be incurred from selling the bond immediately.

As this example makes clear, when the central bank uses historical cost (held-to-maturity) accounting, the decision to sell the bond, or hold it to maturity, has implications for the timing of losses but not their present value. Selling brings losses forward and makes them certain, while holding the debt both pushes the losses into the future and makes them uncertain. Depending on the indemnity agreement

[19] Since this is a government, we ignore the possibility that short-term debt may be difficult and costly to roll over.

between the central bank and the fiscal authority, this could have implications for the temporal pattern of government taxation. We return to this point when we discuss the case of the Bank of England.

Importantly, note that when using fair value accounting, the central bank will realize the losses as they occur. Here, the difference between the two cases, one where the bond is sold and the other where it is held to maturity, is that the central bank will reap gains as the price returns to the face value (100 in the example) as it matures, as well as if interest rates were to fall.

The Sveriges Riksbank and the Bank of Canada are prime examples where the use of fair value accounting gave rise to large losses as interest rates rose. The Sveriges Riksbank reported a loss of SEK 80 billion (roughly 5% of GDP) in 2022, while the Bank of Canada's loss that year was CAD 30 billion (1% of GDP).[20]

Before continuing, it is worth restating that the welfare impact of the central bank's losses (which is largely distributional) should be compared to the macroeconomic stabilization gains from the implementation of the asset purchase policies. These benefits come in the form of higher growth and employment and inflation closer to target. Not only does this increase social welfare, it also raises the net present value of government tax revenue. That is, if we look back at the consolidated balance sheet of the government in Table 2, we can see that this has an unambiguously positive impact as it raises the value of government assets without changing the value of government liabilities, so government net worth rises. Yet another benefit is the positive cash flow resulting from holding the large debt portfolios prior to interest rates increasing. We will discuss this effect in more detail below.

3.4 *Two Digressions*

Before continuing, we will digress and discuss two topics related to central bank balance sheet management: the optimal maturity structure of government debt and the role of seigniorage.

3.4.1 On the Optimal Maturity Structure of Government Debt

As we noted earlier, central bank purchases of long-term domestic sovereign bonds will shorten the maturity of government debt without changing its overall size. This effect can be large. For example, in the case of the United States, Mitra and Sack

[20] See the Riksbank's Annual Report for 2022 and Bank of Canada's Annual Report for 2022. Similar to the case of the Federal Reserve discussed below, both of these central banks have agreements with their respective governments to retain profits for as long as it takes to return capital to an agreed upon level.

(2022) estimate that by mid-2022 the Federal Reserve's purchase of U.S. Treasury securities reduced the average weighted duration of publicly held government debt from 5.1 to 3.6 years. If the initial maturity structure was roughly optimal—and the debt manager does not take actions to reverse the impact of the central bank's actions—this will have social costs.

How large are they? Answering this question is beyond the scope of this paper. Instead, we will simply note the issuance of short- versus long-term government debt involves a tradeoff. As Greenwood et al. (2015a) discuss in detail, determining the optimal maturity structure of government debt requires balancing the benefits of the liquidity services against the deadweight costs of tax rate volatility. The former is the mirror image of the term premium that is evident in long-term debt, while the latter arises from the fact that costs of taxation are convex.

The point at which these benefits and costs balance depends on a host of national characteristics.[21] For example, Greenwood et al. (2015b) argue that there are likely negative externalities associated with the private sector issuance of short-term liquid liabilities. Examples include the possibilities of runs and fire-sales. To reduce these externalities, the government (including the central bank) should issue more short-term liabilities. Another result that does emerge from several studies is that the higher the government debt to GDP ratio, the longer term the average maturity should be.[22]

3.4.2 The Role of Seigniorage

Seigniorage is the ability of the government to finance its activities through an increase in central bank liabilities—commonly known as "printing money." In our context, seigniorage is important because it is added to potential losses when determining central bank overall net income. In addition, it will be present in the future, after the effects of asset purchase policies have ceased, and so it can make up for today's losses. From this intertemporal perspective, we should consider the net present value of future seigniorage as an asset of the central bank. We include it as part of the central bank and the consolidated government balance sheet; we also note that it may be substantial.

So, when does seigniorage arise? The answer depends on several factors. What did the central bank purchase, government or private bonds? What did the central bank issue to make the purchase, currency or interest-bearing reserves?

When the central bank issues non-interest-bearing currency to purchase government bonds—the textbook case—the seigniorage is the growth rate of currency. But the revenue is far lower in all other cases. When the central bank issues interest-bearing reserves to purchase government securities, there is no seigniorage

---

21 See Belton et al. (2018) for an empirical model that delivers the optimal maturity structure of U.S. government debt.

22 See Greenwood et al. (2015a); Bandari et al. (2017); and Mitra and Sack (2022).

at all. And when the central bank uses interest-bearing reserves to purchase private securities, the seigniorage is the carry—which could be negative. So, as the amount of currency in circulation falls, as it has in some jurisdictions, the overall interest margin will fall affecting the amount of seigniorage revenue. In the case where the net interest margin fluctuates around a positive steady state so the net interest margin and the monetary base (currency plus reserves) is roughly proportional to nominal GDP, the level of seigniorage will be proportional to nominal GDP growth.

3.5 The Case of the Bank of England

We now turn to two examples. The first is the Bank of England, which purchased primarily UK gilts.[23] The second is the Federal Reserve, which holds large amounts of both US Treasury securities and government-guaranteed mortgage-backed securities. In both cases, we focus on the flows between the central bank and their respective fiscal authority.

In a letter from 29 January 2009, Chancellor of the Exchequer Alistair Darling set out the terms of the Asset Purchase Facility (APF), a subsidiary of the Bank of England.[24] The letter describes the size of the facility, originally £50 billion; the eligible securities, including corporate bonds, commercial paper, syndicated loans, and certain asset-backed securities; that the facility is financed by borrowing from the Bank of England; and, importantly, that the Government indemnifies the Bank of England, so it bears the risk.

The mechanics of this arrangement are as follows. The Bank of England lends funds to the APF, which uses the proceeds to purchase UK gilts. The facility receives interest income in the form of coupon payments on the gilts and pays interest at the cash rate (the overnight policy rate) to the Bank of England. The UK Treasury receives any surplus and must make up any shortfall.

The consequences of this arrangement are straightforward. During the period of very low policy rates, the facility generated a positive cash flow for the fiscal authority. But, as policy rates rose over the last few years, the flow turned negative. To give a sense of the size of this swing, we can do a simple calculation for 2024. Start with the fact that the nominal holdings at the beginning of 2024 are £639 billion with £46 billion maturing during the year. These holdings yield coupon interest income of £15.2 billion. Next, note that the cost of these bonds, some of which were purchased at a substantial premium, is £744 billion of which £49.6 billion will mature. Using the OIS forward curve from January 2024—5.06% at 6 months

[23] The Bank of England did purchase some private bonds. The maximum amount was roughly £20 billion out of a peak level of £890 billion. Furthermore, at this writing, only £300 million remained. So, we ignore these.

[24] See the letter of 29 January 2009 from Chancellor of the Exchequer Alistair Darling to Bank of England Governor Mervyn King here.

and 4.23% at 12 months—this implies an interest cost of £33.6 billion. So, the net interest expense (the negative carry) of the APF is £18.4 billion. In addition, during the course of the year, £46 billion will mature and generate a realized loss (the purchase price minus the par value) of £3.5 billion. Adding these together, we see that the total loss is £21.9 billion, or roughly 0.8% of UK GDP.

Figure 2 shows the actual and projected transfers between the Bank of England and HM Treasury from 2013 to 2071 as a fraction of UK nominal GDP implied by current holdings assuming no active sales, so all bonds are held to maturity. From 2013 to 2022, the Bank of England made positive transfers that sum to 6.23% of UK GDP. In fact, the average for 2014 to 2022 (ignoring the large positive value in 2013) is 0.44% of UK GDP per year. Looking at the losses, we divide these into the negative carry and the capital loss realized at maturity. For 2023, we have actual numbers. This includes the losses realized on the sale of bonds that had not matured. The total loss of −1.43% of GDP is quite large. Our estimate suggests that roughly half of this is from realized losses associated with selling long-term securities purchased at a premium that were sold at a discount.[25] We also note that the sum of the (undiscounted) losses through 2071 is about −7.8% of GDP. This should be balanced against the combination of profits over the past decade (+6.2% of GDP) and the stabilization benefits from accommodative monetary policy.

The financing arrangements for the APF mean that HM Treasury must make transfers to the Bank of England in compensation for the losses in the Asset Purchase Facility. These payments create a fiscal expenditure—both the negative cash flow and the realized capital losses. At one level, this is purely bookkeeping, as the amounts are exactly what the UK debt manager would have to pay if they had issued debt with the maturity structure of the consolidated balance sheet of the government. This means that the only true economic cost comes from the fact that the debt may be too short term relative to what would have been optimal ex ante.[26] But from a political perspective, there may be a problem as the APF's losses show up as an explicit budget expenditure for the government.

It is worth emphasizing that the estimates in Fig. 2 represent the slowest possible path for the runoff of the APF. Because the Bank of England is choosing to sell bonds before they mature, the losses are being realized more quickly.

[25] Since we do not know the exact purchase price of the lots sold, we compute the realized capital loss using the average purchase premium bond by bond and subtract this from the total published by the Office of National Statistics.

[26] We note that this economic cost—the expected cost of a suboptimal maturity structure—is different from the ex post cost that we report in Fig. 2.

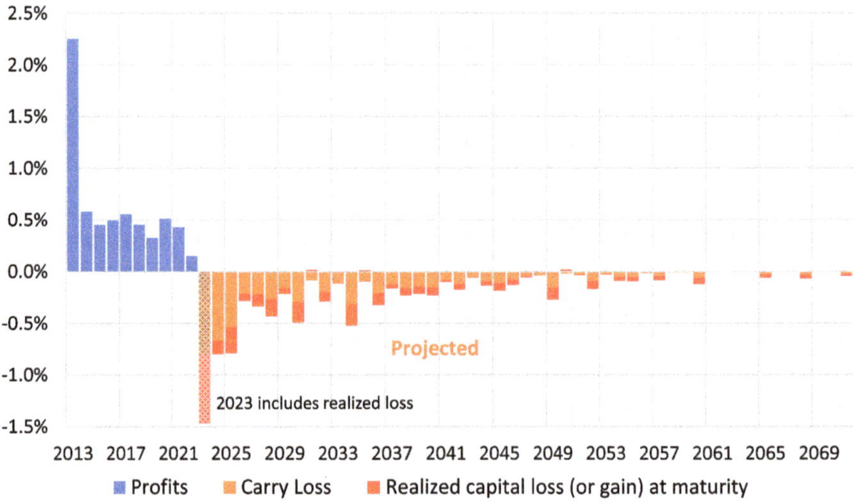

Fig. 2 Bank of England Asset Purchase Facility Net Profits and Losses, 2013 to 2071. Note: Data through 2023 are the net transfers from the Bank of England to HM Treasury as reported by the UK Office of National Statistics. For 2023, the division between the carry loss and the capital loss is the authors' estimate. Data for 2024 to 2071 are authors' estimates based on the information on the holdings of the Bank of England's Asset Purchase Facility, combined with a forward interest curve as published by the Bank of England, assuming that all bonds in the APF are held to maturity. Data for GDP through 2028 are from the IMF. From 2028 on, nominal GDP is assumed to grow at a 3.6% constant rate consistent with assumptions in the Office of Budget Responsibility (2023). Source: UK Office of National Statistics, Bank of England, IMF World Economic Outlook Database, and authors' calculations

The end-of-2023 Asset Purchase Facility Quarterly Report suggests a base case in which the combined maturities plus sales will be roughly £100 billion face value per year until nothing is left.[27] These sales can result in the realization of fairly large losses. To see how large, we note that the bonds currently in the APF were purchased at an average premium of roughly 15%. Sales in 2022 and 2023 were at a discount of 25%. That is, on average, bonds purchased at £115 are being sold for £75.

To understand the overall implications of this, we compare projected measures of the losses with and without sales in Fig. 3. Over the 2024 to 2031 period, undiscounted losses without sales average £9.7 billion per year. By comparison, with sales, the average is £23.8 billion per year. As a percent of GDP, the path with sales averages 0.78% of GDP per year, while the path without sales implies

[27] See https://www.bankofengland.co.uk/asset-purchase-facility/2023/2023-q4

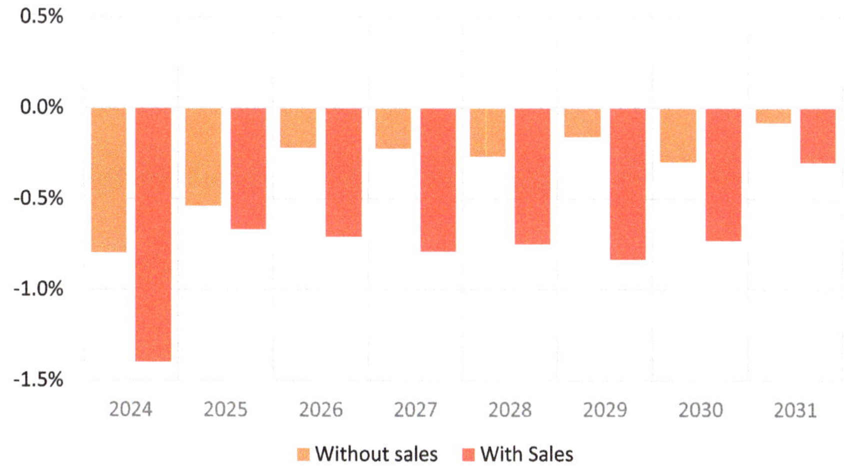

Fig. 3 Bank of England Asset Purchase Facility Net Losses with and without sales, 2024 to 2031. Note: We assume that the APF sells £100bn each year. The total is a combination of bonds that mature, paying the face value, and sales. We assume that the APF sells bonds across the board and measure the total size of sales using the average purchase price. Losses then have three components: negative carry, capital losses from maturing bonds, and capital losses from sales. We assume that the bank sells only bonds with maturities of 2032 and beyond since the other bonds will naturally mature within the time span it takes to unwind the APF. Projected sale prices are calculated by discounting bond cash flows using the forward gilt curve published by the Bank of England. Cost of carry is based on the forward OIS rates. Nominal GDP projections are based on a 3.6% annual growth rate. Source: Bank of England and authors' calculations

average losses of 0.35% of GDP.[28] Two things explain the difference. First, the slower path averages the losses over a far longer period, and second it pushes some of the losses into years when nominal GDP is higher.[29] The smoother path clearly puts less short-run pressure on fiscal finances and may involve smaller deadweight losses of taxation.

To summarize, at the beginning of 2024, the UK's APF has large holdings with significant unrealized losses. The institutional arrangement between the Band of England and HM Treasury means that APF losses are covered by HM Treasury as they occur. The apparent current schedule of bond sales, together with this institutional setup, implies substantial deficits for the fiscal authority.

Indeed, the UK government is well aware of these implications:

> "When the Bank of England voted to implement quantitative tightening in September 2022, it put the UK economy in uncharted territory—particularly in terms of the decision to actively sell gilts back to the market.

[28] Since UK government spending is roughly 45% of GDP, these numbers represent rough 0.8% and 1.7% of total fiscal expenditure.

[29] We note that a smaller level of nominal GDP growth may result in slightly larger future burdens when measured as a percentage of GDP.

> No major central bank has pursued [quantitative tightening (QT)] in this way. Both the Federal Reserve and the European Central Bank have opted only for the passive method of allowing their bonds to mature without replacement." Harriett Baldwin, chair of the House of Commons Treasury select committee, 7 February 2024.[30]

It is possible that active quantitative tightening, as appears to be pursued by the Bank of England, is a deliberate choice in setting monetary policy so as to ensure price stability. This view is suggested by Bank of England Governor Bailey's letter to Harriett Baldwin from December 18, 2023. He states that the "scale and pace of the reduction in the stock of assets in the APF as part of QT are chosen solely to meet the MPC's policy objectives." We note that this choice of policy instrument stands in contrast to other central banks combating high inflation (Fed, ECB) who have chosen to rely primarily on increases in the policy rate.

One potential response by HM Treasury could be to simply roll over the shortfall by issuing new debt. However, this path will increase headline public sector borrowing, which could influence borrowing costs. The result may be that, on top of the quantitative tightening that results from the APF selling bonds there may be concurrent fiscal tightening in response to the APF's realized losses and resulting costs for HM Treasury.

3.6 *The Case of the Federal Reserve*

Turning to the Federal Reserve, institutional arrangements are quite different.[31] When the Federal Reserve System's revenues exceed its operational costs, the Fed transfers the excess to the US Treasury. This was the case in virtually every year until 2023. When losses accrue, however, these are treated as a deferred asset with the agreement that there will be no further transfers to the Treasury until that deferred asset is extinguished.[32] Put slightly different, the Fed keeps track of the losses and then retains earnings until they are completely gone.[33]

---

[30] Full article available here: Bank of England's quantitative tightening is a leap in the dark (ft.com).

[31] See Carpenter et al. (2015) for a detailed discussion of the mechanics and accounting of the Federal Reserve's balance sheet.

[32] Note that there is a separate arrangement associated with the risks associated with the possibility of losses that may arise from the purchase of private securities. Since the Federal Reserve can only purchase and hold assets that are fully government guaranteed, purchases of corporate bonds, commercial paper, and the like can only occur through special purchase vehicles. These facilities require US Treasury indemnification, so that the Federal Reserve cannot sustain any losses. We do not concern ourselves with these types of instruments here.

[33] The Riksbank and the Bank of Canada appear to have similar arrangements where they withhold profits to rebuild their capital. See Riksbank (2024) and Bank of Canada (2020).

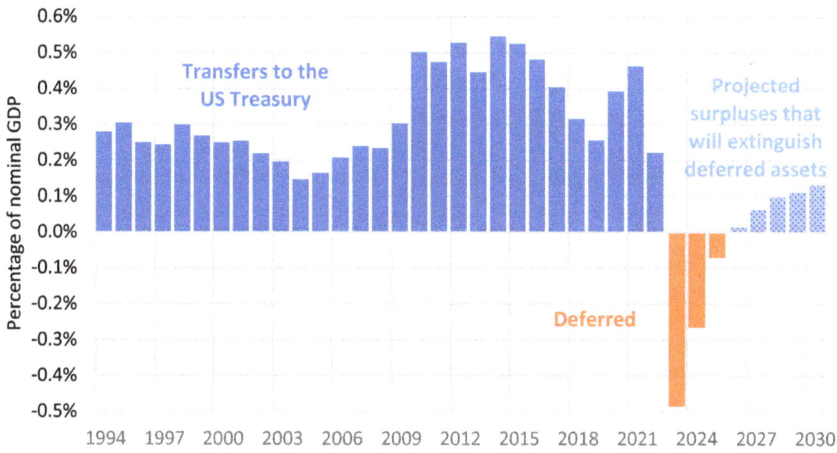

Fig. 4 Federal Reserve Transfers to the US Treasury, 1994 to 2030. Source: Federal Reserve Board H.4.1, Table 6; and Fig. 3, Levin and Skinner (2023). We thank Andrew Levin and Christina Paragon Skinner for sharing their data

Figure 4 plots the Fed's transfers to the US Treasury in blue and its deferred assets in orange.[34] We note that from 2010 to 2021 the average annual transfer to the Treasury was roughly 0.45% of GDP, or USD 84 billion. Levin and Skinner (2023) report projections suggesting that the cumulative deferred assets of the Federal Reserve will still be in the range of USD 100 billion by the end of this decade. That is, the profits from 2026 to 2030 will not be sufficient to balance the losses over the 2023 to 2025 period.

Importantly, however, these numbers appear small. Peak losses are less than one-half of 1% of GDP. If, as we suspect is the case, the asset purchase programs helped to avert a severe recession both following the financial crisis and the pandemic, then the benefits almost surely outweighed the costs.[35]

To summarize, the large asset purchases by the Fed, resulting in the Fed balance sheet peaking at approximately USD 9 trillion, are producing losses in response to higher interest rates. Similar to the case of the UK, there are fiscal implications since transfers from the Fed to the Treasury have now been halted for likely close to ten years. However, foregone transfers are small as a percentage of GDP and small, measured relative to GDP, when compared to the UK's APF losses. Most likely, the difference is due to the longer-maturity bonds purchased by the APF.

[34] Note that these are published weekly in Table 6 of the Federal Reserve's H.4.1 release. They are a liability labeled "Earnings remittances due to the U.S. Treasury."

[35] Benefits of different rounds of QE may have been different. For example, Levin et al. (2022) point out that the first round of pandemic-related QE in March/April 2020 was most likely cost effective, while the second round from May 2020 to March 2022 may not have been.

In both cases—Bank of England and Fed—we calculate *ex post* losses resulting from a shortening of the maturity structure of public debt. Because of the timing of our study, we are focusing on losses and have not balanced these against the previous gains. When the large-scale asset purchase programs were initiated, the carry was positive. Funding the purchases at a close-to-zero interest rate was low cost, while the coupons provided interest income. We therefore emphasize that focusing on current losses misses three important counterbalancing considerations. First, losses were preceded by gains and it may therefore make sense to consider net rather than gross losses. Second, what matters from the perspective of optimal policy is *ex ante* expected gains and losses rather than *ex post* losses. For example, one might argue that interest rates are higher-than-expected today because of high energy costs (due to the Russian invasion of Ukraine) and larger-than-expected supply chain disruptions (due to COVID).[36] Third, as pointed out already, large asset purchase programs most likely reduced the length and severity of two recessions. In addition, higher borrowing costs translate directly into higher returns for the holders of government debt. They are therefore a transfer rather than a direct cost. Correspondingly, we need to consider deadweight costs of taxation, as well as distributional consequences, rather than treating losses directly as reductions of welfare due to, for example, cross-border wealth transfers. This last piece is something that changes when foreigners hold the assets.

4 The Impact of Central Bank Purchases of Foreign Securities

We now turn to the case of an open economy. That is, the public and private sector can hold assets issued by foreigners denominated in foreign currency, and foreigners can hold domestic assets issued in domestic currency. Our interest is in valuation changes that create cross-border wealth transfers.

To focus the discussion, we make the following simplifying assumptions: (1) private sector cross-border investment positions exactly balance in both quantity and duration and (2) the foreign government owns no domestic assets. This allows us to focus on the impact of exchange rate and interest rate changes on the central bank's holdings of foreign assets net of both foreign public sector's holding and the (net) private sector investment position. Adjusting the balance sheet in Panel B of Table 1, we now have the following:

There are two additions. First, we add "Foreign Assets." These could be of any type. These are government bonds, private bonds, equity, and real assets. Second, since the central bank purchased these assets from foreigners and paid for them by creating reserves, we now include commercial bank reserves held by foreigners as a

[36] Bhattarai et al. (2023) suggest that large-scale asset purchases may delay the central bank increasing interest rates, thus reducing losses.

Table 4 Stylized Balance Sheet of the Domestic Central Bank in an Open Economy

Assets	Liabilities
Domestic Government Bonds	Domestic Currency
Domestic Private Bonds	Commercial Bank Reserves held by domestic residents
Loans to Banks	**Commercial Bank Reserves held by foreigners**
PV of Future Seigniorage	Fiscal Authority's Account
Other Assets	Other Liabilities
Foreign Assets	
	Central Bank Net Worth

central bank liability. (This is an obvious short-hand for the fact that foreigners hold deposits at a domestic commercial bank that are backed by the commercial bank's reserves at the central bank.)

Looking at Table 4, we note that, unlike the closed economy case, consolidation of the domestic central bank's balance sheet with that of the domestic fiscal authority has no impact on these foreign assets. Furthermore, changes in the central bank's net worth can now arise from changes in the value of foreign assets. Importantly, this clearly represents a wealth transfer to the foreigners and a loss to the country.

Whether this decline in central bank net worth reduces domestic social welfare depends on the reason that the central bank purchased foreign assets and incurred foreign liabilities. In most cases, the rationale is tied to a desire to stabilize a country's exchange rate in order to ensure the viability of export and import-competing industries.

With this in mind, we can turn to the Swiss example. In September 2011, the Swiss National Bank (SNB) sought to counter a "massive overvaluation" of the franc that posed "an acute threat to the Swiss economy" and "the risk of a deflationary development." Accordingly, it set a floor of CHF 1.20/€, promising to "buy foreign currency in unlimited quantities."[37] Over the next three years, until January 2015, the SNB held to this policy. But achieving this goal required purchasing an enormous quantity of euro-denominated assets. Swiss foreign exchange reserves soared from CHF 281 billion in August 2011 to CHF 508 billion in January 2015—that is, from 44% to 76% of Swiss GDP. While the SNB abandoned the numerical exchange rate floor in January 2015, they continued to purchase foreign assets in an effort to keep their exchange rate from appreciating. The SNB's foreign exchange reserves peaked at nearly CHF 966 billion—more than 125% of Swiss GDP—in early 2022.

This level of foreign exchange reserves induces volatility in the net worth and net income of the central bank for two reasons. First, since the central bank always does its accounting in domestic currency, changes in the exchange rate matter. Second, the prices of the foreign assets change. Together, these can have a large effect.

[37] See https://www.snb.ch/en/publications/communication/press-releases/2011/pre_20110906

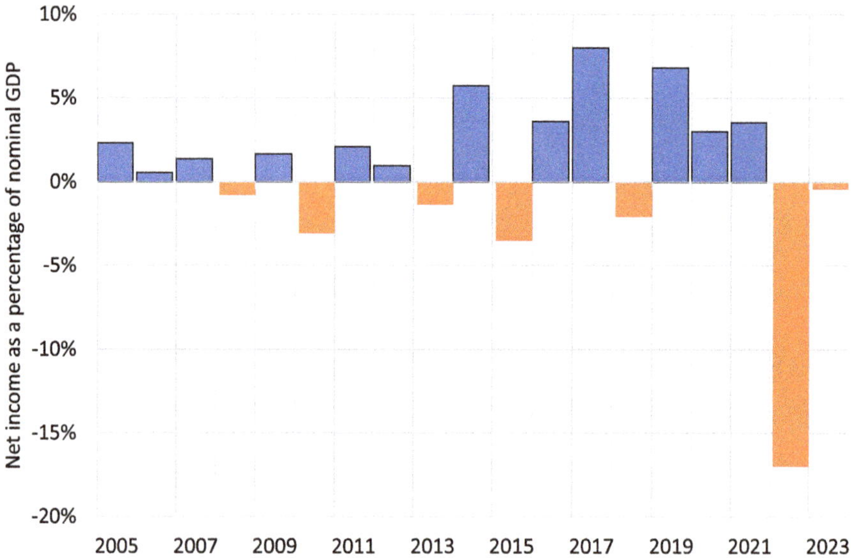

Fig. 5 Swiss National Bank Net Income 2005 to 2023, percent of GDP. Source: Swiss National Bank

To see how large, we plot the Swiss National Bank's net income as a percentage of nominal GDP in Fig. 5. In our view, numbers like +8% and −17%—the maximum and the minimum in the chart—are very large. And recall, these represent transfers between domestic residents and foreigners. Again, we need to balance these against the potential gains associated with the exchange rate policy that began in September 2011. And, in fact, the sum of the net income over the past dozen years is positive. But the volatility would seem to have at least some costs.

Summing up, when a central bank holds substantial foreign exchange reserves, changes in net worth create wealth transfers between domestic residents and foreigners that can be substantial.

We also note that losses were at times quite large (−3.1% of GDP in 2010, −2.5% in 2025 and − 2.1% in 2018) *before* the recent increase in interest rates. Thus, prior to the current discussion of the potential effects of central bank losses, the SNB experienced substantial losses without there being doubts about its ability to conduct monetary policy. One might interpret this as an example of the lack of consequences of central bank losses on central bank operations.

5 Risk Sharing in a Monetary Union

We now turn to the case of the Eurosystem. If each of the national central banks (NCBs) of the member states purchases bonds of its own government and issues liabilities to its domestic banks, then this would be identical to the original closed

Table 5 Stylized Central Bank Balance Sheets in a Two-Country Monetary Union

A. National Central Bank A (NCBA)

Assets	Liabilities
Government A Bonds	Common Currency
Account at CCB	Commercial Bank A Reserves
CCB Net Worth	Fiscal Authority A's Account
	Central Bank A Net Worth

B. National Central Bank B (NCBB)

Assets	Liabilities
Government B Bonds	Common Currency
Account at CCB	Commercial Bank B Reserves
CCB Net Worth	Fiscal Authority B's Account
	Central Bank B Net Worth

C. Common Central Bank (CCB)

Assets	Liabilities
Government A Bonds	NCBA's Account
Government B Bonds	NBCB's Account
	CCB Net Worth

economy case in Sect. 3. But this is not how the asset purchase program operates since the European Central Bank (ECB) buys a fraction of the securities mutualizing any losses. From the perspective of the citizens of a given member state in the euro area, this has characteristics of the open economy case.

To understand the mechanics of how this works, we consider a stylized example in which there are two countries of equal size. Each of the countries has a central bank and a finance ministry that issues domestic bonds. In addition, there is a common central bank (CCB). In this simple example, assume that each national central bank purchases bonds issued by their own government and nothing else. The CCB purchases bonds issued by governments in both countries, issues liabilities in the form of accounts to the NCBs and has net worth split equally between the two NCBs.[38] Changes in the value of its assets flow through to the CCBs net worth, so they are mutualized. Table 5 shows the simplified balance sheets.[39]

To continue, assume that the system decides to purchase 100 bonds. Since the countries are of equal size, this means buying 50 government A bonds and 50 government B bonds. Furthermore, assume that the purchase is allocated so that the CCB owns 20% of the total.[40] This means each NCB purchases 40 of their own country bonds, and the CCB purchases 10 of each country's bonds.

When interest rates change, the value of the government bonds change, and there are valuation effects on all of these balance sheets. But the impact of the mutualization through the CCB only has an impact if interest rates in the two countries change relative to one another. To see why, note that if interest rates move equally, then there is no difference between the NCBs each owning all of the government bonds that the system purchases. But if country A's interest rate

[38] The NCB balance at the ECB may be related to the interbank payments system (TARGET2). See the discussion in Cecchetti and Schoenholtz (2018). https://www.moneyandbanking.com/commentary/2018/7/8/target2-balances-mask-reduced-financial-fragmentation-in-the-euro-area

[39] See Kyriakopoulou and Ortlieb (2021) for a slightly different presentation.

[40] This is the level consistent with the current level of risk sharing in the Eurosystem. See here.

rises by more than country B's, so country A's government bonds decline in value by more than country B's, then country B shares in losses that it otherwise would not have to bear.

In the more realistic case in which there are many countries of varying sizes, the same thing will happen. That is, there will be transfers from countries whose interest rates rose by less to those whose interest rates rose by more. But, in addition to the transfers depending on changes in interest rate differentials, they will also be a function of the relative size of the country.

To get a sense of how large these transfers might be, we can look at the changes in interest rate differentials combined with the holdings of a country's sovereign bonds. Take the example of Italy. The system holds €400 bn of Italian bonds with a weighted average maturity of about 7 years. This means that when Italian bond spreads rise by 1 percentage point, the mutualized losses were $1\% \times 7$ years $\times 20\% \times 400$bn $=$ €5.6bn. These are redistributed according to relative size as measured by the capital key (which combines population and GDP).[41] This means that the transfer from Germany, which represents 21% of the Eurosystem, is on the order of €1.1bn. Of course, when the spread shrinks, the direction of this transfer reverses.

Turning to the cash flows—the seigniorage revenue in the Eurosystem—these are pooled and redistributed based on country size with one important exception. The exception is that as compensation for the risk of holding its sovereign bonds, a national central bank (NCB) retains interest income in excess of the reference rate (set at the main refinancing rate). This means that when NCB's own country sovereigns have a coupon in excess of the reference rate, the NCB retains the excess. As a result, Italy is less likely to experience a cash-flow loss than, for example, Germany or the Netherlands. Looking at the results in Belhocine et al. (2023) we see that this is exactly the case.[42] Those authors projected that for 2023, the Bundesbank would have a loss on the order of 0.6% of German GDP, while the Banca d'Italia would have a very modest profit.

Since our interest is more in the aggregate impact that the distribution, we focus on the profit and loss for the Eurosystem as a whole. Figure 6 reproduces the relevant panel of Belhocine et al. (2023)'s Fig. 14. Here we note that the seigniorage revenue is generally in the range of 0.2% to 0.4% of euro area GDP—similar in magnitude to that of the Federal Reserve. But the losses appear somewhat more modest, as they only occur in 2023 and 2024 and total 0.42% of GDP—roughly half of the total for the Federal Reserve.

In summary, the effects of large-scale asset purchases in the Eurosystem appear quite modest as a percentage of GDP. This is interesting given that the total size

[41] For the most recent computations of the capital key, as well as a discussion of the methodology, see here,

[42] See Belhocine et al. (2023)'s for a detailed description of the risk sharing and income pooling arrangements in the Eurosystem. Their full projections are in Figure 14 on page 18 of the IMF working paper version.

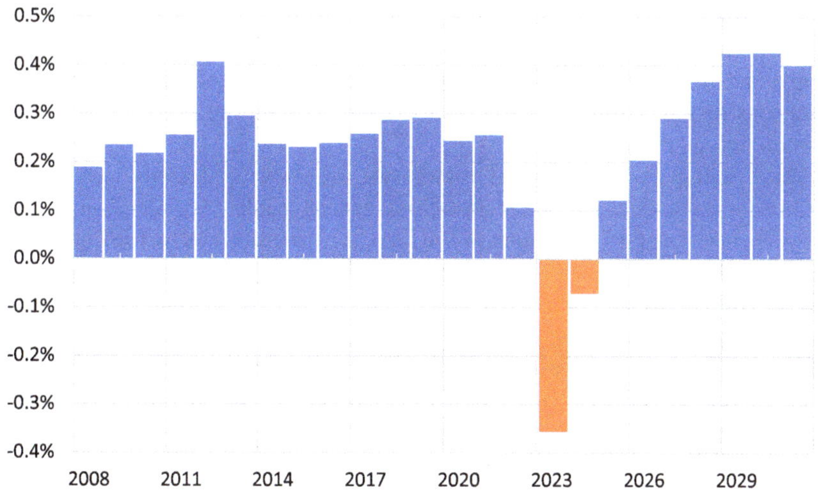

Fig. 6 Eurosystem Profit and Loss, 2000 to 2031, percent of GDP. Note: Projections were constructed in 2022, so the chart does not include actual data for 2023 reported in early 2024. Source: Belhocine et al. (2023), Fig. 14 bottom right panel. We thank Nazim Belocine, Ashok Vir Bhatia, and Jan Frie for sharing their data

of asset purchases is comparable to the US, while GDP is about one-third lower. It is likely that the difference is due to the large share of longer-term refinancing operations (LTRO) making up Eurosystem assets.

Given the modest size of losses, the fact that there is a combination of country-specific losses resulting from NCBs purchasing domestic bonds and mutualized losses is not as crucial.[43] Indeed, as pointed out, those countries holding bonds with larger spreads had smaller losses, compensating them for market-perceived differences in risk. Also, even for small effects on the severity and duration of recessions, benefits of asset purchase programs will have exceeded costs.

6 Conclusion

In this paper, we make three contributions to the literature on consequences of quantitative easing policies to central bank balance sheets. First, we propose merging the balance sheets of the central bank and the fiscal authority into one consolidated government balance sheet. This clarifies the consequences of central bank asset purchases, emphasizing that these actions have fiscal consequences.

[43] Belhocine et al. (2023)'s projections suggest that the Banque de France, Bundesbank, De Nederlandsche Bank, and Banca de España will face losses, the Banca d'Italia will not.

Second, using the consolidated balance sheet approach, we classify central bank purchases into three groups—domestic government bonds, domestic private sector bonds, and foreign securities. We trace out the effects of all three—a change in maturity structure resulting in potentially higher variation of tax liabilities as well as intra- and inter-country transfers.

Third, using ex post realized losses, we are able to quantify and describe differences in losses and transfers across central banks. For this purpose, we consider four examples: The Bank of England, the Federal Reserve, the Eurosystem, and the Swiss National Bank. In the first three, the losses are relatively small, ranging from 0.3 and 1.5% of GDP in a given year. By contrast, the Swiss National Bank is sustaining losses up to 17% of GDP. However, compared to the potential gains of avoiding more severe recessions in the face of the Global Financial Crisis and the Global Pandemic as well as earlier benefits from holding high-yielding securities funded by low-interest reserves, losses are most likely smaller.

Institutional arrangements also play an important role. We note that realized losses may have different effects depending on accounting treatments and on indemnification policies. If losses appear on the balance sheet only when sales are made, the timing of sales affects the timing of losses. This is true in the case of the Bank of England, which is currently selling a substantial fraction of bond holdings every year. In contrast, timing of sales is not relevant for the timing of losses if fair value (mark-to-market) accounting is used. Then, once the losses appear, they may become part of a deferred asset (e.g., Fed) or need to be paid by the fiscal authority in real time. The timing of fiscal consequences thus is related to the institutional arrangements.

References

Adler, G., Castro, P., & Tovar, C. E. (February 2016). Does central bank capital matter for monetary policy? *Open Economy Review, 27*(1), 183–205.

Archer, D., & Moser-Boehm, P. (April 2013). *Central bank finances*. BIS Papers No 71.

Bandari, A., Evans, D., Golosov, M., & Sargent, T. J. (April 2017). *The Optimal Maturity of Government Debt*. Unpublished manuscript, University of Chicago.

Bank of Canada, Indemnity Agreement (Provincial Bond Purchase Program) (7 May 2020).

Barro, R. J. (November–December 1974). Are Government Bonds Net Wealth? *Journal of Political Economy, 82*(6), 1095–1117.

Barro, R. J. (October 1979). On the determination of the public debt. *Journal of Political Economy, 87*(5), 940–971.

Belhocine, N., Bhatia, A. V., & Frie, J. (July 2023). *Raising rates with a large balance sheet: The Eurosystem's net income and its fiscal implications*. IMF Working Paper No WP/23/145.

Belton, T., Dawsey, K., Greenlaw, D., Li, H., Ramaswamy, S., & Sack, B. (October 10, 2018). *Optimizing the maturity structure of U.S. Treasury debt: A model-based framework*. Brookings Institution.

Bhattarai, S., Eggertsson, G. B., & Gafarov, B. (2023). Time consistency and duration of government debt: A model of quantitative easing. *The Review of Economic Studies, 90*(4), 1759–1799.

Bohn, H. (December 1990). Tax smoothing with financial instruments. *American Economic Review, 80*(5), 1217–1230.

Buiter, W. (May 2008). *Can central banks go broke?*. CEPR Policy Insight No 24.

Buiter, W., Cecchetti, S. G., Dominguez, K., & Serrano, A. S. (January 2023). *Stabilising financial markets: Lending and market making as a last resort*. Advisory Scientific Committee of the European Systemic Risk Board Report No. 13.

Cantú, C., Cavallino, P., De Fiore, F., & Yetman, J. (March 2021). *A global database on central banks' monetary responses to Covid-19*. BIS Working Paper, No 934.

Carpenter, S., Ihrig, J., Klee, E., Quinn, D., & Boote, A. (March 2015). The federal reserve's balance sheet and earnings: A primer and projections. *International Journal of Central Banking, 11*(2), 237–283.

Cecchetti, S. G., & Kermit L. S. (9 July 2018). *TARGET2 balances mask reduced financial fragmentation in the euro area*.http://www.moneyandbanking.com/

Cecchetti, S. G., & Tucker, P. M. W. (1 June 2021). *Understanding how central banks use their balance sheets: A critical categorization*. VoxEU.

Chaboud, A., & Leahy, M. (March 8, 2013). *Foreign central bank remittance practices*. Memo to the FOMC (published January 11, 2019).

Committee on the Global Financial System. (March 2023). *Central bank asset purchases in response to the COVID-19 crisis*. CGFS Papers No. 68.

Del Negro, M., & Sims, C. A. *When does a central bank's balance sheet require fiscal support?* Federal Reserve Bank of New York Staff Report No. 701, Revised March 2015.

Du, W., Forbes, K., & Luzzetti, M. (February 2024). *Quantitative tightening around the globe: What have we learned?* 2024 US Monetary Policy Forum Report.

Gagnon, J. E. (April 2016). *Quantitative easing: An underappreciated success. PIIE Policy Briefs* 16–4.

Greenlaw, D., Hamilton, J. D., Harris, E., & West, K. D. (June 2018). *A skeptical view of the impact of the fed's balance sheet*. NBER Working Paper, no. 24687.

Greenwood, R., Hanson, S. G., Rudolph, J. S., & Summers, L. H. (2015a). The optimal maturity of government debt. In D. Wessel (Ed.), *The $13 trillion question: How America manages its debt* (pp. 1–41). Brookings Institution Press.

Greenwood, R., Hanson, S. G., & Stein, J. C. (2015b). A comparative advantage approach to government debt maturity. *Journal of Finance, 70*, 1683–1722.

Lagarde, C. (19 November 2020). *Committee on economic and monetary affairs monetary dialogue*.

Levin, A. T., Lu, B. L., & Nelson, W. R. (2022). *Quantifying the costs and benefits of quantitative easing*. No. w30749. National Bureau of Economic Research.

Levin, A. T., & Skinner, C. P. (December 2023). *Central bank undersight: Assessing the fed's accountability to congress*. Mimeo.

Lucas, R. E., & Stokey, N. L. (1983). Optimal fiscal and monetary policy in an economy without capital. *Journal of Monetary Economics, 12*(1), 55–93.

Kyriakopoulou, D., & Ortlieb, P. (27 January 2021). *Does central bank capital matter?* OMFIF Commentary.

Mitra, S., & Sack, B. (27 July 2022). *Projecting the structure of US Treasury debt*. Brookings Institution Commentary.

Nordström, A., & Vredin, A. (December 2022). *Does central bank equity matter for monetary policy?* Sveriges Riksbank Staff Memo.

Office of Budget Responsibility. (November 2023). *Economic and fiscal outlook*. U.K. Crown.

Perera, A., Ralston, D., & Wickramanayake, J. (September 2013). Central bank financial strength and inflation: Is there a robust link? *Journal of Financial Stability, 9*(3), 399–414.

Pinter, J. (November 2018). Does central bank financial strength really matter for inflation? The key role of the fiscal support. *Open Economy Review, 29*(5), 911–952.

Reis, R. (June 2015). *Different types of central bank insolvency and the central role of seigniorage*. NBER Working Paper No. 21226.

Riksbank. (18 September 2024). *Consultation response on the memorandum new conditions for the Riksbank's financing*.
Wessels, P., & Broeders, D. (2022a). *On the capitalisation of central banks*. De Nederlandsche Bank Occasional Studies Volume 20–4.
Wessels, P., & Broeders, D. (September 2022b). *Central bank capital*. SUERF Policy Brief 420.

Open Access This chapter is licensed under the terms of the Creative Commons Attribution 4.0 International License (http://creativecommons.org/licenses/by/4.0/), which permits use, sharing, adaptation, distribution and reproduction in any medium or format, as long as you give appropriate credit to the original author(s) and the source, provide a link to the Creative Commons license and indicate if changes were made.

The images or other third party material in this chapter are included in the chapter's Creative Commons license, unless indicated otherwise in a credit line to the material. If material is not included in the chapter's Creative Commons license and your intended use is not permitted by statutory regulation or exceeds the permitted use, you will need to obtain permission directly from the copyright holder.

Central Bank Capital and Shareholder Relationship

Matteo Bonetti, Dirk Broeders, Damiaan Chen, and Daniel Dimitrov

Abstract In pursuing its mandate, a central bank assumes financial risks through its monetary policy operations. Central bank capital is a critical tool in mitigating these risks. We investigate the concept of central bank capital as a mechanism for risk sharing with its shareholder. Adopting an option pricing framework, we explore the setting where the central bank commits to distributing dividends when its capital is robust, while the shareholder may be called upon to recapitalize the bank during adverse economic conditions when its capital is negative. Our analysis dissects the trade-offs inherent in these options, seeking a mutually beneficial agreement that disincentivizes deviation for either party. This equilibrium is essential for safeguarding the independence and credibility of the central bank in executing monetary policy effectively.

Keywords Central bank capital · Contingent claim analysis · Risk management · Shareholder · Sequential games

We thank Guido Ascari, Maurice Bun, Silvia Caserta, Jan Willem van den End, Jan Kakes, René Rollingswier, Jan Smit, Razvan Vlahu, Sweder van Wijnbergen, and DNB's seminar participants for the useful comments and discussions. The views expressed in this paper are those of the authors and do not reflect the views of De Nederlandsche Bank, or the Eurosystem.

M. Bonetti · D. Chen · D. Dimitrov
De Nederlandsche Bank, Amsterdam, The Netherlands
e-mail: M.Bonetti@dnb.nl; d.h.j.chen@dnb.nl; d.k.dimitrov@dnb.nl

D. Broeders (✉)
European Central Bank, Frankfurt, Germany
e-mail: Dirk.Broeders@ecb.europa.eu

© The Author(s) 2025

D. Broeders et al. (eds.), *Central Bank Capital in Turbulent Times*,
Contributions to Finance and Accounting,
https://doi.org/10.1007/978-3-031-73549-3_5

1 Introduction

Owned typically by the government, central banks operate within a framework that involves accepting financial risks to implement monetary policy. Central bank capital can play a key role in absorbing these risks. A key question then arises: How much capital should a central bank have relative to the risks it bears in monetary policy operations and other activities such as reserve management and lending of last resort? One perspective suggests that maintaining capital is irrelevant for a central bank, as long as it can continue to issue legal tender and receives unconditional fiscal support from the government (Reis, 2015a; Hall & Reis, 2015). However, from a different perspective, adequate capital levels are essential for a central bank to establish independence and to maintain policy credibility. From this standpoint, capital serves as an instrument ensuring effective policy implementation (Stella, 2005; Klüh & Stella, 2008; Benigno, 2020; Wessels & Broeders, 2023).

The question of what the adequate levels of central bank capital are is becoming increasingly pertinent as central banks' worldwide report losses due to rapid changes in monetary policy stance (Bell et al., 2023; Belhocine et al., 2023). Furthermore, quantitative easing is evolving into a standard tool of monetary policy, consequently heightening financial risks on central banks' balance sheets. Central banks are therefore keen to evaluate capital adequacy, given that these novel monetary policy instruments are riskier and may yield lower profitability in contrast to conventional tools. A prolonged period of losses can impair their capital positions and may ultimately undermine their ability to fulfill their mandate. In this context, the literature on central banking underscores the importance of fiscal support from the government in the form of recapitalization (Del Negro & Sims, 2015; Benigno & Nisticò, 2020). However, capital policy as a contract between the central bank and its shareholder is still widely unexplored.

In this chapter, we examine this contract as a financial risk-sharing agreement between the central bank and its shareholder.[1] This arrangement entails mutual acceptance of obligations. First, the central bank distributes dividends to the shareholder during periods of robust capitalization. Second, the shareholder, often implicitly, pledges fiscal support by committing to recapitalize the bank, should asset values drop significantly relative to liability values, jeopardizing the credibility of its monetary policy.

[1] Without loss of generality, we consider a scenario where the sole shareholder is the government, a common assumption reflecting the prevailing reality in many cases, as the state often holds exclusive ownership. It is noteworthy, however, that in practical terms the ownership structure of central banks varies. Stocks of central banks in Belgium, Greece, Japan, South Africa, Switzerland, and Turkey are traded on a stock exchange. Moreover, in certain instances such as in the USA, the central bank is partially owned by commercial banks, adding an additional layer of complexity to their ownership dynamics, see, e.g., Archer and Moser-Boehm (2013). The European Central Bank is fully owned by the national central banks in the euro area, with no governments directly backing it.

To analyze the risk-sharing arrangement, we employ models that are typically used for credit risk and equity valuation (Merton, 1974; Leland, 1994; Black & Cox, 1976). Through this approach, we delve into the dynamics between the central bank and its shareholder, enabling a comprehensive evaluation of the risks assumed by each party. From the central bank's perspective, the obligation to pay dividends in the future, conditional on having sufficient buffers, is a short call option on the central bank's assets. The recapitalization guarantee, again from the central bank's perspective, is a long put option on its assets. The value of equity is therefore the result of a bargaining problem for the central bank and the shareholder on the key features of these two options. In this fashion, we translate Merton's model, commonly used to evaluate default risk, into a context where insolvency is defined not in terms of the ability to pay liabilities, but in terms of the ability to keep up with policy objectives. We take a three-step approach in our analysis.

First, we introduce an economic definition of central bank equity. In contrast to capital defined in accounting terms as the value of total assets minus liabilities, we define equity as accounting capital minus the value of the dividend payment option plus the value of the recapitalization option. These options are implicitly defined, as they do not appear in the central bank's reported balance sheet, and they are not traded on any market. As one would expect, then, holding everything else fixed, a higher value of central bank assets means a higher value of the dividend option and a lower value of the recapitalization option. Conversely, lower asset values lower the value of the dividend option and increase the value of the recapitalization option. Second, we explore the risk-sharing implications of the capital policy, where the central bank and its shareholder establish the terms for dividend distribution and recapitalization. In our setting, these terms are defined by the strike prices (or "strikes") of the implicit options, which dictate when the options are exercised. Third, we formalize the negotiation process wherein the central bank and its shareholder establish terms for dividend distribution and recapitalization via a Stackelberg game. The goal is to derive a contract from which neither party would have incentives to deviate. Such an equilibrium agreement ensures the central bank's independence while simultaneously securing a commitment from the shareholder to provide fiscal support when necessary.

Following this three-step approach, we first find that the dynamics of a central bank's accounting capital and the economic value of its equity are remarkably different. The dividend and recapitalization options smooth the impact of changes in asset value on equity. Second, we demonstrate that capital policy can have implications about the risk appetite of central banks, depending on the institutional setting. For example, an undercapitalized central bank with fiscal backing may be incentivized to enhance the value of its equity by taking on more risk in monetary operations. Conversely, a well-capitalized central bank without strong fiscal backing may exhibit hesitancy in engaging in unconventional monetary policy, as it fears that doing so could deplete its capital position, while any surpluses would flow to the shareholder in the form of dividends. Third, using our framework, we demonstrate that the capital policy in equilibrium depends on how decision rights are allocated between the shareholder and the central bank. A negotiation, for instance, in which the central bank sets the recapitalization conditions, and the shareholder sets the dividend conditions, will result in a relatively high recapitalization threshold and a low dividend payment threshold. This means high protection against capital shortfalls, as recapitalization is more likely to be triggered. However, it also implies less ability to rebuild capital by retaining profits, as, in return, the shareholder would require a lower dividend payment threshold to agree on the arrangement. These findings underscore the necessity of well-designed institutional frameworks to align the risk incentives of the central bank and its shareholders, ensuring stability and resilience in the financial system.

The central bank's capital structure problem is distinct in several notable ways that are worth discussing before setting up our model. First, the unique ability of a central bank to create reserves ensures that it will never run out of liquidity in its own currency. As a result, there are no bankruptcy proceedings in the conventional sense for central banks and having negative capital is completely feasible. However, a central bank that experiences a large drain on its capital, may need to resort to issuing reserves to service the costs on its ongoing liabilities. This inevitably would affect its ability to curb inflation and as a result would jeopardize its credibility. That is why fiscal support in the form of recapitalization is needed to safeguard its credibility.[2]

At the same time, the asset-liability structure of a central bank is very specific and has evolved in recent years. While liabilities are typically short term, assets are either short term, when created through lending operations or through the central bank's standing facilities, or long term and subject to repricing risk, when created through quantitative easing or other asset purchase programs. This exposes the central bank to specific asset-liability mismatches. Unlike commercial banks, however, central banks do not hedge these risks, as that would go against the monetary stance which requires purchasing these assets in the first place. In this chapter we abstract from the maturity dimension of interest rate risk and model it through a generic risky asset representing purchase programs. This allows us to keep the model abstract and tractable, while still retaining the key features relevant for valuing the options implicit in the balance sheet.

In terms of the related literature, our paper contributes to the debate on central bank capital and fiscal support (Reis, 2015a; Del Negro & Sims, 2015; Hall & Reis, 2015; Benigno, 2020) by showing how dividend and recapitalization arrangements between the central bank and government are made. We also relate to the growing literature on the effect of non-conventional monetary policy and central bank losses

[2] There is some heterogeneity in the academic literature on what central bank insolvency entails precisely. Reis (2015b) covers a number of definitions from the point of view of valuing the central bank's promise to generate seigniorage while keeping in line with its resource constraint. Similarly, there are different ways to approach central bank credibility and independence. Blinder (2000) provides an overview and relates credibility to inflation bias—the tendency of central banks to lose policy credibility and generate excess inflation when they lack independence from the fiscal authority. Here, without engaging in these discussions in detail, we use the terms insolvency, credibility, and independence in the context of the balance sheet of the central bank as a tool in effectively supporting its inflation objectives.

(Chiacchio et al., 2018; Benigno & Nisticò, 2020; Goncharov et al., 2023) and to the literature on central bank independence (Barro & Gordon, 1983; Eijffinger et al., 1996; Binder, 2021). Further, the model presented in this chapter relates to the literature on commercial bank recapitalization (DeMarzo & Sannikov, 2006; Décamps et al., 2011; Peura & Keppo, 2006; Moreno-Bromberg & Rochet, 2018), albeit with substantial differences given the specificity of the central bank operations and objectives discussed earlier.

The structure of this chapter is as follows. In Sect. 2, we introduce the assumptions that underpin our analysis of the risk-sharing arrangement between the central bank and the shareholder. Section 3 outlines the model used to determine the equilibrium capital policy in potential negotiations between the central bank and the shareholder. Next, in Sect. 4, we present numerical results derived from the optimal policy. In Sect. 5, we explore several real-world cases of capital policy implementation. Finally, Sect. 6 provides concluding remarks.

2 Model

We develop a static, one-period model in the spirit of Merton (1974). We assume that during the period under examination the central bank will not implement new monetary policy measures and the amount of banknotes in the economy is fixed. Our approach is further based on a number of simplifying assumptions which keep the focus of the analysis on risk-sharing arrangement between the central bank and the shareholder:

- All information is public and becomes available according to a standard filtration $\mathcal{F}_t$ generated by a Brownian motion W_t.
- Markets are complete and frictionless. The central bank's assets and liabilities are readily tradeable and liquid.
- We assume partial equilibrium dynamics. This means that the development of asset prices and the risk-free rate are purely exogenous, and any shocks introduced by the central bank's policies before the start of the period have already been priced in by markets.
- At time t the central bank and the shareholder agree on the capital policy. Similarly to the standard Merton model, any uncertainty resolves at time T and the European-type options embedded in the central bank's capital structure mature.
- There is no discretionary expansion or contraction of the central bank's balance sheet during the analysis period. Any central bank intervention has happened beforehand and is already priced into the interest rates. The money supply in the form of banknotes is fixed.
- The shareholder keeps its commitment. Thus, we abstract from the risk of political interference once the agreement is agreed upon, and assume that the state has deep pockets and is able and willing to fulfill the recapitalization commitment in all states of the world.

2.1 The Central Bank Balance Sheet

Based on these assumptions, and under the additional presumption that assets and liabilities on the balance sheet are valued on a marked-to-market (MTM) basis, we can now describe the stylized model of the central bank (Table 1).

The central bank utilizes open market operations and asset purchase programs to implement its monetary policy. Total assets can be categorized into these two main components: lending operations (M_t) and asset purchase programs (P_t).[3] Total assets are then defined as

$$A_t = M_t + P_t. \tag{1}$$

The evolution of lending operations M is given by

$$dM_t/M_t = rdt, \tag{2}$$

where r is the risk-free rate. The risk-free nature of r is derived from the fact that loans to commercial banks are well collateralized through high-quality assets or through haircuts which are applied whenever collateral risk needs to be managed.

The value of the purchase programs evolves with the price changes of the risky assets under the physical risk measure as

$$dP_t/P_t = (r + \lambda\sigma)dt + \sigma dW_t, \tag{3}$$

where λ is the price of risk, or risk premium, per unit of asset volatility σ, and dW_t is a Brownian increment.

We define the share of risky assets in the balance sheet as $\omega = P_t/A_t$. The evolution of total assets can then be written as

$$\begin{aligned} dA_t/A_t &= dM_t/A_t + dP_t/A_t \\ &= (1-\omega)dM_t/M_t + \omega dP_t/P_t \\ &= (r + \omega\lambda\sigma)\,dt + \omega\sigma dW_t. \end{aligned}$$

Liabilities consist of a fixed amount of banknotes N and reserves R_t. Reserves are deposits held by commercial banks at the central bank. Total liabilities are then given by

$$L_t = N + R_t. \tag{4}$$

[3] We ignore for the purposes of this study other central bank activities that may require capital such as reserve management and acting as the lender of last resort.

Table 1 Central bank's accounting (Marked-to-Market) balance sheet

Assets (A_t)		Liabilities (L_t)	
Lending operations	M_t	Banknotes	N
Asset purchase program	P_t	Reserves	R_t
		Capital	B_t

The central bank forgoes interest costs through its privilege of issuing banknotes, while on the reserves it pays the risk-free rate. This implies that total liabilities grow only through the interest rate that has to be paid on reserves

$$dL_t = rR_t dt. \tag{5}$$

We define the level of the central bank's capital in accounting terms as the net asset position:

$$B_t = A_t - L_t. \tag{6}$$

As a result, changes in capital can be written as

$$\begin{aligned} dB_t &= dA_t - dL_t \\ &= dM_t + dP_t - dR_t \\ &= \underbrace{(M_t + P_t - R_t)rdt}_{\text{Seigniorage}} + \underbrace{P_t\lambda\sigma dt}_{\text{Risk Premium}} + \underbrace{P_t\sigma dW_t}_{\text{Financial Risk}}. \end{aligned} \tag{7}$$

From Eq. (7), it follows that the change in capital comes from the central bank earning risk-free seigniorage profits by issuing banknotes, the risk premium obtained by investing in the risky asset, and the asset risk that is injected into its balance sheet as a result of holding the purchase program assets.

It is worthwhile discussing some caveats of our model before we proceed further. First, we simplify reality in a number of ways to enhance the tractability of the model. We treat the asset purchase programs P_t as a homogeneous asset class with a single risk driver. In reality, these programs can consist of long-term government bonds, commercial bonds, asset-backed securities, covered bonds, or even equity, as is the case with the Bank of Japan.[4] Second, we do not discuss the motivations behind the asset purchases, which in practice may come as a response to an extreme market shock.[5] From that point of view, the asset price log-normality assumption

[4] Charoenwong et al. (2021) discuss the Bank of Japan's asset purchase programs. For implementation in the U.S.A., see Di Maggio et al. (2020). Benigno et al. (2023), among others, discuss the purchase programs initiated by the ECB in response to the Covid-19 pandemic shock.

[5] Central banks have utilized large-scale asset purchase programs, commonly known as Quantitative Easing (QE), since the Global Financial Crisis. These programs, such as the ECB's Public

embedded in the Merton model may seem troublesome. It is, in theory, possible to extend the risk dynamics of our model, for instance, by incorporating stochastic variance to address market turbulence or stochastic interest rates to reflect term-structure risk. However, we refrain from doing so here, as we are not concerned with the triggers of asset purchases or their interaction with asset dynamics, a research question posed, for instance, in Broeders et al. (2023). In our model, the size of asset purchases is exogenous and appears in the central bank's balance sheet as a legacy from previously fulfilled policy. Here, we aim to emphasize the option-type structure of central bank capital, which remains conceptually consistent regardless of the underlying risk factor dynamics.

Furthermore, we assume that the central bank's balance sheet is continuously marked to market, while in reality assets may also be accounted for as held to maturity (HTM). This is the case, for instance, of bonds held under the asset purchase programmes of the Eurosystem. Conceptually, however, the MTM and the HTM accounting differ only with respect to the timing of the recognition of profits and losses. To provide an example, an upward shift in the yield curve will immediately be recognized as a loss under MTM accounting by revaluing all bonds held on the asset side of the balance sheet; at the same time, losses will be recognized only gradually under HTM accounting when cash outflows associated with funding costs (interest rates on reserves) increase potentially above the cash inflows from the HTM assets (coupons received on the bonds held to maturity).

2.2 Capital Policy

Capital acts as a buffer to absorb the risks taken by the central bank to implement monetary policy. We examine the concept of central bank capital as the result of a risk-sharing arrangement with the shareholder. In our chapter, the central bank and its shareholder agree on a capital policy for the duration of one period. This policy has two features that reflect the risk-sharing arrangement. First, the central bank and the shareholder agree on the parameters of the dividend policy. If the bank is well capitalized, it will pay a dividend. Concretely, any assets above a multiple κ_C of liabilities are paid in the form of a dividend to the shareholder. Second, the central bank and the shareholder agree on the parameters of a recapitalization. Following the premises of structural finance, we assume that at time T the central bank needs to be recapitalized by the shareholder if its assets fall below a multiple of κ_Π of its

Sector Purchase Programme (PSPP), are designed to ease the monetary stance by reducing interest rates. However, central banks may also initiate asset purchase initiatives in response to various triggers. For instance, programs like the ECB's Securities Markets Programme (SMP) were there to ensure sufficient depth and liquidity in dysfunctioning segments of the sovereign bond markets, and the Pandemic Emergency Purchase Programme (PEPP) was introduced in response to the Covid-19 pandemic to support the monetary transmission process by alleviating extreme financial market distress.

liabilities, i.e., if $A_T \leq \kappa_\Pi L_T$. Below this threshold, the central bank is in jeopardy of not being able to fulfill its monetary policy objectives and therefore it needs to be recapitalized by the shareholder.

We take the perspective of the central bank. From this perspective the future dividend payment is represented by a short call option on the central bank's assets. The payoff at maturity T of the call option is given by

$$C_T = \max\{0, A_T - \kappa_C L_T\}. \tag{8}$$

The option to recapitalize is a long put option on the central bank's assets. We explore the case in which the central bank is recapitalized so that all liabilities L_T are covered with sufficient assets A_T. This entails that the shareholder injects $L_T - A_T$ to recapitalize the bank.

The payoff at maturity T of the put option is given by

$$\Pi_T = \max\{0, L_T - A_T\}. \tag{9}$$

Note that the put option is triggered, whenever $A_T \leq \kappa_\Pi L_T$. This setting cannot be analyzed using regular options but rather "gap options" (Hull, 2012). Hence, the strike that triggers the option is not the strike that determines the payoff.

It is important to note that the implementation of recapitalization can vary in practice. The most straightforward approach involves a bond transfer directly from the shareholder to the central bank's balance sheet in return for an equivalent capital stake in the bank. However, recapitalization can also manifest itself in subtler forms. For instance, the central bank might record losses as deferred assets, essentially creating a claim on the shareholder without an immediate cash transfer, as exemplified by the approach taken by the US Federal Reserve (Carpenter et al., 2018). Gradually, these deferred assets are mitigated by retaining future central bank earnings, essentially meaning that the shareholder recapitalizes the central bank by forfeiting future dividends. In our context, the specific assets utilized for recapitalizing the central bank have no relevance, as we do not model the post-maturity developments.

So far we have used capital to denote the central bank's net assets in accounting terms, without the two options on its implicit balance sheet. We now introduce the term "equity" to refer to the central bank's net assets including the two options. Factoring in these options, we can write the value of equity at time t as the sum of capital and the recapitalization option minus the dividend option

$$E_T = B_T + \Pi_T - C_T. \tag{10}$$

The options are implicit as they do not appear on the central bank's MtM accounting balance sheet. Nevertheless, we can now present the central bank's economic balance sheet including the implicit options as in Table 2.

Based on this, we can determine the value of equity at the end of the period. The thick red line in Fig. 1 shows the equity value E_T as a function of the value of the central bank's assets A_T at time T. Note that the red line is discontinuous at the

Table 2 Central bank's balance sheet including the implicit options

Assets		Liabilities	
Lending operations	M_t	Banknotes	N
Asset purchase program	P_t	Reserves	R_t
Recapitalization option	Π_t	Dividend option	C_t
		Equity	E_t

strike of the put option ($\kappa_\Pi L_T$) due to the fact that the option's exercise and the payoff are disconnected. The black dashed line shows capital B_T as a function of assets at maturity. Equity and capital overlap in between the option strike multiples.

2.3 Valuation of Central Bank Equity

At time t, we define the value of central bank equity as the current value of net assets plus the market value of the embedded recapitalization option, net of the market value of the contingent obligation to pay dividends:[6]

$$E_t = A_t - L_t + \Pi_t - C_t. \tag{11}$$

Conceptually, the idea of valuing equity through the options embedded on a firm's balance sheet goes back to Merton (1974), who relates the value of a firm's equity to the value of the implicit call option that the shareholders have on its assets. It is important to note that the capital structure of a central bank diverges from that of a typical firm for two key reasons. First, whereas shareholders of a firm benefit from limited liability and can choose to let the firm default if recapitalization is not projected to yield profits, such recourse is unavailable for central banks. The shareholder of a central bank is more inclined to recapitalize it, given the role of the central bank in the economy, without the option of default as an exit strategy. In fact, the central bank's equity resembles an option strategy referred to by traders as a "collar," in which the investor holds a long out-of-the-money call and a short out-of-the-money put on the same underlying asset.

Second, unlike a commercial enterprise, the central bank can display negative equity on its balance sheet without creditors demanding back their claims. This resilience is sustained by the trust held by counterparties, who recognize that the central bank's liabilities are ultimately backed by its shareholder. Furthermore, the shareholder has no incentive to disengage, even in situations where the central

[6] Formally, the value of equity can be seen as the discounted expected value of the central bank's payoff at period T, defined as $E_t = e^{-r_t(T-t)}\mathbb{E}_t^{\mathbb{Q}}(A_T - L_T + \Pi_T - C_T)$, where $\mathbb{E}_t^{\mathbb{Q}}(.)$ denotes an expectation under the risk-neutral distribution of asset returns. See Shreve (2000) for details on risk-neutral asset pricing.

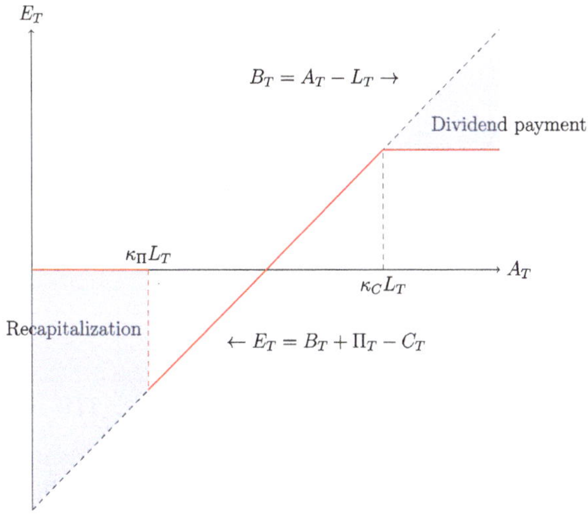

Fig. 1 Central bank equity payoff at maturity

bank's assets fall below its liabilities. This commitment stems from the central bank's pivotal institutional role in society to offer price or exchange rate stability.

The values of the embedded call and put payoffs can then be determined through the well-known Black and Scholes relations as follows:

$$C_t = N(d_{1,C})A_t - N(d_{2,C})\kappa_C L_t^* \tag{12}$$

$$\Pi_t = N(-d_{2,\Pi})L_t^* - N(-d_{1,\Pi})A_t, \tag{13}$$

where

$$d_{1,i} = \frac{1}{\omega\sigma\sqrt{T-t}}\left[\ln\left(\frac{A_t}{\kappa_i L_T}\right) + \left(r + \frac{1}{2}(\omega\sigma)^2\right)(T-t)\right] \tag{14}$$

$$d_{2,i} = d_1(\kappa_i) - \omega\sigma\sqrt{T-t}. \tag{15}$$

The indicator $i = \{C, \Pi\}$ refers to the call and put options, respectively. Furthermore, L_t^* is the terminal value of liabilities, discounted at the risk-free rate or $L_t^* = (R_T + N)e^{-r(T-t)} = Ne^{-r(T-t)} + R_t$. Note that the risk on the asset side of the balance sheet is driven by the fraction ω that the central bank invests in the risky assets. Therefore we scale the volatility factor in the Black and Scholes pricing formula accordingly ($\omega\sigma$).[7]

[7] To verify our formulas, recall the well-known Black and Scholes relation. For example, the price of a call option with strike K and underlying value S_t can be written as $C_t = N(d_1)S_t - N(d_2)Ke^{-rt}$. In our case, specifically, the strike becomes $K = \kappa_C L_T = \kappa_C(N + R_t)$, where $R_t = R_t e^{r(T-t)}$. Then, we can absorb the discount factor into L_t^*, such that $Ke^{r(T-t)} =$

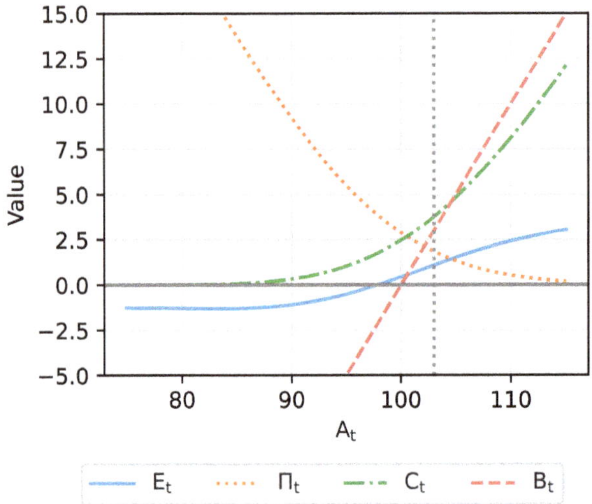

Fig. 2 Equity value as a function of asset value. *Note*. This figure shows the value of equity (E_t), the dividend option (C_t), the recapitalization option (Π_t), and accounting capital (B_t), as a function of the central bank's asset value. The dotted vertical line shows the initial asset value ($A_t = 103$). The dividend and recapitalization policy parameters for the call and put options are $\kappa_C = 1.05$ and $\kappa_\Pi = 0.90$, respectively. The remaining parameter values are given in Annex A.1

It is important to note that the valuation of the put option follows a modification of the standard Black and Scholes formula. When the option is triggered, the shareholder does not pay the difference between the asset value and the strike price, but rather pays a higher amount such that capital is replenished back to zero. Equation (13) reflects this feature through the fact that the strike term in front of $N(-d_{2,\Pi})$ is not equal to $\kappa_\Pi L_t^*$ (as it would have been in case of a plain-vanilla option) but equal to L_t^*. This derivative can be priced as a gap-type option, which disconnects the option trigger κ_Π from the payout level. We assume that the central bank is recapitalized up to 100% of its liabilities when assets drop below the trigger level $\kappa_\Pi L_T$.[8]

We are now able to determine the value of the policy options, which consequently influences the value of the central bank's equity. To initiate the calibration process of the model, we set the total liabilities at a standardized level of $L_t = 100$, while total assets will vary. We set the dividend and recapitalization policy parameters ("strike multiples") for call and put options at $\kappa_C = 1.05$ and $\kappa_\Pi = 0.90$, respectively. The remaining numerical values are presented in Annex A.1. Figure 2 shows how the value of equity E_t varies for different asset levels A_t. The figure also shows

$\kappa_C \left(Ne^{-r(T-t)} + R_t\right) = \kappa_C L_t^*$. The discount factor is canceled out from the reserves portfolio R_t but is maintained on the banknote liabilities. This also makes intuitive sense, as the issuance of banknotes allows a central bank to finance its assets thorough a cost-free liability.

[8] See for example Hull (2012) for a formal derivation of the Black and Scholes pricing function of gap options.

capital B_t and the value of the dividend option C_t and recapitalization option Π_t. Since any losses beyond the $\kappa_\Pi L_T$ are (more than fully) covered by the shareholder, the equity value is higher than capital for low asset values. Conversely, for high asset values the equity is below capital, as the former takes into account future dividend payments. Therefore the dynamics of a central bank's accounting capital and the economic value of its equity are remarkably different. The dividend and recapitalization options smooth the impact of changes in asset value on equity.

2.4 Policy Parameters

We now turn to the problem at hand and assume that the central bank and the shareholder negotiate the capital policy by setting the key parameters of the dividend option and the recapitalization option. Negotiations can help align the interests of the central bank with those of the government and the public. After all, central bank capital comprises public funds.[9]

In our setting, this means that the central bank and the government agree on a particular set of policy parameters for the dividend and recapitalization policy $\{\kappa_C, \kappa_\Pi\}$. We are therefore interested in how the values of the dividend option and the recapitalization option change with respect to these key policy design parameters.

Intuitively, a higher strike, κ_C, lowers the price of the call option as it raises the probability that the call will expire worthless and the shareholder will receive no dividend. Similarly, a higher strike of the put, κ_Π, increases the chances of recapitalization, so it increases the value of the put. Mathematically, we can show this by evaluating the first derivatives of the option values with respect to the strike parameters as follows (cf. Annex A.3 for details):

$$\begin{aligned} C_{\kappa_C} &\equiv \frac{\partial C_t}{\partial \kappa_C} = -N(d_{2,C})L_t^* < 0; \\ \Pi_{\kappa_\Pi} &\equiv \frac{\partial \Pi}{\partial \kappa_\Pi} = (\kappa_\Pi - 1)L_t^* N(-d_{2,\Pi})\frac{\partial d_{2,\Pi}}{\partial \kappa_\Pi} > 0 \text{ for } \kappa_\Pi < 1. \end{aligned} \tag{16}$$

3 Equilibrium Capital Policy: Theory

So far, we have treated the two main policy parameters, the strike price or threshold of the dividend payment option, κ_C, and the strike price of the recapitalization option, κ_Π, which together govern the capital policy, as given. Now, we turn to the

[9] In a broader context, the government, as a shareholder, may seek to ensure that the central bank's policies regarding dividends and recapitalization are in line with economic goals and fiscal responsibilities.

problem of setting these two parameters. For that, we will rely on a bargaining game. First, we examine the payoffs and objectives of the central bank and the shareholder as functions of the dividend and recapitalization thresholds. Second, we establish a number of constraints that the two thresholds need to satisfy. Third, we provide the equilibrium solution in the form of a Stackelberg game to coordinate the actions of the shareholder and the central bank.

3.1 Payoffs and Objectives

When analyzing payoffs and objectives, it is clear that any transfers between the central bank and the shareholder represent a reallocation of existing assets and are therefore a zero-sum game in valuation terms. However, the assets may serve different purposes for each entity, with the central bank needing capital for effective implementation of monetary policy and independence and the government seeking revenue for public expenditures.

To simplify the analysis, we assume that both the central bank and the shareholder are risk neutral, implying that agents do not require additional compensation for taking risk and only care about maximizing their expected payoff. This enables us to sidestep the conversation about the degree of risk aversion exhibited by each agent, and our estimates will ultimately be unaffected by the quantification of risk premiums.

The central bank's payoff at the end of the period will be a function of the accumulated buffers, net of any dividends paid out to the shareholder in good states of the world and net of any recapitalization funds received in bad states of the world. In that sense, it is equivalent to the value of central bank equity defined in Eq. (10). Since the choice of the policy parameters governs the value of the contingent transfers from and to the central bank, this payoff can be written as a function of κ_C and κ_Π. With risk neutrality in mind, the beginning of period discounted expected payoff becomes

$$\rho_{CB}(\kappa_C, \kappa_\Pi) \equiv B_t + \Pi_t - C_t. \tag{17}$$

The central bank prefers to have a high strike price for the dividend option and also a high strike price for the recapitalization option. This is illustrated in Fig. 3 by the arrows in the bottom-left corner. Technically, this follows from the central bank's objective function which is increasing in both strike prices, as we have that

$$\frac{\partial \rho_{CB}}{\partial \kappa_C} = -C_{t,\kappa_C} > 0$$
$$\frac{\partial \rho_{CB}}{\partial \kappa_\Pi} = \Pi_{t,\kappa_\Pi} > 0,$$

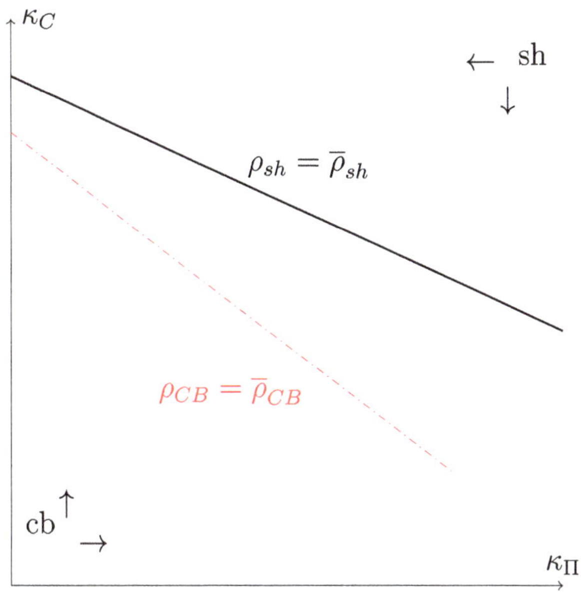

Fig. 3 Indifference curves in terms of policy parameters κ_Π and κ_C

where C_{t,κ_C} and Π_{t,κ_Π} are the partial derivatives defined in Eq. (16) of the call and put pricing functions.

To illustrate the trade-offs between the dividend payment and recapitalization thresholds, we conceptualize the idea of an *indifference curve*. We do that by plotting on a curve the combinations of the two thresholds between which each party, the central bank or respectively the shareholder, is indifferent. In Fig. 3, each line presents the combinations of the policy parameters that deliver a given equity value for the central bank ($\overline{\rho}_{CB}$) and a given payoff for the shareholder ($\overline{\rho}_{sh}$).

Then, we can show that for a fixed payoff level $\overline{\rho}_{CB}$ the indifference curve of the central bank will be downward sloping. Formally, an indifference curve is constructed by finding the marginal change in κ_C compensated by a corresponding change in κ_Π that leaves the payoff of the corresponding party fixed. Mathematically, we have

$$
\begin{aligned}
d\rho_{CB} &= \frac{\partial \rho_{CB}}{\partial \kappa_C} d\kappa_C + \frac{\partial \rho_{CB}}{\partial \kappa_\Pi} d\kappa_\Pi = 0 \\
\implies \frac{d\kappa_C}{d\kappa_\Pi} &= \left. \frac{\partial \rho_{CB}/\partial \kappa_C}{\partial \rho_{CB}/\partial \kappa_\Pi} \right|_{\rho_{CB}=\overline{\rho}_{CB}} < 0.
\end{aligned}
$$

Similarly, the shareholder's profit function at time t is defined by the value of the call option on the central bank's assets, net of the value of the recapitalization put

$$\rho_{sh}(\kappa_C, \kappa_\Pi) = C_t - \Pi_t. \tag{18}$$

Again, we can show that the period t value of the shareholder payoff is decreasing in both strike levels, as we have that $\frac{\partial \rho_{sh}}{\partial \kappa_C} < 0$ and $\frac{\partial \rho_{sh}}{\partial \kappa_\Pi} < 0$. Consequently, the slope of the indifference curve for the shareholder will also be negative, as illustrated with the red dashed line in Fig. 3. In optimizing its payoff, the shareholder will aim to shift its indifference curve down and to the left. In other words, the central bank will try to maximize the strike levels of the two options, while the shareholder, mirroring the central bank's objective, will try to minimize them.

3.2 *Central Bank and Shareholder Constraints*

Before the central bank and the shareholder can negotiate and decide on the capital policy, they need to factor in that the choice of the policy parameters $\{\kappa_C, \kappa_\Pi\}$ is restricted in practice. We therefore define the domain of admissible values for the central bank's equity. There are four main dynamics that determine this domain.

3.2.1 The Central Bank's Credibility Constraint at the Start of the Policy Period

First, the central bank should ex ante be adequately financed to function as a credible and effective monetary authority (Bolt et al., 2024). This means that a central bank can have negative equity, but it should have a minimum amount of assets relative to its liabilities. We define η as a proportion of the central bank's liabilities as this implicit distress boundary beyond which the policy objectives of the central bank are jeopardized. Then, we can write formally the lower bound condition on the central bank equity as

$$B_t + \Pi_t - C_t \geq \eta L_t. \tag{19}$$

It is generally understood that a central bank can continue to operate with negative equity as long as credible fiscal support is in place. Therefore, for the purposes of our analysis going forward, we assume that $\eta < 0$.

In the context of our paper, we assume that the distress boundary η is known and fixed. In practice, it is likely to be determined by factors such as the perceived ability of the central bank to maintain inflation and economic stability, policy consistency, transparency, and independence from political interference. To abstract away from any dynamics beyond the scope of this chapter, we refrain from theorizing the foundations of η and accept the existence of a lower bound as given. Nevertheless, the literature offers various approaches to defining the point at which a central bank breaks, a situation of policy insolvency. Bolt et al. (2024) use a global games approach to determine the point in terms of economic fundamentals at which public trust in the currency backed up by the central bank is undermined. Reis (2013, 2015b) discusses different types of central bank insolvency in terms of the resource constraint that a central bank faces and its ability to generate seigniorage over time balanced by the limit on money demand from the public. The inverse relationship between money demand and inflation induces a Laffer-type curve with a maximum level of acceptable inflation, beyond which the public will reduce its money holdings, thus refusing to fund the central bank (Cagan, 1956; Easterly et al., 1995).

In our interpretation, the critical threshold for a central bank lies in its ability to uphold its policy objectives, particularly in ensuring price stability. Note, however, that an equilibrium capital policy may suggest the need for earlier recapitalization. To address this nuanced dynamic, we advocate for a separation between the strike price of the recapitalization option (κ_{Π}) and the point where the central bank is no longer credible (η) in the next subsection.

3.2.2 The Central Bank's Credibility Constraint at the End of the Policy Period

Second, the central bank should be adequately financed at the end of the period. To that end we have to ensure that recapitalization is triggered at levels of assets where the central bank is still credible, and not below the credibility threshold η. For the central bank credibility constraint to hold at this trigger point, we must ensure that the level of accounting capital at time T just before recapitalization is such that $B_T = A_T - L_T \geq \eta L_T$. As indicated in Fig. 1, recapitalization is triggered at level of assets $A_T = \kappa_{\Pi} L_T$. This implies

$$\kappa_{\Pi} L_T - L_T \geq \eta L_T$$

or

$$\kappa_{\Pi} \geq \eta + 1. \tag{20}$$

This imposes a lower bound for κ_{Π}, which ensures that given recapitalization, it occurs at a point that can still save the central bank's credibility.[10]

[10] Note that this condition is compatible with Eq. (19)—since the call option in this scenario is worthless, we can write

$$B_T + \Pi_T - C_T \geq \eta L_T.$$

Taking expectations under the risk-neutral measure $\mathbb{Q}$ and discounting both sides at the risk-free rate bring us to Eq. (19).

3.2.3 The Shareholder's Participation Constraint

Third, from the shareholder's point of view, and in order for the capital policy to be enforceable, we need to ensure that the value of the dividend option exceeds the value of the recapitalization option by a minimum amount of θ, scaled by the size of liabilities:

$$C_t - \Pi_t \geq \theta L_t. \tag{21}$$

Take for instance the minimum level $\theta = 0$. This signifies that the shareholder is only willing to support the central bank if the present discounted value of future dividends equals the present discounted value of any recapitalization. A positive θ indicates that the shareholder demands to receive more dividend payments from seigniorage profits than it is prepared to provide in backing.

3.2.4 Additional Threshold Conditions

To complete our set of constraints, we argue that it only makes sense to pay dividends if assets are higher than liabilities ($A_t \geq L_T$). At the same time, it only makes sense to pay dividends to the shareholder in states of the world when the central bank is not being recapitalized. We thus constrain the trigger of the recapitalization option below an asset-liability ratio of 100%. As a result, we have[11]

$$\kappa_C \geq 1 \tag{22}$$

$$\kappa_\Pi \leq 1. \tag{23}$$

Figure 4 combines all the constraints and shows the colored region of feasible combinations of the policy parameters $\{\kappa_\Pi, \kappa_C\}$.

3.3 Equilibrium Solution

Building on the preceding section, we now establish the negotiation dynamics which determine the central bank's capital levels. First, we look at a situation in which one of the two players holds all the decision power over both the recapitalization and

[11] We ignore in Eq. (20) that the credibility constraint holds at time T by construction when the call is exercised. If we relax the assumption that $\eta < 1$, however, we need to make sure also that κ_C does not break the viability constraint in period T when the call is exercised, such that with $A_T > \kappa_C L_T$:

$$A_T - L_T - (A_T - \kappa_C L_T) > \eta L_T.$$

This would then imply a condition $\kappa_C \geq \eta + 1$ which is stricter than $\kappa_C \geq 1$ when η is assumed to be positive.

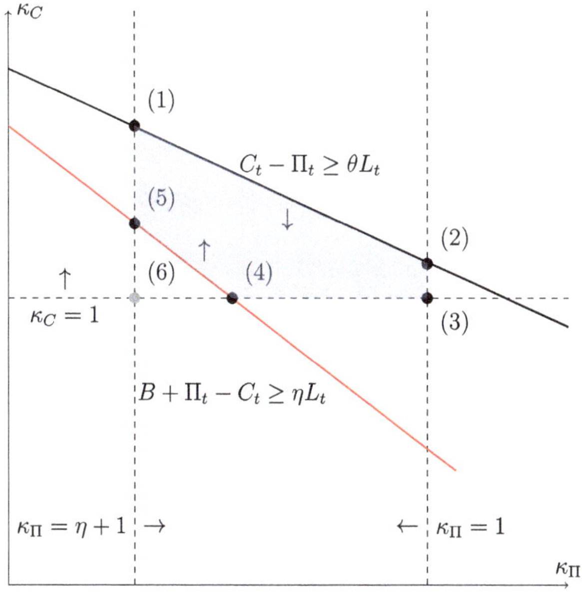

Fig. 4 Constraints and feasible combinations of policy parameters

the dividend payment parameter and the other player complies given its constraints. Then, we look at a situation where the decision of each parameter is allocated to one player, and each player acts strategically in a Stackelberg style leader–follower game-theoretic setting.

3.3.1 One Player Dominates the Decision

First, assume that one player can set both policy parameters. In this scenario, we have two options: Either the central bank possesses all bargaining power and the shareholder must accept the arrangement, or the shareholder sets the parameters to maximize its payoff, and the central bank is required to accept the conditions. Formally, we can write the optimization problem for both cases as

$$\begin{aligned} &\max_{\kappa_C, \kappa_\Pi} \{\rho_i(\kappa_C, \kappa_\Pi)\}, \text{ subject to} \\ &\kappa_C, \kappa_\Pi \in \mathcal{A}, \end{aligned} \tag{24}$$

where $i = \{cb; sh\}$ is the indicator of the payoff function of the player who dominates the decision process with the objectives of the two players being defined as $\rho_{cb} = B_t + \Pi_t - C_t$, while $\rho_{sh} = C_t - \Pi_t$. $\mathcal{A}$ is then the set of feasible outcomes outlined in Sect. 3.2. We now look at the two corner solutions that are possible in terms of negotiation power. For that we look at Fig. 4 that shows the colored area or combinations of the policy parameters $\{\kappa_C, \kappa_\Pi\}$ that the central bank and shareholder can choose from.

First, if the central bank sets both policy parameters, it will aim to decrease the value of the dividend option and to increase the value of the recapitalization option as much as possible. As a result, it will provide a solution that exactly satisfies the shareholder's minimum required payoff, such that $C_t - \Pi_t = \theta L_t$. Substituting this in the central bank's objective function, we get that at the optimum, the payoff of the central bank is $\rho_{cb} = B_t - \theta L_t$. As a result, any combination of κ_c and κ_Π that lies on the shareholder's minimum participation requirement is optimal when it also satisfies the rest of the constraints. So, graphically, the solution is any point between and including points (1) and (2) in Fig. 4.

Second, if instead the shareholder is capable of setting the two policy parameters, it will try to increase the value of the dividend option and reduce the value of the recapitalization option. This means it will set κ_C and κ_Π at any point between (4) and (5) in Fig. 4. On this line segment the central bank can just fulfill its credibility constraint. Note that in this stylized example, we have assumed that the central bank's credibility constraint (the red line in Fig. 4) lies above the point where $\kappa_C = 1$ and $\kappa_\Pi = \eta + 1$. This depends solely on the parameterization of the model. If that is not the case and the central bank credibility constraint is not binding, the shareholder will instead simply pick point (6), setting $\kappa_C = 1$, the lowest possible value, and $\kappa_\Pi = \eta + 1$, the lowest possible recapitalization trigger threshold at which the central bank would still be credible (Cf. Sect. 3.2.2).

In reality, each of the two parties may be unwilling to grant the other the full control over setting the threshold parameters. Therefore, we will see in the next section how the equilibrium changes if instead the rights over each separate policy parameter are split between the two counterparties, such that each player can set one policy parameter in a way that optimizes its payoff.

3.3.2 Each Player Sets One Policy Parameter

In this section, players are endowed with the responsibility of sequentially choosing one policy parameter each, akin to a Stackelberg game. In this strategic setting, the initial player takes the lead by making the first move, operating under the assumption that its decision will be observed and factored into the subsequent moves of the second player. The equilibrium is contingent on the identity of the initial mover and the extent of authority each player wields in determining a specific parameter. The power that the leader has in a Stackelberg game relative to the follower is akin to the power that a counterparty has to set the terms in a negotiation.

The conventional methodology of backward induction can be applied to solve the game. First, we determine the reaction function of the follower with respect to any of the first mover's potential choices. Then, given that reactions are common knowledge, the leader picks out of the follower's reaction function the best choice with respect to his own payoff. In all cases, the players can choose only from the feasible region.

To illustrate, assume that the central banks is a first mover in setting the recapitalization parameter (κ_Π), while the shareholder follows by setting the dividend policy parameter (κ_C). Then, the algorithm that is used to find the equilibrium point can be separated into two main steps: First we solve the follower's optimal problem (in this case the shareholder) and then solve the leader's optimization. We can formalize this as:

1. First, based on any κ_Π within the reach of the central bank, we find the optimal choice of κ_C for the shareholder. This provides the shareholder's optimal reaction function which we denote as $\tilde{\kappa_C}(\kappa_\Pi)$. The function represents the choice of κ_C, which maximizes the shareholder's payoff function, given a κ_Π. Mathematically, this is the solution of the following optimization

$$\tilde{\kappa}_C(\kappa_\Pi) = \arg\max_{\kappa_C \in \mathcal{A}} \rho_{sh}(\kappa_C, \kappa_\Pi).$$

2. Then, given the shareholder's reaction function, we derive the leader's optimal choice, i.e., the κ_Π which maximizes its payoff, given that the shareholder picks κ_C according to the reaction function established in the previous step. Formally, this is

$$\tilde{\kappa}_\Pi = \arg\max_{\kappa_\Pi \in \mathcal{A}} \rho_{cb}(\tilde{\kappa}_C(\kappa_\Pi), \kappa_\Pi).$$

The final equilibrium is then the point $\{\tilde{\kappa}_\Pi, \tilde{\kappa}_C(\tilde{\kappa}_\Pi)\}$.

The same algorithm can also be used in the other cases, simply adjusting the payoff functions and the leader and the follower, and adjusting the decision parameter over which each party has control. Using this approach, we can now distinguish a number of settings for the Stackelberg game. The equilibrium solution will depend on which party is the first mover and which party has authority over which of the two decision parameters:

- The central bank is the first mover and sets the policy parameter for recapitalization, (κ_Π), with the idea that the shareholder will choose the dividend policy parameter, denoted as κ_C, optimally in response. There are two steps in this procedure. First, we determine the reaction function of the shareholder, who will choose the lowest feasible value for κ_C when confronted with κ_Π by the central bank. The solid black line segments on the lower left edge of the feasible region in Fig. 5a illustrate this reaction function. Second, with the knowledge of this reaction function, the optimal choice for the central bank as a first mover is to choose κ_Π at the level of solution point (3).
- The shareholder is the first mover and sets κ_Π. Then the central bank will set the dividend policy parameter κ_C optimally as a response. Again, we can find the equilibrium solution through backward induction. First, we determine the reaction function of the second mover, the central bank, which gives $\kappa_C(\kappa_\Pi)$. In Fig. 5b this is the black line between points (1) and (2), which provides the optimal response of the central bank for any potential choice of κ_Π by the

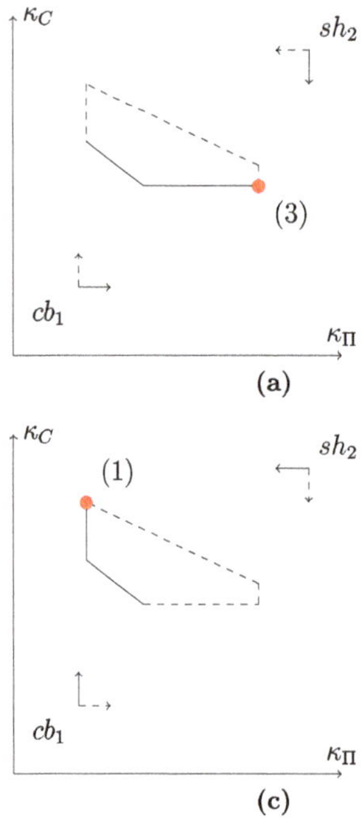

Fig. 5 Stackelberg solutions. *Note*. This set of figures shows the reaction function of the second mover and the equilibrium in the Stackelberg game. The subscripts indicate whether the party is a first or a second mover. The arrows indicate the direction in which the player wants to move the two parameters of the game, with the solid arrow indicating the variable over which the player has decision power

shareholder. Now, determining the optimal κ_Π by the shareholder, it is important to remember that the line segment (1) to (2) actually lies on a shareholder indifference curve (Cf. Sect. 4.1). This means that the shareholder will be indifferent between any point on the reaction function of the central bank, so the equilibrium outcome is any point on the line segment between (1) and (2).

- The central bank is the first mover to set κ_C with the knowledge that the shareholder will set κ_Π optimally as a response. The reaction function of the second mover $\kappa_\Pi(\kappa_C)$ consists of the solid black line segments representing the lower-right edge of the feasible region in Fig. 5c. Then the optimal choice for the central bank is choosing κ_C at the level of point (1), which indicates the equilibrium.
- The shareholder sets κ_C first, and the central bank optimally sets κ_Π as a response. The reaction function of the second mover consists of the solid black line segments on the upper-right edge of the feasible region in Fig. 5d. With the knowledge of the reaction function, the shareholder picks the highest feasible value for κ_Π, and the equilibrium is at point (3).

Table 3 Stackelberg equilibrium combinations

First mover	Central bank (CB)		Shareholder (SH)	
Who sets which policy				
– Dividend policy	SH	CB	SH	CB
– Recapitalization policy	CB	SH	CB	SH
Equilibrium impact on thresholds				
– Dividend payment threshold	Lower	Higher	Lower	Higher
– Recapitalization threshold	Higher	Lower	Higher	Higher
Equilibrium point	(3)	(1)	(3)	(1) to (2)

Table 3 summarizes all possible equilibria. As illustrated, what is more important in the process of setting the recapitalization conditions is not so much which party moves first in the game, but rather how the decision rights over the policy parameters are allocated. If the central bank has power over the dividend policy (κ_C), the equilibrium ends up with a relatively low level of the capitalization threshold (top left on Figs. 5b and d) and a relatively high value of the dividend threshold. In economic terms, this means that the central bank does not have much protection against negative buffers as the recapitalization option is less likely to be exercised. However, it can also accumulate a high capital without paying dividends to the shareholder, as the dividend option is also less likely to be triggered.

In contrast, if the central bank has the power over the recapitalization policy (κ_Π), the equilibrium has a relatively high recapitalization threshold and low dividend threshold (bottom-right in Figs. 5a and d). In that case, the central bank has better protection against negative buffers as the recapitalization option is more likely to be triggered. However, it is also more likely to pay dividend to the shareholder. Moreover, at the equilibrium point (3) in Fig. 4, we have that $\kappa_\Pi = \kappa_C = 1$. In this case, the position of the shareholder in the recapitalization is similar to a long position in the net assets of the central bank: Any positive buffers are paid out to the shareholder, and any negative buffers are recapitalized. One can also see that through the put–call parity: The payoff for the shareholder becomes $C_t - \Pi_t = A_t - L_t^*$.

3.4 *Risk-Shifting Implications*

The setting presented so far enables us to assess how risks are distributed between the central bank and its shareholder. An intriguing question arises: Once the capital thresholds are set, and abstracting from policy objectives, does the central bank have an incentive to take more risk onto its balance sheet, thereby transferring risk toward the shareholder, who ultimately provides the downside protection? Similarly, does a central bank have an incentive to reduce risk taking to limit the upside dividend potential for the shareholder?

To study the risk-shifting implications, we look at how the economic value of equity changes when the share of risky assets on its balance sheet increases. Notably, the central bank has the authority to determine the risk profile of its assets by engaging in purchase programs rather than traditional lending operations. In our model this is captured through the weight of risky assets (ω). We can then examine this question by looking at how equity value changes through the repricing of the dividend and recapitalization options, when the share of risky assets changes.

In option pricing, the sensitivity to risk is commonly referred to as "vega" and can be evaluated through the partial derivatives of the Black–Scholes option valuation functions. We can thus show that for a given strike level, the vega for both the call and put options is given by

$$\nu_t = \frac{\partial C_t}{\partial(\omega\sigma)} = \frac{\partial \Pi_t}{\partial(\omega\sigma)} = A_t\sqrt{T-t}N'(d_{1,i}) > 0 \tag{25}$$

with $i = \{C, \Pi\}$ being an indicator for the call or the put option.[12]

To analyze this, note that the values of the dividend and the recapitalization options are increasing in the asset's return volatility, which is determined by the share of risky assets ω. Intuitively, a higher share of risky assets increases the asset return volatility on the balance sheet of the central bank, which increases the likelihood that one of the two options will be exercised. Furthermore, in Fig. 6a, we show how vega for the call and put options in our model changes as a function of how deep in the money each of the options is.[13] In our setting, the moneyness, or how close the assets currently are to the strike parameters, is determined by the value of capital B_t, the "underlying." It follows from the figure that the vega is nonlinear in the underlying, and in each case it peaks at the corresponding strike. As the strike of the put option is lower than the strike of the call (by construction the recapitalization threshold is lower than the dividend payment threshold), the call vega is shifted to the right. This implies that with high central bank capitalization the dividend payment option is close to or in the money and will be more sensitive to risk than the recapitalization option, which in that case is out of the money. The opposite happens for an undercapitalized bank.

Going back to our original question, we can evaluate the sensitivity of the equity value to changes in ω as:

$$\frac{\partial E_t}{\partial(\omega\sigma)} = -\frac{\partial C_t}{\partial(\omega\sigma)} + \frac{\partial \Pi_t}{\partial(\omega\sigma)}.$$

[12] Strictly speaking, the vega is defined as the partial derivative of the option value with respect to σ in the literature. The ω and σ in our setting, however, are multiples of each other, and ω governs the degree of risk that the central bank takes.

[13] See Annex A.1 for details on the model calibration.

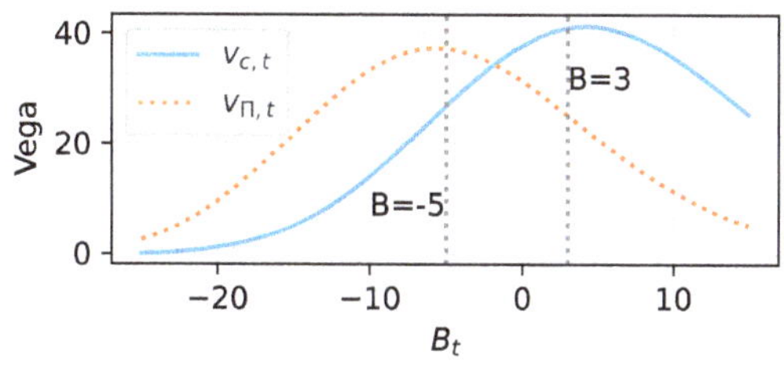

(a) Vega

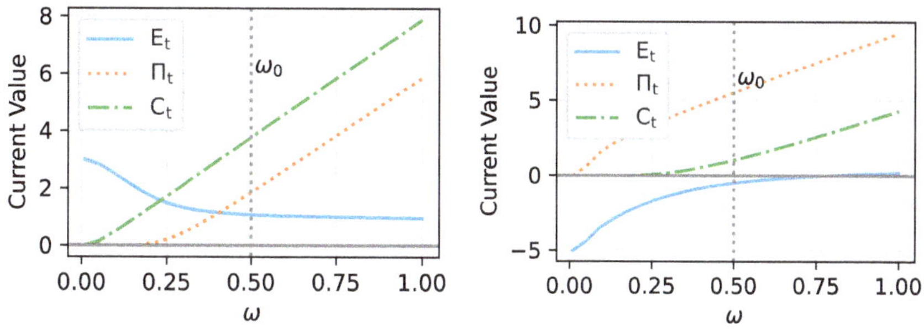

(b) Equity value for $B_t/L_t = 3\%$ (c) Equity value for $B_t/L_t = -5\%$

Fig. 6 Option and equity value as a function of risk. *Note.* This set of figures shows the value of the embedded call and put options in the implied balance sheet of the central bank, and the value of the implied equity, as a function of the share of risky assets, holding everything else fixed. (**a**) shows the situation for a well-capitalized bank with an initial accounting capital of $B_t = 3$; (**b**) shows an undercapitalized bank with an accounting capital of $B_t = -5$; (**c**) shows the vegas of the two options given $\kappa_\Pi < \kappa_C$

We then identify two separate situations graphically outlined in Fig. 6a through the two bell-shaped curves representing the vegas of the embedded call and put options. First, assuming that the central bank is well capitalized (in this example with capital $B_t = 3$), the recapitalization option (the put) will be further out of the money than the dividend payment option (the call). As a result, the call's vega will dominate over the put's vega. The result is shown in Fig. 6b, where we show the impact of changing the risk profile for a well-capitalized central bank. In this case increasing the assets' risk profile by investing more in risky assets increases the value of the call option (dashed curve) more than value of the put option (dotted line) and thus reduces the equity value. Ergo, the central bank has no incentive to shift risks toward the shareholder.

However, if the central bank is undercapitalized ($B_t = -5$), as illustrated in Fig. 6c, the recapitalization option will be closer to at-the-money, and the value of the put will increase faster with the level of asset risk than that of the call. As a result, in that case, the central bank would be able to increase the value of its equity by taking more risk.

On an intuitive level, when considering a central bank with ample capital reserves, an increase in asset risk tends to raise the probability of distributing dividends more significantly than the likelihood of requiring recapitalization. Conversely, an undercapitalized central bank exhibits the opposite effect: Heightened asset risk increases the chances of breaching the recapitalization threshold and necessitating an infusion from its shareholder. Consequently, overly capitalized central banks may not fully utilize the expansion of their balance sheets, such as through an Asset Purchase Program, as any surplus generated must be allocated to shareholder payouts. Conversely, undercapitalized central banks might find advantages in assuming higher risk levels due to the potential value associated with the recapitalization option.

This suggests that without adequate institutional frameworks in place, a central bank operating with insufficient capital might be inclined to respond excessively to its policy objectives, banking on the assurance of a shareholder bailout. Conversely, an excessively capitalized central bank might be tempted to be too conservative in its actions, and aware that any surplus during prosperous periods would mostly benefit the shareholder.

As the central bank has authority over the composition of the assets on its balance sheet and can take on financial risk through the use of outright asset purchases, our findings stress the importance of sound risk management practices. More broadly, while the central bank is entitled to operational independence from the shareholder for optimally achieving its policy objectives, we highlight the need for democratic accountability and transparency in justifying the choice of tools which may potentially exhaust its capital. In the short term, the central bank functions autonomously from the government to pursue its monetary policy goals. However, in the long run, the government exercises control over the central bank's operations and role through its authority to appoint board members and enact legal or statutory amendments (Wessels & Broeders, 2023).

Note that potential risk shifting is not inherently contradictory to the central bank's mandate. For example, macroeconomic factors may compel a central bank to pursue unconventional monetary policy decisions regardless of its capital position. This effectively transfers risk from the central bank's capital to its shareholder. Moreover, any undesirable risk-shifting incentives that are not welfare-improving are likely to be tempered in the presence of well-functioning institutions which ensure central bank accountability. For the sake of brevity and clarity in this chapter, we defer the modeling of this penalty to future work.

4 Equilibrium Capital Policy: Numerical Evaluation

Now that we have outlined the main features of the model, we proceed to evaluate numerically the equilibrium solution for the capital policy under the initial conditions outlined in Annex A.1. In the following sections we first look at the properties of the payoff functions of the two players in the model and outline the feasible region they face. We then solve numerically for the equilibrium capital structure of the central bank using the backward induction approach outlined earlier. Finally, we verify the sensitivity of the solution to variations in the participation threshold of the central bank, and to the central bank's initial capital buffers.

4.1 Indifference Curves

We defined in Sect. 4.1 the payoff functions of each counterparty in the model. Figure 7 shows the indifference curves for the central bank and the shareholder. Each line presents combinations of the policy parameters that deliver a given equity value for the central bank (Fig. 7a) and a given payoff for the shareholder (Fig. 7b). The numbers along the lines represent the payoff along each indifference curve based on the given calibration. As we indicated analytically earlier, we can verify quantitatively here that the central bank will aim to move in a north–west direction, while the shareholder will move east–south to maximize its payoff.

4.2 Feasible Region for the Policy Parameters

In Fig. 8 we plot the feasibility region in terms of combinations of the policy parameters $\{\kappa_C, \kappa_\Pi\}$ for the model calibration in Annex A.1. In Panel (a) we assume that the central bank has an initial accounting capital B_t equal to 3% of the current liabilities. This is consistent with a central bank that is relatively well capitalized and potentially close to the dividend payment region.

The central bank's credibility condition is given by the blue line. All combinations of $\{\kappa_C, \kappa_\Pi\}$ that are on or above this curve satisfy this constraint.

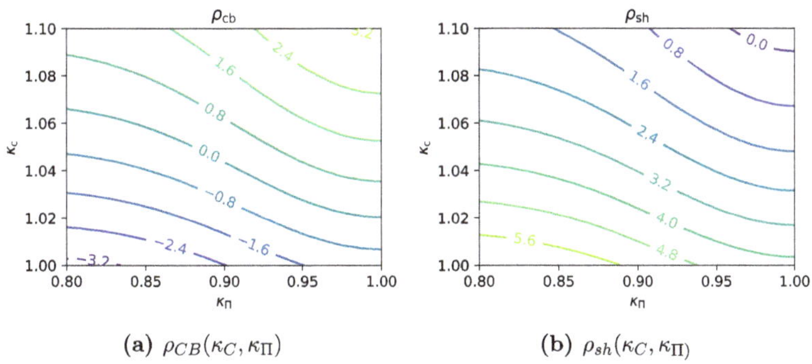

(a) $\rho_{CB}(\kappa_C, \kappa_\Pi)$ (b) $\rho_{sh}(\kappa_C, \kappa_\Pi)$

Fig. 7 Indifference curves. *Note*. This set of figures shows the indifference curves underlying the risk-neutral objective functions of the central bank and shareholder risk-neutral objective curves

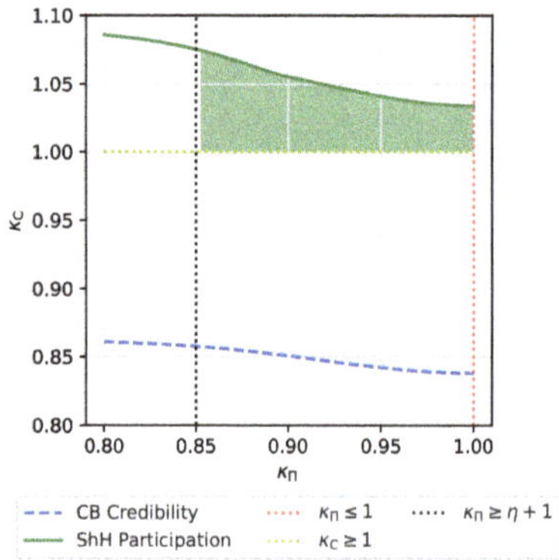

(a) $B_t/L_t = 3\%$

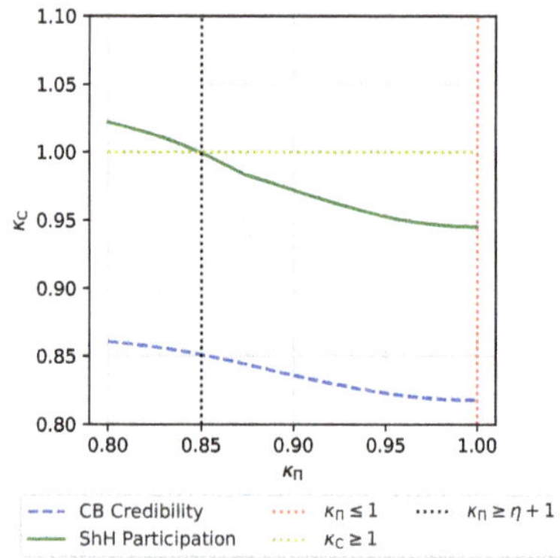

(b) $B_t/L_t = -2\%$

Fig. 8 Feasible region. *Note*. This set of figures shows the feasible region (shaded area) with (**a**) positive buffers; and (**b**) negative buffers, holding everything else fixed

The shareholder's participation constraint is given by the solid green curve. All combinations of $\{\kappa_C, \kappa_\Pi\}$ that are on or below this curve satisfy the participation constraint. Further, the constraint that the central bank only pays dividends if assets are higher than liabilities ($\kappa_C \geq 1$) is given by the green dotted line, and the constraint that the central bank only pays dividends when it is not being recapitalized ($\kappa_C \geq \kappa_\Pi$) is given by the red dotted line. The feasible region is now given by the green area. Note that the central bank's credibility condition is not affecting the feasible region.

In Panel (b) we assume a lower capital B_t equal to -2% of liabilities. Lower capital shifts down the shareholder's participation constraint (the solid green curve). This occurs as, ceteris paribus, lower buffers make the put option held by the central bank more expensive. In order to compensate, the shareholder would demand lower strikes for the call and/or the put in order to get back to its reservation value set in Eq. (19) by θL_t. In this case, the curve is shifted down so much that the feasible region is a single point at $\kappa_C = 1$ and $\kappa_\Pi = 0.85$.

4.3 Equilibrium

Figure 9 illustrates the solution of the Stackelberg game. We examine in particular the setting which is most in line with central bank independence: The central bank is the first mover, and it has the authority to set the recapitalization threshold, κ_Π. In response, the shareholder sets an optimal threshold for paying dividends, κ_C. As outlined in Sect. 3.2, there are no informational frictions between the two counterparties, so in setting κ_Π the central bank already anticipates the optimal reaction function of the shareholder.

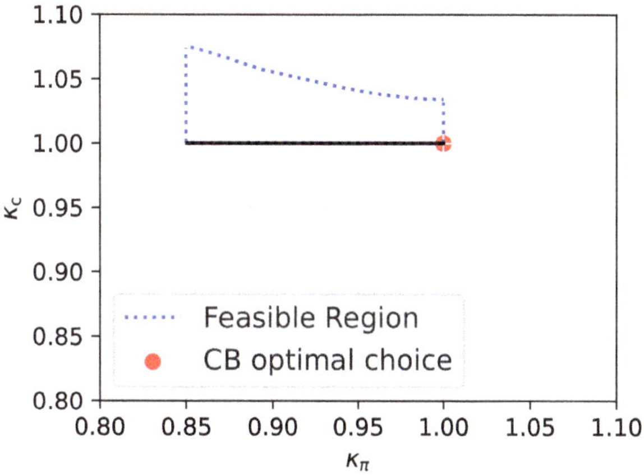

Fig. 9 Stackelberg equilibrium solution. *Note*. This figure shows the edge of the feasible region (dotted), the optimal reaction function of the shareholder as a Stackelberg follower (solid line), and the final optimal solution with the central bank being a Stackelberg leader (single dot)

Under this arrangement, we find that the shareholder will stick to a demand of keeping the dividend payment threshold at 100% of the assets. In equilibrium, then, the central bank will also demand that it is recapitalized if liabilities fall below 100%.

4.4 Sensitivity Analyses

The equilibrium is influenced by many factors. In the following subsection, we look at how the equilibrium capital policy changes when some of the key input parameters are varied. The game setting is again in line with the arrangement discussed in Sect. 4.3.

First, we evaluate the sensitivity of the solution to the participation threshold θ, a parameter which is not directly observable in reality. At the same time, it shifts the shareholder's participation constraint and thus can affect the equilibrium results. A higher θ implies a stronger position of the shareholder, and thus a stricter participation constraint. In that case, as the shareholder becomes stronger, its participation curve (cf. Fig. 4) will shift down, demanding more value from the call option or less value from the put option, or equivalently lower strikes for each of the options. As a result, the feasible region shrinks, and the central bank is left with fewer options to move the solution point to the utmost right direction in the κ_C region. As the lowest possible value for κ_C is fixed at 100%, the central bank can only agree to reduce the value of the strike if that becomes needed. Figure 10a then shows the equilibrium solutions for the two parameters. As θ increases, at some point the shareholder and the central bank will agree on a κ_Π that will be below

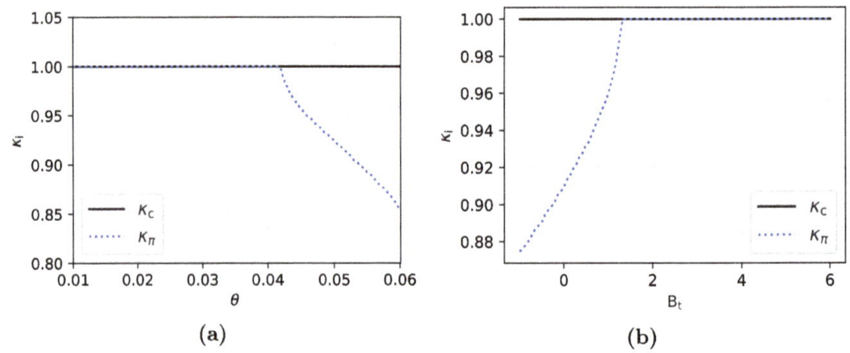

Fig. 10 Stackelberg equilibrium (CB chooses first). *Note*. This set of figures shows that a stricter shareholder's participation constraint affects the choice of optimal recapitalization and dividend payment thresholds. In this game, the central bank moves first, picking the optimal value of κ_Π. In the first chart, we vary θ; in the second, we vary the current level of buffers

100%. If θ increases further, there may be no solution left in the feasible region, leaving the two parties without agreement.

Second, we can evaluate, under the same setting, the impact of the initial capital B_t on the Stackelberg equilibrium. As indicated in Sect. 4.2, higher B_t shifts down the shareholder participation curve. Then, as soon as it becomes a binding constraint, the equilibrium condition will also change as indicated in Fig. 10b. Since κ_C is at its minimum possible value of 100% already, it does not change.

5 Policy Evaluation

In this chapter, we present a generalization of the capital policy. In practice, central banks around the world have heterogeneous capital policies. In this section, we first discuss four cases and show how they fit into our model: the Federal Reserve System (Fed); the Bank of England (BoE); Sveriges Riksbank; and De Nederlandsche Bank (DNB). Next, we consider the policy implications of recapitalization.

5.1 Capital Policies in Practice

We begin by considering the **Fed**. Recapitalization is not explicitly a component of the legislative framework established with the US Treasury. There is, however, a ceiling to the surplus that the Fed can hold.[14] The Fed's income statement presents these cumulative payments to the US Treasury as "*Earnings remittances to the Treasury*." In practice, these remittances are paid weekly, and the annual report states the sum of all weekly payments over the year. If earnings are not sufficient to provide for the cost of operations, payment of dividends, and maintaining a surplus, negative remittances will be booked in the Fed's balance sheet as a deferred asset.[15] The deferred asset position will be reduced and eventually cancelled out by future earning remittances. The working assumption of this framework is that the net present value of future remittances to the US Treasury is positive through the Fed's seigniorage income and will at some point offset the deferred asset.

The **BoE**, on the other hand, has an explicit memorandum of understanding with its shareholder, the UK Treasury, which sets a capital target level of GBP 3.5 billion, which is deemed sufficient to allow the BoE to perform its monetary policy and financial stability functions. Similarly to our stylized setting presented earlier, the BoE memorandum establishes a floor and a ceiling level of capital (GBP 0.5 billion and GBP 5.5 billion, respectively). If the BoE's capital falls below the floor, the UK Treasury is committed to providing capital injections. At the same time, a flexible dividend-sharing arrangement is established, which states that when capital falls below the target, but remains above the floor, the BoE retains any net income completely. When the capital is above the target, but below the ceiling, half of the net income is retained and half is distributed to the UK Treasury. When the capital is above the ceiling, the net income is completely transferred to the UK Treasury (Bank of England, 2018).

The floor and ceiling framework established by the BoE is captured very well by our setting presented in Sect. 2. In fact, using the notation of our model, we can combine the value of the central bank liabilities as of 2023 and the size of the floor to establish that[16]

$$\kappa_\Pi = \frac{\text{Floor} + L_T}{L_T} = \frac{0.5 + 1070}{1070} = 1.0005.$$

Similarly, we can derive the strike price of the dividend option, κ_C, from the ceiling capital:

$$\kappa_C = \frac{\text{Ceiling} + L_T}{L_T} = \frac{5.5 + 1,070}{1,070} = 1.005.$$

[14] "*The Federal Reserve Act requires that aggregate Federal Reserve Bank surplus does not exceed a cap. After providing for the costs of operations, payment of dividends, and the amount necessary to maintain the surplus cap, any residual net earnings will be remitted to the US Treasury*." Cf. Federal Reserve Board (2024).

[15] See, for example, Table 6 in Federal Reserve Board (2023).

[16] Remember that the put option is triggered at $\underline{A}_T = \kappa_\Pi L_T$. We can then derive the strike price of the recapitalization option, κ_Π, by noting that the recapitalization threshold value of assets, $\underline{A}_T$, is the sum of BoE floor capital and the value of liabilities.

Similarly, **Sveriges Riksbank** has an explicit capital framework in place specifying the rules for recapitalization. Effective from 2023, the Sveriges Riksbank Act sets a target level for its capital at the level SEK 60 billion and a baseline at SEK 40 billion. The target level of SEK 60 billion is intended as an appropriate upper limit and is adjusted upward by inflation each year.

Furthermore, the Act requires the Riksbank to petition the Swedish parliament for capital restoration through recapitalization if it falls below a minimum threshold of SEK 20 billion. This means that in years in which the Riksbank reports capital lower than the target level, any profit shall be retained to replenish it. In years in which the Riksbank reports capital above the target level, part of the profit is retained to adjust the target capital to inflation growth, but the excess profit is distributed to the state. If the capital falls below the minimum threshold, the Riksbank is obliged to request recapitalization from the state. While the act also foresees certain exceptions to this general rule, in principle, the state then has to restore capital up to the baseline level (Sveriges Riksbank, 2023).

Again, we can easily map the Riksbank's capital framework onto our stylized model. Using 2022 annual report data leads to $\kappa_\Pi = \frac{20+1,437}{1,437} = 1.01$. By setting the target capital as the threshold for dividend payouts, we obtain $\kappa_C = \frac{60+1,437}{1,437} = 1.04$.

DNB also has an explicit capital policy in place with target capital of EUR 9.4 billion, which is also linked to GDP and grows yearly by 3.9%. The annual growth rate is revised every five years and currently represents a ten-year moving average of the growth rate of Dutch GDP. There is no explicit recapitalization level. There are, however, two relevant floors: First, dividend payments are forbidden if capital falls below EUR 0.5 billion (the issued capital); second, EU legislation mandates that Member States must ensure their national central banks maintain sufficient financial resources and adequate "net equity" to fulfill their duties. Net equity encompasses various elements, including capital, the general reserve fund, revaluation accounts, any accumulated losses from previous periods, and any profit or loss for the current year. Should the net equity fall below the statutory capital or even turn negative, government intervention is required to inject the central bank with capital, ensuring that it reaches at least the level of statutory capital within a reasonable period of time. Using DNB's 2022 target capital as the threshold above which dividends can be paid in full, we obtain $\kappa_C = \frac{9.4+480}{480} = 1.0195$. κ_Π can be approximated by assuming that recapitalization would occur if capital falls below the issued capital. In this case, using 2022 annual report data, we obtain $\kappa_\Pi = \frac{0.5+480}{480} = 1.001$.

Table 4 provides an overview of these capital policies and the actual positions with recent annual report data. For the BoE, Sveriges Riksbank, and DNB, the put option is out of the money, as κ_Π is below the ratio (A_t/L_t), indicating that recapitalization conditions are not yet met. However, in the case of Sveriges Riksbank, this is only the case because the government already provided recapitalization at the end of 2022. On the other hand, the call option is in the money for the BoE, as κ_C is just below the ratio (A_t/L_t). The call option is also in the money for Sveriges Riksbank, although this is a mechanical consequence of the capital injection from

Table 4 Different central banks' capital policies at the end of 2022

Central bank	Imposed strike put option (κ_Π)	Imposed strike call option (κ_C)	Actual position (A_t/L_t)
Federal Reserve	1.0*	1.0*	1.049
Bank of England	1.0005	1.005	1.0051
Sveriges Riksbank	1.01	1.04	1.0435
De Nederlandsche Bank	1.001	1.0195	1.0177

Notes: All numbers in the table are based on figures from the annual reports of the central banks, or official documentation describing the agreement between the shareholder and the central banks. *In the case of the Federal Reserve, the thresholds are implicit because dividend payments occur nearly continuously, and recapitalization automatically takes place through the creation of deferred assets on the balance sheet

the government. In practice no dividend has been paid in 2022. The call option is out of the money for DNB, as κ_C is above the ratio (A_t/L_t), so DNB did not pay any dividend in 2022. We need to be aware, however, that comparing central banks is not straightforward, as they may be subject to different accounting rules governing the way assets and liabilities are valued.

5.2 *Recapitalization*

Although we do not explicitly model this, it is important to know how recapitalization works in practice. In the event that a central bank experiences losses surpassing its capital, it will initially reflect either a negative capital on the liability side or a positive loss carried forward on the asset side of its balance sheet (Buiter, 2024). Both scenarios essentially signify a claim of the central bank on the government, assuming the government is the sole owner of the central bank.

Subsequently, two options become available. First, the government can directly inject funds into the central bank to settle the claim immediately. The simplest method for recapitalizing a central bank involves transferring a government bond to the central bank in exchange for an equity stake of equal value. This transaction results in an increase in the central bank's balance sheet size. Second, the central bank can record negative equity as deferred assets, also known as losses carried forward. Over time, these losses can be reduced by retaining future profits, effectively recapitalizing the central bank as the government forgoes future dividends.

It should be noted, however, that recapitalizing a central bank through government intervention can yield unintended consequences. First, it may jeopardize the central bank's independence, potentially compromising its ability to make impartial monetary policy decisions. Government influence might prioritize short-term political considerations over long-term economic stability. Second, recapitalization could strain the government's fiscal position, diverting resources from essential public services or exacerbating existing budgetary pressures. Additionally, the terms of the contract between the central bank and the shareholder are likely to resemble a repeated game setting, given that central bank management faces reelection at regular intervals or when governments change. These unintended consequences may discourage the central bank from seeking recapitalization, thereby potentially forgoing the exercise of the put option.

6 Conclusion

This chapter discusses how a central bank manages financial risks through capital as a buffer for risk taking in monetary policy operations. It explores the central bank's capital formation resulting from a risk-sharing arrangement with the government, using an option pricing perspective and the tools from finance. We investigate the trade-offs between dividend payouts in favorable states of the world and recapitalizing the central bank in unfavorable states, deriving equilibrium solutions through Stackelberg games where both parties negotiate optimal dividend and recapitalization policies. The findings of this study have several significant policy implications for central banks and their shareholders, typically governments, in managing financial risks and optimizing their capital policies.

First, understanding central bank capital as a result of a risk-sharing arrangement emphasizes the importance of effective risk management strategies. Policymakers should carefully evaluate the trade-offs associated with paying dividends during prosperous periods and holding recapitalization options for challenging economic states. This awareness can guide the formulation of robust risk-sharing agreements that strike an optimal balance between risk absorption and financial stability.

Second, we document the risk incentives embedded in the balance sheet of central banks. In accordance with option pricing theory, we observe that the value of both the dividend payment and recapitalization options rises with the level of balance sheet risk. In the context of central banking, risk primarily stems from the proportion of risky assets within monetary portfolios, such as those acquired through an asset purchase program. We find, however, that an increase in risk will have different implications for the value of equity of a well-capitalized versus an undercapitalized central bank. The initial level of buffers determines which of the two options will dominate.

Building on this, our paper also highlights a coordination problem between the central bank and the government. As a next step, we look for the trade-offs and optimal arrangement in which the recapitalization and dividend payment thresholds are set, as a result of a negotiation game. We establish the solution from which neither party has incentives to deviate. From that point of view, coordination is endogenous and is essential in negotiating dividend and recapitalization policies that align with overall economic objectives. Recognizing central bank capital as the result of a dynamic negotiation game, we highlight the ex ante arrangements contingent on changing economic conditions.

The application of the Stackelberg game provides insights into the strategic interactions between central banks and shareholders in setting policy parameters. Policymakers may consider this perspective when formulating policies, acknowledging that each counterparty's decision influences the other's strategy. This strategic awareness can lead to more informed decision-making in negotiations regarding dividend and recapitalization policies.

The framework that we outline is only an initial attempt to handle the recapitalization arrangement between the central bank and the shareholder from a finance point of view. There is ample room for further research that can build on the current paper. First, we recognize that a dynamic version of the model would be able to capture the temporal aspect of the problem, as central banks have the ability to rebuild buffers and vary the size of monetary assets over time through the ability to generate seigniorage. Furthermore, central bank capital can be put within a macro framework that would allow evaluation of the wider welfare implications of different capital policies by also capturing the relationship between inflation, monetary policy, and interest rates through the business cycle.

A Annex

A.1 Calibration

To determine the equity value we apply the calibration given in Table 5. The model horizon, denoted as T, represents the option maturity set at one year. The bank's composition is characterized by banknotes (N), reserves (R_t), and total assets (A_t) with values of 20, 75, and 100, respectively. The accounting capital (B_t) is therefore at 5. The percentage share of the risky asset denoted as ω is set at 50%. The

Table 5 Baseline model calibration

Variable	Notation	Value
Model horizon (option maturity in years)	T	1
Banknotes	N	25
Reserves	R_t	75
Total assets	A_t	103
Accounting capital	B_t	3
Share invested in the risky asset	ω	50%
Standard deviation of the risky asset's return	σ	20%
Risk-free rate	r	5%
Dividend (call) strike multiple	κ_C	1.05
Recapitalization (put) strike multiple	κ_Π	0.95
Shareholder participation threshold	θ	2.5%
Central bank credibility threshold	η	− 15%

standard deviation of the risky asset's return (σ) is specified as 0.2, and the risk-free rate (r) is set at 5%. Additionally, dividend and recapitalization strike multiples for call and put options are set at $\kappa_C = 1.05$ and $\kappa_\Pi = 0.9$, respectively. The shareholder participation threshold (θ) and the central bank credibility threshold (η) are established at 2.5 and -15, providing a comprehensive overview of the model's parameterization.

A.2 Inverse Option Price

In the chapter, we need to solve for the strike multiples κ_Π and κ_C that are optimal with respect to the payoffs of each counterparty given its constraints in terms of the value of the call and put options. For this purpose, it is useful to define the inverse function $C_t^{-1}(x)$ for any $x > 0$. It will provide the strike multiples consistent with a Black and Scholes option call price of x, holding the other parameters in the model fixed. Since the Black and Scholes call and put prices are monotonously decreasing, and increasing, respectively, with respect to the strike multiples, this allows us to define the inverse. We infer the functional form numerically through a root-finding procedure. Figure 11 plots how the inverse option values are derived for certain choices of the option multiples κ_C and κ_Π.

We wrote the condition under which the central bank operates as

$$B_t + \Pi_t - C_t \geq \eta L_t. \tag{26}$$

We need to solve for the strike values. As a result, we need to rewrite the condition in terms of the dividend strike multiple as

$$\begin{aligned} C_t &\leq B_t + \Pi_t - \eta L_t \\ \kappa_C &\geq C_t^{-1}\left(B_t + \Pi_t - \eta L_t\right), \end{aligned}$$

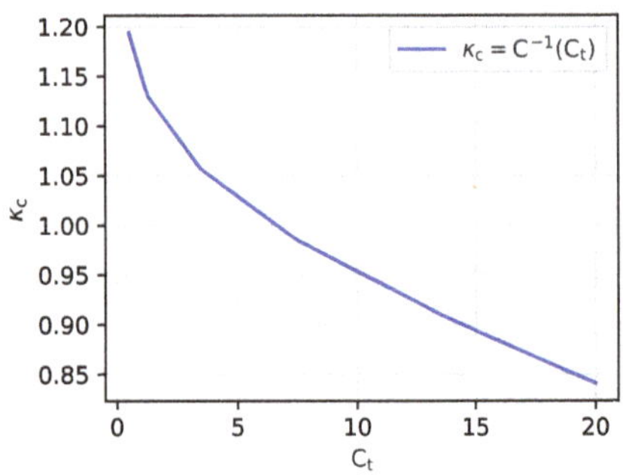

Fig. 11 The inverses option value functions. *Note*. This figure shows the inverse call and put values as function of the strike multiples κ_Π and κ_C using the calibration from Table 5

where the last line follows from the fact that the value of a call option is monotonously decreasing in the strike.

We can find the line at which the above inequalities are binding numerically by examining the inverse Black and Scholes prices.

Similarly, we can rewrite the shareholder's participation constraint in Eq. (21) in terms of the size of the dividend strike multiple

$$\kappa_C \leq C_t^{-1}(\Pi_t + \theta L_t)$$

where we make use of the fact that Π_t is a monotonously increasing function, while C_t is a monotonously decreasing function with respect to its strike. Again, using the numerical procedure outlined earlier, we can find the curve along which the condition is binding.

A.3 *Call and Put Derivatives with Respect to the Strikes*

From the density of the standard normal distribution,

$$N'(x) = \frac{1}{\sqrt{2\pi}} \exp\left(-\frac{1}{2}x^2\right),$$

we can show that $d_{1,i}$ and $d_{2,i}$ from the Black–Scholes formulas in Eq. (12) and Eq. (13) satisfy

$$\begin{aligned}\ln N'(d_{1,i}) - \ln N'(d_{2,i}) &= -\ln \frac{A_t}{\kappa_i L_t^*} \\ \Longrightarrow N'(d_{1,i})A_t &= \kappa_i L_t^* N'(d_{2,i}).\end{aligned}$$

Using this property and the fact that $\frac{\partial d_{1,i}}{\partial \kappa_i} = \frac{\partial d_{2,i}}{\partial \kappa_i}$, we can find the derivative of the call option price in Eq. (12) with respect to the strike multiple as follows:

$$\begin{aligned}\frac{\partial C_t}{\partial \kappa_C} &= -N'(d_{1,C})A_t \frac{\partial d_{1,C}}{\partial \kappa_C} - N'(d_{2,C})\kappa_C L_t^* \frac{\partial d_{2,C}}{\partial \kappa_C} - N(d_{2,C})L_t^* \\ &= \underbrace{\left(N'(d_{1,C})A_t - N'(d_{2,C})\kappa_C L_t^*\right)}_{=0} \frac{\partial d_{1,C}}{\partial \kappa_C} - N(d_{2,C})L_t^* \\ &= -N(d_{2,C})L_t^* < 0.\end{aligned} \tag{27}$$

Similarly we can derive the derivative of the put option price in Eq. (13) with respect to the strike multiple as follows:

$$
\begin{aligned}
\frac{\partial \Pi_t}{\partial \kappa_\Pi} &= -\left(N'(-d_{1,\Pi})A_t \frac{\partial d_{1,\Pi}}{\partial \kappa_\Pi} - N'(-d_{2,\Pi})L_t^* \frac{\partial d_{2,\Pi}}{\partial \kappa_\Pi}\right) \\
&= \left(N'(d_{1,\Pi})A_t - N'(d_{2,\Pi})L_t^*\right)\frac{\partial d_{1,\Pi}}{\partial \kappa_\Pi} \\
&= \underbrace{(\kappa_\Pi - 1)}_{<0}\underbrace{N'(d_{2,\Pi})L_t^*}_{>0}\underbrace{\frac{\partial d_{1,\Pi}}{\partial \kappa_\Pi}}_{<0} > 0.
\end{aligned}
\tag{28}
$$

To see the sign of the put option derivative, note that

$$
\frac{\partial d_{1,\Pi}}{\partial \kappa_\Pi} = -\left(\frac{1}{\kappa_\Pi \omega \sigma \sqrt{T-t}}\right) < 0
$$

and that by assumption $\kappa_\Pi < 1$.

References

Archer, D., & Moser-Boehm, P. (2013). Central bank finances. *BIS papers, No. 71.*

Bank of England. (2018). Exchange of letters between the governor and chancellor on the bank's financial framework. https://www.bankofengland.co.uk/letter/2018/banks-financial-framework-june-2018.

Barro, R. J., & Gordon, D. B. (1983). Rules, discretion and reputation in a model of monetary policy. *Journal of Monetary Economics, 12*(1), 101–121.

Belhocine, N., Bhatia, A. V., & Frie, J. (2023). Raising rates with a large balance sheet: The Eurosystem's net income and its fiscal implications. *IMF Working Paper, No. 145.*

Bell, S., Chui, M., Gomes, T., Moser-Boehm, P., & Pierres Tejada, A. (2023). Why are central banks reporting losses? Does it matter? *BIS Bulletin, No. 68.*

Benigno, P. (2020). A central bank theory of price level determination. *American Economic Journal: Macroeconomics, 12*(3), 258–283.

Benigno, P., & Nisticò, S. (2020). Non-neutrality of open-market operations. *American Economic Journal: Macroeconomics, 12*(3), 175–226.

Benigno, P., Canofari, P., Di Bartolomeo, G., & Messori, M. (2023). The ECB's asset purchase programme: Theory, effects, and risks. *Journal of Economic Surveys, 37*(3), 890–914.

Binder, C. C. (2021). Political pressure on central banks. *Journal of Money, Credit and Banking, 53*(4), 715–744.

Black, F., & Cox, J. C. (1976). Valuing corporate securities: Some effects of bond indenture provisions. *The Journal of Finance, 31*(2), 351–367.

Blinder, A. S. (2000). Central-bank credibility: Why do we care? How do we build it? *American Economic Review, 90*(5), 1421–1431.

Bolt, W., Frost, J., Shin, H. S., & Wierts, P. (2024). The bank of Amsterdam and the limits of fiat money. *Journal of Political Economy, 132*(12), 3919–3941.

Broeders, D., de Haan, L., & Willem van den End, J. (2023). How quantitative easing changes the nature of sovereign risk. *Journal of International Money and Finance, 137*, 102881.

Buiter, W. (2024). Central banks need to be honest about their losses. *Project Syndicate.*

Cagan, P. (1956). The monetary dynamics of hyperinflation. In M. Friedman (Ed.), *Studies in the quantity theory of money* (pp. 25–117). Chicago: The University of Chicago Press.
Carpenter, S., Ihrig, J., Klee, E., Quinn, D., & Boote, A. (2018). The Federal Reserve's balance sheet and earnings: A primer and projections. *The International Journal of Central Banking, 52*, 230–244.
Charoenwong, B., Morck, R., & Wiwattanakantang, Y. (2021). Bank of Japan equity purchases: The (non-) effects of extreme quantitative easing. *Review of Finance, 25*(3), 713–743.
Chiacchio, F., Claeys, G., & Papadia, F. (2018). Should we care about central bank profits? Technical report, Bruegel Policy Contribution.
Décamps, J.-P., Mariotti, T., Rochet, J.-C., & Villeneuve, S. (2011). Free cash flow, issuance costs, and stock prices. *The Journal of Finance, 66*(5), 1501–1544.
Del Negro, M., & Sims, C. A. (2015). When does a central bank's balance sheet require fiscal support? *Journal of Monetary Economics, 73*, 1–19.
DeMarzo, P. M., & Sannikov, Y. (2006). Optimal security design and dynamic capital structure in a continuous-time agency model. *The Journal of Finance, 61*(6), 2681–2724.
Di Maggio, M., Kermani, A., & Palmer, C. J. (2020). How quantitative easing works: Evidence on the refinancing channel. *The Review of Economic Studies, 87*(3), 1498–1528.
Easterly, W. R., Mauro, P., & Schmidt-Hebbel, K. (1995). Money demand and seigniorage-maximizing inflation. *Journal of Money, Credit and Banking, 27*(2), 583–603.
Eijffinger, S. C., De Haan, J., et al. (1996). The political economy of central-bank independence. *Princeton Special Papers in International Economics, No. 19.*
Federal Reserve Board. (2023). Federal Reserve Balance Sheet: Factors Affecting Reserve Balances. https://www.federalreserve.gov/releases/h41/20230831/.
Federal Reserve Board. (2024). Credit and Liquidity Programs and the Balance Sheet. https://www.federalreserve.gov/monetarypolicy/bst_fedsbalancesheet.htm.
Goncharov, I., Ioannidou, V., & Schmalz, M. C. (2023). (Why) do central banks care about their profits? *The Journal of Finance, 78*(5), 2991–3045.
Hall, R. E., & Reis, R. (2015). Maintaining central-bank financial stability under new-style central banking. Technical report, National Bureau of Economic Research.
Hull, J. (2012). *Options, futures, and other derivatives* (7th edn.). Prentice Hall.
Klüh, U. H., & Stella, P. (2008). Central bank financial strength and policy performance: an econometric evaluation. *IMF Working Paper, No. 2008/176*, 2008(176).
Leland, H. E. (1994). Corporate debt value, bond covenants, and optimal capital structure. *The Journal of Finance, 49*(4), 1213–1252.
Merton, R. C. (1974). On the pricing of corporate debt: The risk structure of interest rates. *The Journal of Finance, 29*(2), 449–470.
Moreno-Bromberg, S., & Rochet, J.-C. (2018). *Continuous-time models in corporate finance, banking, and insurance: a user's guide*. Princeton University Press.
Peura, S., & Keppo, J. (2006). Optimal bank capital with costly recapitalization. *The Journal of Business, 79*(4), 2163–2201.
Reis, R. (2013). The mystique surrounding the central bank's balance sheet, applied to the European crisis. *American Economic Review, 103*(3), 135–140.
Reis, R. (2015a). Comment on: "When does a central bank's balance sheet require fiscal support?" by Marco Del Negro and Christopher A. Sims. *Journal of Monetary Economics, 73*, 20–25.
Reis, R. (2015b). Different types of central bank insolvency and the central role of seigniorage. Technical report, National Bureau of Economic Research.
Shreve, S. E. (2000). *Stochastic calculus for finance II: continuous time models*. Springer.
Stella, P. (2005). Central bank financial strength, transparency, and policy credibility. *IMF Staff Papers, 52*(2), 335–365.
Sveriges Riksbank. (2023). The framework for the Riksbank's equity in the new Sveriges Riksbank act. https://www.riksbank.se/en-gb/markets/riksbanks-balance-sheet/the-framework-for-the-riksbanks-equity-in-the-new-sveriges-riksbank-act/.
Wessels, P., & Broeders, D. (2023). Central bank capital management. *Journal of Risk Management in Financial Institutions, 16*(3), 304–3015.

Open Access This chapter is licensed under the terms of the Creative Commons Attribution 4.0 International License (http://creativecommons.org/licenses/by/4.0/), which permits use, sharing, adaptation, distribution and reproduction in any medium or format, as long as you give appropriate credit to the original author(s) and the source, provide a link to the Creative Commons license and indicate if changes were made.

The images or other third party material in this chapter are included in the chapter's Creative Commons license, unless indicated otherwise in a credit line to the material. If material is not included in the chapter's Creative Commons license and your intended use is not permitted by statutory regulation or exceeds the permitted use, you will need to obtain permission directly from the copyright holder.

Part II
Central Bank Capital and Changes in the Policy Environment

Consequences of Last-Resort Policy for Central Bank Balance Sheets

Kathryn M. E. Dominguez

Abstract Pandemic-era financial instability required central banks around the world to expand their roles as lenders of last resort and, in some cases, become market makers of last resort. These extraordinary interventions stabilized financial markets by restoring funding and market liquidity, while at the same time greatly expanding central bank balance sheets and increasing central bank risk exposure. This paper examines the implications of pandemice-era last-resort policy interventions on central bank balance sheets, providing a comparative analysis of expanded asset holdings, subsequent balance sheet reductions as part of quantitative tightening, and announcements of losses. The evidence suggests that markets have had a benign view of central bank losses due to the measures taken in extraordinary circumstances. The impacts of last-resort policies during the pandemic do not seem to have diminished central banks' ability to achieve monetary policy and financial stability objectives.

Keywords Central bank losses · Lender of last resort · Market maker of last resort · Pandemic-era last-resort policy interventions

1 Introduction

March 2020 marked the start of the Covid-19 pandemic in most countries. Governments put in place lock-down measures in order to reduce the spread of the virus, and as businesses closed, panic took hold in financial markets driving a dash for cash. Policymakers around the globe soon realized that traditional levels of countercyclical monetary and fiscal stimulus would not be enough to stabilize their economies. The extraordinary circumstances required extraordinary measures. Central banks responded with expansions of last-resort facilities that included

K. M. E. Dominguez (✉)
University of Michigan, Ann Arbor, MI, USA
e-mail: kathrynd@umich.edu

© The Author(s) 2025

D. Broeders et al. (eds.), *Central Bank Capital in Turbulent Times*,
Contributions to Finance and Accounting,
https://doi.org/10.1007/978-3-031-73549-3_6

liquidity support to financial and non-financial institutions as well as large-scale asset purchases (LSAPs). These announcements, especially those that promised to do "whatever-it-takes," stabilized markets and led to significant reductions in long-term government bond yields (Dominguez & Foschi, 2024). This paper examines these last-resort central bank actions, focusing on the consequences for balance sheets and implications for future policy actions.

Policies that are labeled "last resort" are not ones that are used frequently in normal times, they are meant to be stabilizers in times of distress. The primary goal of central bank policies in non-crisis times is to maintain price (and sometimes exchange rate) stability by controlling the supply of money and influencing interest rates. Although the operational approach to the policies that central banks use differ, the goal of low inflation over a long-run period is widely shared. In times of crisis, inflation may become a secondary concern to the more immediate need to provide stimulus and restore liquidity in systemically important financial markets. This is when unconventional and last-resort policies may be required.

Quantitative easing (QE) is the unconventional policy that is relevant if central banks need to provide additional stimulus at a time when policy interest rates are already at or close to zero.[1] Last-resort interventions in illiquid financial markets are needed to restore the flow of credit and limit impacts on the real economy. These financial market interventions can be indirect, providing loans to market participants through enhanced lender of last resort (LOLR) facilities, or direct, by making outright purchases of illiquid assets as a market maker of last resort (MMLR). In the midst of the pandemic, central banks intervened using policies that had features of unconventional and last-resort policy.[2] Buiter et al. (2023) document the ways in which the objectives of these central bank pandemic-era programs were often difficult to categorize. Expansions of QE programs provided aggregate demand stimulus, as well as stabilizing targeted markets using features of MMLR.

Central bank policy announcements during the early stages of the pandemic were meant to calm markets and provide stimulus with little benefit of historical precedent.[3] In those early months, there was limited data to help forecast how quickly the Covid-19 virus might spread, the impacts on global health and mortality, how long lock-downs would need to continue, and how household and firm behavior would change in these new circumstances. Monetary and fiscal authorities across the

---

[1] Vissing-Jorgensen (2023) analyzes the optimal size of central bank balance sheets when interest rates are no longer at the zero-lower-bound, focusing on the role of convenience yields.

[2] Hauser (2023) discusses some of the downside risks for central banks that use these new tools to stabilize financial markets. Fruzzetti et al. (2023) examine impacts on credit risk of Eurosystem monetary policy and emergency liquidity assistance operations over the period 2010 to 2022.

[3] Two papers that provide historical policy context were published during and after the worst of the Covid-19 pandemic. Anderson et al. (2020) examine the effect of liquidity support during the 1918 influenza pandemic. Ferguson et al. (2023) examine financial crises in the past 400 years for 17 central banks, and show that balance sheet expansions of at least 15% after a financial crisis leads to a cumulative increase in real GDP of 21% over the subsequent three years relative to a no-support counterfactual.

globe responded quickly and decisively in an attempt to cushion economies as much as possible in the face of extreme uncertainty and dramatic declines in economic activity. Even with these extraordinary policy measures, global GDP fell by over 3% in 2020, the sharpest decline since the initial declines of the Great Depression in the 1930s.

Almost as quickly as the pandemic disrupted every aspect of life in 2020, access to vaccines and the lifting of most public health-related restrictions in 2021 led global economic activity to rebound.[4] At the same time global inflation, which had remained low in most advanced economies in the years between the 2008 financial crisis and the pandemic, began to rise, ultimately peaking at 10.7% for the OECD countries in October 2022.[5] The rebound in economic activity and increases in inflation led central bankers to again respond quickly, shifting from expansionary to contractionary stances. Forward guidance at the early stages of the pandemic had indicated that the extraordinary policies would end, but most central banks expected to shift to a neutral stance, not contraction.

This paper describes the extraordinary central bank policies that were put in place during the pandemic as well as the policies that followed in 2021 when central banks returned their focus to stabilizing prices. The pandemic-era policies led to substantial expansions of central bank balance sheets, which have been only partially reduced in the subsequent few years.

2 Central Bank Last-Resort Policies During the Pandemic

As the implications of economic and financial market distress in the early days of the pandemic started to be felt around the globe, central banks reacted quickly with announcements of new and expanded programs. Two lessons learned from previous crises were to "go fast and go big"[6] and promise to do whatever-it-takes.[7] Many central banks already had sovereign bond asset-purchase programs in place as part of QE policy, making expansions of those programs relatively straightforward.

Table 1 lists the dates of the first announcement by all the central banks that expanded existing programs or introduced new sovereign bond purchasing programs, starting on March 12, 2020 with the Bank of Canada, the European Central Bank, the Bank of Mexico, and the Federal Reserve. The table documents the number of pandemic-era sovereign bond purchasing announcements made by

[4] In contrast, the Great Depression lasted more than a decade, beginning in 1929 and not ending until World War II in 1941.

[5] OECD monthly inflation (CPI) doi: 10.1787/eee82e6e-en (accessed on 19 May 2024).

[6] Baily et al. (2020) examine the Bank of England's balance sheet expansion after the 2008 financial crisis through 2019 and suggest that going "big" and "fast" improves QE effectiveness in the midst of a crisis.

[7] Mario Draghi is credited with first using the promise to do whatever-it-takes in 2012 during the European debt crisis.

Table 1 Central Bank sovereign bond asset-purchase Announcements during the pandemic

Country	Date of first announcement	Number of announcements	Number WIT	% WIT
Canada	3/12/2020	11	2	18%
Euro Area	3/12/2020	10	5	50%
USA	3/12/2020	8	4	50%
Mexico	3/12/2020	2	0	0%
Japan	3/13/2020	4	2	50%
Israel	3/15/2020	3	0	0%
Sweden	3/16/2020	3	1	33%
Poland	3/16/2020	2	2	100%
Chile	3/16/2020	3	0	0%
India	3/18/2020	5	2	40%
UK	3/19/2020	3	1	33%
Australia	3/19/2020	9	6	67%
Korea	3/19/2020	5	0	0%
Romania	3/20/2020	1	0	0%
Thailand	3/22/2020	1	0	0%
Colombia	3/23/2020	3	2	67%
New Zealand	3/23/2020	5	0	0%
South Africa	3/25/2020	1	1	100%
Turkey	3/31/2020	2	1	50%
Indonesia	4/1/2020	3	0	0%
Hungary	4/7/2020	20	4	20%
Philippines	4/10/2020	1	0	0%
Total		105	33	31%

Source: Announcement data from Cantu et al. (2021), classification as whatever-it-takes (WIT) by Dominguez and Foschi (2024)

each central bank (105 in total) and, of these, how many involved open-ended promises to do whatever-it-takes (33%).[8]

In some countries, central bank sovereign bond purchases in the early days of the pandemic were good examples of MMLR policy. In March 2020, investors shifted from initially increasing their demand for safe assets like sovereign bonds to dashing-for-cash. As a consequence, sovereign yields in many advanced economies, including the USA, Germany, the UK, and Japan, rose and then, just as quickly, fell in the span of a week.[9] Market distress in the U.S. Treasury market was disproportionately high, likely due to the central role of the dollar in global financial markets. Along with serving as an MMLR by purchasing Treasuries, the Federal

[8] Categorization of whatever-it-takes by Dominguez and Foschi (2024) is based on central bank press releases, press conference statements, and subsequent news coverage.

[9] Vissing-Jorgensen (2021) documents the turmoil in the U.S. Treasury market during March 2020 and concludes that Federal Reserve purchases of Treasuries ($1T in 2020Q1) caused the reduction in yields and restored market function.

Reserve reopened swap lines with an expanded list of countries and established a temporary Foreign and International Monetary Authorities (FIMA) repo facility to help reduce pressures in global dollar funding markets.[10]

The contribution of sovereign bond asset purchases to expanding central bank balance sheets during the pandemic was much larger than it was during the 2008 crisis, and purchases were more frontloaded. One concern that this raises is that these programs may have been perceived as financing fiscal spending in some countries. Issuance of sovereign debt rose during the pandemic, as did the share of this debt held by central banks. Hooley et al. (2023) describe that among the central banks that purchased sovereign bonds, "net purchases represented more than 10 percent of the outstanding debt stock in 20 percent of cases and more than fully covered the government's additional borrowing requirements in 10 percent of cases" (page 8).

The dates of the first announcement by central banks of sovereign bond asset purchase programs in Table 1 suggest that there were significant peer effects. All the announcements occurred within a 30-day span, with multiple announcements made on some days. This close timing is likely to have reduced the potential negative cross-country spillovers that would have been expected if only a few countries had announced policies. Figure 1 shows that although the Fed was one of the early whatever-it-takes announcers of LSAP programs, the dollar strengthened against most currencies starting in mid-March 2020 when investors dashed-for-dollar-cash. Emerging market currency values experienced some of the largest declines against the dollar in 2020, though by early 2021 they had largely returned to their pre-pandemic valuations.

Financial market reactions to the central bank announcements listed in Table 1 were significant and this was especially true for announcements that were open-ended. Dominguez and Foschi (2024) find that on average whatever-it-takes announcements lowered 10-year bond yields by 47 basis points more than size-limited announcements, and all the first announcements made by central banks significantly impacted yields. Interestingly, announcements had stronger impacts on bond maturities that went well beyond the time by which asset-purchases would have stopped. Bernardini and Conti (2023) examine the impacts of the subsequent purchases of assets by the ECB. They find that the pace of ECB purchases increased when euro-area financial market conditions deteriorated, that purchases were frontloaded, and the total amount purchased was often considerably smaller than markets had anticipated based on the bond yield reactions to ECB announcements.

Many of the same central banks that expanded their sovereign bond asset-purchasing programs during the pandemic also launched a series of open-ended

[10] The Federal Reserve permanently responded to the March 2020 turmoil in the Treasury market in July 2021 when it established the Standing Repo Facility (SRF) for primary dealers and eligible depository institutions. Likewise, the FIMA Repo Facility was made a standing facility on July 28, 2021 for central banks and other international monetary authorities with accounts at the Federal Reserve Bank of New York to exchange Treasuries for cash at an administrated rate.

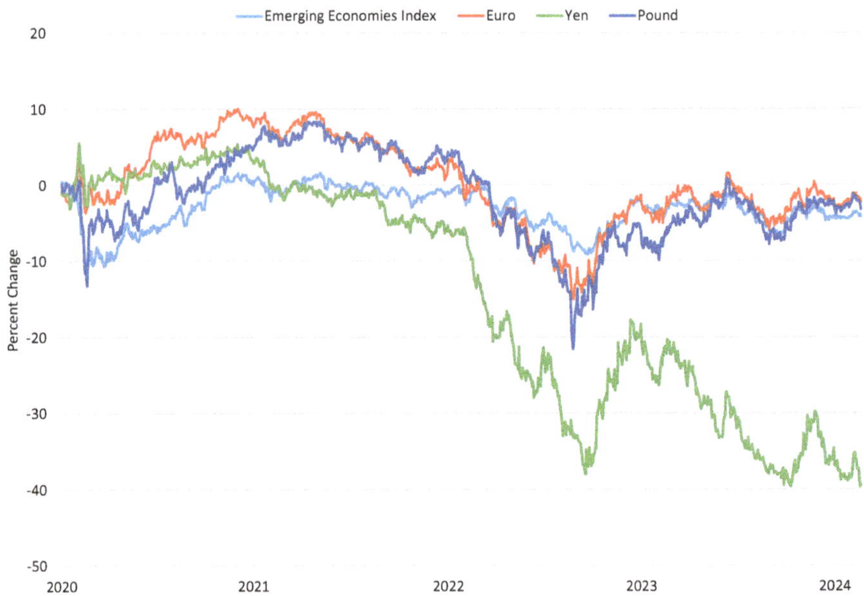

Fig. 1 Currency values against the dollar. Source: FRED daily nominal dollar indices, 2020 = 100

long-term refinancing operations (LTROs) for banks at subsidized rates as well as enhanced lender-of-last-resort (LOLR) facilities that extended credit to primary dealers in a range of asset markets and provided targeted lending to non-bank financial institutions and nonfinancial firms. The design of pandemic-era LOLR facilities often seems to have prioritized the first part of Bagehot's principles of lending in a liquidity crisis: to lend freely, at a penalty rate, against good collateral.[11] The penalty rate and high-quality collateral are meant to reduce moral hazard as well as central bank risk exposure. Buiter et al. (2023) describe the appropriate penalty rate as "below the one available in disorderly markets, but above an estimate of what would prevail in markets in normal times" (page 26). In practice during the pandemic central banks often reduced the penalty rates on their LOLR facilities and accepted a wider range of collateral, in an effort to encourage borrowers.

Table 2 lists the dates of the first announcement of pandemic-era enhanced LOLR facilities. In some cases announcements were expansions of already existing facilities (for example, repo program amounts were increased and maturities were lengthened), some were reactivated crisis-era facilities (an example is the Fed's Term Asset-Backed Securities Loan Facility (TALF)), and others were new programs often targeted to specific financial markets, institutions, or borrowers.

[11] Bagehot's (1873) advice to central banks in a crisis was to "lend to merchants, to minor bankers, to this man and that man" (page 25), this was followed by the phrase "whenever the security is good." He also states that this type of lending be done at a "very high rate."

Table 2 First announcements by central banks of enhanced LOLR during the pandemic

Country	Date of first announcement	Lending Operation/Facility	Size
USA	3/9/2020	Repurchase Agreements	
UK	3/11/2020	Term Funding Scheme with additional incentives for SMEs	
Canada	3/12/2020	Term Repo operations	
Chile	3/12/2020	Repo operations	
Colombia	3/12/2020	Repo operations	
Euro Area	3/12/2020	Targeted Longer-Term Refinancing Operation III	€1.2tn
Korea	3/12/2020	Lending facilities	
Japan	3/13/2020	Funds-supplying and repo operations, Security Lending Facility	
Sweden	3/13/2020	Onward lending to non-financial corporations	SEK 500bn
Israel	3/15/2020	Repo operations	
Hungary	3/16/2020	Liquidity providing operations	HUF 2,5tn
India	3/16/2020	Long-Term Repo Operations	INR 1tn
New Zealand	3/16/2020	Standing facilities	
Philippines	3/16/2020	Rediscounting (standing credit) facility	
Poland	3/16/2020	Discount Credit, Repo Operations	
Turkey	3/17/2020	Targeted additional liquidity facilities	
Australia	3/19/2020	Term Funding Facility to Support Lending to Australian Businesses	AUD 90bn
Indonesia	3/19/2020	Repo operations	
Mexico	3/20/2020	Ordinary Additional Liquidity Facility	
Romania	3/20/2020	Repo operations	
South Africa	3/20/2020	Repo operations	
Thailand	3/22/2020	Mutual funds liquidity facility	THB 1tn

Source: Announcement data from Cantu et al. (2021)

Traditional and enhanced LOLR operations are financed with bank reserves in the same way as central banks finance asset purchases, leading to balance sheet expansions.[12] In non-crisis periods LOLR loans are sources of central bank balance sheet risk, and in times of crisis this risk is elevated because borrowers are inevitably riskier, the distinction between illiquidity and insolvency is less clear, and the

[12] Liquidity provision does not require central bank balance sheet expansion. For example, swaps of risky assets held by the public for safer assets held by the central bank will not impact the size of the balance sheet, but will increase its riskiness.

quality of collateral may be difficult to measure. Enhanced LOLR loans during the pandemic were offered to a wider range of institutions, often at preferential terms, greatly increasing their risks.

Globally, the amounts of central bank LOLR support to financial institutions during the pandemic was significant. Hooley et al. (2023) describe that the median increase in LOLR lending to the "financial sector during 2020 and 2021 was 4½ percent of GDP for AEs and 1¾ percent of GDP for EMEs" (page 20). The level of LOLR support to the non-financial sector was much smaller, in large part because take-up was low. The loans made by two of the non-financial sector LOLR facilities offered by the Fed (the Primary Market Corporate Credit Facility and Municipal Liquidity Facility) amounted to a small fraction of their authorized amounts.[13]

In non-crisis periods central banks rarely serve as market makers of last resort (MMLR), and even in crisis periods, LOLR facilities are usually the first of the last-resort lines of defense. Buiter et al. (2023) detail the circumstances under which LOLR measures are unable to restore financial market liquidity, requiring central banks to directly purchase the relevant assets. These circumstances involve situations when there is extreme uncertainty about asset quality, borrower solvency, counterparty availability, or impacts of regulatory constraints on market makers. In all these cases MMLR is likely to be the only feasible option for central banks. Although some of the early pandemic MMLR interventions involved sovereign bond markets, it was largely distressed markets for private sector securities that required outright purchases by central banks.

Many central banks are prohibited by law to purchase private sector securities. The Federal Reserve Act only allows the Fed to buy and sell assets that are direct obligations of, or guaranteed by, the US government. As a result, the Fed was required to invoke Sect. 13.3 of the Federal Reserve Act to address "unusual and exigent circumstances" in order to establish its commercial paper, corporate credit, and municipal liquidity facilities. In the UK, purchases of private securities were made through a wholly-owned subsidiary of the BOE with full Treasury indemnification. The Bank of Canada also purchased private-sector securities with a government indemnity.[14]

Table 3 lists the central banks that established pandemic-era non-sovereign bond asset purchase programs, along with announcement dates and program details. All 22 central banks that established sovereign bond purchase programs also established enhanced LOLR facilities, but only 13 central banks established facilities that purchased private sector assets. Outside of crises, interventions in private-sector asset markets are well outside traditional central bank operational frameworks. In the midst of the pandemic, however, central banks served as MMLR in some of these markets to avoid the potential damage to the real economy that distress

[13] The Fed's corporate-credit facilities lent only $14bn, a fraction of the $750bn available.

[14] In most cases when governments guaranteed central bank purchases of private assets only the credit risk was transferred from the central bank to the Treasury, interest rate and liquidity risk remained with the central bank (Hooley et al., 2023, page 31).

Table 3 Central Bank announcements of non-sovereign asset-purchase programs during the pandemic

Country	Date of Announcement	Program/Facility	(Initial) Size
Canada	3/13/2020	Bankers' Acceptance Purchase Facility (BAPF)	min bank credit rating
	3/16/2020	Canada Mortgage Bond Purchase	$500 billion weekly
	3/24/2020	Provincial Money Market Purchase Program (PMMP)	40-percent purchase limit
	3/27/2020	Commercial Paper Purchase Program (CPPP)	Open-ended
	4/15/2020	Provincial Bond Purchase Program (PBPP)	Up to 50 billion
	4/15/2020	Corporate Bond Purchase Program (CBPP)	Up to 10 billion
	4/30/2021	Securities Repo Operations (SROs)	4000 million
Chile	3/19/2020	Bank Purchase Program	limited
	7/30/2020	Cash Purchase Operations Program	US$10 billion
	7/30/2020	Bank Deposit Purchase Program	US$8 billion
Colombia	3/23/2020	Purchase of Private Titles of Credit Establishments	10 trillion
Euro Area	3/18/2020	Corporate Sector Purchase Program (CSPP)	Open-ended
	9/22/2020	Sustainability-linked bonds Purchases	limited
UK	3/17/2020	Covid Corporate Financing Facility (CCFF)	Open-ended
	4/2/2020	Corporate Bond Purchases	>10 billion
Hungary	4/7/2020	Mortgage Bond Purchase Program	limited
Israel	7/6/2020	Corporate Bond Purchase Program	15 billion
India	10/9/2020	State Development Loans (SDLs)	limited
Japan	3/16/2020	Corporate Bond Purchases	<2 trillion yen
	3/16/2020	Stock Purchases	<12 trillion yen
Korea	5/20/2020	Commercial Paper Purchase Program	10 trillion
	7/17/2020	Corporate Bond Purchases	8 trillion

(continued)

Table 3 (continued)

Country	Date of Announcement	Program/Facility	(Initial) Size
Sweden	3/20/2020	Covered Bonds Purchase	10 billion
	3/26/2020	Commercial Paper Purchase	4 billion
	4/22/2020	Municipal Bond-purchasing Program	15 billion
	5/8/2020	Commercial Paper Purchase	32 billion
Thailand	4/7/2020	Corporate Bond Stabilization Fund	limited
USA	3/17/2020	Commercial Paper Funding Facility (CPFF)	10 billion
	3/23/2020	Primary Market Corporate Credit Facility (PMCCF)	Open-ended
	3/23/2020	Secondary Market Corporate Credit Facility (SMCCF)	Open-ended
	4/9/2020	Municipal Liquidity Facility (MLF)	Open-ended
	7/23/20	Emergency Lending Facilities	limited

Source: Announcement data from Cantu et al. (2021)

in systemic financial markets could inflict. Boneva et al. (2022) study the BOE Corporate Bond Purchase Scheme and find strong evidence that purchases improved liquidity of purchased bonds. Knock-on impacts on portfolio rebalancing across markets may also improve liquidity more broadly (Delgado & Gravelle, 2023). Announcements of central bank purchase programs are likely to bid up the prices of targeted assets, causing yields to decline, and leading investors to switch to alternative assets potentially easing wider financial conditions.[15] Along with the potential improvements in market liquidity, it is worth noting that private-sector asset purchase programs are likely to increase central bank balance sheet risk because the underlying assets will be inherently riskier than sovereign bonds.

3 Central Bank Balance Sheets and Quantitative Tightening

The QE, enhanced LOLR, and MMLR programs announced in 2020 dramatically expanded central bank balance sheets. Figure 2 shows that the biggest increases were in Japan, the USA, and the Euro Area. The month in which balance sheets peaked differs across countries, but in all cases it was in 2021.

Dramatic global rebounds in economic activity as well as increases in inflation in 2021 led central banks to end pandemic interventions sooner than anticipated. The lessons from the slow recovery experience after the 2008 financial crisis suggested that withdrawing support too early was a mistake. This may explain why there was little advance discussion of balance sheet "normalization" even as economic conditions began improving in late 2020. As Du et al. (2024) describe, "at the start of 2021, the Fed was not expected to liftoff until well into 2024, and then not to begin QT until 2024 at the earliest" (page 10). Instead, the Fed announced its first interest rate increase since 2018 on March 16, 2022. Table 4 lists the dates on which central banks first announced they would begin quantitative tightening (QT). Interestingly, it was emerging market (EM) countries, like Mexico, that were the first-movers. Few EM central banks had pre-existing LSAPs in place before the pandemic,[16] their programs tended to be significantly smaller in size than those in AEs, and they started winding down the programs more quickly. The Bank of England was the first AE central bank to announce a shift to QT in February 2022, and this followed quickly on their announcement to end QE (in December 2021).

---

[15] Alridge et al. (2023) review the potential costs of central bank interventions and find evidence that LSAPs may inadvertently negatively impact market liquidity if they remove a large share of the targeted assets from the market or, if they increase the concentration of asset holdings among price-inelastic investors.

[16] Hungary and Colombia are two EMs that had pre-existing asset-purchase programs. One of the reasons EMs had not previously used QE is that their policy rates were not at the zero-lower-bound. It was also the case that in many EMs (including Brazil and Chile) there were legal restrictions on central bank purchases of public debt.

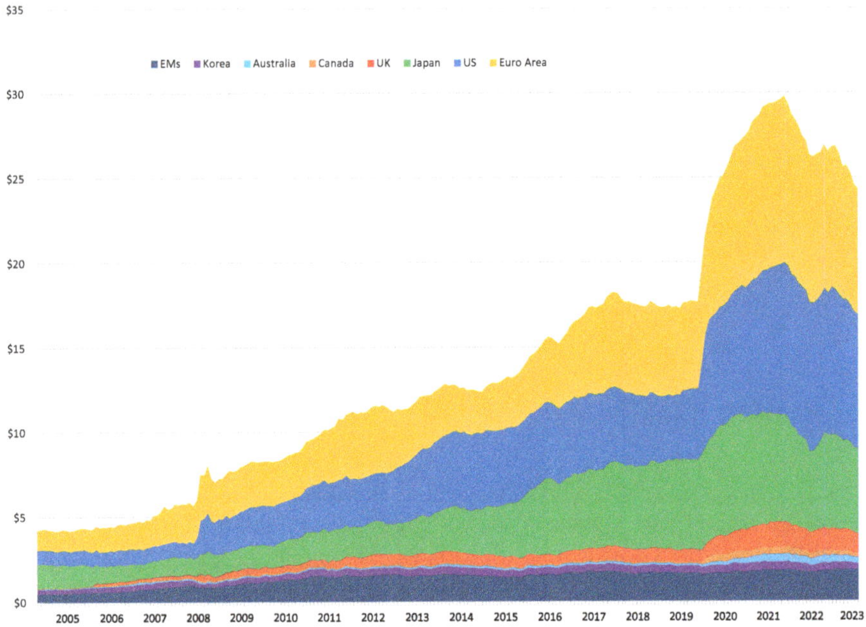

Fig. 2 Central Bank total assets (Trillions of US$). Source: Central Bank total asset data from FRED and IMF IFS, domestic currency translated into USD using IMF IFS monthly end-of-period exchange rates

Although all central banks that had QE programs shifted course in 2021, approaches to QT varied. Most countries began QT with a "passive" approach, not replacing assets that matured with new assets. "Active" QT, involving selling assets before they mature, followed in some cases. Central bank QT programs also differ on the pace and size of sales, as well as the composition and maturities of assets that are sold. The BOE started with sales of corporate bond holdings; the Fed QT program involves sales of mortgage-backed securities as well as Treasuries. The largest share of assets on most central bank balance sheets are sovereign bonds, so they make up the largest share of global QT sales.

Table 4 shows that central bank asset holdings have fallen significantly from their peaks in 2021 as a result of QT. The Bank of Canada has reduced the size of their balance sheet by the largest percentage, at almost 50%, and the size of most other AE central bank balance sheets have fallen by around 25%. Du et al. (2024) find that market reactions to central bank announcements of the start of QT, and the subsequent implementation of QT plans, have been significantly smaller than those associated with QE.[17] This asymmetry in reaction is presumably what central banks

[17] Ludvigson (2022) examines high frequency market reactions to fourteen pre-pandemic Fed QT announcements (over 2013–2019), and finds larger effects on financial market variables, but no evidence of accompanying changes in expectations for the macro-economy or inflation.

Table 4 Central Bank QE and QT announcements and balance sheet changes

Country	Date of first QE announcement during the pandemic	Peak balance sheet date	% increase in assets: Dec 2019 to peak	Date of first QT announcement	% decrease in assets: peak to Oct 2023	First increase in policy rate
Canada	3/12/2020	Feb-21	400%	4/13/2022	48%	Mar-22
Euro Area	3/12/2020	Feb-22	89%	12/15/2022	25%	Jul-22
USA	3/12/2020	Apr-22	115%	3/16/2022	11%	Mar-22
Mexico	3/12/2020	Oct-21	26%	6/24/2021	5%	Jun-21
Japan	3/13/2020	Jan-21	30%	NA	27%	Mar-24
UK	3/17/2020	Oct-21	98%	2/3/2022	24%	Dec-21
India	3/18/2020	Oct-21	41%	NA	10%	May-22
Australia	3/19/2020	Mar-22	277%	5/3/2022	29%	May-22
Korea	3/19/2020	Dec-21	18%	NA	24%	Aug-21
Thailand	3/22/2020	Nov-21	19%	NA	15%	Aug-22
Turkey	3/31/2020	Nov-21	51%	NA	4%	Sep-20
Indonesia	4/1/2020	Dec-21	43%	NA	6%	Aug-22

Source: Asset purchase announcement dates from Cantu et al. (2021), Central Bank total asset data from FRED and IMF IFS, domestic currency translated into USD using IMF IFS monthly end-of-period exchange rates

intended. The objective of QE at the start of the pandemic was to calm markets and provide stimulus, whereas the objectives of QT are to unwind the operations without disrupting market liquidity.

As QT continues, and especially as riskier holdings mature or are sold, central balance sheets and their risk exposures are expected to decline. How far this process will go depends on how QT impacts liquidity as reserves fall. Acharya et al. (2023) examine the impacts on US banking system liquidity during periods of Fed QE relative to periods of QT, and find evidence of an asymmetry. Liquidity rises during QE together with increases in reserves, but does not fall during QT as reserves decline. Instead, banks attempt to maintain liquidity by substituting bond purchases for reserves. This behavior will increase financial fragility when deposits decline or bond valuations fall and every bank needs liquid assets (dashing for cash) at the same time. This concern over the optimal level of reserves, and the implications for liquidity is the subject of ongoing analysis and debate at central banks.[18]

4 Central Bank Losses and Credibility

Central banks are unique, in that they can continue to operate with a negative equity position. Solvency in the conventional sense doesn't apply to them. Central banks create their own liabilities, in the form of bank reserves, guaranteeing that they can never run short of funding. A number of central banks, including the Czech National Bank, the Bank of Israel, Banco de Mexico, and Banco Central de Chile, have successfully operated despite having ongoing negative equity.

Outside of crises, most advanced economy central banks make profits, and depending on the arrangement they have with the fiscal authority, net income is typically either distributed in the form of dividends or remitted to the government. The evaluation of central bank finances depends importantly on the treatment of unrealized gains and losses. Table 5 shows the range of accounting and distribution rules used by different central banks that make comparisons across countries difficult.

Although most central banks rarely experience significant losses, when they do, it is inevitably in tightening cycles when the value of balance sheet assets is declining. Central banks that use fair value accounting will regularly mark-to-market assets on their balance sheet and will therefore record an unrealized loss due to valuation changes more quickly than central banks that use a historic value approach. The consequences of recording unrealized losses will, in turn, depend on distribution rules. Central banks that are required to immediately remit unrealized gains and losses may find that subsequent changes in asset value will partially or fully reverse

[18] Lane (2023) examines the role of central bank reserves in the new steady state that emerges after crisis conditions have ended, focusing on the appropriate level of ECB reserves after QT and the expiration of the ECB's Targeted Longer-Term Refinancing Operations program.

Table 5 Central Bank accounting and distribution rules

Category	Approach	Examples
Accounting approach	Fair value: mark-to-market, changes go directly to P&L	RBA, BOE
	Fair value: mark-to-market, changes go to equity account	SARB
	Historic value: changes in market value not recognized until sold	Fed, ECB[a]
Income recognition and distribution rules	Full and automatic transfers	BOE
	Fixed or contingent distributions	BOC, Fed
	Discretionary risk buffers	BOJ, ECB
	Distribution smoothing	SNB
	Automatic loss coverage	BOK

[a]The ECB uses fair value accounting for assets denominated in foreign currency, and historic value (purchase price adjusted for any premium or discount and amortized over the asset's maturity) for euro-denominated assets

Sources: Archer and Moser-Boehm (2013), Chaboud and Leahy (2013), Bell et al. (2023), and Goncharov et al. (2024)

those distributions, leading to volatile remittances. Other central banks explicitly smooth remittances by treating unrealized gains differently than losses (building up a buffer to absorb valuation losses), or by making allocations to accounts for provisions or reserves that can be drawn down when needed.

In 2021, when many central banks shifted from expansionary to contractionary monetary policy to bring down post-pandemic inflation, interest rates increased, leading to significant asset valuation losses on central bank balance sheets.[19] The BOE and the RBA, two central banks that use fair value accounting, were unsurprisingly among the first central banks to announce losses in 2022. Table 6 lists the dates on which central banks announced post-pandemic losses, in the case of Canada this was the first time it had experienced a net loss.

The Bank of Canada Act does not allow the Bank to accumulate earnings to offset losses, so the government implemented legislative amendments in 2023 to allow the Bank to temporarily retain net income, rather than remitting it to the Government of Canada. This allowed the BOC to use its future income to offset its accumulated losses and hold off on remittances until sufficient equity has been restored. Likewise, the Federal Reserve Act requires the Reserve Banks to remit excess earnings to the U.S. Treasury after providing for operating costs, payments of dividends to member banks, and retention of a sufficient amount to maintain a surplus equal to the amount of capital paid in by members. In periods when

[19] Humann et al. (2023) examine the central bank rate-tightening cycles in the 1970s and 1980s and find that they were able to avoid the losses experienced by many of the same central banks post-pandemic. They attribute the difference in outcomes to smaller initial balance sheets and the lack of bank reserve remuneration.

Table 6 Announcements of post-pandemic Central Bank losses

Country	Date of announcement of losses	Statement
UK	3/31/2022	The value of the Bank of England's Asset Purchase Fund Facility's liabilities exceeded the value of its assets by 40b
Australia	9/21/2022	In 2021/22 the Reserve Bank recorded an accounting loss of $36.7 billion. This will be recorded as accumulated losses on the Bank's balance sheet, meaning that the Bank has negative equity.
Canada	2/14/2023	In 2022Q3, the difference between the interest the Bank pays on settlement balances and what it receives on its bonds turned negative. As a result, the Bank is facing a temporary net loss for the first time in history.
Japan	3/1/2023	The Bank of Japan had an unrealized loss of 157.1 billion yen on its record-high government bond holdings in fiscal 2022 for the first such loss in 17 years
Euro Area	2/22/2024	The European Central Bank's (ECB's) audited financial statements for 2023 show a loss of €1266 million which will be carried forward on the ECB's balance sheet to be offset against future profits.
USA	3/26/2024	The Reserve Banks' 2023 sum total of expenses exceeded earnings by $114.3 billion, its largest operating loss ever, forcing the US central bank to forgo remittances to the Treasury

Source: Central Bank press releases

earnings are not sufficient to provide for those costs, a deferred asset is recorded.[20] Table 7 shows the Federal Reserve's annual gains and losses starting in 2019, when it remitted $54.9 billion to the Treasury. Although the Fed had cumulative unrealized losses starting in 2022, it was not until 2023 that it stopped remittances and created a deferred asset of $116 billion (resulting in a cumulative deferred asset for 2023 of $133 billion).[21] The size of the deferred asset represents the amount of reduction in future remittances to the Treasury that is needed to rebuild reserves. Nordstrom and Vredin (2022) note that, relative to other countries, the USA has low equity and in most years transfers most of its profits to the Treasury. They compare post-pandemic losses across five central banks (Sweden, Australia, USA, New Zealand,

[20] One consequence of this deferred asset approach is that however much the Fed losses on its balance sheet, it will not experience negative equity.

[21] See the Board of Governors Press Release on 12 January 2024: https://www.federalreserve.gov/newsevents/pressreleases/other20240112a.htm

Table 7 Annual Federal Reserve Balance Sheet Gains and Losses (billions)

	2019	2020	2021	2022	2023
Cumulative gains (losses), net	160	353	127	(1080)	(948)
Total Capital	38	149	60	57	51
Balance Sheet, total assets	4173	7358	8756	8569	7835
Remittances (deferral) to Treasury	54.9	86.9	109	59	(116)

Notes: Cumulative net gains (losses) are unrealized
Source: Federal Reserve System Audited Annual Financial Statements, 2019–23

and the Netherlands) based on 2021 annual accounts and find that estimated losses are highest for the USA.[22]

The Bank of England (BOE) uses fair value accounting but holds the assets it acquired through quantitative easing in a special purpose vehicle, the Bank of England Asset Purchase Facility Fund. BOE profits are distributed to the government, but losses are retained on the balance sheet.

Although the central bank losses to date could be a concern,[23] Cecchetti and Hilscher (2024) argue that focusing on these losses in isolation is misleading. It ignores the transfer of asset valuation changes between the bank and the fiscal authority. In the case of sovereign bonds, any valuation losses for the central bank will be offset by an equal-sized gain for the fiscal authority. Consolidating the balance sheets of central banks with the domestic fiscal authority therefore appropriately shifts the focus to the maturity structure of central bank asset holdings as well as the transfer of interest rate risk to future taxpayers when the central bank purchases private sector assets. The muted reaction of markets to announcements of losses suggests that, even in the absence of changes in the institutional approach to balance sheet consolidation, central bank credibility has not been diminished.

5 Conclusions

The rapid expansion and ongoing gradual reduction in central bank balance sheets are direct consequences of pandemic-era crisis interventions and the subsequent global economic rebound. Market reactions to the announcements of the extraordinary last-resort policies were remarkably positive. Yields on long-term bonds fell as central banks promised to do whatever-it-takes, and the potential downsides of balance sheet expansion did not destabilize markets.

[22] This information is provided in Table 1 on page 17 of Nordstrom and Vredin (2022). Similarly, Belocine et al. (2023) forecast Eurosystem national central bank balance sheet gains and losses through 2031.

[23] See Kazuo (2023) for the Bank of Japan's perspective on losses.

There may yet be longer-term costs for central banks if the pandemic-era actions have increased benchmark expectations for last-resort policy, forcing policymakers to use extraordinary measures in ordinary cyclical downturns. This would increase moral hazard and potentially make future crises more likely. Further, the legacy of expanded balance sheets and higher inflation may make it difficult for central banks to respond to the next crisis. The banking tumult in March 2023 may be a counter-example. The Fed and the SNB were able to calm financial markets in that episode by again using last-resort policies and expanding balance sheets, without losing control of inflation.

The benign reactions to central bank announcements of losses suggest that markets are not concerned about the ongoing ability of central banks to achieve their monetary policy and financial stability objectives. It is likely that this is in part due to the fact that the crisis was caused by a pandemic and did not arise endogenously from within the financial system. Central banks have also benefited from the synchronicity of the global policy cycle, which has reduced the negative spillover effects that often arise during crises. Sovereign bond markets continue to function smoothly, even as central banks have significantly reduced their purchases. Exchange rates have remained relatively stable since 2023, and markets seem to have priced in future reductions in policy interest rates in most countries.

References

Acharya, V., Chauhan, R., Rajan, R., & Steffen, S. (2023). *Liquidity dependence and the waxing and waning of central bank balance sheets*. NBER working paper 31050.

Aldridge, P., Cimon, D., & Vala, R. (2023). *Central Bank crisis interventions: A review of the recent literature on potential costs*. Bank of Canada Staff Discussion Paper 2023–20, 11 December.

Anderson, H., Chang, J.-W., & Copeland, A. (2020). *The effect of the central bank liquidity support during pandemics: Evidence from the 1918 Influenza pandemic*. Federal Reserve Bank of New York Staff Reports, no. 928, May.

Archer, D., & Moser-Boehm, P. (2013). *Central Bank Finances*. BIS Papers No 71, April.

Bagehot, W. (1873). *Lombard Street: A Description of the Money Market*. Henry S. King & Co., London, Great Britain, reprinted by Charles Scribner's Sons, New York, 1897.

Bailey, A., Bridges, J., Harrison, R., Jones, J., & Mankodi, A. (2020) *The central bank balance sheet as a policy tool: past, present and future*. Bank of England Staff Working Paper No. 899 (December). https://www.bankofengland.co.uk/-/media/boe/files/working-paper/2020/the-central-bank-balance-sheet-as-a-policy-tool-past-present-and-future.pdf

Bell, S., Chui, M., Gomes, T., Moser-Boehm, P., & Tejada, A. P. (2023). *Why are Central Banks Reporting Losses? Does it Matter?* BIS Bulletin No 68, February. https://www.bis.org/publ/bisbull68.pdf

Belocine, N., Bhatia, A., & Frie, J. (2023). *Raising rates with a large balance sheet: The eurosystem's net income and its fiscal implications*. IMF Working Paper No WP/23/145, July.

Bernardini, M., & Conti, A. (2023). *Announcement and implementation effects of Central Bank asset purchases*. Banca D'Italia working paper 1435.

Boneva, L., Elliott, D., Kaminska, I., Linton, O., McLaren, N., & Morley, B. (2022). The impact of corporate QE on liquidity: Evidence from the UK. *Economic Journal, 132*(648), 2615–2643.

Buiter, W., Cecchetti, S., Dominguez, K., & Sanchez Serrano, A. (2023). *Stabilising financial markets: Lending and market making as a last resort*. Advisory Scientific Committee of the European Systemic Risk Board Report No. 13, January.

Cantú, C., Cavallino, P., De Fiore, F., & Yetman, J. (2021). *A global database on central banks' monetary responses to Covid-19*. BIS Working Paper, No 934, March.

Cecchetti, S., & Hilscher, J. (2024). Fiscal consequences of central bank losses. In D. Broeders, A. Houben, & M. Bonetti (Eds.), *Central bank capital in turbulent times – The risk management dimension of novel monetary policy instruments. Contributions to finance and accounting*. Springer.

Chaboud, A., & Leahy, M. (2013). *Foreign Central Bank Remittance Practices*. FOMC memo, March. https://www.federalreserve.gov/monetarypolicy/files/FOMC20130308memo09.pdf

Delgado, M., & Gravelle, T. (2023). *Central bank asset purchases in response to the covid-19 crisis*. BIS Committee on the Global Financial System Papers No 68.

Dominguez, K., & Foschi, A. (2024). Whatever-it-takes policymaking during the pandemic. *Journal of International Economics, 149*, May.

Du, W., Forbes, K., & Luzzetti, M. (2024). *Quantitative tightening around the globe: What have we learned?* US Monetary Policy Forum Report, February.

Ferguson, N., Kornejew, M., Schmelzing, P., & Schularick, M. (2023). The safety net: Central bank balance sheets and financial crises, 1587–2020. CEPR Discussion Paper No. 17858. CEPR Press, Paris & London. https://cepr.org/publications/dp17858

Fruzzetti, M., Gariano, G., Palazzo, G., & Scalia, A. (2023). The cost of unconventional monetary policy measures. A risk manager's perspective. In A. Scalia (Ed.), *Financial risk management and climate change risk. Contributions to finance and accounting*. Springer. https://doi.org/10.1007/978-3-031-33882-3_2

Goncharov, I., Novotny-Farkas, Z., & Pizzo, C. (2024). Accounting policies, distribution rules and the financial performance of central banks. In D. Broeders, A. Houben, & M. Bonetti (Eds.), *Central bank capital in turbulent times – The risk management dimension of novel monetary policy instruments. Contributions to finance and accounting*. Springer.

Hauser, A. (2023). *A journey of 1000 miles begins with a single step: Filling gaps in the central bank liquidity toolkit*. Speech at a Market News International Connect Event, Chartered Accountants' Hall, London. Published on 28 September 2023.

Hooley, J., Khan, A., Lattie, C., Mak, I., Salazar, N., Sayegh, A., & Stella, P. (2023). *Quasi-fiscal implications of central bank crisis interventions*. IMF Working Paper WP/23/114.

Humann, T., Mitchener, K., & Monnet, E. (2023). *Do disinflation policies ravage central bank finances?* CEPR Discussion Paper No. 18246. https://cepr.org/publications/dp18246

Kazuo, U. (2023). *Central bank finances and monetary policy conduct, speech at the 2023 autumn annual meeting of the japan society of monetary economics*, 30 September.

Lane, P. (2023). *Central bank liquidity: A macroeconomic perspective*. Welcome address at the ECB Conference on Money Markets, 9 November.

Ludvigson, S. (2022). Market reactions to the federal reserve's balance sheet normalization plans. *Brookings Papers on Economic Activity*, Fall: 243–258.

Nordstrom, A., & Vredin, A. (2022) *Does central bank equity matter for monetary policy?* Sveriges Riksbank Staff Memo, December.

Vissing-Jorgensen, A. (2021). The treasury market in spring 2020 and the response of the federal reserve. *Journal of Monetary Economics, 124*, 19–47.

Vissing-Jorgensen, A. (2023). *Balance Sheet Policy above the ELB*. ECB Forum on Central Banking, June 2023.

Open Access This chapter is licensed under the terms of the Creative Commons Attribution 4.0 International License (http://creativecommons.org/licenses/by/4.0/), which permits use, sharing, adaptation, distribution and reproduction in any medium or format, as long as you give appropriate credit to the original author(s) and the source, provide a link to the Creative Commons license and indicate if changes were made.

The images or other third party material in this chapter are included in the chapter's Creative Commons license, unless indicated otherwise in a credit line to the material. If material is not included in the chapter's Creative Commons license and your intended use is not permitted by statutory regulation or exceeds the permitted use, you will need to obtain permission directly from the copyright holder.

New Perspectives on Quantitative Easing and Central Bank Capital Policies

Tobias Adrian, Christopher Erceg, Marcin Kolasa, Jesper Lindé, Roger McLeod, Romain Veyrune, and Pawel Zabczyk

Abstract Central banks have come under increasing criticism for large balance sheet losses associated with quantitative easing (QE), and some observers have also argued that QE helped fuel the post-COVID-19 inflation boom. In this paper, we reconsider the conditions under which QE may be warranted considering the recent high inflation experience. We emphasize that the merits of QE should be evaluated based on the macroeconomic stimulus it provides and its effects on the consolidated fiscal position, and not simply on central bank profits or losses. Using an open economy DSGE model with segmented asset markets, we show how QE can provide a sizeable boost to output and inflation in a deep recession and improve the consolidated fiscal position—even if the central bank experiences considerable losses. However, the commitment-based features of QE and the possibility that upside inflation risks are bigger than recognized pre-pandemic call for more caution in using QE closer to full employment. We then consider how central banks might modify their policies for allocating profits to the government in light of large-scale losses. In short, we suggest that a more forward-looking and risk-based approach may be desirable in helping protect central bank financial autonomy and ultimately independence.

Keywords Central bank balance sheet · Central bank losses · DSGE model · Quantitative easing

This paper represents the view of the authors and not those of IMF Staff, IMF Management, or of the IMF Executive Board.

T. Adrian (✉) · C. Erceg · M. Kolasa · J. Lindé · R. McLeod · R. Veyrune · P. Zabczyk
International Monetary Fund, Washington, DC, USA
e-mail: TAdrian@imf.org

© International Monetary Fund 2025

D. Broeders et al. (eds.), *Central Bank Capital in Turbulent Times*, Contributions to Finance and Accounting,
https://doi.org/10.1007/978-3-031-73549-3_7

1 Introduction

Central banks spent much of the decade after the Global Financial Crisis focused on how to achieve their goals in an environment of limited policy space and asymmetric downside risks. Unconventional monetary policy tools—including quantitative easing (QE) and forward guidance—were incorporated fully into the central bank arsenal with the expectation that they would frequently be used. Policy strategies were modified to better address asymmetric risks from the effective lower bound. The view that the Phillips Curve was flat meant little need to take account of upside inflation risks in implementing these strategies. For example, in the United States, the Federal Reserve adopted an asymmetric form of average inflation targeting that promised to make up for persistent inflation undershoots of its target, but not overshoots.

The recovery from the COVID-19 pandemic involved many surprising developments that suggest some need to rethink this pre-pandemic playbook. The rapid surge in inflation points to the potential for significant nonlinearities in the Phillips Curve and underscores the need to take more account of upside inflation risks (Gopinath, 2022). While QE was likely instrumental in supporting recovery from the COVID-19 pandemic, it may have been continued for too long, and contributed to overheating and the post-COVID-19 inflation boom. Additionally, central bank forward guidance about QE may have inhibited a timelier liftoff of policy rates (Orphanides, 2023).

QE also exposed central bank balance sheets to much greater maturity risk. Heightened exposure to duration risk is an intended outcome during times of depressed demand, aiming at easing financial conditions by reducing term premia. As part of the mechanics of QE, central banks exposed themselves to this risk in order to reduce it in the marketplace. As a result, in a rising interest rate environment, many central banks have experienced large losses. While central banks can operate with realized losses and negative capital, the public backlash against these losses can be difficult to manage. In some cases, a weak central bank balance sheet or persistent decline in its remittances to the treasury could potentially undermine central bank credibility and independence.

In this paper, we consider whether and how the use of QE might be refined considering the pandemic experience (Gopinath, 2023). A key question is what the appropriate circumstances are to use QE.[1] During the period following the Global Financial Crisis, QE was used initially when economies faced very deep recessions but was later also used to boost inflation and inflation expectations after unemployment had declined close to historic lows. Is QE likely to be warranted in the latter circumstances? We also consider how the modalities of QE might be adjusted to minimize some of the risks, including through the use of escape clauses.

[1] QE may be used to reduce financial stress and improve market functioning—as in 2008–2009 and during the early phases of the pandemic—or to provide macroeconomic stimulus after policy rates have been reduced to their effective lower bound. Our paper focuses on the latter case.

We argue that the right methodological approach to address these questions about the merits of QE should take a broad-based societal perspective rather than focus on the balance sheet losses often highlighted in the financial press (other economists have raised a similar point, e.g., English and Kohn, 2022). This should involve assessing the macroeconomic benefits against the consolidated fiscal costs, as well as take account of other factors affected by QE that may matter for societal welfare (e.g., distributional effects). The consolidated fiscal costs include central bank losses, but also "subtract out" the benefits to government's fiscal position from any initial central bank profits from QE, as well as the effects on government tax revenue, expenditure, and debt-servicing costs. These benefits to the government can be sizeable, and more than offset central bank losses. Hence, it is misleading to simply focus on central bank losses when considering the costs of QE.

To be sure, the central bank would not be expected to take account of the effects of QE on the government's consolidated fiscal position when using QE any more than it would when adjusting the policy rate. In either case, its decisions about how and when to use its tools should be governed by its mandate(s), and hence aimed at ensuring macroeconomic and financial stability. But understanding the societal benefits of QE is presumably very important to those legislative and executive branch officials with oversight of the central bank, who must decide what powers ("tools") to delegate to the central bank and the circumstances in which the central bank may utilize these tools (Tucker, 2018). In general, these societal benefits include the macroeconomic benefits, but also depend on the consolidated fiscal costs and other factors such as distributional effects. Accordingly, providing an assessment of these societal benefits under different economic conditions should be helpful for this delegation choice.

Toward this end, our paper uses a quantitative model that can help gauge some of the key benefits of QE, including effects on the macroeconomy, consolidated fiscal balance, and central bank profits. While our model does not provide a full assessment of the factors likely to encompass the societal benefits of QE, it is nevertheless useful in capturing the salient considerations, and, in particular, underscores how a focus on central bank profits is problematic.

More specifically, we use an open economy DSGE model to help evaluate the benefits and costs of QE under different conditions, and also draw on related evidence in the literature. Our model builds on the framework of Kolasa and Wesolowski (2020), which incorporates bond market segmentation that allows QE to affect term premiums. The model also accounts for behavioral discounting as in Gabaix (2020) to mitigate the "forward guidance puzzle," incorporates bond market segmentation, and embeds a nonlinear Phillips Curve as in Harding, Lindé, and Trabandt (2022, 2023).

We show that QE is likely to have substantial macroeconomic benefits in a deep recession and liquidity trap, even while calibrating the model so that the effects of asset purchases on term premiums are quite modest from the perspective of the empirical literature. Moreover, the consolidated fiscal position of the government typically improves significantly, as the faster recovery in output boosts the primary balance, debt service costs fall due to lower interest payments, and increases in the price level lower the real value of existing debt. The central bank also typically makes profits, at least provided the yield curve is upward sloping. Interestingly, while central bank profits could turn significantly negative if the policy stance needs to be adjusted unexpectedly fast—as during the past 2 years—the consolidated fiscal position still tends to show considerable improvement.

QE is considerably less attractive when the central bank faces a "shallow" liquidity trap, where interest rates are pinned at zero mainly because inflation and inflation expectations are running well below target, even while output is close to potential, and the unemployment rate is not very elevated. A number of countries faced such conditions prior to the pandemic. Our simulations show that while a "small dose" of QE is still likely to be beneficial if the economy evolves roughly in line with the modal outlook, even relatively modest shocks that put upward pressure on inflation (say from fiscal expansion) can make the QE counterproductive, causing the economy to overheat and contributing to increasing inflationary pressures.

Importantly, our simulations aim to capture how some of the "commitment" aspects of QE—including forward guidance that the policy rate won't likely be raised until well after QE ends—can amplify overheating. As emphasized by Orphanides (2023), the forward guidance typically associated with QE can make it difficult for central banks to respond nimbly to overheating pressures. While this might seem inconsequential if the Phillips Curve was very flat, our simulations suggest more problems if the Phillips Curve is nonlinear and upside inflation risks more pronounced—risks that seem more material considering the recent inflation surge.

The central bank can also easily experience significant losses in these circumstances relative to a deep recession, though the implications for the consolidated fiscal positions may still be favorable. All in all, our analysis suggests substantial benefits of QE in a deep recession, despite some risk of sizeable central bank losses. But more caution is required when using QE in circumstances closer to full employment, and it is important to give thorough consideration to other approaches such as pushing interest rates negative before turning to QE.

While central bank losses should not serve as a litmus test for whether QE is desirable from a societal perspective, such losses may weaken the financial autonomy of the central bank and possibly undermine both its credibility and independence. Accordingly, we next turn to whether central banks should modify their capital policies—how they allocate profits between building their own capital and distributions to the government—to account for bigger and riskier central bank balance sheets. Current policies were typically designed decades ago when central bank balance sheets were small, cash-in-circulation the main liability, and central banks were almost always profitable (aside from those exposed to FX risk). But QE has exposed central banks to asset duration risk and resulted in big losses, with risks arising both from policy actions such as QE and from simply operating a floor system.

As is well-recognized, if a central bank has full operational independence, its monetary policy strategy and implementation should not depend on its capital or distributions to the government, and some central banks have operated effectively with negative capital for decades. But in practice, a weak financial position or inability to make profits and distributions to the government may affect operational independence. The central bank may be exposed to more political incursions, including on budgetary and personnel decisions. Or the central bank may feel compelled to view policy decisions with an eye to its balance sheet, possibly inducing it to put a "higher bar" on the use of QE. Hence central bank governance frameworks typically put a high weight on maintaining central bank financial autonomy. The importance of financial autonomy for independent decision-making has been underscored in a recent extensive survey of senior central bank officials in Adrian, Khan, and Menand (2024b).

There are currently a wide range of approaches in distributing central bank profits to the government that depend on the legal framework. For instance, distributions in some countries depend on the level of central bank capital relative to the statutory minimum. If capital is below the minimum, central bank profits must go to building capital, while profits are distributed to the government once capital exceeds the minimum. In other countries, the allocation is determined through bilateral negotiations between the central bank and the government. But the broad aim is similar. If there are shortfalls, the central bank should rebuild capital either organically through profit retention or possibly turn to a government-sponsored recapitalization if capital falls well below the regulatory minimum. These approaches are aimed at supporting the financial autonomy of the central bank, and have the appeal of simplicity, but are not risk-based or forward-looking.

Our paper explores the merits of modest departures from existing frameworks that could potentially help reduce the risks to central bank autonomy that could come from a weak capital position or high variability in its distributions to the government (especially a prolonged suspension of distributions). Notably, QE tends to generate large initial central bank profits followed by a sharp decline that could possibly translate into big cumulative losses. It seems natural to try to smooth through some of this volatility and retain some profits rather than fully distributing large upfront profits to the government.

Accordingly, we explore how central banks could modify their capital policies to take a more risk-based approach. A dynamic capital policy would involve quantifying key sources of risk and making profit allocation decisions to build capital to "provision" against shocks.[2] Central banks could use a range of models to conduct such balance sheet assessments. IMF staff have developed an approach based on the model of Hall and Reis (2015) that allows for an assessment of credit, maturity, and foreign exchange risk. Scenario analysis—or "stress tests"—can be used to gauge the risks posed by large balance sheets in the steady state due to shocks (e.g., from an inflation surge that requires policy tightening), as well as from prospective actions such as new QE programs. These tests could then help inform decisions about provisioning. A central bank experiencing large "windfall" gains from a decline in policy rates, for instance, might opt to hold on to some of these

[2] In this paper, we interpret "provisioning," as involving the creation of financial buffers through the temporary suspension in profit distributions to the government, which differs from its strict accounting definition in the International Financial Reporting Standards (IFRS).

profits—and offset future potential losses rather than simply remit them all to the Treasury.

We see considerable appeal of a risk-based approach. Even so, this approach has significant complexities. For instance, in deciding how much of its profits to retain, should the central bank look at the modal outlook or to tail risks, which may require much higher provisioning? And governments may be averse to central banks building up a war chest through retaining a large share of profits.

Our aim in this paper is simply to illuminate some alternatives to the approaches currently taken, while recognizing that there may be—for good reasons—substantial differences in the approaches ultimately taken (Tucker, 2018). Some central banks may view themselves as likely to have high operational independence irrespective of their capital position or their likely distributions to the government. Under these conditions, they may favor retaining a simple approach. Other central banks may regard financial weakness as posing risks to their ability to take mandate-consistent actions, including to use tools such as QE, and may see more appeal in risk-based approaches.

The remainder of the paper is organized as follows. Section 2 provides some background on how quantitative easing was used after the Global Financial Crisis, and on its effectiveness. Section 3 considers the lessons of the recent inflation surge for the future use of QE, while Sect. 4 considers how some of the modalities of QE might be adjusted to minimize risks to central bank credibility (e.g., through the increased use of escape clauses). Section 5 considers how central bank capital policies might be modified to account for the risks posed by bigger and more leveraged central bank balance sheets. Finally, Sect. 6 concludes.

2 Quantitative Easing Before the Pandemic

Quantitative easing (QE) became a key component of the toolkit of central banks during and after the Global Financial Crisis. Given the sharp downturn in activity, central banks lowered interest rates to the zero lower bound. The major central banks, including the Federal Reserve, Bank of England, Bank of Japan, and European Central Bank, also turned to QE—complemented with forward guidance—to provide support to the macroeconomy and boost inflation.

Quantitative easing involves central banks purchasing longer-term government bonds and financing those purchases through the issuance of reserve money. Because reserve money is a short-term liability, QE can be regarded as tantamount to shortening the maturity structure of public debt, which tends to lower term premiums through portfolio balance channels. In addition, central banks have also purchased private assets such as mortgage-backed securities and corporate bonds to lower risk premiums. While similar actions by Treasuries—such as swapping short for long-term debt—would presumably elicit similar effects through portfolio channels, an important argument for delegating QE to central banks is that it strengthens the impact through "signaling" channels, including by underscoring the central bank's aim to maintain accommodative policy.

QE was initially used in the context of a sharp economic downturn driven by a rapid tightening of financial conditions. The expectation was that the large balance sheet expansions associated with QE were temporary measures meant to address the exceptional circumstances of the Global Financial Crisis, and that balance sheets would gradually be "wound down" as conditions normalized. Central banks expected to maintain corridor-based operational frameworks, under the assumption that they would return to conventional interest rate policy as their primary policy tool.

These expectations were belied by the slow subsequent recovery in advanced economies and drag from the unfolding debt crisis in Europe, and major central banks launched an array of QE programs to spur recovery and nudge inflation closer to their targets. Moreover, even as financial conditions eased and economic recovery progressed, policymakers became increasingly concerned that a decline in the neutral rate of interest (r*) would severely limit policy space even as activity and employment fully recovered. As a result, central banks were very cautious unwinding QE, and only the Federal Reserve ended up reducing the size of its balance sheet. Other major central banks proceeded to expand their balance sheets in the 2016–2019 period—even as unemployment moved toward historic lows—given concerns that a continued downward drift in inflation expectations below target would further limit policy space and given concerns about downside risks. Thus, the Bank of England launched a QE program following the Brexit referendum in 2016, the ECB embarked in renewed quantitative easing in the fall of 2019, and the BoJ progressively expanded the breadth of its yield-curve control framework to include equity.

The upshot was that QE—in concert with forward guidance—de facto became the primary tool used by a number of advanced economy central banks for providing monetary accommodation through most of the period between the GFC and the pandemic. Central banks viewed QE as a good, even if imperfect, substitute for conventional monetary policy. Their views were well-grounded in substantial empirical and model-based evidence showing that QE had sizeable effects on term and risk premiums, especially in periods of financial stress, and could provide macroeconomic stimulus when conventional policy space was limited.

Importantly, the way that QE programs were structured and communicated to the public evolved considerably through time, as central banks sought to better link QE with policy objectives. In particular, central banks moved from using a fixed timetable for QE purchases that was insensitive to economic conditions to a more state-contingent approach in which the duration and pace of QE depended on economic conditions and progress on inflation—essentially a QE reaction function.

Central banks also aimed to improve effectiveness through deepening the link between QE and the reaction function for the policy rate. Intuitively, if policy rates were expected to react a lot to the decline in term and risk spreads induced by QE, QE would have little effect on bond yields and hence on activity. Conversely, QE effectiveness could be enhanced by convincing markets that the policy rate wouldn't be likely to react much. Based on this reasoning, central banks indicated that policy rates were unlikely to be raised until well after QE ended, and that policy rate adjustment was likely to be gradual even after liftoff. Because asset purchase programs were viewed as mainly operating through stock effects—and hence had to remain in place for a long time to have their intended effect—this communication, in effect, guided markets to expect that policy rates would be very low for several years.

Structural models helped central banks identify the potential benefits of adopting an interest rate reaction function consistent with gradual liftoff as well as quantifying the gains. For instance, the research of Engen, Laubach, and Reifschneider (2016) showed how the effects of a given-sized QE program on unemployment are much larger under a calibration of the Taylor rule implying a more gradual liftoff of policy rates than a standard Taylor rule. They argued that the Fed's communication after the Global Financial crisis evolved in a way consistent with this more accommodative form of the Taylor rule.

Central banks generally perceived that some degree of commitment could enhance the stimulus from QE (Bernanke, 2017). Using evocative language from Greek mythology, the president of the Federal Reserve Bank of Chicago Charles Evans and his colleagues described this as "Odyssean" forward guidance: just as Odysseus tied himself to the mast to resist bewitchment by Circe, central banks could promise to keep policy rates low—at least to a point—even if economic conditions called for raising interest rates under their normal reaction function (Campbell et~al., 2012). These commitments were perceived as being relatively low cost to central bank credibility insofar as economic recovery was expected to be gradual, and there seemed little risk of an inflation surge given that the Phillips Curve appeared very flat. Indeed, rather than liftoff earlier than markets anticipated, slow progress on inflation and the perception of pronounced downside risks led central banks to repeatedly push back the expected date of liftoff from the effective lower bound.

On the financial side, central banks typically made sizeable profits from QE. While it was recognized that QE required the central bank to take leveraged positions that in principle could result in losses if central banks had to raise policy rates sharply, such an outcome was viewed as unlikely. And even with very low long-term yields, the yield curve remained sufficiently upward sloping to keep interest margins profitable and generate ongoing central bank profits that were distributed to Treasuries. Given the boost to the economy and hence positive effects on government fiscal positions, the effects of QE were even more favorable from a consolidated perspective.

The perception that QE was an indispensable tool in delivering stimulus when conventional policy was constrained—as well as a widespread belief that a low r* was likely to seriously constrain policy space going forward—were key factors leading central banks to shift toward floor-based operating systems in the years prior to the pandemic. A highly attractive feature of a floor system is that it allows a central bank to rapidly scale up its balance sheet through expanding reserves when needed—while keeping the policy rate from falling too low—but also to tighten policy when appropriate without having to liquidate assets. Thus, the perception that the ELB was often likely to bind, and that QE was critical in such circumstances was a major catalyst in shifting away from the lean balance sheets and corridor systems that had been used for decades before the Global Financial Crisis.

3 Implications of the Inflation Surge for the Use of QE

Central banks in advanced economies largely followed the pre-pandemic playbook in deploying QE over the pandemic period. Large-scale asset purchases were initially used to support market functioning when financial markets came under severe pandemic-related stress in the spring of 2020 and were accompanied by a raft of liquidity-support measures. Once financial stresses eased, central banks indicated that they would continue to expand their balance sheets through QE operations to provide macroeconomic stimulus. QE was complemented by sharp interest rate cuts that pushed policy rates to their effective lower bound, and by forward guidance suggesting that policy rates would remain tethered to their effective floor for a prolonged period (often several years).

QE was undertaken by a broader group of advanced economy central banks than had used QE before the pandemic, as well as a couple of emerging markets. Central banks at the time projected a very slow recovery in employment and return of inflation to target. For example, the ECB staff projections in September 2020 saw unemployment hovering near 9% by late 2022, and inflation just nudging over 1%. While forecast uncertainty was viewed as very high, the forward guidance of central banks was predicated on the belief that inflation was likely to remain well below target in most plausible scenarios, and that risks were skewed to the downside.

Thus, central banks felt comfortable in making longer-horizon promises about the policy rate path, and in omitting the "escape clauses" that had often accompanied QE prior to the pandemic. And markets broadly shared this pessimistic outlook: participants in the September 2020 NY Fed Survey of Primary Dealers saw only a 1% chance that the federal funds rate would rise above 2% by end-2023, which was still below the level viewed as normal in the long-run.

In the event, a rapid surge of inflation that began in 2021 forced central banks to tighten policy much earlier than expected. While the inflation appears to have been mainly driven by supply factors in many economies, especially outside of the United States, stronger-than-expected recoveries also helped boost inflation, making central banks feel confident that sharp tightening was warranted.

Given that QE heavily exposed central banks to maturity mismatch—they had bought assets when yields on long-term bonds were at record lows and often significantly negative—the sharp rise in interest rates and inversion of the yield curve has caused central banks to experience very sizeable losses. These losses, in concert with the inflation spike itself, have created a significant public backlash against QE—to the effect that central banks overdid their policy support, amplifying inflation pressure while accumulating losses that ultimately must be borne by taxpayers. Perhaps more subtly, central banks have been criticized for the modalities of QE, as forward guidance that policy rates wouldn't be raised until QE ended may have delayed a more timely liftoff (see Orphanides, 2023).

This experience suggests the need to consider possible lessons for the future use of QE. Under what conditions is QE likely to be desirable to use, and when should central banks be more cautious about deploying it? And if central banks do decide to use QE, should they change the modalities of how they implement and communicate it?

In reassessing the benefits and costs of QE, it seems crucial to not simply fixate on the implications for central bank balance sheets—as often seems the case in political debates and in the press. QE should be evaluated by considering the benefits it can have in achieving core central bank stabilization objectives—including to lower unemployment and raise inflation in the context of a recession—as well as its consolidated fiscal costs. Critically, the latter should include not only central bank losses, but also sizeable initial gains, as well as the effects on government debt arising through lower interest payments, higher tax receipts, and lower expenditures.

From a broad perspective, there would still seem to be substantial benefits from using QE in a deep recession of the sort experienced in the wake of the Global Financial Crisis. For a given scale of QE, the effects on term and risk premiums would likely be larger than in a shallow recession, especially if financial conditions hadn't completely normalized. And such QE would be unlikely to engender noticeably earlier or faster liftoff, resulting in much of the decline in term premiums translating into lower yields, and boosting its effectiveness. On the fiscal side, the stimulus to activity and reduction in yields should reduce government debt, and any adverse effects on central bank profits would likely be limited as long as policy rates remained fairly low for some time.

The more difficult question focuses on the merits of QE in a "shallower trap" or recession, in which inflation may be running considerably below target, but employment or output slack is very modest. In this situation, central banks may have well-grounded concerns about downside risks, including that inflation expectations could drift down and further limit policy space. But the recent inflation surge is highly suggestive of the potential importance of nonlinearities in the Phillips Curve that may reflect changes in price-setting when the economy is running hot or inflation is already running high, as in recent models by Benigno and Eggertsson (2023) and Harding et al. (2023). Such nonlinearities may reflect in part the presence of fixed factors of production at the sectoral level that can imply large effects of demand stimulus on key input prices (in the spirit of Lorenzoni and Werning, 2023). While QE in the pre-pandemic period was increasingly predicated on the belief that the Phillips Curve was very flat, recent experience suggests a material risk that QE could push the economy into a region of overheating if initiated in a shallow liquidity trap.

3.1 Illustrative Model Simulations

To provide more clarity about the conditions in which QE may be appropriate, it is helpful to draw upon simulations of a two-country New Keynesian DSGE model with several key frictions that make it potentially desirable to use QE. First, building on Chen et~al. (2012) and Kolasa and Wesolowski (2020), the model incorporates portfolio transaction costs and restricts some agents from trading both short- and long-term bonds. This segmentation of the bond market is critical for allowing large-scale asset purchases by the central bank—or QE—to affect term premiums. Second, the model incorporates behavioral discounting as in Gabaix (2020). Allowing some agents to be myopic limits the traction that central banks can get from making commitments about future conventional policy after the effective lower bound no longer binds; without such discounting, central banks could simply rely on forward guidance and not have to worry about using QE (as emphasized in the "forward-guidance" puzzle literature, e.g., Del Negro et~al., 2015). Finally, on the aggregate supply side, the model embeds a nonlinear Phillips Curve in which inflation rises more sharply with output when the economy is already running hot (with this "banana shape" reflecting convexities in price-setting as in Harding et~al., 2022, 2023). The model is parameterized to be conservative in the effects of QE, and to imply standard effects of conventional monetary and fiscal policy shocks.[3] Further details on the model, including its parameterization, is provided in Adrian et~al. (2024a).

It is useful to assess the effects of QE in a liquidity trap generated by economic conditions of varying severity. In one case, QE is implemented in a very deep liquidity trap associated with a severe recession in which the output gap is deeply negative, and inflation is well below target. Roughly speaking, this scenario would be similar to that prevailing in the aftermath of the GFC, where financial conditions had improved but unemployment ran far above its long-run level. The second scenario considers QE in a much shallower liquidity trap in which output is only modestly below potential while inflation runs about 0.8 percentage points below target. This is reasonably similar to the situation that a number of advanced economy central banks faced before the pandemic in which inflation seemed stuck well below target even as unemployment moved toward record lows. In either situation, the recession is driven by mix of supply and demand shocks (of varying size),[4] and

[3] For QE, we calibrate the model to imply effects on output that are somewhat smaller than the empirical papers by academic scholars surveyed in Fabo et~al. (2021). This meta-analysis notes that the effectiveness of QE is found to be notably smaller by academics than central bank economists, so by benchmarking our model to their evidence excluding central banks, we take a conservative view on the effectiveness of QE.

[4] The deep liquidity trap is mainly driven by large negative demand shocks, with some contribution of favorable supply shocks representing additional wage moderation. The demand shocks used to construct the shallow trap are smaller while wage moderation drivers are amplified. The more sizable supply component in the shallow trap scenario allows us to achieve a larger inflation decline relative to target amid a moderate downturn in economic activity.

the central bank is assumed to follow a Taylor-style interest rate reaction function subject to an ELB constraint (here assumed to be 0) on the short-term policy rate. QE is assumed to be implemented gradually, with the stock of assets held by the central bank peaking at 10% of baseline GDP after a year. This sequence of purchases reduces the term premium initially by about 50 basis points.

In the deep recession scenario, QE clearly has sizeable macroeconomic benefits. As seen in Fig. 1, QE boosts output (upper left panel) by about 0.8% relative to baseline after six quarters and inflation (upper right panel) by 0.2 percentage points. This stimulus reflects that markets expect the central bank to progressively expand its balance sheet through asset purchases, so that the term premium declines persistently (middle right panel). The macro stimulus induces a slightly earlier liftoff of the policy rate (middle left panel). Even so, this offset is relatively modest, so that most of the decline in the term premium passes through to longer-term yields.[5]

On the fiscal side, the strong stimulus to output boosts the government's primary balance substantially, reduces interest payments, and results in a large reduction in government debt. The central bank also makes profits, with the central bank's capital rising about 0.5% after 5 years (lower right panel). The central bank profits reflect that long-term yields—while declining substantially—remain well above the policy rate that is pinned at zero for several years and then rises only gradually to its long-run level. As a result, the consolidated fiscal position (lower left panel) improves substantially by about 5% of baseline GDP after 5 years (difference between solid line and dashed line in panel e), of which the bulk reflects increased tax revenue. The consolidated position includes central bank profits, which are assumed to be remitted immediately in our model. In effect, QE more than pays for itself insofar as the macro stimulus is accompanied by falling government debt.

This "holy trinity" of significant macroeconomic benefits, a boost to government revenues, and positive central bank profits seems a reasonable characterization of the central bank experience with QE in the aftermath of the GFC. Moreover, in a deep recession, the macro and fiscal benefits are likely to remain substantial even if there are shocks that occur after the implementation of a QE program that would call for faster policy rate hikes under normal conditions. In particular, given that the central bank would like to set a deeply negative policy rate if constrained by the ELB, modest-sized aggregate demand shocks—such as from fiscal expansion—would not push toward significantly earlier liftoff, and the benefits of QE from a macro perspective and consolidated fiscal perspective would be similar to those in Fig. 1. Central bank profits would be diminished a bit but would still be likely positive (if the policy rate does not have to markedly overshoot its steady-state level).

Even so, as suggested by recent experience, very large shocks could materially affect the benefits of a given QE program, especially if they induced a rapid recovery

[5] While our focus in this paper is on monetary policy, fiscal stimulus can also play a critical role in supporting economic recovery and is likely to be particularly effective in these circumstances when conventional monetary policy is constrained by the effective lower bound.

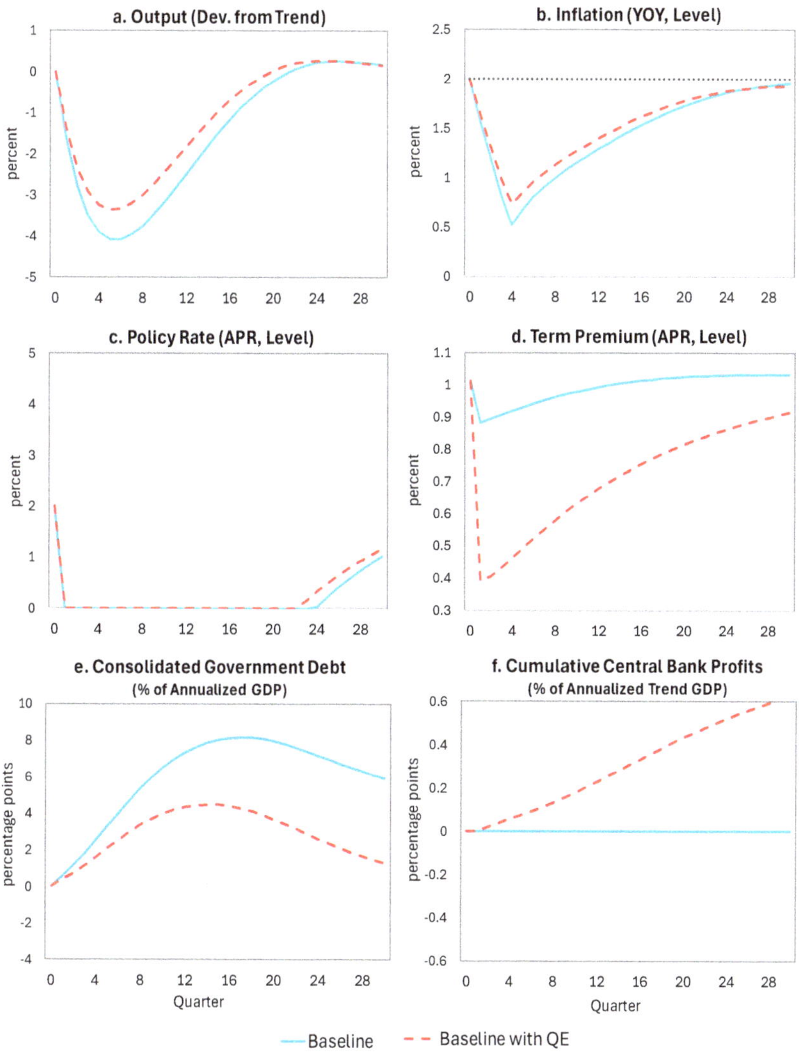

Fig. 1 Ex ante: deep liquidity trap. Note: The panels compare baseline (solid) paths of the respective variables in a deep liquidity trap to those from an alternative scenario (dashed lines) in which QE equal to 10% of GDP is also deployed. Source: IMF staff calculations

and inflation surge that pushed the central bank to raise policy rates well above their normal long-run level. Under these circumstances, the central bank could face large losses. But even in these circumstances where the "ex post" benefits of QE are lower than envisioned, QE would still be likely to have significant beneficial effects, especially in the plausible case in which the stimulative shocks take some time to affect the macroeconomy.

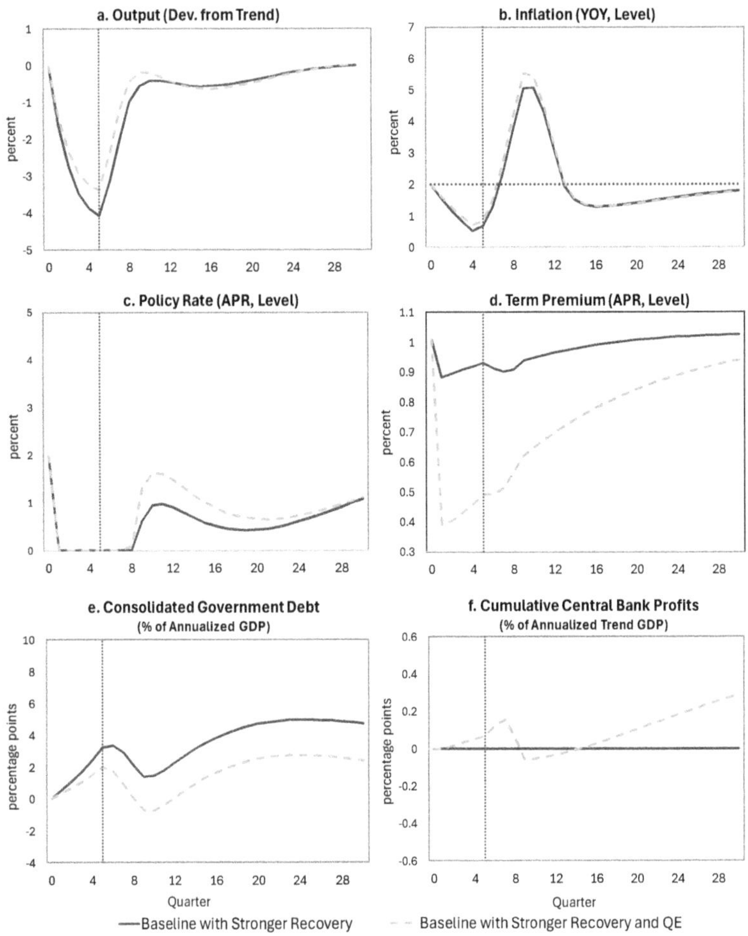

Fig. 2 Ex post: deep liquidity trap. Note: The panels compare paths of the respective variables in a deep liquidity trap with a stronger recovery (solid lines) to those from an alternative scenario (dashed lines) in which QE equal to 10% of GDP is also deployed. Source: IMF staff calculations

In this vein, Fig. 2 shows the effects of QE relative to a baseline (solid lines) that is initially identical to the recession in Fig. 1 but incorporates a much faster recovery in output and inflation driven by a mix of positive demand and adverse cost-push shocks, which materialize one and a half year after the initial shock. QE still provides substantial macro benefits, also from this ex-post perspective—boosting output and inflation when the economic slack is sizeable, and the welfare benefits are presumably highest. While the eventual overheating and overshoot of the inflation target require a sharp rise in the policy rate that pares back central bank profits significantly, the consolidated fiscal position still improves considerably. These results underscore the robustness of QE in a deep trap, and the importance of looking at the consolidated fiscal position in assessing the fiscal consequences.

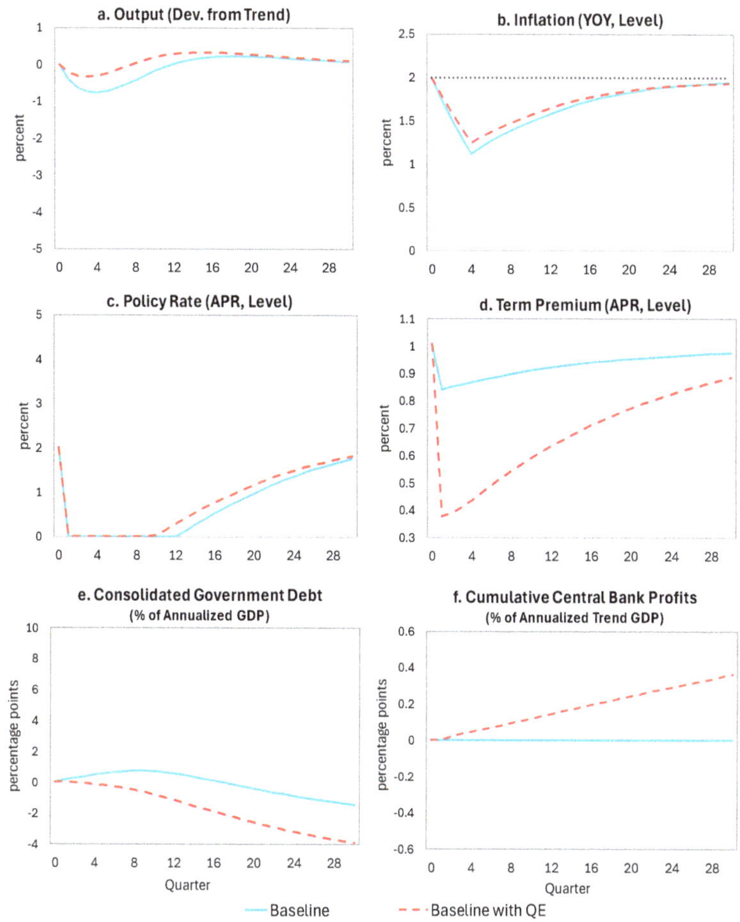

Fig. 3 Ex ante: shallow liquidity trap. Note: The panels compare baseline (solid blue) paths of the respective variables in a shallow liquidity trap to those from an alternative scenario (dashed red lines) in which QE equal to 10% of GDP is also deployed. Source: IMF staff calculations

Turning to the case of a shallow liquidity trap with a smaller economic decline and below target inflation shown in Fig. 3, QE still appears beneficial provided that the economy evolves reasonably in line with the modal outlook (i.e., that it would stay close to baseline absent QE). As illustrated in Fig. 3, the baseline without QE has a negative output gap of a little less than 1% and inflation is about 0.8 percentage points below target. A modest-sized QE program is helpful in closing the output gap in this scenario and in boosting inflation, and the implications for the consolidated fiscal position remain favorable. In fact, the central bank experiences some improvement in its capital position, as the yield curve remains upward sloping (with the policy rate only converging gradually to its long-run level).

However, there are several noteworthy differences between the effects of QE in a shallow liquidity trap compared to the deep liquidity trap case considered earlier. First, a given-sized QE program has less "bang for the buck" in reducing long-term yields and hence in boosting output and inflation, reflecting that the stimulus from QE tends to cause policy rates to rise more quickly than in a deep liquidity trap. Thus, the output rise is only about two-thirds as large in Fig. 3 as in Fig. 1.

Second, there is more risk that QE can be counterproductive in a shallow liquidity trap if even modest upside inflation risks—such as from fiscal stimulus—materialize. This is illustrated in Fig. 4, which shows the effects of QE against the backdrop of the same initial baseline as in Fig. 3, but with stimulative shocks hitting a few quarters after QE is initiated. While QE is initially modestly beneficial as in Fig. 3, its marginal impact is to overheat the economy once it recovers faster than envisioned than when QE was first undertaken (the baselines without QE are shown by the solid lines in Figs. 3 and 4, respectively).

Moreover, the commitment element of QE can additionally fuel the overheating and makes the central bank much less nimble in responding to the upside inflation surprise. As discussed in Sect. 2, QE typically involves some guidance about how long it is likely to last, as well as a conditional promise to delay hiking rates until well-after QE ends. The second simulation (dashed line) in Fig. 4 aims to capture the latter channel by assuming the central bank keeps policy rates on hold for several quarters after the new shocks hit (comparing the dashed line to the solid line). In effect, the central bank may feel "locked into" keeping policy rates low even when it would otherwise raise them quickly, which accounts for much of the overheating effects of QE in our scenario. In practice, central banks may also feel constrained by the guidance they give about the likely duration of QE program, including both from concerns about credibility and financial stability. These risks associated with the low nimbleness of QE are clearly higher when upside inflation risks are more pronounced, as would be the case if the Phillips Curve is nonlinear and the QE is initiated reasonably close to full employment.

A third point to note about QE in a shallow trap is that it is more likely to result in central bank losses (lower right panel) given a greater likelihood that policy rates would eventually have to be raised well above neutral. In our simulation, it still turns out that QE reduces government debt from a consolidated perspective (lower left panel). However, the fiscal implications could be less favorable in the event the central bank felt it was necessary to shift its reaction function and act more forcefully. This would amplify central bank losses and could cause the consolidated fiscal position to deteriorate. Such an outcome would be more likely if the nonlinearities in the Phillips Curve were more pronounced—and lead to more persistent inflation effects—than in our model.

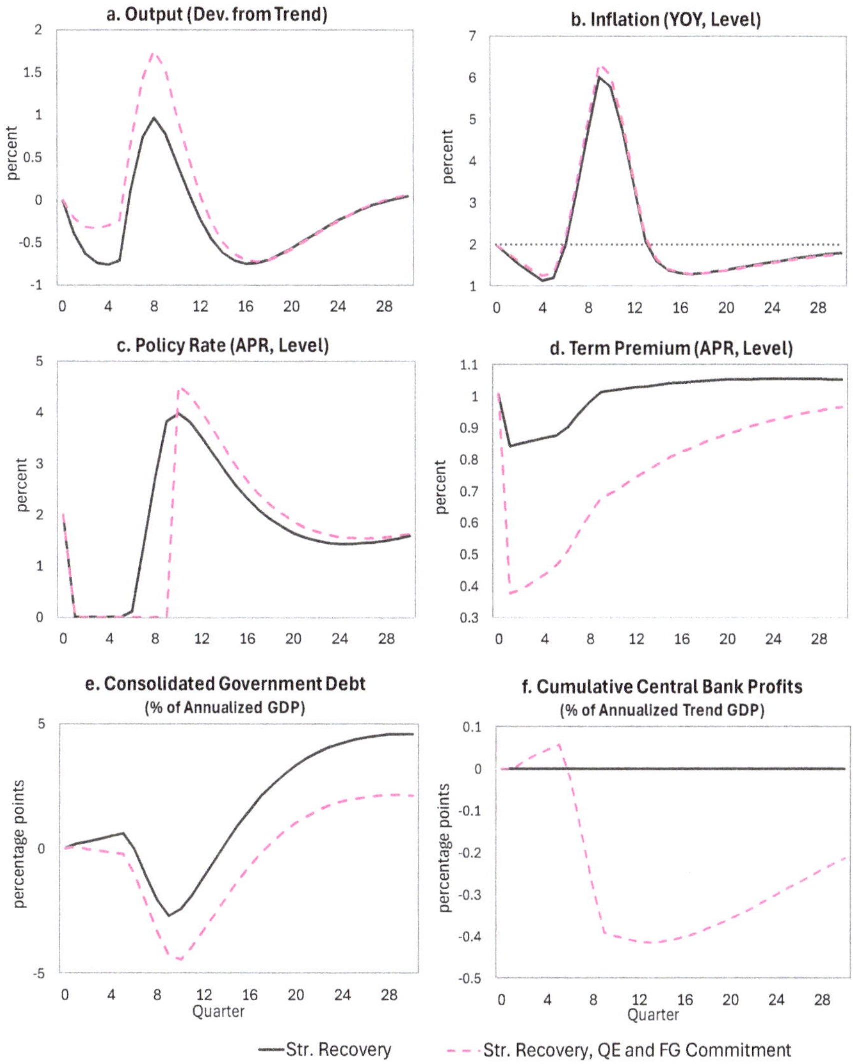

Fig. 4 Ex post: shallow liquidity trap with forward guidance commitment. Note: The panels compare paths of the respective variables in a shallow liquidity trap with a stronger recovery (solid lines) to those from an alternative scenario (dashed lines) in which QE equal to 10% of GDP is also deployed and in which the central bank feels "locked into" keeping policy rates low even when it would otherwise raise them quickly. Source: IMF staff calculations

4 The Modalities of QE and Some Alternatives

The previous section has highlighted conditions under which QE is likely to be welfare-improving, and conditions under which more caution is required. But a closely related question involves the appropriate modalities of QE, including how central banks should communicate conditional commitments about the duration of QE or a QE reaction function, and about policy rate adjustment after QE. This issue seems particularly relevant given that upside inflation risks seem much more material than was recognized before the pandemic.

As discussed earlier, the macroeconomic benefits of QE hinge significantly on communication that reinforces the market's view that: (1) QE will remain in effect for a prolonged period (which should push down term premiums more); (2) policy rate adjustment will not begin until well after QE ends; and (3) policy rate adjustment is likely to be gradual after it commences. The inflation surge and heightened risk of nonlinearities in the Phillips Curve suggest a need for central bank communication to be clearer in recognizing the possible need to exit QE early and raise policy rates faster.

Such an outcome is considerably more likely in a shallow liquidity trap, where there would seem a particularly strong case for using "escape clauses" to signal conditions that could terminate QE early and call for faster policy adjustment, perhaps well before net purchases ceased. Without such escape clauses, central banks could feel somewhat constrained from responding as aggressively as needed to a surge in inflation and/or macroeconomic overheating due to concerns about a loss to their credibility. Orphanides (2023) has argued in the case of the recent inflation surge, central banks could become "trapped" by their own forward guidance, and their slow exit from QE could in turn generate macroeconomic instability. At the same time, such escape clauses may shorten agents' expectations about how long the central bank will keep policy rates at the effective lower bound, making QE even less potent in affecting long-term yields and economic activity in a shallow liquidity trap.

The upshot is that the central banks could reasonably feel quite confident about using QE in a deep trap where the risk of early termination and rapid liftoff is small. Hence, a given-sized QE program would tend to impart larger macro stimulus "when it is needed most," have favorable fiscal effects and be less likely to adversely affect central bank balance sheets. In contrast, the benefits of QE in a shallow liquidity trap are likely to be noticeably smaller as markets recognize a greater chance that the central bank may have to depart from a gradualist approach to removing accommodation.

In deciding whether to use QE, central banks would also want to take account of the potential challenges of reversing it through QT. Acharya et~al. (2023) argue that scaling down balance sheets may be more challenging that building them up, so that QT presents considerable risks to financial stability and market functioning. Forbes and Du et~al. (2024) are somewhat more sanguine based on the experience of QT thus far, but caution that significant problems may emerge as reserves decline further.[6]

[6] Erceg et~al. (2024) show that an exit strategy that relies more heavily on QT than policy rate hikes can have more adverse spillovers to other economies under some conditions (by generating sharper adjustments in exchange rates and term premiums).

Given that QE requires longer-term commitments to be effective that can be problematic to make in a shallow trap, central banks may give more consideration to negative rates, or to simply relying on forward guidance without tying it to QE. On negative rates, several central banks pushed interest rates to levels below zero for a prolonged period, with the ECB setting its policy rate at minus 50 basis points and Swiss National Bank holding its policy rate at minus 50–75 basis points for several years. Empirical evidence suggests that transmission was quite effective compared to conventional policy, with negative rates showing substantial passthrough to both lending and deposit rates (Brandao-Marques et al., 2024). These policy adjustments did not generate the financial stability risks that were often feared, suggesting some scope to push in this direction before turning to QE. Even so, moving rates to moderately negative levels may not deliver the stimulus needed to deliver on central bank mandates, and pushing much further on this dimension could cause financial stability risks to surface.

5 How Should Central Bank Capital Policies be Modified to Account for Bigger and Riskier CB Balance Sheets?

While we have argued that the consolidated fiscal position is the appropriate way to assess the fiscal costs of QE from a societal perspective, it is important to safeguard against risks to the central bank's financial position. For an appropriately independent central bank, the capital position should have no bearing on its ability to carry out its mandated objectives. However, in practice, a weak financial position or inability to make profits and distributions to the government may increase the risk that the central bank is exposed to incursions on its independence. For instance, central banks might feel pressured to put a higher bar on the use of QE, or even in taking conventional policy actions (raising interest rates).

The importance of financial autonomy as a core aspect of good central bank governance has long been recognized and incorporated into central bank laws. However, the capital policies of most advanced economy central banks were developed in an environment of "lean" balance sheets in which they faced little credit, maturity, or FX risk. Because their liabilities were largely non-interest bearing—consisting mostly of currency in circulation—central banks could invest in interest-bearing securities and almost always make a profit (Stella, 2008). In this environment, capital policies seemed of little consequence, at least for advanced economy central banks not exposed to FX risk, and capital distribution policies were often quite mechanical.

However, the large losses central banks have taken in the wake of balance sheet actions—especially QE and FX accumulation—are raising interest in whether and how central banks might adjust capital policies going forward. How should they be adapted to manage heavily leveraged balance sheets? Central banks face greater balance sheet risks both because of discretionary actions such as using QE to fight recessions, but also because they have changed their operating frameworks toward floor systems. Floor systems require larger steady-state balance sheets and hence are more exposed to shocks.

5.1 Current Capital Policies

As a prelude to addressing these questions, it is helpful to first delve a bit more into existing capital policies, where there is wide variation across central banks. Some central banks are legally required to maintain a minimum level of capital that may be specified as a fixed nominal amount in the domestic currency—such as 20 billion krona in the case of the Riksbank—or as a percentage of some component of monetary liabilities.

There is also wide variation in approaches to distributing central bank profits to the government. Some central banks make distributions that depend on the level of capital relative to the statutory minimum: in this case, all profits typically are used to build central bank reserves if capital is below the minimum, while profits are distributed to the government once that level is exceeded. In other cases, the law establishes that a fixed percentage of the profits goes to reserves and the rest to the government—with the horizon sometimes extending to several years in an effort to smooth through short-term variability in profits. In other cases, there is no specific rule for distributing profits, and the distribution is the result of a negotiation between the central bank and the government. In practice, many central banks have distributed a large share of their profits to the government even in the past few years (see Fig. 5).

A common feature of most capital distribution policies—including the setting of minimum capital levels when applicable and the approach to distributing profits—is that they typically are not risk-based. When capital shortfalls do materialize, they are addressed by organically rebuilding central bank capital through profit retention (mainly seigniorage) and sometimes complemented by recapitalizations by the government. Such recapitalizations may be required by central bank law but are often done by the government on a more discretionary basis.

While the mechanical approaches to profit distribution seem understandable given that most advanced economy central banks faced little balance sheet risk before the Global Financial Crisis, there is some precedent for more risk-based approaches. Notably, some small and highly open advanced economy as well as emerging market central banks have developed capital policies that provision against exchange rate risk. For example, the Norges Bank developed a risk-based approach in the early 1990s after experiencing sizeable foreign exchange losses (Stella, 2008). During the past couple of years, a number of central banks have moved toward more risk-based provisioning to account for greater balance sheet risks after the massive balance sheet expansions during COVID-19, including by some euro-system central banks. For instance, the Bundesbank stopped paying remittances to the German

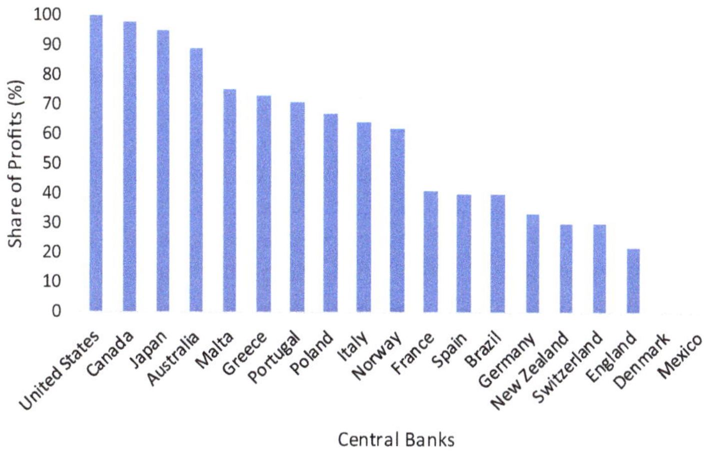

Fig. 5 Distributions of Central Bank Profits to the Government (average over 2019–2022). Note: The central banks of the following countries were included (listed in alphabetical order): Australia; Brazil; Canada; Denmark; UK; France; Germany; Greece; Italy; Japan; Malta; Mexico; New Zealand; Norway; Poland; Portugal; Spain; Switzerland; USA. Profits for all Euro area countries are calculated as distributable net profits plus risk provision. Source: IMF staff calculations based on audited financial statements of respective central banks

Ministry of Finance in 2020 to help build buffers to withstand losses, and the Central Bank of the Netherlands did so in 2021.

5.2 *Key Facets of a Risk-Based Approach*

In light of the risks associated with larger balance sheets, central banks may want to consider the merits of moving toward a more dynamic approach that determines an adequate capital level (or perhaps range) on a forward-looking basis that takes account of key sources of risk. Specifically, a dynamic capital policy would allow for the suspension of profit distributions when needed to build the central bank's capital to provision against shocks (even if current profits are positive and capital above the statutory minimum).

Implementing a dynamic capital policy would involve quantifying key risks to the central bank's capital position, including from credit risk, maturity mismatch, and foreign exchange risk. This process can be viewed as a form of "stress-testing" by analogy to the exercises applied to commercial banks insofar as it would help gauge how central bank capital would evolve in a range of scenarios.

Even so, the interpretation of the results would be very different than for a commercial bank, for which negative capital would signal insolvency. A central bank could instead use the stress-testing approach to assess the risk that its capital would dip to levels below the statutory minima and trigger a potentially long suspension of distributions to the government. Such outcomes could pose material challenges to its ability to carry out its mandated objectives (perhaps making it difficult to initiate a QE program) or even operate effectively (if it faces heavy budgetary pressures).

The risks posed by a weak financial position to central bank independence appear to be well-recognized by central bankers. A recent paper by Adrian, Khan, and Menand (2024b) that aimed to weigh the aspects of de jure central bank independence that matter most for de facto independence in policymaking ranked financial autonomy at the very top of the list, even ahead of independence of the central bank board from government officials. Thus, decisions about how to distribute central bank profits between the general reserves of the central bank (a component of statutory capital) versus the government (the "shareholder") can be quite consequential.

While central banks may employ different approaches to stress-test their balance sheets, IMF staff have developed a quantitative framework that can potentially facilitate these efforts. The IMF staff approach builds on the model of Hall and Reis (2015), which considers central bank capital as exposed to three key sources of risk: (1) interest rate risk; (2) credit risk; and (3) exchange rate risk. The staff's "central bank stress-testing" model (CBST model) projects the profits and capital path of a central bank in a wide range of macroeconomic scenarios. The scenario analysis can help a central bank gauge an adequate capital level (or comfort range) that would allow it to absorb large but plausible shocks without pushing capital to very low levels likely to create political pressures (either directly or because it would imply a suspension of distributions to the government).

Stress-testing can be used both to assess risks arising from shocks—such as an inflation surge—as well as of central bank policy actions. Notably, the shift of major central banks to floor operating systems has translated into much larger balance sheets that are exposed to both credit and maturity risk, especially from shocks that cause the yield curve to invert. Stress-testing can help the central bank quantify this risk in a range of scenarios that might involve inflation running well above or below its target. Implementation does require a range of specific model assumptions, such as about the form of the monetary policy reaction function, as well as empirical relationships specifying how policy rate changes affect the yield curve. Thus, a more aggressive monetary policy reaction to inflation would mean a sharper interest rate hike in response to an inflation surge, and bigger central bank losses. The stress test could also gauge the effects of policy actions such as QE both under the modal outlook, and in shock scenarios.

The results could help inform central bank decisions about how to allocate profits and may entail building capital to well above statutory minimums. For instance, a central bank running a floor system and experiencing large profits due to a decline in policy rates—perhaps because of a recession that was expected to be short-lived—may want to retain some of these profits to build capital to counter the risk that the policy rate could eventually rise enough to generate significant losses.

From an institutional perspective, the central bank would typically have a "risk unit" that would develop and maintain the underlying model, as well as prepare the stress tests that would help quantify the central banks' exposure to balance sheet risk. The Board of the central bank would provide oversight of the stress-testing framework and could draw on the stress-test results to inform its decision about profit distributions. Of course, the Board members might have a range of views about how to proceed, but the stress test would help them think through the implications of different options.

5.3 What Is the Right Breadth of Risk-Based Provisioning?

An appealing feature of central bank stress testing is that it can help central banks better assess risks to their capital position in an environment of large balance sheets and help insulate them against key risks. This approach can help central banks gauge how much of any "unusual" profits they should retain to offset losses down the road. Such provisioning should reduce the risk that a central bank gets "forced into a hole" and potentially has to request a Treasury recapitalization to maintain credibility.

Such an approach is also helpful for public accountability to help better gauge whether central bank actions such as QE seem warranted based on benefit/cost criteria. Of course, as we have emphasized, such an evaluation should necessarily also take account of both the benefits to macroeconomic and financial stability as well as the implications for the government's fiscal position.

But there are a number of open questions that central banks will have to consider. These range from technical issues about how to model various components of balance sheet risk to deciding how to link the stress test results to provisioning decisions.

One fundamental question concerns the appropriate breadth of provisioning. Should the central bank aim to provision ex ante to account of a wide range of actions that it might take in crisis circumstances, or stick to provisioning against "core" risks associated say with operating a floor system and managing FX reserves? The former case would not only entail complex scenario design—about which tools might be used in various situations, and about initial conditions such as the slope of the yield curve—but also to assign probabilities to these scenarios. On the other hand, assessing and provisioning against core risks seems much more straightforward.

A second issue is the role of the Treasury and legislative branch in vetting the stress-testing and provisioning choices. What if the Treasury disagrees with the central bank and perceives that the central bank faces much lower risks of capital losses? Or if it believes that the central bank should not be using certain tools such as QE as readily, reserving these for more exceptional circumstances? Such dynamic provisioning is likely to entail more bilateral discussion between the central bank and government than under the simple mechanical rules central banks have typically followed in the past. It will be important for the central bank to have a high degree of transparency with the government about its stress testing framework and the decision-making process for provisioning.

A third and related issue is that the governmental authorities overseeing the central bank may worry about agency problems associated with the central bank building a large war chest based on their own risk assessment. Such a war chest may weaken the central banks' internal governance, perhaps allowing it to expand employment excessively and move into new areas. Or it may encourage the central bank to put too low a bar on actions that may have some economic benefits but come with substantial political economy risks.

5.4 Whether to Move Toward More Risk-Based Capital Policies?

The approach that central banks favor in deciding whether to move to a more risk-based approach should presumably depend on the risks they perceive of a weak financial position, as well as their perception of the backing they have from their Treasury or legislature to "leverage" their balance sheet and take actions that pose balance sheet risks. Of course, in practice, any decisions to modify existing approaches would likely be made in close concert with the governmental authorities to whom the central bank is accountable, and is likely to require legislative changes (Tucker, 2018). The legislative framework will need to be clear on the application of this risk-based approach.

Some central banks may view the risk that their policy independence is constrained by their balance sheet position as very low and prefer to retain their current strategy of remitting most or all their profits provided that capital is above the statutory floor. They may view a simple approach to distributing profits as appealing given its simplicity and transparency and prefer not to modify it in light of the pandemic-related surge in inflation—especially given the unusual nature of that event. The risks associated with a floor system may be perceived as small given that the term structure is usually upward-sloping, and, importantly, they may perceive that they would have strong governmental backing for using their full arsenal of tools if needed even if this entailed additional balance sheet losses. Even a central bank in this position, however, may find enhanced transparency about its actions—that would involve central bank stress-testing as well as gauging macroeconomic and fiscal effects of its balance sheet policies—as desirable for solidifying public support and maintaining appropriate accountability.

But some central banks may have stronger concerns that a weak capital position, especially if persistent, could undermine their ability to achieve mandated objectives, and thus weaken both their policy effectiveness and credibility. Weak central bank capital, for instance, may make them feel that the bar for using balance sheet policies was unduly high from a social welfare perspective. These concerns would likely be heightened for central banks that have limited seigniorage revenue, so that rebuilding capital organically would be a very slow process. In these circumstances, the central bank could regard it as particularly desirable to adjust its capital policies to reduce the risk of further weakening its capital position (and would presumably seek government backing to do so).

As discussed above, a key question in implementing a more forward-looking approach to capital policy is the breadth of risks to take into account in determining distributions to the Treasury. With much larger and more leveraged balance sheets under floor operating systems even in normal times, the volatility of profits is much larger as a share of GDP, and it would seem reasonable that central banks adjust their distribution policy to take this into account. Thus, if the central bank holds a sizeable portfolio of long-term Treasuries with a coupon of 3.5% and it reduces its policy rate from 3% (say the "steady state level") to 2% given a cyclical slowdown, it could use some of these windfall gains to build its capital cushion against possible future losses when interest rates rise. While many central banks already "smooth through" profit volatility by basing distributions on average profits over a multi-year backward window, a forward-looking approach could have quite different implications insofar as it would be based on an evaluation of future risks.

Central banks may also consider provisioning for risks associated with the prospective large-scale use of balance sheet policies in the future, including liquidity support and QE. But given the political economy difficulties of provisioning ex ante for a range of contingencies noted earlier, central banks may find it desirable to use scenario analysis to strengthen political support for providing equity backstops from the Treasury to help address significant risks to macroeconomic and financial stability when they arise. Such "ex post" backstops are desirable insofar as they not only protect the central bank's balance sheet, but also signal political support for the central bank's actions. Of course, the government would have to decide ex post what sort of central bank actions to backstop, and the magnitude of the support they are willing to provide, possibly relying on a stress testing exercise like the one proposed for the central bank.

In the event a crisis does emerge, a forward-looking policy can again be helpful in buttressing the central bank's capital position. In this event, a central bank could use scenario analysis to consider how its capital position would evolve while taking account of government backstops (which are often only partial). Given that central bank profits—especially in the early phases of programs such as QE—are often sizeable, reflecting that policy rates are very low, retaining a large share to offset future sharp declines would help buttress the central bank's capital position through the recovery period.

6 Conclusion

This paper aims at providing a preliminary assessment of the implications of the recent inflation surge for the use of central bank quantitative easing and its capital policies (including distributions to the government). We emphasize four key points.

The first is that QE policies are likely to have substantial benefits in a deep recession in which policy rates are expected to be constrained by the ELB for a protracted period. QE boosts output and inflation and improves the consolidated fiscal position of the government. Thus, QE is likely to be a very useful tool in the event that the ELB again becomes severely binding.

The second is that—in light of the recent experience of high inflation—more caution is warranted in using QE in a shallow liquidity trap in which the central bank mainly faces a low inflation problem. While QE may appear beneficial ex ante, there is considerable risk that QE may cause overheating ex post given important nonlinearities in the Phillips Curve, the potential for an outsized easing of financial conditions, and that other inflation-raising shocks may hit after the deployment of QE. Negative interest rates may be preferable in these circumstances.

The third is that the duration risk that central banks take on with QE has the intended outcome of fueling risk-taking, which compresses term premia and eases financial conditions more broadly. But a side effect is to make central banks highly exposed to losses if interest rates rise substantially. We argue that the benefits of QE are often significantly positive even when the central bank experiences losses, as can occur if the recovery from recession is unexpectedly fast and the yield curve inverts. Even so, the losses still represent a potential headwind for central bank credibility and may ultimately weaken its independence, at least in some cases.

The fourth point is that central banks should consider reassessing their capital policies—including for distributing profits to the government—in light of much riskier balance sheets. Many central banks have retained simple distribution policies that were developed in an environment of small balance sheets and little duration (or credit) risk. Central banks that believe that their capital positions and profit distributions to the government have little bearing on how they carry out their mandate may opt to retain these strategies. However, other central banks may benefit from taking a more forward-looking approach to assessing balance sheet risks and for helping them decide how to allocate profits between building capital and distributions to the government. Allowing central banks greater flexibility in this regard can help protect their financial autonomy and support their independence, and appears high on the agenda for central bank reforms.

References

Acharya, V., Chauhan, R. S., Rajan, R., & Steffen, S. (2023). *Liquidity dependence and the waxing and waning of Central Bank balance sheets*. NBER Working Paper No. 31050. https://www.nber.org/papers/w31050

Adrian, T., Erceg, C., Kolasa, M., Lindé, J., & Zabczyk, P. (2024a). *Fiscal costs and benefits of QE*. IMF Working Paper, forthcoming.

Adrian, T., Khan, A., & Menand, L. (2024b). *A new measure of central Bank Independence*. IMF Working Paper no. 2024/035. International Monetary Fund. https://www.imf.org/en/Publications/WP/Issues/2024/02/23/A-New-Measure-of-Central-Bank-Independence-545270

Benigno, P., & Eggertsson, G. (2023). *It's Baaack: The surge in inflation in the 2020s and the return of the non-linear Phillips Curve* (NBER Working Paper no. 31197). https://www.nber.org/papers/w31197

Bernanke, B. (2017). *Monetary policy in a new era.* Paper prepared for a conference on Rethinking Macroeconomic Policy at the Peterson Institute of International Economics on October 2, 2017. https://www.brookings.edu/wp-content/uploads/2017/10/bernanke_rethinking_macro_final.pdf

Brandão-Marques, L., Casiraghi, M., Gelos, G., Kamber, G., & Meeks, R. (2024). Negative interest rate policies: A survey. *Annual Review of Economics, 16.* https://doi.org/10.1146/annurev-economics-080323-042145

Campbell, J., Evans, C., Fisher, J., & Justiniano, A.. (2012). Macroeconomic effects of Federal Reserve forward guidance. *Brookings Papers on Economic Activity*, Spring, pp. 1–54. https://www.brookings.edu/wp-content/uploads/2012/03/2012a_evans.pdf

Chen, H., Cúrdia, V., & Ferrero, A. (2012). The macroeconomic effects of large-scale asset purchase programmes. *Economic Journal, 122*(564), 289–315. https://www.jstor.org/stable/pdf/23324225.pdf

Du, W., Forbes, K., & Luzzetti, M. *Quantitative tightening around the globe: What have we learned?* Paper prepared for the U.S. Monetary Forum on February 28, 2024. https://www.federalreserve.gov/newsevents/speech/files/waller20240301a.pdf

English, W., & Kohn, D.. (2022). What if the Federal Reserve Books Losses because of its quantitative easing? *Brookings Institution "Up Front" blog*, June 1, 2022. https://www.brookings.edu/articles/what-if-the-federal-reserve-books-losses-because-of-its-quantitative-easing/

Erceg, C., Kolasa, M., Lindé, J., Mumtaz, H., & Zabczyk, P. (2024). *Central Bank Exit Strategies: Domestic Transmission and International Spillovers.* IMF Working Paper No. 2024/073, International Monetary Fund. https://www.imf.org/en/Publications/WP/Issues/2024/03/29/Central-Bank-Exit-Strategies-Domestic-Transmission-and-International-Spillovers-546938

Fabo, B., Kempf, E., Jančoková, M., & Pástor, L. (2021). Fifty shades of QE: Comparing findings of central banks and academics. *Journal of Monetary Economics, 120*, 1–20. https://www.sciencedirect.com/science/article/abs/pii/S0304393221000398

Gabaix, X. (2020). A behavioral new Keynesian model. *American Economic Review, 110*(8), 2271–2327. https://doi.org/10.1257/aer.20162005

Gopinath, G. (2022). *How will the pandemic and war shape future monetary policy?* Presentation prepared for the Jackson Hole Symposium on August 26, 2022. https://www.imf.org/en/News/Articles/2022/08/26/sp-gita-gopinath-remarks-at-the-jackson-hole-symposium

Gopinath, G. (2023). *Three uncomfortable truths for monetary policy.* Remarks prepared for the European Central Bank Forum on Central Banking on June 28, 2023. https://www.imf.org/en/News/Articles/2023/06/26/fdmd-speech-sintra-3-uncomfortable-truths

Hall, R., & Reis, R. (2015). *Maintaining central Bank financial stability under new-style central banking.* NBER Working Paper No. 21173. https://www.nber.org/papers/w21173

Harding, M., Lindé, J., & Trabandt, M. (2022). Resolving the missing deflation puzzle. *Journal of Monetary Economics, 126*(C), 15–34. https://www.sciencedirect.com/science/article/pii/S0304393221000969

Harding, M., Lindé, J., & Trabandt, M. (2023). *Understanding post-COVID inflation dynamics.* IMF Working Paper No. 2023/010. International Monetary Fund. https://www.imf.org/en/Publications/WP/Issues/2023/01/20/Understanding-Post-COVID-Inflation-Dynamics-528404

Kolasa, M., & Wesolowski, G. (2020). International spillovers of quantitative easing. *Journal of International Economics, 126*, 103330. https://www.sciencedirect.com/science/article/pii/S0022199620300477

Orphanides, A. (2023). *The forward guidance trap.* Institute for Monetary and Economic Studies, Bank of Japan. Discussion Paper No. 20234-E-6, Tokyo. https://www.imes.boj.or.jp/research/papers/english/23-E-06.pdf

Stella, P. (2008). *Central Bank Balance Sheet Strength, Policy Constraints, and Inflation.* IMF Working Paper No. 2008/049. https://www.imf.org/en/Publications/WP/Issues/2016/12/31/Central-Bank-Financial-Strength-Policy-Constraints-and-Inflation-21718

Tucker, P. (2018). *Unelected power: The quest for legitimacy in central banking and the regulatory state.* Princeton University Press.

The opinions expressed in this chapter are those of the author(s) and do not necessarily reflect the views of the International Monetary Fund, its Board of Directors, or the countries they represent

Open Access This chapter is licensed under the terms of the Creative Commons Attribution 3.0 IGO license (https://creativecommons.org/licenses/by/3.0/igo/), which permits use, sharing, adaptation, distribution and reproduction in any medium or format, as long as you give appropriate credit to the International Monetary Fund, provide a link to the Creative Commons license and indicate if changes were made.

Any dispute related to the use of the works of the International Monetary Fund that cannot be settled amicably shall be submitted to arbitration pursuant to the UNCITRAL rules. The use of the International Monetary Fund's name for any purpose other than for attribution, and the use of the International Monetary Fund's logo, shall be subject to a separate written license agreement between the International Monetary Fund and the user and is not authorized as part of this CC-IGO license. Note that the link provided above includes additional terms and conditions of the license.

The images or other third party material in this chapter are included in the chapter's Creative Commons license, unless indicated otherwise in a credit line to the material. If material is not included in the chapter's Creative Commons license and your intended use is not permitted by statutory regulation or exceeds the permitted use, you will need to obtain permission directly from the copyright holder.

Central Bank Capital and Independence: A Quantitative Case Study

David Vestin, Anders Vredin, and Magnus Åhl

Abstract inancial independence for central banks is often taken to mean that their profits should be high enough to cover their operating costs, and that there should be financial buffers to cover unexpected losses so that the central bank does not have to be recapitalized too often. In this paper, we present a case study on these questions by describing the experiences of Sveriges Riksbank. Since the Riksbank became more independent in 1999, there have been three formal reviews initiated by the Swedish parliament. In 2023 a new Riksbank Act came into effect, incidentally right after the Riksbank's equity was completely eroded. On 2 April 2024, the Riksbank, in line with the new law, asked the parliament for a recapitalization. In this paper, we describe the factors that have been viewed as important for the judgements about how much capital the Riksbank needs, and present a method for estimating the probability of recapitalization. Volatility in financial prices, in combination with the current legislated framework and likely scenarios for the Riksbank's future balance sheet, lead to relatively high estimated probabilities for future recapitalizations.

Keywords Central bank · Central bank balance sheet · Central bank capital · Central bank independence · Central bank losses · Central bank recapitalization

The opinions expressed in this article are the sole responsibility of the authors and should not be interpreted as reflecting the views of Sveriges Riksbank. The authors are grateful for fruitful discussions with Jan Alsterlind, Matteo Bonetti, Dirk Broeders, Aino Bunge, Mattias Danielsson, Jens Iversen, David Kjellberg, and Carina Selander.

D. Vestin · A. Vredin (✉)
Sveriges Riksbank, Stockholm, Sweden
e-mail: anders.vredin@riksbank.se

M. Åhl
National Institute of Economic Research, Stockholm, Sweden

© The Author(s) 2025
D. Broeders et al. (eds.), *Central Bank Capital in Turbulent Times*,
Contributions to Finance and Accounting,
https://doi.org/10.1007/978-3-031-73549-3_8

1 Introduction

Practical experiences together with theoretical and empirical research have resulted in a general agreement that central banks should have a high degree of independence. But independence is a matter of degree, and also has many dimensions. Consequently, it also varies across countries.[1]

In the EU, four types of independence are monitored (see e.g. ECB, 2022): functional, institutional, personal, and financial. Institutional independence, for instance, includes prohibition against instructions from governments to national central banks. Financial independence means that member states may not put their national central banks in a position where they have insufficient financial resources and inadequate equity to carry out their tasks within the European System of Central Banks (ESCB).

Central banks are not, and cannot be, 100% independent.[2] One reason is that central banks' decisions have implications for fiscal policy. There is a direct channel since central banks' profits are at least to some degree transferred to the state. The numerous indirect links may be even more important: a central bank's decisions on monetary policy and financial stability affect the fluctuations in the general level of economic activity and thereby government revenue, expenditure, and debt. Effects from monetary policy on income distribution and the allocation of resources may lead to changes in fiscal policy, just like the effects of fiscal policy on inflation and economic activity may lead to changes in monetary policy.

In principle, the central bank's independence in policy making is not necessarily closely tied to the central bank's financial independence. There are no strong direct links between the central bank's capital and monetary policy. On the other hand, there are indirect links that may be important.[3] The central bank's profits or losses, or other implications of monetary policy for fiscal policy, may lead to decisions by the parliament or the government to change the governance of the central bank. Experiences from "unconventional" monetary policies since the great financial crisis (GFC) obviously have raised new questions about central banks' independence and the links between monetary policy and fiscal policy.[4]

While it is easy to reach agreement about central bank independence in principle, it is thus much more difficult to define appropriate levels for the various dimensions of independence in practice.

[1] See e.g. Dincer and Eichengreen (2014) and Archer and Moser-Boehm (2013).

[2] See Wessels and Broeders (2022) for a discussion of this issue.

[3] See Nordström and Vredin (2022) for a brief literature review.

[4] Central bank acts have recently been changed in, e.g., New Zealand (2022) and Sweden (2023). A recent review of the Reserve Bank of Australia (2023) included proposals for changes in governance and legislation. In July 2023 the Bank of England's Court announced that there will be "a review into the Bank's forecasting and related processes" and "an independent and objective look at the processes which underpin the MPC's policy decisions". Levin and Skinner (2024) present suggestions to "restore effective oversight of the Fed's monetary policymaking".

In this paper, we will shed light on some fundamental principal questions by presenting a case study of the central bank in Sweden, Sveriges Riksbank. The Riksbank gradually became more independent during the 1990s and a new Riksbank Act came into effect in 1999. Since then, there have been more or less continuous discussions about the Riksbank's need for capital, including three formal reviews initiated by the parliament. A new law including target levels for the Riksbank's equity came into effect in 2023, incidentally right after the Riksbank's equity had been completely eroded through decreases in the market values of bond holdings after the increase in interest rates during 2022. On 2 April 2024 the Riksbank, in line with the new law, asked the parliament for a recapitalization.

We describe the factors that have been viewed as important for the judgements, in Sweden, about how much capital a central bank needs. The paper is structured as follows. In Sect. 2, we present arguments on why central banks need equity at all. In Sect. 3, we summarize the various reviews of the Riksbank's capital needs 2000–2019 and the different assumptions made behind the judgements of the Riksbank's capital needs. Section 4 presents a method that can be used to measure the implications of various factors on the desired level of financial independence, measured as the probability of a recapitalization. Section 5 includes a summary and lessons from the Swedish experiences.

2 Why Is There a Need for Central Bank Equity at All?

A central bank can—as any private bank—fund its expenditures by issuing deposits, which in the case of the central bank are typically labelled "reserves"—i.e., the balances held by the banks and other financial market participants at the central bank. In contrast to a private bank, the central bank is not constrained by regulatory requirements applied to private banks, or restrained by market forces such as creditors' willingness to lend. In this sense, the central bank does not require capital in order to function, and it is tempting to suppose that this implies that negative capital is just a technical accounting effect that we should not worry about. As stressed by Del Negro and Sims (2015), however, this all depends on how the negative capital relates to future expected earnings potential. If the present value of future net profits exceeds the current negative capital, then the central bank will in expected value be able to recapitalize itself without the need for government intervention. Both the US as well as the key countries in the Eurozone are currently in this situation due to the high value of future seigniorage.[5] But other countries such as Sweden are not—there the outstanding stock of currency has fallen short of 1% of GDP which barely covers operational costs.

[5] See Belhocine et al. (2023) for a discussion of the Eurozone and Cavallo et al. (2019) for a discussion of the Fed.

If, however, future discounted surpluses fall short, the central bank will in expected value be forced to make a choice. It may either pay interest on the steadily increasing debt/negative capital and continue to pursue its inflation target. Or it may set the policy rate to zero to prevent further increases in the negative capital and let spiralling inflation reduce the real value of debt to the point where the real debt has been sufficiently eroded, just like in the case when public debt has outgrown future surpluses—a version of the fiscal-theory of the price-level.[6] According to the fiscal-theory of the price-level, Leeper (1991), the former solution requires that the consolidated balance sheet of the government remains stable, which in turn requires that the government would accumulate ever growing claims on the private sector. If this is ruled out, as in both Del Negro and Sims (2015) as well as in Hall and Reis (2015), fiscal dominance ensues and will result in exploding inflation. Thus, in practice, both these cases require the central bank to give up on its price stability mandate. Del Negro and Sims (2015) draw the conclusion that a stable equilibrium requires an automatic recapitalization rule that will restore the capital of the central bank in case of a negative shock.

In the presence of an automatic rule, there is no need for a particular level of capital, neither as a source of revenue generation nor for buffer use. From a purely financial perspective, if this is the case, there is no problem operating with negative capital for a while. This just amounts to the central bank borrowing against the collateral of the government backing. The timing of when the government choses to inject capital to reverse the trend becomes a technical matter.

If, however, no such automatic recapitalization rule exists—as is the case for most central banks—capital functions as a cushion that both serves as a revenue-generating vehicle as well as a buffer for balance-sheet risk. The more capital the central bank has, the less likely is it to encounter the point where an injection is needed to restore financial health. That is, the probability of a recapitalization depends on the amount of capital that the central bank holds. Of course, it is the combination of capital, the amount of risk, other funding sources and so forth that determines the probability of a recapitalization. We will take the perspective of Kjellberg and Vestin (2019) and Wessels and Broeders (2022), who assume that we may formally operationalize the notion of financial independence in terms of the probability that a recapitalization is needed in the coming, say, 5–10 years. If the capital framework of the central bank specifies explicit rules concerning when a recapitalization should occur, as is the case for the Riksbank (from 2023), this probability can be computed by simulating the future evolution of interest rates, exchange rates and other variables of importance for the evolution of the profits or losses of the central bank.[7] If no explicit rule is in place, we have to do with some

[6] An alternative is to set the rate on *a part of* the reserves to zero. Both the ECB (see ECB, 2023) as well as the SNB has recently adopted a zero remuneration of required reserves without losing the ability to control shorter term market rates.

[7] The Riksbank Act stipulates when a recapitalisation should be petitioned for by the Riksbank, not necessarily how the petition should be handled by the parliament nor when the recapitalisation should be effective.

notion such as the one in Del Negro and Sims (2015)—compute the risk that future expected surpluses fall short of current negative capital.

Assuming that there is a probability which is deemed consistent with a sufficient degree of financial independence, we may now approach the problem of determining how much capital the central bank should hold from two perspectives—as a source of earnings and as a buffer for risk. We start by noting that if seigniorage revenue is ample, future income may certainly buffer for potential losses, reducing or even eliminating the need for capital from both these perspectives. Here we restrict ourselves to a situation where this is not the case, such as the present circumstances in Sweden.

First, in terms of revenue generation, capital is a cost-free form of funding on the liability side of the balance sheet that allows a corresponding amount of some revenue-generating asset on the asset side of the balance sheet. For example, the central bank may use a capital injection to purchase short-term riskless notes. The interest income on those notes will add to revenue, and capital will not add to expenses. In this case, we will have a risk-free addition to income, though of course the size of the contribution will vary with the interest rate. Whether the central bank needs capital in this capacity depends on the other income sources. If the stock of outstanding cash—the other major cost-free item on the liability side—is large, no further capital may be required, and it may even be possible to operate with negative capital.

Second, starting from a level of capital K that is at least sufficient for revenue-generating purposes, any additional capital A can be used as a buffer for balance-sheet risk. That is, given an amount of capital K + A, the central bank can afford to lose A without threatening its financial independence. The appropriate size of A depends on the riskiness of the assets held on the current balance-sheet, or on the risk that the central bank wants to be able to handle without further accumulation of equity. If the legal framework of the central bank forces recapitalization at a certain minimum level of capital, and such recapitalizations are viewed as costly by the governors, the buffer A must be calibrated to the risks on the balance-sheet even if the *expected* future surpluses from the assets covers expected future costs.

For many decades preceding the financial crisis 2008–2009, most western central banks have operated with relatively small balance-sheets, where cash has been one of the major items on the liability side. This interest-rate free liability has provided the bulk for central bank financial independence, by delivering a steady stream of seigniorage income which for most central banks has been far exceeding operating costs, allowing the central bank to distribute large profits to its owner, the government. This, perhaps, has led to a bit of complacency concerning income streams and risks on the central banks' balance sheets.

Two simultaneous developments have recently altered this state, rather dramatically, not least in the Swedish case. First, the risks on the balance-sheet have increased dramatically due to large-scale asset purchases and—to a lesser extent—increases in the foreign exchange (FX) reserve. Second, the usage of cash has been declining over the past decade or so, and currently the outstanding stock is below 1% of GDP, leading to a lower seigniorage revenue.

These developments highlight the dual possible roles of capital as safeguards of financial independence for the central bank: a source for revenue to fund operating expenses and as a buffer for financial risk.

Against this backdrop, we now proceed to describe the evolution of the Swedish discussion, first in terms of the formal enquires leading up to a revised Riksbank Act in place since January 1, 2023, and then in terms of showing simulations modelling the risks in relation to required equity. Note that in the case of the Riksbank, there are three types of interest-rate-free liabilities on the balance-sheet: currency (notes and coins), revaluation accounts and equity. The latter term refers to the amount injected into the central bank by the owners (share capital according to the definition in Archer & Moser-Boehm, 2013) plus the cumulated sum of retained earnings.

3 Reviews of Sveriges Riksbank's Capital Needs During the Era of Central Bank Independence

After a banking and currency crisis of 1990–1992, which forced the Riksbank to abandon the pegged exchange rate regime, monetary and fiscal policy were gradually reformed.[8] An explicit inflation target of 2% was announced by the Riksbank (the Governing Council) in 1993. Changes in the Riksbank Act to make the Riksbank more independent were made from 1999. During 1994–2000 the Swedish fiscal policy framework was also reformed.

The reforms achieved the objectives. Average inflation declined from above 8% per year during 1974–1992 to below 2% per year 1993–2021. Government debt, which had increased from around 20% of GDP in the early 1970s to around 80% in 1995, declined to around 40% in 2020.

Before the present Riksbank Act came into effect in January 2023, the level of the Riksbank's capital was not regulated by law. The earlier Riksbank Act however stated that the General Council (consisting of only external members) each year should make proposals to the Riksdag (the parliament) on the allocation of the profit of the Riksbank.[9] Since 1988 the General Council in practice followed a rule that 80% of a 5-year moving average of the Riksbank's profit was distributed to the government budget.[10] Exceptions were made in 2001 and 2002, when the parliament decided to make extra transfers to the government budget amounting to SEK 20

[8] The Riksbank gradually became more independent also during the 1980s. For more details on the regime shifts in Sweden, see Bylund et al. (2024).

[9] Unlike most other central banks, Sveriges Riksbank is not an authority under the government but under the parliament. After each general election, the parliament forms a number of committees, including the General Council of the Riksbank. Since 1999 the General Council appoints the Executive Board of the Riksbank. The history of the Riksbank, the oldest existing central bank in the world, is described in Wetterberg (2009).

[10] The rule was decided by the Governing Council in 1988 and approved by the parliament in 1989. See SOU (2007, p. 171) and Gardholm and Gerwin (2011).

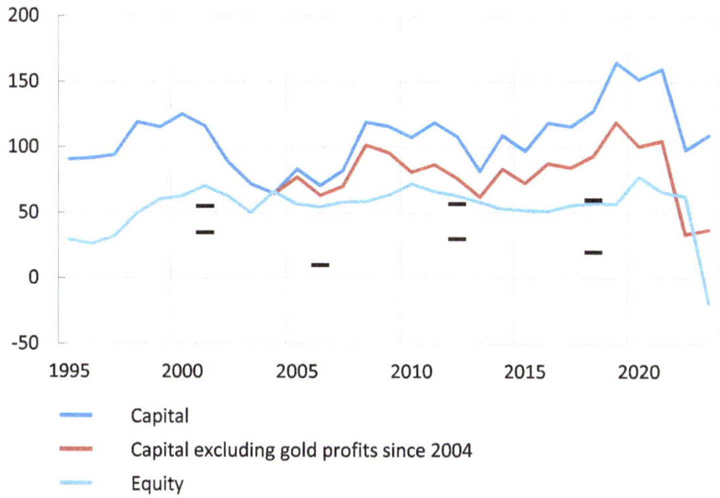

Fig. 1 The Riksbank's equity and total capital. Note: SEK billion. The short horizontal black lines show the recommended levels of equity from the different reviews presented in Sect. 3. Sources: Sveriges Riksbank, Ernhagen et al. (2002), SOU (2007, 2013, 2019)

billion per year (corresponding to around 30% of the Riksbank's equity each year, and around 0.8% of GDP) (Figs. 1 and 2).[11]

The background and process for the extra transfers are described in Sect. 3.1. The European Commission and the ECB argued in 2002 that the extra transfers showed that the Riksbank Act had to be reformed to include formal rules about the allocation of the Riksbank's profit, in order to be consistent with financial independence. This led to a review of the Riksbank's financial independence in 2006–2007, chaired by Ingrid Bonde, "the Bonde review", which is summarized in Sect. 3.2. This did not, however, lead to any new legislation. Another review was conducted in 2011–2013, chaired by Harry Flam, "the Flam review", which is summarized in Sect. 3.3. Neither this review led to any changes. After a more general review of the Riksbank Act in 2017–2019, summarized in Sect. 3.4, a new Riksbank Act including a target level for the Riksbank's equity came into effect in 2023. The Riksbank Act now includes a target level for the Riksbank's equity and as long as that level is achieved, all profits will be distributed to the government budget.

During 2022 the Riksbank's reported losses exceeded the Riksbank's equity which thus became negative in 2023. Following the new Act, the Riksbank handed

---

[11] According to the Riksbank Act, both from 1999 and the new Act from 2023, the Executive Board makes the decision on the Riksbank's annual budget, and only informs the Governing Council, the parliament (the Finance Committee) and the National Audit Office about its decision. Figures 1 and 2 show the developments of Riksbank's capital, profits and transfers to the state. Table 1 shows the Riksbank's balance sheet, operating costs and GDP (in current prices) for the years discussed in Sects. 3 and 4.

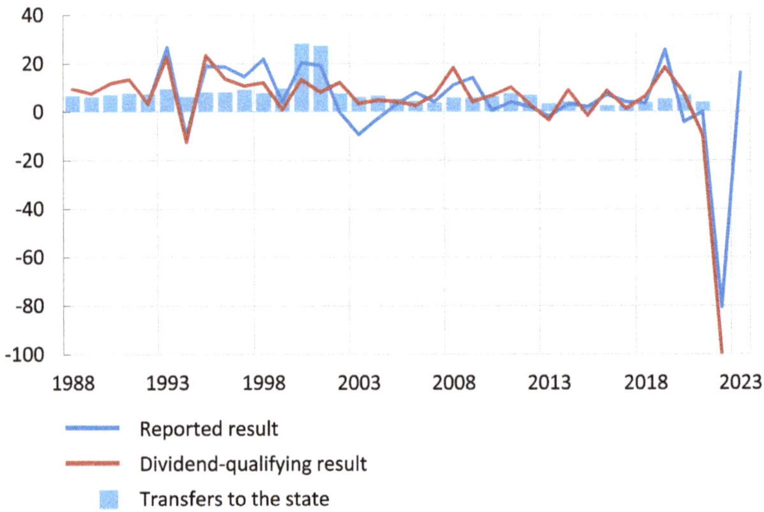

Fig. 2 The Riksbank's annual profits and transfers to the government budget. Note: SEK billion. The dividend-qualifying result is no longer relevant since 2023, when the new Riksbank Act came into effect. Transfers to the state have been zero for 2022 and 2023. Source: Sveriges Riksbank

in a petition for a capital injection from the parliament on 2 April 2024. Section 4 presents methods the Riksbank have used during this process, to analyse the implications of various factors on the need for a recapitalization.

3.1 Extra Transfers to the Government Budget During 2001 and 2002

In February 2001, the Governing Council decided to propose an extra transfer of SEK 20 billion (around 30% of equity, around 0.8% of GDP) to the government budget. In February 2002 the Governing Council proposed a further transfer of SEK 20 billion. The background was that the Finance Committee in the Swedish parliament in May 2000, in their annual assessment of the Riksbank's monetary policy and governance, had raised questions about the applied rule for the allocation of the Riksbank's profit and the resulting increased level of the Riksbank's equity, see Fig. 1.[12] The Finance Committee declared that they did not see these principles as self-evident also for the future.[13] This led the Governing Council to request an

[12] Note that the definitions in Fig. 1 differ from those used in Archer and Moser-Boehm (2013).

[13] The increase in total capital partly reflected unrealized profits from a depreciation of the krona. As regards monetary policy, the Finance Committee's assessments over the years have typically avoided to make any evaluations of the Executive Board's policy decisions. In May 2000, the

analysis of these matters from the Executive Board, which was delivered in January 2001.

The Executive Board's conclusions were that an expected normal level of the Riksbank's annual profit was SEK 10 billion per year and that the applied rule for allocation of the profit should be maintained. This would add SEK 2 billion to the Riksbank's equity each year, which would be consistent with an expected stable real level of equity at SEK 100 billion if the inflation target of 2% was achieved. This, in turn, would allow a one-time extra transfer of SEK 20 billion to the government budget during 2001.[14] The Governing Council also made this proposal to the Finance Committee.[15]

When the Finance Committee in May 2001 in their turn proposed the extra transfer to the parliament, they also decided that the Governing Council ought to propose an extra transfer of around SEK 20 billion also the following year. The Finance Committee's judgements (i.e., not formal decisions) were that such a transfer would not have negative implications for the Riksbank's monetary and exchange rate policies, and that the applied 80/20 rule henceforth should be followed. This led the Governing Council to request updated analyses from the Executive Board, which were delivered in January 2002.

This time the Executive Board came to the conclusions that an extra transfer of SEK 0–20 billion was possible, but that no such transfer ought to be made if the existing level of preparedness should be maintained, and that changes in the Riksbank Act should be made to clarify the Riksbank's capital needs, increase the predictability of the decisions on the allocation of the profit, and increase the consistency with the EU Treaty. The Governing Council's decision was to propose an extra transfer of SEK 20 billion just like the previous year, based, among other things, on the assumption that the 80/20 rule henceforth should be followed. The Governing Council thus followed the Finance Committee's earlier recommendation.

While there was a high degree of agreement about the extra transfer in 2001 in the Executive Board, the Governing Council and the Finance Committee, there was more disagreement about the transfer in 2002. First, a minority in the Finance Committee objected to the Committee's decision (in May 2001) to suggest a further transfer. The minority argued that the reason for the suggestion was expected deficits in the government's budget, and that a transfer would threaten the Riksbank's

---

Finance Committee, among other things, noted that the Riksbank had made reasonably good forecasts and that the Riksbank showed a relatively high degree of transparency in an international comparison. The Finance Committee's assessments have been based both on annual assessments submitted by the Riksbank itself and on external evaluations by international experts about every 5 years.

[14] The Riksbank's equity was SEK 63 billion by the end of year 2000 and total capital SEK 125 billion, including also revaluation accounts (SEK 42 billion) and the profit during 2000 (SEK 20 billion).

[15] The Riksbank's equity (unlike total capital) did not decrease by SEK 20 billion (see Fig. 1), because the money was taken from a balancing (revaluation) account and the profit made during year 2000. See the Riksbank's annual report for 2001, ars01eng.pdf (riksbank.se), p. 48.

independence. Second, a minority in the Governing Council objected to the majority's decision in February 2002 to follow the Finance Committee's suggestion. The minority partly based their objection on the Executive Board's judgement that no extra transfer ought to be made if the existing level of preparedness should be maintained. The minority also argued that the further transfer was not consistent with the Riksbank's legislated independence and should not be made.

Since the composition of both the Finance Committee and Governing Council—as always—reflected the composition of the parliament, the different views reflected different political judgements. But the Riksbank also provided some economic analyses as input to the process (on request from the Governing Council). The Executive Board thus partly based their arguments on analyses presented by Ernhagen et al. (2002). They argued that the Riksbank needed equity amounting to SEK 10 billion to cover operating costs, and another SEK 25–45 billion as a buffer against potential losses from, e.g. acting as a lender of last resort.[16] They also argued that the 55 billion of accumulated unrealized profits in the Riksbank's balance sheet by the end of 2001 should not be regarded as an addition to the Riksbank's equity. The Riksbank's total capital at the time of SEK 117 billion (see Table 1 and Fig. 1) was thus SEK 7–27 billion above the interval of SEK 90–110 billion arrived at in these calculations. As noted above, the Executive Board's conclusion was that an extra transfer of SEK 0–20 billion was possible, but that no extra transfer ought to be made if the existing level of preparedness should be maintained.

The convergence report from the European Central Bank (ECB, 2002, p. 45) "reiterates the need to codify the rules on profit distribution" stressed by the European Monetary Institute in 1996 and 1997. At that time, the Swedish government had argued that "the determination of the disposition of the profit is undertaken on objective grounds" (i.e., the 80/20 rule) and that "The Government takes it for granted that this shall also be the case in the future". The government therefore did not share EMI's views on the need to codify the rules. In light of the extra transfers made during 2001 and 2002, the ECB (2002) however argued that the financial independence of the Riksbank should be safeguarded.

3.2 *The Bonde Review, 2006–2007*

In April 2006, the government (with the same political composition as in the events described in the previous sub-section) gave Ingrid Bonde, general director of the Financial Supervisory Authority (an authority under the government, unlike

[16] The recommended interval for SEK 35–55 billion, is indicated by short horizontal black lines in Fig. 1. The Riksbank's operating costs in 2001 were SEK 0.8 billion, see Table 1. Ernhagen et al. noted that seigniorage could be used to cover operating costs. If the use of notes and coins would decline to zero, so would the costs for production and distribution of notes and coins, which amounted to around SEK 0.3 billion. Therefore, equity of SEK 10 billion would be sufficient to cover the remaining operation costs if the return on equity was 5%.

Table 1 The Riksbank's balance sheet

	2001 (Ernhagen et al.)	2006 (Bonde)	2011 (Flam)	2018 (Review of RB Act)	2023
SEK assets	69	7	0	392	630
FX	148	167	300	488	419
Gold	17	22	44	46	84
Other	2	4	4	8	123
Total assets	236	200	348	934	1256
Currency	107	112	100	62	58
Equity	71	55	67	57	−18
Other capital	46	16	52	71	128
Debt	0	14	104	714	993
Other	12	3	25	30	94
Total liab.	236	200	348	934	1256
Operat. costs	0.9	0.7	0.7	0.9	1.4
Nominal GDP	2504	3122	3728	4828	5487[a]

[a] Nominal GDP year 2021

Note: SEK billion, assets and liabilities at end of year. Years are chosen to describe the conditions at the times of the different reviews

Source: Sveriges Riksbank

Sveriges Riksbank) the task to review the Riksbank's profit allocation and capital. The review should lead to proposals on new legislation for the principles of the profit allocation. The proposals should, among other things, build on analyses of the Riksbank's equity needs, future structures of the balance sheet and the capital and the effects for the Riksbank and the state of different profit allocation systems.

The listed objectives for the review included that the Riksbank should be financially independent but not over-capitalized.

The main conclusions from the Bonde review presented in June 2007 were:[17]

- The Riksbank should hedge its FX reserve fully, in order to lower the need of a capital buffer to cover losses from exchange rate fluctuations.
- A formal recapitalization rule was not necessary, since the cost of keeping enough capital in the Riksbank was considered to be low.
- In principle, the Riksbank's activities are long run sustainable even if equity is negative, since notes and coins constitute a source of positive cash-flow and cost-free financing.
- The Riksbank needs a cost-free source of financing of SEK 60–74 billion.[18] Since the stock of notes and coins at the time was SEK 110 billion, the Riksbank's need for equity (for technical and credibility reasons) was small, SEK 10 billion. This implied that a transfer to the government budget of around SEK 50 billion could be made.[19]
- Alternatively, if notes and coins are not viewed as an appropriate source of cost-free financing,
  - The equity needed was estimated to be SEK 60 billion,
  - The Riksbank should annually make transfers to the government budget corresponding an interest rate on the stock of notes and coins.
- In both alternatives, all profits made by the Riksbank resulting in a higher equity level than SEK 10 billion (Alt. 1) or SEK 60 billion (Alt. 2) should be transferred to the government budget.

The Bonde review argued that the need of foreign exchange reserves was small, given the flexible exchange rate regime, and furthermore should be fully hedged. A foreign exchange reserve therefore did not imply any large need for buffer capital. The review did not see any significant need of buffers for other risks either, given the size of cost-free financing provided by notes and coins.

In its comments on the Bonde review (from February 2008) the Riksbank argued, among other things, that there was a risk that the use of notes and coins in the future could go down, lowering the seigniorage, and that a situation with negative

[17] See SOU (2007), pp. 10–15.

[18] See SOU (2007), p. 127, for a decomposition.

[19] The recommended level of SEK 10 billion is shown by a short horizontal black line in Fig. 1. The Riksbank's equity when the Bonde report was published was around SEK 58 billion (see SOU (2007), p. 153), somewhat higher than by the end of 2006 (SEK 55 billion, see Table 1).

equity should be avoided. The Riksbank therefore argued for a modified version of Alternative 2, where the initial level of equity (SEK 60 billion) should be adjusted annually with the growth in nominal GDP and where the transfers to the government budget should be zero if equity was below the targeted level.[20]

When Ingrid Bonde delivered her report in June 2007, there had been a change in government after the general election in 2006 (and hence also in the composition of the General Council). The report did not lead to any changes in legislation.

3.3 *The Flam Review, 2011–2013*

In the aftermath of the financial crisis 2008–2009, the Executive Board decided to strengthen the foreign exchange reserve by SEK 100 billion (from around 200 billion to around 300 billion) which implied a persistent increase in the balance sheet. The increase was financed via the National Debt Office and hence also contributed to an increase in (gross) public debt.[21]

Against the background of the experiences from the financial crisis, the government in October 2011 gave Harry Flam, professor at Stockholm University, the task to make a new and updated review of the Riksbank's equity needs. This time a number of questions related to the FX reserve were added:[22] How large the reserve should be, how it should be financed, and what responsibility the National Debt Office should have in supporting the Riksbank's borrowing in foreign currency. The government recognized that there were trade-offs between the different objectives of financial independence for the Riksbank, financial stability and public debt management (e.g., its level and costs). The implications of the Riksbank's balance sheet for public debt may in turn have consequences for fiscal policy.

The main conclusions from the Flam review presented in January 2013 were:[23]

- The equity needed was estimated to be SEK 30 billion and total interest-free and inflation-protected capital (including the stock of notes and coins) SEK 75 billion.
- This proposal was based on the ideas that:

[20] The Bonde review's proposal was that the targeted level should be adjusted annually with inflation, but not with the growth of the real economy.

[21] During the financial crisis 2008–2009, the Riksbank provided loans to banks in USD amounting to USD 30 billion. Using the average SEK/USD exchange rate during 2008–2009, this amounted to SEK 213 billion. Using the average exchange rate during 2023 it would amount to SEK 318 billion. For more detailed descriptions of the Riksbank's policy decisions during the global financial crisis, see Elmér et al. (2012), Berg et al. (2018), and Bylund et al. (2024). In December 2012, the Executive Board decided about a further increase of the FX reserve amounting to SEK 100 billion.

[22] See SOU (2013), pp. 195–209. The terms of reference for the earlier Bonde review did not explicitly mention that any rules for the foreign exchange reserve should be analysed, but a significant part of the conclusions from that review concerned this issue.

[23] See SOU (2013), pp. 15–18.

- A normal real return on the Riksbank's capital is 1% per year.
- Operating costs normally amount to SEK 0.75 billion.
- Equity of SEK 30 billion is needed to cover risks related to last-resort lending to banks and fluctuations in the price of gold and interest rates on holdings of foreign bonds.
- The exchange rate risk in the FX reserve is fully hedged, so no extra equity (buffer) is needed for this purpose. Without hedging, an additional equity capital of SEK 27 billion would be required.

- New injections of capital should be made if total interest-free capital falls SEK 10 billion below the targeted level of SEK 75 billion, or if equity falls below SEK 20 billion.
- There should be a limit on the Riksbank's FX reserve of SEK 200 billion (indexed to GDP in current prices).
- The limit on the FX reserve (SEK 200 billion) together with the target for total interest-free capital (SEK 75 billion) gives a limit also for how much the Riksbank should be allowed to borrow via the National Debt Office in normal times (SEK 125 billion). The review also included, among other things, a judgement that SEK 73 billion could be transferred from the Riksbank to the government budget.[24]

The Flam review's estimate of the Riksbank's need for an FX reserve in normal times was higher than the Bonde review's, which is hardly surprising given the experiences from the global financial crisis. The Flam review was also somewhat less optimistic about the future development of the stock of notes and coins and therefore about seigniorage. Still, the two reviews reached largely the same conclusions about the Riksbank's need for equity and total capital. They argued that the risk of losses on the FX reserve should be hedged and that the risk of other losses was relatively small.

In its comments on the Flam review (in June 2013), the Riksbank repeated an argument presented in connection with the earlier Bonde review: it is possible to implement monetary policy in normal times with very different levels of equity. The appropriate level of equity and financial independence is rather determined by the need for security margins desirable for the purpose of financial stability. The Riksbank argued that the global financial crisis had shown that the need for equity and an FX reserve varies over time, in particular due to the banking system's need for liquidity support in foreign currency, and that the Riksbank therefore needs flexibility to determine these levels. Rather than specifying certain levels,

[24] At the time, the stock of notes and coins amounted to around SEK 100 billion and equity plus other capital (revaluation accounts) to around SEK 120 billion, see Table 1. The Flam review did not suggest that the whole difference between SEK 120 and 30 billion should be transferred to the government budget. See SOU (2013), pp. 166–167.

the Riksbank Act should regulate the processes for how decisions on equity, profit allocation, the FX reserve and its financing, etc., should be made. For instance:

- The Riksbank should have the right to increase the FX reserve through borrowing via the National Debt Office under the precondition that the decision was based on a broad and transparent process including consultations with the General Council, the Ministry of Finance and the National Debt Office.
- The Riksbank should have the right to increase its capital through financial provisions, after consultation with the General Council.
- Transfers to the government budget exceeding the Riksbank's profit during the preceding year should not be allowed without approval from the Riksbank.

The Riksbank argued that its own proposals, in contrast to the Flam review's, were consistent with EU rules on financial independence.

This time, in contrast to the situation after the Bonde review, there was disagreement within the Riksbank. Two members of the Executive Board did not share the majority's views but supported the principles behind the Flam review. They argued that the Riksbank's financial independence would be higher with the rules proposed in the review, compared to the more discretionary processes suggested by the Riksbank. They also argued that a high level of the FX reserve could create moral hazard problems in the financial system and suggested that there should be higher liquidity requirements on banks instead. The General Council also disagreed with the Executive Board's suggestions. The General Council argued that the level of the Riksbank's capital should not be decided by the Executive Board, but that a target level should be included in the law. The General Council suggested that the level of the total capital (equity plus unrealized profits) in 2012, SEK 108 billion, should be the target level. The General Council also argued that an increase or decrease in the FX reserve should be determined jointly by the Executive Board and the General Council.[25]

3.4 *Review of the Riksbank Act, 2017–2019*

Like in the case of the Bonde review, the Flam review did not lead to any changes in legislation. Instead, the government in December 2016 appointed a committee (a parliamentary committee, this time) for a complete review of the Riksbank Act. A new review of the whole Act had been discussed on different occasions in the parliament's Finance Committee since the Riksbank became more independent in 1999. In 2010, the Riksbank's Executive Board and Governing Council together suggested a broad review of the Swedish rules for the financial system (see Gernandt

---

[25] It was suggested in the Flam review (SOU, 2013, p. 126) that decisions on the Riksbank's borrowing of foreign currency via the National Debt Office should be taken after consultation with the General Council, but no such rule was included in the actual proposals for changes in the law.

et al., 2010), against the background of the experiences from the GFC. In their review of the Riksbank's monetary policy, Goodfriend and King (2016) argued for a review of the Riksbank Act, primarily in order to clarify the Riksbank's responsibilities for the exchange rate regime and for financial stability.

3.4.1 Terms of Reference

The committee should analyse and propose changes in the legislation that they thought were necessary in a number of areas beyond Riksbank capital, which we do not comment on here. Regarding capital and financial independence, the European Commission had expressed a view that the rules for profit distribution were not consistent with financial independence. As described above, the Governing Council had the responsibility to make a proposal to the parliament. The Commission argued that the decision should be made by the Riksbank. In addition to the original terms of reference from December 2016, referring to the European Commission's views, further terms were added in October 2017. The review should also take the government's referral to the Council on Legislation from March 2017, with proposals on the Riksbank's financial independence and balance sheet, based on the Flam review, into account (including consultation comments from others). The review should lead to suggestions on the Riksbank's possibilities to increase the FX reserve through borrowing from the National Debt Office, and on how the existing loans should be repaid when a new law had come into effect.[26]

The conclusions from the review of the act regarding institutional and financial independence—with proposals on the Riksbank's need for capital and an FX reserve—will be summarized in Sect. 3.4.2.

3.4.2 Proposals on Capital and FX Reserve[27]

The parliamentary committee suggested that a target level for the Riksbank's equity, SEK 60 billion (indexed to the CPI) should be laid down in law. Profits leading to a level of equity higher than the target level should be transferred to the government budget. If losses lead to a level of equity lower than 1/3 of the targeted level (i.e., SEK 20 billion initially), the Riksbank should petition the parliament to restore equity. Capital should then normally be restored to a base level corresponding to 2/3 of the target level (i.e., SEK 40 billion initially, the midpoint between the target level and the lower threshold)—unless unrealized gains on the balance sheet (revaluation

[26] In this part, the new review should take the government's referral to the Council on Legislation, based on the Flam review, into account.

[27] A summary of the review of the Riksbank Act is available in English, see SOU (2019), pp. 59–78.

account) justify restoration to a lower level or not at all.[28] If required to secure the Riksbank's ability to be self-financing in the long term, the petition may be for an amount corresponding to, at most, the amount restoring equity to the target level. In the review of the act it was also noted that the General Council and the Executive Board have a general right to petition the parliament concerning increases in the target level of capital, or for a capital injection even if the level of capital exceeds the minimum threshold.

The assumptions and conclusions in the review of the Riksbank act did not differ very much from those of the Flam review.[29] For instance, the assumptions about normal levels of operating costs (around SEK 0.85 billion) and the real interest rate (1%) were similar. In the new review no presumption of FX hedging was made, although the review recommended the Riksbank to analyse this issue. Even if FX risk continued to be quantitatively important, and the Riksbank had decided in December 2012 to increase the FX reserve further, it was argued in the review that no buffer was needed to cover FX risk over and above the unrealized gains in the revaluation account. On the other hand, the new review put more weight on the risk of rapidly declining seigniorage. The judgement was made that the stock of notes and coins could be halved (i.e., decrease by around SEK 30 billion, see Table 1), and yet ensure a sufficient level of interest-free financing (SEK 85 billion) with equity at its target level.

At the time of the review of the act, the Riksbank had large holdings of domestic government bonds (see Table 1) due to the Riksbank's asset purchases for monetary policy reasons. In contrast to the situations in the earlier reviews, this involved high exposure to interest rate changes. The conclusion in the review was that the revaluation account provided a sufficient buffer for this risk, especially since it was also suggested that the Riksbank should have the right to ask for more capital than the target level if needed.

In the parliamentary committee's review of the Riksbank Act, it was clear that they saw a possible conflict, or a trade-off, between the central bank's financial independence and fiscal policy:[30]

> In assessing what constitutes an appropriate capital buffer for the Riksbank, needs to safeguard its ability to self-finance should also be weighed against the cost of the state tying up capital in the Riksbank. The larger the Riksbank's equity, the more capital is tied up by the central government in the Riksbank. There is a risk that the state will tie up capital in the Riksbank that crowds out borrowing opportunities. Given that the central government's borrowing opportunities are limited, every government krona tied up in the Riksbank is in some sense one krona less in financial room for maneuver. In a situation where public finances are weak, this may imply a more significant limitation.

---

[28] In contrast to the Flam review, no automatic recapitalisation rule was thus suggested. The arguments for discretion rather than a fixed rule can be found in SOU (2019), pp. 1269–1270.

[29] The arguments in the review also closely followed the government's referral to the Council on Legislation based on the Flam review.

[30] Translation from p. 1235 in SOU (2019).

3.4.3 The Riksbank's Comments[31]

In its consultation response to the proposals for a new Sveriges Riksbank Act, the Executive Board argued that the model for the Riksbank's equity did not provide sufficient financial independence for the Riksbank. The probability that the Riksbank would need to be recapitalized within the coming 10 years was too great.[32]

The Board stressed that the composition and size of the Riksbank's balance sheet have shown relatively wide variation historically. The Board thought that it is difficult to predict which balance sheet will be needed. The Board argued that the risks of a large balance sheet also in the future, of financial losses due to fluctuations in interest and exchange rates, and of declining seigniorage had been underestimated in the review. The level of equity should not be limited to a level that involves a significant risk for recapitalization in the near future—such as 5–10 years.[33] The Board argued that it was not appropriate to legislate a specific level of equity at all. Instead, the Board advocated that the 80/20 model for profit should be confirmed by law (with some amendments).

The Riksbank's consultation response included an annex with scenario analyses, building on a framework presented by Kjellberg and Vestin (2019). Quantitative analyses were used to illustrate the effects of different assumptions about the long-term real interest rate, the slope of the yield curve, the outstanding stock of notes and coins, etc. In a "main scenario", the Riksbank's ability to finance its operations via a combination of equity and seigniorage appeared to be satisfactory. Taking historical uncertainty into account, however, a time series model gave a 30% probability of a recapitalization (equity below SEK 20 billion) during the first 10 years of the simulations. The annex showed how the probability was affected by various assumptions. The annex also noted that if the 80/20 model for profit allocation would be used instead of the proposed changes to the law, the probability of low equity would not be much affected, but such a model would give the Riksbank more flexibility to retain profits in situations where equity was considered to be too small.

Given the later development, to which we now turn, it is especially interesting to note some reasoning in the Executive Board's consultation response and the annex related to possible future developments of the interest rate. First, in historically normal circumstances, a higher interest rate level has led to higher profits for the central bank, when assets have been largely financed through interest-free equity and

[31] Here we summarize the comments of the Riksbank on the initial proposal. For a more recent discussion of how the new law has worked, see Thedéen (2024).

[32] The Governing Council supported the new profit allocation model and target level for the Riksbank's equity, but also noted that there are risks for higher costs and lower income due to a rapid decline of the use of cash, lower long-term interest rates or higher financial risks in the Riksbank's balance sheet.

[33] The idea that the degree of financial independence can be measured by the probability of recapitalisation within a certain horizon has also been presented by, among others, Kjellberg and Vestin (2019) and Wessels and Broeders (2022). This was also noted in the review of the act, SOU (2019), p. 1235.

currency. When the central bank to a higher degree finances asset purchases through interest-bearing reserves the effect may be less positive and even negative. The Executive Board noted that if interest rates were to rise in line with the assumptions in the review of the act, the Riksbank's earning capacity would be at the intended level—but the loss-absorbing capacity would be much lower due to financial losses when assets are valued according to market prices. If, on the other hand, interest rates would remain low, capital buffers would be unaffected, but the Riksbank's capacity to finance itself from revenue would become weak, especially if the stock of notes and coins declines. Second, the annex contained explicit examples of changes in interest and exchange rates that would trigger a recapitalization of the Riksbank with the proposed new law.

4 Model-Based Simulations of the Probability of Recapitalization

In 2022, the Riksbank reported a loss of SEK 81 billion in the profit and loss account.[34] The reported loss was almost exclusively due to assets' market values falling below the respective purchase values, because of rising interest rates. Both FX and SEK assets contributed to the loss.

The financial loss from assets and liabilities, mark-to-market, led to a drop of equity for the accounting year 2023 to SEK −18 billion, far below 1/3 of the targeted level and, thus, triggered a process where the Riksbank needs to make a petition to the parliament for a capital injection.[35] On 2 April 2024, the Riksbank submitted a proposal for a restoration of equity to the base level, i.e., 2/3 of the targeted level.[36]

As noted in the previous sections, there is large uncertainty about how much capital a central bank needs, partly because the degree of financial independence is affected by many factors whose development is highly uncertain, and partly because the proper definition of financial independence itself is uncertain. The latter issue has to some extent been solved in Sweden, since the Riksbank Act from 2023 includes a target level for equity, and a minimum level that determines when requests for recapitalization should be made. Given this minimum level, it is, in principle, possible to measure the probability of a recapitalization based on models of the factors that affect the central bank's capital. In this section, we present a

[34] In the same accounting year, a depreciating krona increased the market value of the currencies in the Riksbank's FX reserve. However, these unrealized profits were booked to revaluation accounts and, hence, did not affect the reported result. The Riksbank's total capital, including revaluation accounts, decreased from SEK 161 billion to SEK 99 billion; see Fig. 1 and Annual Report for Sveriges Riksbank 2022, pp. 87–89.

[35] In 2023, the Riksbank's result reported in the profit and loss account was a profit of SEK 16 billion. Total capital increased from SEK 99 billion to 110 billion. See Figs. 1 and 2.

[36] See The Riksbank proposes that equity be restored to the statutory base level | Sveriges Riksbank.

framework for such analyses and quantitative examples of how the probability of a recapitalization of the Riksbank is affected by different factors and assumptions. The framework has been developed at the Riksbank during the last decade and has earlier been used in the analyses by Kjellberg and Vestin (2019) and Kjellberg and Åhl (2022).

The models and assumptions are presented in Sect. 4.1. Some illustrative scenarios based on specific alternative assumptions about the future developments of interest rates and exchange rates are presented in Sect. 4.2. Estimates of the probability of recapitalization based on the more general uncertainty about a larger number of factors are presented in Sect. 4.3.

4.1 Models and Assumptions

Before we present a more ambitious quantitative analysis of the questions at hand in Sect. 4.3, it is useful to discuss some important mechanisms in terms of a simpler framework. Equation (1) below provides a simple relation which takes us quite far in understanding the importance of different factors for the net interest income of a central bank. Equations (2) and (3) define a law of motion for the capital as a function of the net interest income and operating costs. These relations constitute the foundation for the quantitative model exercises presented later.

$$\text{Interest net}_t = r_t^a \cdot \text{Assets}_t - r_t^p \cdot \text{Interestbearing liabilities}_t \tag{1}$$

$$\text{Result}_t = \text{Interest net}_t - \text{Operating cost}_t \tag{2}$$

$$\text{Equity}_{t+1} = \text{Equity}_t + \text{Result}_t - \text{Dividend}_t + \text{Capital injection}_t \tag{3}$$

r_t^a is the average return on assets. In the case of the Riksbank, the assets consist almost exclusively of bonds in domestic and foreign currency (SEK assets and FX) and gold; see Table 1. The gold holdings are managed in a passive way, i.e., the strategy is to never buy, sell or rent out the gold and it, thus, yields no return reported in the profit and loss statement. When applying Eq. (1) in analyses of the development of the Riksbank's financial result and equity we must therefore either adjust r_t^a down to compensate for this, or exclude the gold from the assets factor.

r_t^p is the interest the Riksbank pays on its interest-bearing liabilities, consisting almost exclusively of debt to the banks (central bank reserves); interest bearing liabilities = assets – currency – total capital, see Table 1. Equity thus affects net interest income since increased equity (i.e., a profit not distributed to the state as dividends, or a capital injection from the state) can be used to either purchase more return-yielding assets or replace interest-bearing debt, thus improving net interest income. Vice versa, decreased equity (losses or dividend payments) weakens net interest income.

In the case of the Riksbank, r_t^p is very close to the policy rate.[37] Furthermore, it is fair to approximate the Riksbank's assets with a portfolio of government bonds with different maturities and in different currencies.[38] The return on government bonds, r_t^a, connects to the policy rate, r_t^p, through the expectation hypothesis and a term premium, i.e., $r_{t,k}^a = \sum_{i=0}^k E_t\left[r_{t+i}^p\right] + \mathrm{TP}_{t,k}$, where $r_{t,k}^a$ is the market yield at time t on a government bond maturing in k periods and $\mathrm{TP}_{t,\,k}$ is the corresponding term premium at time t. $\mathrm{TP}_{t,\,k}$ is unobserved and challenging to estimate.

On average, one can expect the difference between the return on the Riksbank's assets and the interest on its interest-bearing debt to be given by a long-run average term premium. Since a fairly large share of the bonds are in foreign currencies (FX reserves, see Table 1), changes to and trends in exchange rates and interest differentials between Sweden and the rest of the world (affected by expected exchange rate changes and risk premia) also affect the return r_t^a.

This discussion shows that the Riksbank's financial result and equity should be determined by the following factors, all to be found more or less explicitly in Eqs. (1)–(3):

- Level and trend in operating costs.
- The average risk-free short interest rate (i.e., the policy rate).
- The average term premium.
- Foreign interest rates, exchange rate changes and currency risk premia.
- The distribution of the assets' duration (which affect r_t^a given the previous three factors).
- The size of the balance sheet (i.e., assets).
- The share of liabilities bearing interest, i.e., the difference between total liabilities and interest-free liabilities. Interest-free liabilities consist of
  - Currency (outstanding stock of banknotes and coins)
  - Equity
  - Other capital (provisions, revaluation accounts)

This framework, and relations similar to Eqs. (1)–(3), were used, more or less explicitly, in all the reviews summarized in Sect. 3. Different assumptions about the factors above, and the associated risks, led to different conclusions about the development of the Riksbank's financial result and equity. Table 3 describes the assumptions made in a baseline scenario used in the analyses below.

In order to do a quantitative analysis of the development of the Riksbank's equity under different conditions, we need an analytically and empirically relevant framework that helps us illustrate key risks going forward. Ideally, we would like to have a model where all variables are endogenous. For instance, the size of the

[37] The majority of the reserves are week-long Riksbank certificates yielding exactly the policy rate. A smaller share is overnight deposits yielding the policy rate minus 10 bp.

[38] The Riksbank currently holds some bonds subject to larger credit risk, but with shorter duration. According to the communicated plan, the Riksbank will hold these to maturity and not reinvest as the portfolio shrinks.

central bank balance sheet will respond to future monetary policy decisions, e.g., about asset purchases (QE) triggered by the lower bound on the policy rate; the demand for currency depends on the evolution of payment markets; and so forth. In practice, we have to make simplifying assumptions reflecting what we can handle in terms of endogenous variables, and then do robustness exercises on the variables we treat as exogenous. Our modelling approach consists of two parts—a Bayesian VAR model and a balance-sheet module.

The BVAR model we use is fairly standard and utilizes steady-state priors as introduced by Villani (2009). It consists of foreign variables and domestic (Swedish) variables, where the former are block exogenous in the sense that foreign variables are allowed to affect domestic variables, but the opposite is not true. Table 2 lists the variables in the BVAR model and the corresponding steady-state prior and posterior distributions (in terms of 90% probability intervals). The estimation uses a monthly data sample covering 1997m9–2024m2 and four lags.

Table 2 Variables included in the BVAR model

Variable	Transformation	Steady-state prior (90%)	Steady-state posterior (90%)
Foreign			
US inflation	1200*Logdiff	[1.9, 2.1]	[1.92, 2.08]
US unemployment		[5, 7]	[4.88, 6.42]
US 3 m gvmt yield		[2.4, 2.6]	[2.41, 2.58]
US 2y gvmt yield		[2.55, 2.75]	[2.57, 2.74]
US 10y gvmt yield		[3.1, 3.3]	[3.16, 3.33]
S&P 500 stock index	1200*Logdiff	[0, 10]	[0.67, 8.57]
Euro area (EA) inflation	1200*Logdiff	[1.9, 2.1]	[1.93, 2.10]
EA unemployment		[5, 7]	[5.48, 7.58]
German 3 m gvmt yield		[2.4, 2.6]	[2.41, 2.57]
German 2y gvmt yield		[2.55, 2.75]	[2.59, 2.76]
German 10y gvmt yield		[3.1, 3.3]	[3.08, 3.25]
STOXX stock index	1200*Logdiff	[0, 10]	[0.08, 7.93]
USD/EUR exchange rate	Log	[−0.14, −0.12]	[−0.14, −0.12]
Gold price	1200*Logdiff	[−10, 10]	[−5.55, 9.41]
Domestic			
Inflation (CPIF)	1200*Logdiff	[1.99, 2.01]	[1.99, 2.01]
Unemployment		[5, 7]	[6.45, 7.81]
3 m gvmt yield		[2.4, 2.6]	[2.42, 2.58]
2y gvmt yield		[2.55, 2.75]	[2.57, 2.73]
10y gvmt yield		[3.1, 3.3]	[3.10, 3.26]
OMXS30 stock index	1200*Logdiff	[0, 10]	[1.51, 9.45]
USD/SEK exchange rate	Log	[2.25, 2.30]	[2.24, 2.28]
Mortgage spread 2y		[0, 1.5]	[0.33, 0.96]
Mortgage spread 5y		[0, 1.5]	[0.50, 1.23]

Table 3 Baseline assumptions in model-based simulations

Assumption	Value
QE portfolio (SEK)	Gradually towards zero
FX assets	Stable around SEK 400 billion in constant prices
Gold assets	Managed passively, yielding no reported profit or loss
Banknotes and coins	Stay at the current nominal level
Normal policy rate	2.5% (i.e., 0.5% real rate)
Normal term premium	70 bp for 10y maturity
Duration, FX assets	4 years (same as current value)
Exchange rates	No long-term trend
Regional interest differentials	Zero
Growth rate of operating costs	2% (as inflation target)

The balance-sheet module, so-called BRA module, takes as given a future evolution of financial prices (yield curves and exchange rates).[39] These can be exogenous assumptions, as is the case in Sect. 4.2, or provided by the BVAR model, as is the case in Sect. 4.3. Also the development of currency (outstanding stock of banknotes and coins), operating costs and the Riksbank's decisions to change the other items on the balance-sheet are input to the BRA module. The assumptions made in a baseline scenario are provided in Table 3.[40] The calculations are in line with the framework presented in Eqs. (1)–(3), but with additional sophistication. The BRA module also attempts to capture accounting rules, as closely as practically possible, such as the principle of mark-to-market and the use of revaluation accounts. For example, if a simulation implies an increase in longer-term interest rates, this is translated into price effects on the government bonds that the Riksbank holds. Furthermore, for the December month of each year in a simulation, the algorithm computes an annual profit and loss statement, and employs rules for

[39] One important aspect is how the term premium is modelled. In a scenario, consisting of exogenous assumptions for the policy rates, the term premium at the beginning of the scenario is calculated as the difference between the actual market rate and the scenario-implied expected average policy rate over the corresponding period. Throughout the scenario, the term premium is assumed to gradually return to its normal level. As a consequence, neither the term premium nor longer rates "jump" to new levels in a scenario, as policy rates can be assumed to do. Also consequently, the starting level of the term premium can differ between different scenarios starting at the same point in time, depending on the (assumed) expected development of the policy rates. In the BVAR model, used for simulation, rates of different durations are included, so the development of the term premium is implicit. However, steady-state prior assumptions are applied, consistent with an average term premium in line with a historical average.

[40] It deserves to be noted, e.g., that the stock of outstanding currency is kept fixed (deemed consistent with current forecasts) and that the QE portfolio is assumed to trickle down according to the current plan communicated by the Executive Board. See e.g. Monetary policy report March 2024 (riksbank.se), Figure 33. We hence do not capture additional risk in the form of future asset purchases (or a change in the current speed of portfolio adjustments) motivated by monetary policy. The size of the FX reserve is kept fixed at a level consistent with the current holdings of the Riksbank.

profit distribution and so forth. The algorithm also keeps track of the implications of cash-flows from bond holdings and interest expenses on debt (reserves), etc.

4.2 *Illustrative Scenarios*

In Sect. 4.3, we use the BVAR model and the BRA module to estimate the probability of recapitalization by simulations of 2000 forecasts for the period 2024m3–2059m12, subject to model shocks consistent with the empirical evidence. Before looking at the probabilities generated by the simulations, it is illustrative to describe a few specific scenarios. These scenarios are not based on simulations from the BVAR model. Instead, they show how the Riksbank's balance sheet evolves under specific assumptions (i.e., scenarios) for interest rates, exchange rates and exogenous balance-sheet variables like banknotes and coins and operating costs.[41]

Figure 3 shows the future paths for the short-term interest rate, the policy rate, and the exchange rate (SEK/USD) in our baseline scenario together with alternative scenarios with higher and lower levels for the interest rate and the exchange rate. Policy rates in Sweden, the USA, and the euro area are assumed to be temporarily higher or lower (around 1 percentage point) than in the baseline scenario. Other assumptions are unchanged from the baseline scenario.

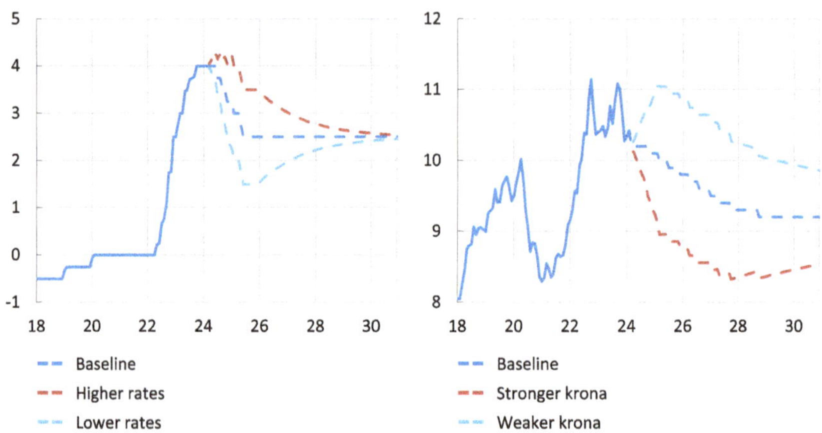

Fig. 3 Assumptions for baseline and sensitivity scenarios. Note: Policy rate in Sweden in per cent (left panel) and SEK per USD (right panel). Source: The Riksbank: The Riksbank proposes that equity be restored to the statutory base level | Sveriges Riksbank

[41] The scenarios are the same as in the petition, The Riksbank proposes that equity be restored to the statutory base level | Sveriges Riksbank. In these scenarios, higher equity than the target level was not assumed to lead to dividend payments from the Riksbank to the state.

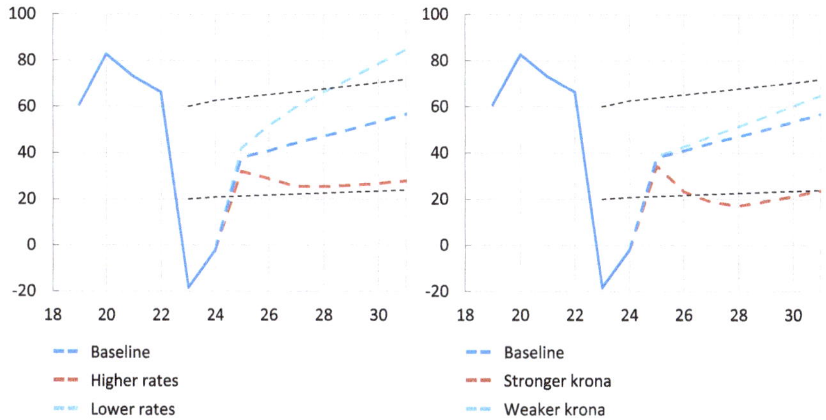

Fig. 4 Equity development in baseline and sensitivity scenarios. Note: SEK billion. The dotted black lines indicate the target level and 1/3 of the target level, indexed with steady-state inflation of 2%. Source: The Riksbank: The Riksbank proposes that equity be restored to the statutory base level | Sveriges Riksbank

Figure 4 shows the resulting development for the Riksbank's equity in the baseline scenario and the alternative scenarios. All scenarios assume that the Riksbank receives a capital injection of SEK 44 billion in 2024, in line with the Executive Board's recent petition to the parliament, bringing equity close to the so-called base level (2/3 of the target level), i.e., the midpoint of the tolerance interval between the target level and the minimum level that gives rise to a petition (1/3 of the target level).[42]

We can learn a few things from these scenarios. Starting with the baseline scenario, profits are made and equity is expected to increase towards the target level at a slow pace. One important reason why profits are positive is that a majority of the FX assets are US government bonds, currently yielding a higher return than the Swedish policy rate.[43] This difference disappears only gradually, although the long-term assumptions are symmetric between the countries (see Tables 2 and 3).

We see from the left-hand panel in Fig. 4 that higher or lower interest rates have significant effects on the Riksbank's equity. With lower interest rates, equity grows fast enough to reach the target level in a few years. In the scenario where interest rates instead increase rapidly, losses are made initially and equity falls close to but not below the minimum level.

[42] Equity here includes balanced profits, so the profit for the accounting year 2024 also affects the equity level for 2024.

[43] This corresponds to r_t^a currently being higher than r_t^p in Eq. (1). According to the theory of uncovered interest parity (UIP), this difference should be compensated by (expected) changes in the exchange rate. The UIP, however, rarely holds empirically.

In the alternative scenarios with a weaker and stronger krona, the Riksbank's reported profit is of course also affected. Although the exchange-rate assumptions are symmetric around the baseline scenario (see the right-hand panel in Fig. 3), the effects on equity are far from symmetric (right-hand panel in Fig. 4). The explanation is that although a weaker krona increases the market value of the Riksbank's FX assets, this does not affect the reported result and thus the equity. Instead, the valuation gains are booked to revaluation accounts on the liability side of the balance sheet. In the scenario where the krona strengthens, there are some initial buffers available in the revaluation accounts but not enough to absorb the total valuation loss. Therefore, losses are reported in the profit and loss statement, bringing equity below the minimum level.[44]

While the illustrative scenarios reported in this section disregard the legislated principles for dividend payments and capital injections, the simulations reported in Sect. 4.3 do not. In the simulations, if equity increases above the target level, a dividend corresponding to the difference is paid to the state, bringing equity back to the target level. Similarly, if losses are made so that the equity falls below the minimum level (1/3 of the target level), a capital injection is assumed to bring equity to the base level (2/3 of the target level).

The baseline scenario shows the development of the Riksbank's equity in a scenario with no further shocks. In reality, financial prices are volatile due to shocks hitting different parts of the economy. The intention of the alternative scenarios in this subsection is to illustrate the effects of alternative developments, but these specific alternative paths are arbitrary and isolated, and do not take the co-variance of relevant variables into account. We can, however, do this in a more structured way using BVAR simulations.

4.3 Simulations of the Probability for Recapitalization

In this section, we present results from using the BRA model and the BVAR model in combination. We use the framework to calculate probabilities, given the legislated capital framework and historical correlations, of recurring petitions for capital injections.

We use the BVAR model to simulate 2000 scenarios for the period 2024–2059. It is useful to make a distinction between what happens in the near term and in the long term. The main reason is that in the near term, the balance sheet is dominated by the SEK-denominated bonds in the QE portfolio. The current view of the Riksbank is, however, that this portfolio will gradually diminish.[45] The QE portfolio is associated

[44] This should trigger another petition to the parliament for a capital injection, but the scenarios in the petition of 2024 disregarded this aspect.

[45] Swedish government bonds are actively sold at a pace of SEK 6.5 billon per month, with a bias towards longer maturities. The covered, municipal and corporate bonds have shorter maturities and

with substantial interest-rate risk. From around 2027, the balance sheet is expected to have more of a "steady-state" nature. There is of course some probability that asset purchases will be used again in the future. This is, however, very difficult both to predict and to implement in our models in an appropriate way. Ideally, the simulation would include an endogenous response with QE if the policy rate reaches an effective lower bound, but at the present we abstract from this.

In the simulations, we focus on the probability of future petitions for recapitalization, i.e., the probability of equity falling below the minimum level (1/3 of the target level). We also look at the probability of dividend payments, since it is of course also possible that the Riksbank will make profits leading to equity reaching the target level and therefore also to dividends to the state.

We perform several sets of simulations; one based on our baseline assumptions and a number of "sensitivity checks" where we deviate from the baseline assumptions in one dimension (one explanatory factor) at a time. The baseline assumptions are listed in Table 3 and can also to some extent be read from the steady-state priors in Table 2.

In the simulations reported in Tables 4 and 5, we assume that the Riksbank receives a capital injection during 2024 such that its equity returns to the base level (2/3 of the target level) in line with the Riksbank's petition from 2 April 2024.[46] Figure 5 gives a flavour of the importance of this assumption. The figure illustrates how the probability of equity falling below the minimum level and, thus, triggering another petition for a recapitalization within 3 years, may be affected by the size of the capital injection in 2024. According to the modelling framework used here, a capital injection of less than SEK 20 billion would almost certainly not be enough to prevent another recapitalization in the near term. A capital injection of above SEK 70 billion, on the other hand, could under the same assumptions decrease the probability of another near-term recapitalization to below 10%.

Our main results are reported in Table 4 for the near term and Table 5 for the longer term. From Table 4, focusing first on the baseline column, we see that the currently large balance sheet, with substantial financial risk, is associated with an estimated relatively high probability, 33%, of the accounting year 2024 triggering a new recapitalization, even if a recapitalization to the base level is made during this year. As the QE portfolio and, hence, the interest rate risk, decreases, so does the probability of another near-term recapitalization. For the years 2025–2026 the probability of a recapitalization is actually lower than the annual probability in the long run (see Table 5). This is likely due to the current relatively favourable situation with US yields being substantially higher than the Riksbank's policy rate, a positive effect on the Riksbank's profits which is expected to decrease over time.

---

will thus disappear to a great extent within a few years. See Monetary policy report March 2024 (riksbank.se), Figure 33.

[46] See The Riksbank proposes that equity be restored to the statutory base level | Sveriges Riksbank.

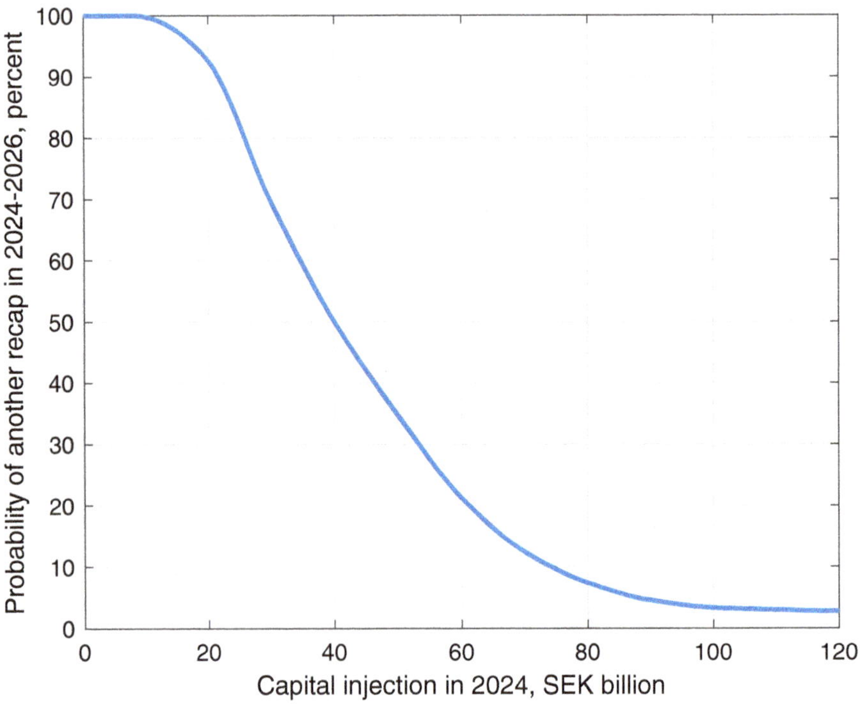

Fig. 5 Near-term probability of recapitalization as a function of capital injection in 2024

Table 4 Recapitalization and dividend probabilities in the near term. Note: All values are probabilities in per cent. Green and red numbers indicate a financial situation that is better or worse, respectively, compared to the baseline. See below for an explanation of columns (i)–(vii)

	Baseline	(i)	(ii)	(iii)	(iv)	(v)	(vi)	(vii)
2024								
Recap	33	33/33	33/33	39/33	33/33	31/36	35/33	19
Dividend > 0	0	0/0	0/0	0/0	0/0	0/0	0/0	0
2025								
Recap	11	11/11	11/11	18/8	12/11	7/14	12/12	8
Dividend > 0	4	4/4	4/4	1/5	3/4	1/12	3/4	1
2026								
Recap	8	8/8	8/8	15/5	9/7	4/12	9/8	5
Dividend > 0	17	17/17	17/17	7/21	13/17	7/32	15/16	4

We can also see that the estimated probability of the Riksbank distributing profits as dividends to the state, i.e., equity exceeding the target level, increases from 0% in 2024 to 17% in 2026, in the baseline scenario. There are thus "good" scenarios in which the Riksbank makes substantial profits in the near future, but these are, judging from historical patterns in the data, rather unlikely.

On top of the uncertainty caused by the volatility in financial prices, captured by the BVAR model's input to the BRA module, there is substantial uncertainty about

Table 5 Recapitalization probability and dividend size in the longer term, 2027–2059. Note: Green and red numbers indicate a financial situation that is better or worse, respectively, compared to the baseline. See below for an explanation of columns (i)–(vii). Average dividend payments are calculated in constant prices. Explanation to numbered columns in Table 4 and this table, alternative assumptions in simulation: (i) Growth rate of operating cost: 5/0% per year: (Baseline: 2%). (ii) Growth rate of notes and coins in circulation: 2/−5% per year: (Baseline: 0). (iii) Normal real interest rate: +/− 75 bp: (Baseline: 0.5%). (iv) Steady-state term premium, 10-year maturity: 20/120 bp: (Baseline: 70 bp). (v) Average duration in FX assets: 1.5 /7 years: (Baseline: 4 years). (vi) Interest differential Sweden—rest of the world: +/− 50 bp, implemented half and half on normal interest rate and term premium: (Baseline: no difference). (vii) Increased target level for equity: SEK 90 billion (In this simulation, also the capital injection of 2024 is assumed to be higher, to 2/3 of the new target level. This is contradicting the petition handed in by the Riksbank to the parliament on 2 April 2024 and should be viewed as hypothetic): (Baseline: SEK 60 billion)

	Baseline	(i)	(ii)	(iii)	(iv)	(v)	(vi)	(vii)
Annual pr. Recap (%)	14	15/14	14/15	16/13	16/13	14/17	15/14	10
Avg. annual div. (SEK bn)	4.4	4.0/4.5	4.6/4.1	6.0/3.4	5.2/7.1	4.5/7.3	3.5/6.1	3.7

the assumptions underlying the baseline simulations in Tables 4 and 5. Columns (i)–(vii) are attempts at addressing and analysing this uncertainty, varying one potentially important assumption at a time.[47] In Table 4 we see that a higher normal interest rate level increases the probability for another near-term recapitalization (column iii). The reason is that the higher the normal interest level is, the more likely are near-term interest rate hikes, which would lower the market value of the Riksbank's assets (as in 2022). Further, a decrease in the interest-rate risk by lowering the average duration for the FX assets, from around 4 years to 1.5 years, would lower the risk of another recapitalization through lower volatility of the market values of the assets (column v). However, this would also lower the expected return on the assets, and therefore also the probability of dividend payments to the state in the near term. An increase in the target level from SEK 60 to 90 billion (column vii) would both improve the Riksbank's net interest income and increase the distance to the legislated level for a new petition (which would also increase, but not by as much in absolute terms), thus substantially lowering the probability of a recapitalization.

Shifting the focus to the longer run and what could be considered as more of a steady-state situation, Table 5 shows that in the baseline scenario we can expect an average probability of a recapitalization of 14% each year, i.e., a recapitalization around every seventh year. The sensitivity analysis shows that the probability is only marginally affected by variations in the assumptions about the explanatory factors. From Table 5 we also see that the long-term yearly average dividend payment from the Riksbank to the state is SEK 4.4 billion (in constant prices), slightly below the average in the 2000s. The simulation exercise predicts that a volatile result, stemming from volatile financial prices, will give rise to *both* periods of good profits

[47] Ideally, we would like to analyse the combined uncertainty of all the assumptions. However, the complexity of the issue prevents us from doing this for the time being.

and dividends *and* periods leading to recurring needs for recapitalization according to the current legislated framework.

While it is complicated to understand all the intricate details about accounting rules and the exact composition of the balance-sheet, the basic risks to Riksbank's capital are fairly easy to grasp. The Riksbank has purchased a large portfolio of bonds, currently around SEK 1000 billion, with a predetermined (in nominal terms) return. The portfolio includes foreign bonds—currently worth around SEK 400 billion—denominated in primarily USD and EUR. This portfolio was funded with a small amount of interest-free liabilities (capital and currency) and the rest with reserves remunerated close to the variable policy rate. Around 75% of the currency reserve is unhedged. Thus, the two main risks from an economic perspective are that the short-term interest rate rises, which increases the interest expense on the reserves, and that the exchange rate appreciates against the USD and the EUR. If the short-term interest rate increases by 1 percentage point the annual increase in interest payments is currently around SEK 10 billion. Of course, the balance sheet is projected to decline in the coming years and then the future increase in interest payments will be correspondingly lower. Second, if the exchange rate appreciates by 5%, the unhedged component, of around SEK 340 billion, would lose around SEK 17 billion in value.

If capital is increased to SEK 40 billion, a loss of around SEK 20 billion would be sufficient to trigger a new recapitalization. It is clear from the above figures that a combination of slightly higher interest rates and a stronger currency could easily result in losses of such magnitudes. This is reflected in relatively high estimated probabilities of recapitalization in Tables 4 and 5.

Two practical issues affect the computations. First, assets are valued mark-to-market at year-end such that unrealized losses must be written down and hence affecting equity. This has the implication of front-loading the triggering of a recapitalization. Assume for example that current and expected short-rates are increased by 1 percentage point such that the yield on the bond portfolio increases by 1 percentage point. The duration in the portfolio is currently around 3.5 years, such that the drop in value would correspond to (the duration times the increase in yield) 3.5%, or SEK 35 billion. In terms of cash-flow, the increased interest payment on the reserves would be spread over the remaining life-time of the bonds. But with the accounting rules, the entire loss would be written down the first year-end. This will have a tendency to front-load recapitalizations. On the other hand, there is currently a rather large surplus on the revaluation accounts for USD (SEK 20 billion), EUR (SEK 2 billion), and other currencies (SEK 8 billion). Thus, the appreciation of the krona exchange rate would have to be rather larger than the 5% in the example above before actually triggering a decline in capital sufficient to trigger a recapitalization.

Of course, in the simulations discussed above, there is a correlation between exchange rate appreciations and interest rate increases further complicating a full understanding of the results, but the basic logic is apparent from the above reasoning. As long as assets are valued according to mark-to-market and there is substantial interest and exchange-rate risk on the Riksbank's balance sheet, the current tolerated interval for equity can be expected to lead to recurring recapitalizations (but also to recurrent dividends being paid out when profits lead to higher equity than the target level).

5 Summary and Conclusions

Both theoretical arguments and practical experiences show that *there is large uncertainty about how much capital a central bank needs to be sufficiently "financially independent"*. There seems to be wide agreement, in principle, that the central bank should have financial strength that makes the probability low that it will have to ask the government or parliament for more resources in the short or medium term. At a minimum, capital should be sufficient to generate a return so that the central bank can cover its operating costs for the foreseeable future (10 years?). If a target level for capital has been decided, recapitalizations should ideally be automatic in order to minimize the risk of political influence on the central bank's policy decisions.

In practice, these issues are very difficult, as our descriptions of the Swedish experiences clearly show. Different assumptions about, e.g., the normal levels of interest rates, the size and structure of the balance sheet, and the central bank's costs have large implications for the equity needed.

It is not realistic to assume that there will be automatic recapitalizations. In consequence, a satisfactory level of financial independence requires that the central bank not only cover its operational costs, but that there also are buffers that make it possible to restore equity to the targeted level when there have been unexpectedly large losses. The discussions in Sweden reflect *very different views on the need for buffers*. Some arguments have been made that the central bank should take so low risks that buffers are not needed. Other arguments have been that interest-free financing in the form of notes and coins constitutes a sufficient buffer.

The difference between financial and institutional independence is not clear. The different assessments of the Riksbank's need for equity have involved analyses of the size and structure of the Riksbank's balance sheet, e.g. the size, financing and risk of the FX reserves. The Flam review proposed an upper limit for the FX reserve and on the Riksbank's borrowing in foreign currency via the National Debt Office. The General Council argued that decisions on the size of the FX reserve should be taken jointly by the Executive Board and the General Council.[48] The latest review of the Riksbank Act resulted in new explicit restrictions on the Riksbank's possibilities to issue own debt in foreign currency and to purchase other assets than domestic government paper.

Restrictions on policy independence often reflect fiscal policy considerations. This seems to have been the case when the parliament decided on extra transfers from the Riksbank in 2001 and 2002. Fiscal policy considerations were also explicit

[48] The central bank does not have complete control over FX reserves in all countries.

in the terms of reference for the Flam review 2011. The new restrictions in the Riksbank Act from 2023 reflect a desire to limit the Riksbank's risk-taking.

Economic analyses can provide very useful input to the political decisions. *Given a targeted minimum level of equity, the probability of petitions for recapitalization can be estimated.* Quantitative analyses of the Riksbank's situation suggest that the probability of recapitalization is relatively high, especially in the short term before the size of the balance sheet has declined. The Riksbank's responses to low inflation before and during the pandemic, and the increased FX reserve to promote financial stability, have led to substantial risks associated with fluctuations in interest rates and exchange rates. At the same time, expected future revenue in the form of seigniorage is low in an historical and international perspective. This has led to an increasing probability of losses (and, with the new law, recapitalizations) also in the longer run. Natural volatility in financial prices, in combination with the current legislated framework and likely scenarios for the Riksbank's future balance sheet, thus lead to relatively high estimated probabilities for recurring petitions to the parliament for capital injections—according to the modelling framework presented here.

The Swedish experiences support the hypothesis by Kjellberg and Vestin (2019, p. 31), that "*The amount of equity the central bank is allowed to retain can be said to reflect the size of risks that the politicians can accept that the bank takes*". The fundamental uncertainty about all factors that influence the central bank's need for capital also leaves much room for disagreement, and hence for political influence on the central bank. *It is unavoidable that estimates of how much capital—"financial independence"—a central bank needs are influenced by political judgements.*

References

Archer, D., & Moser-Boehm, P. (2013). Central Bank Finances, BIS Papers No 71.

Belhocine, N., Bhatia, A. V., & Frie, J. (2023). *Raising rates with a large balance sheet: The Eurosystem's Net income and its fiscal implications*. IMF working paper WP/23/145.

Berg, C., Meyersson, P., & Molin, J. (2018). Dramatic years in Sweden and globally: Economic developments 2006–2017. *Economic Review, 4*, 19–34.

Bylund, E., Iversen, J., & Vredin, A. (2024). Monetary policy in Sweden after the end of Bretton woods. *Comparative Economic studies 66*, 535–590.

Cavallo, M., Del Negro, M., Frame, W. S., Grasing, J., Malin, B. A., & Rosa, C. (2019). Fiscal implications of the Federal Reserve's balance sheet normalization. *International Journal of Central Banking, 15*(5), 255–306.

Del Negro, M., & Sims, C. (2015). When does a Central Bank's balance sheet require fiscal support? *Journal of Monetary Economics, 73*, 1–19.

Dincer, N., & Eichengreen, B. (2014). Central Bank Transparency and Independence: Updates and new measures. *International Journal of Central Banking, 10*(1), 189–253.

ECB. (2002). Convergence report 2002.

ECB. (2022). Convergence report, June 2022.

ECB. (2023). *ECB adjusts remuneration of minimum reserves*. Press release July 27.

Elmér, H., Guibourg, G., Kjellberg, D., & Nessén, M. (2012). The Riksbank's measures during the financial crisis—Evaluation and lessons learnt. *Economic Review* 2012:3, Sveriges Riksbank, 1–24.

Ernhagen, T., Vesterlund, M., & Viotti, S. (2002). How much equity does a central bank need? *Economic Review* 2002:2, Sveriges Riksbank, 5–18.

Gardholm, H., & Gerwin, J. (2011). The Riksbank's dividend in the past two decades. *Economic Commentary* no. 2, Sveriges Riksbank.

Gernandt, J., Pagrotsky, L., & Ingves, S. (2010). Urgent need for new financial regulations and tools. *Economic Commentary* No. 1, 2010, Sveriges Riksbank.

Goodfriend, M., & King, M. (2016). *Review of the Riksbank's Monetary Policy 2010–2015*, Sveriges Riksdag, 2015/16: RFR7.

Hall, R., & Reis, R. (2015). *Maintaining Central-Bank financial stability under new-style central banking*. NBER Working Paper 21173.

Kjellberg, D., & Åhl, M. (2022). The Riksbank's financial results and capital are affected by higher interest rates. *Economic Commentary*, No 8 2022, Sveriges Riksbank.

Kjellberg, D., & Vestin, D. (2019). The Riksbank's balance sheet and financial independence. *Economic Review* 2019:2, Sveriges Riksbank, 5–41.

Leeper, E. M. (1991). Equilibria under 'active' and 'passive' monetary and fiscal policies. *Journal of Monetary Economics, 27*(1), 129–147.

Levin, A. T., & Skinner, C. P. (2024). *Central Bank Undersight: Assessing the Fed's accountability to congress*. Economics Working Paper 23120, Hoover Institution, Stanford University.

Nordström, A., & Vredin, A. (2022). *Does central bank equity matter for monetary policy?* Staff memo, Sveriges Riksbank.

SOU. (2007). Riksbankens finansiella oberoende, SOU 2007:51.

SOU. (2013). Riksbankens finansiella oberoende och balansräkning, SOU 2013:9.

SOU. (2019). En ny riksbankslag, SOU 2019:46.

Thedéen, E. (2024). A year with the new Riksbank Act. Speech given at the Stockholm Centre for Commercial Law, Stockholm University, January 18.

Villani, M. (2009). Steady-state priors for vector autoregressions. *Journal of Applied Econometrics., 24*, 630–650. https://doi.org/10.1002/jae.1065

Wessels, P., & Broeders, D. (2022), On the capitalisation of central banks. *Occasional Studies, 20*(4), De Nederlandsche Bank.

Wetterberg, G. (2009). *Money and power*. Atlantis and Sveriges Riksbank.

Open Access This chapter is licensed under the terms of the Creative Commons Attribution 4.0 International License (http://creativecommons.org/licenses/by/4.0/), which permits use, sharing, adaptation, distribution and reproduction in any medium or format, as long as you give appropriate credit to the original author(s) and the source, provide a link to the Creative Commons license and indicate if changes were made.

The images or other third party material in this chapter are included in the chapter's Creative Commons license, unless indicated otherwise in a credit line to the material. If material is not included in the chapter's Creative Commons license and your intended use is not permitted by statutory regulation or exceeds the permitted use, you will need to obtain permission directly from the copyright holder.

The Impact of Central Bank Digital Currency on Central Bank Profitability, Risk Taking and Capital

Ulrich Bindseil, Marco Marrazzo, and Stephan Sauer

Abstract With digital payments becoming more and more popular, many central banks are investigating the issuance of retail central bank digital currency (CBDC) as a new central bank monetary liability in addition to banknotes and commercial bank reserves. CBDC will have broadly the same central bank balance sheet and profit implications as the issuance of banknotes. While the decision to issue CBDC is often thought to likely increase the size of the central bank balance sheet, the net impact of digitalization on the central bank balance sheet size could also be negative, as CBDC's design feature could limit its take-up as store of value and banknotes in circulation may decline. We use scenario analyses to illustrate the key drivers of the impact of CBDC on central bank profitability, with the part of CBDC not created from an exchange of banknotes being an important factor in this respect. The central bank's financial risk implications of CBDC can be managed within well-established frameworks and such implications depend primarily on the balance sheet size and asset composition impact. The paper concludes with a discussion how the profit and risk channels affect central bank capital.

Keywords Central bank balance sheet · Central bank capital · Central bank digital currency · Central bank profitability

---

The paper benefitted from comments by Katrin Assenmacher, Luca Bortolussi, Harald Deinhammer, Thomas Garcia, Polychronis Karakitsos, Antonella Pellicani, Alexandru Penciu, Doris Schneeberger, Oscar Soons, Nacho Terol and earlier discussions on this topic with Gabriel Andrade, Olaf Barning, Matteo Bonetti, Dirk Broeders, Giovanni Candura, Fernando Monar, Manuel Muñoz, Karl Pochet, Pedro Tomé and members of the Eurosystem Risk Management Committee. We also thank the participants of the workshop for the discussion. The views expressed are those of the authors and do not necessarily reflect those of the European Central Bank or the Eurosystem. All remaining errors are ours.

U. Bindseil · M. Marrazzo (✉) · S. Sauer
European Central Bank, Frankfurt, Germany
e-mail: Pasquale_Marco.Marrazzo@ecb.europa.eu; stephan.sauer@ecb.europa.eu

© The Author(s) 2025

D. Broeders et al. (eds.), *Central Bank Capital in Turbulent Times*,
Contributions to Finance and Accounting,
https://doi.org/10.1007/978-3-031-73549-3_9

1 Introduction

Modern central banks are unique from the perspective of capital needs for at least two reasons: *first*, their right to issue legal tender in the absence of any convertibility promise implies that they are not threatened by illiquidity and financial insolvency, providing them additional leeway in terms of balance sheet structure relative to a company without this privilege.[1] Therefore, central banks can operate rather orderly and maintain their ability to implement monetary policy (e.g. change the level of short-term market interest rates via their money market operations) regardless of temporary fluctuation in their profitability, capital and net equity (see, e.g., Bell et al., 2023; European Central Bank, 2023b). *Second,* they are normally structurally profitable because of the exclusive right, provided to them by law, to issue unremunerated central bank money while being able to match these with remunerated assets.

Both of these factors relate to their privilege to issue central bank money. However, the only central bank money issued to the general public has been for a while in the form of banknotes,[2] and banknotes are being used less and less for payments (European Central Bank, 2022), thereby reducing their demand for transaction purposes. While most of the banknotes in circulation are understood to serve store of value functions (see Devigne et al., 2023), the lesser usability of banknotes for payments could eventually weaken their attractiveness as store of value.

In this paper, we will directly focus on how the introduction of central bank digital currency (CBDC) may affect the central bank's balance sheet, profitability, risks, capital and net equity. We will not review specifically the general literature on the relevance of central bank profits and capital (see e.g. Bindseil et al., 2004; Archer & Moser-Boehm, 2013; Goncharov et al., 2023; Stella, 1997; Wessels & Broeders,

[1] Convertibility of central bank money had been the norm for centuries and ended for most countries only with the demise of the Bretton Woods system. Moreover, many central banks still operate under a fixed exchange rate regime in which they commit to convert their own currency into a foreign currency. In that case, the required level of capital that should suffice to prevent a run on the central bank can be modelled, for example in a model like Bindseil and Lanari (2022), which models asset liquidity in the sense of the ability of a (central) bank to sell assets in the short term without this inflicting fire sale losses depleting capital.

[2] Cash also comprises coins, which are usually minted by governments/treasuries, thus not a central bank liability, and quantitatively much less relevant than banknotes. In the euro area, the Governing Council of the ECB approves the overall value of the coins to be put into circulation annually. Only banknotes in circulation are on the ECB and the Eurosystem balance sheets, whereas coins in circulation are included only on the consolidated public sector balance sheet (combining the central bank and government balance sheet) for euro area countries. The same separation applies for the United States. In December 2023, there were 1567.2 billion euros banknotes and 33.5 billion euros coins denominated in euro in circulation (https://www.ecb.europa.eu/stats/policy_and_exchange_rates/banknotes+coins/circulation/html/index.en.html)

2022; ECB, 2015).[3] This focus on the effects on the *central bank* distinguishes our paper from various papers on CBDC (e.g. Adalid et al., 2022; Bindseil, 2020), in which the financial stability implications of CBDC, and thus its effects on the *commercial bank* balance sheets, are at the centre of attention. Throughout this paper, the term "CBDC" exclusively refers to CBDC available to households ("retail CBDC").[4]

Section 2 recalls the reasons for central banks to issue CBDC, and what central banks working at an advanced stage on such CBDC have announced so far with regard to the design features of CBDC. Both aspects are crucial for the rest of the paper, as both have profound implications on the future scenarios regarding the total central bank money in circulation, and thus central bank balance sheet length, profitability and risk taking. Section 3 looks at the CBDC impact on central bank profitability, using scenario analysis for the Eurosystem as an example. Sections 4 and 5 elaborate on the financial risk and capital implications, respectively. Section 6 concludes.

2 CBDC: A Future Monetary Liability of Central Banks

2.1 The "Endogeneity" of the CBDC Issuance Decision and Emerging CBDC Design Features

The pros and cons of CBDCs have been debated intensively since 2016, and the perception has emerged in the meantime that the majority of central banks will eventually deploy their monetary liabilities also in digital form to the general public. In essence, CBDC would preserve the advantages of central bank money in a digital age, in which people will pay less and less with banknotes. The availability and use of central bank money has served economies and societies well for several centuries. Not renewing the form of central bank money available to all in a digital age would imply to largely give up the well-tested two-layer monetary system based on a co-existence of central bank and commercial bank money.

Key advantages of preserving, also in a digital age, the availability of central bank money include the following: The continued availability of an ultimate risk-free medium of settlement; maintaining relevant the convertibility promise defining

[3] The specific literature on central bank solvency and mechanisms for safeguarding central bank independence is reviewed in Box 2 of ECB (2021), focusing on ways to avoid that financial losses of central banks and a subsequent lack of fiscal transfers to recapitalise the central bank would risk failures to achieve the monetary policy objectives.

[4] Central banks and market participants also discuss the potential introduction of "wholesale CBDC" as tokenised assets to settle transactions between financial institutions in new ways; the central bank balance sheet implications of wholesale CBDC are ultimately equivalent to already existing (digital) deposits of banks with central banks ("reserves") and outside the scope of this paper.

commercial bank money, which is essentially a promise to convert a claim into central bank money at sight; have available for citizens a digital means of payment designed from a public good perspective; the availability and usability of central bank money adds to competition in an industry with network effects and thus typically a predominance of few players which will unavoidably try to abuse their market power; CBDC strengthens strategic sovereignty if the dominant private players in the payment markets are foreign-owned companies. Money and payments are a function of universal importance for a society built on the division of labour, or, as argued by Simmel (1900), it is even at the very core of modern society. Therefore, the continued availability in a digital age of an effective form of public money appears as an obvious choice.

While the decision of a central bank to issue CBDC will certainly affect its balance sheet, profitability, risk taking and capital, it must not be overlooked that such a decision would be endogenous to the general transformation of payment habits of society, and that these changes will in any case have a profound impact on central bank balance sheets: in an ever more digitalized society, the use of cash is likely to decline and may end up being ultimately marginalized, implying also an eventual decline in the circulation of banknotes, which in turn could reduce central bank balance sheet sizes, seigniorage income[5] and profitability. A decision to issue CBDC appears in this context as a means to preserve, i.e. stabilize, the role of central bank money, against the alternative scenario in which the role of central bank money diminishes due to the declining use of banknotes. In that latter case, the central bank would not only discontinue a large part of its services to society, but also would see its balance sheet size, seigniorage and profitability shrink.

Certainly, the effects of the issuance of CBDC on central bank balance sheets and profitability will depend on key features of CBDC, which are design parameters set by the central bank. Apart from the general attractiveness as a means of payment (in this respect, central banks should do the utmost to make CBDC as attractive as possible to use), key design choices that will affect the amount of circulation of CBDC will be:

- *Remuneration*: from a liquidity and safety perspective, CBDC is potentially a highly attractive form of investment. If in addition CBDC would exhibit rates of return similar to private forms of money or money substitutes, then large flows of investment into CBDC would be likely. For this reason, and also to emphasize that CBDC is conceived primarily as a means of payment and not as a store of value, central banks who have started to offer CBDC (e.g. People's Bank of China; India) or who have published their potential design choices (e.g. ECB,

[5] The term seigniorage is not uniquely defined in the literature. In general, and in this paper, seigniorage refers to the revenue from money creation. Broader definitions equate seigniorage with central bank profits. Narrower definitions of seigniorage focus on the profit from the creation of banknotes (see, e.g., the ECB explainer "what is seigniorage?", https://www.ecb.europa.eu/ecb/educational/explainers/tell-me/html/seigniorage.en.html, accessed 1 February 2024).

Bank of England) have all set a zero remuneration rate, making CBDC in this respect similar to banknotes.

- *Limits*: since market interest rates can get as low as zero (or even negative), the zero remuneration has not been considered sufficient by central banks to prevent that CBDC could become a large-scale store of value with potential implications for the economy and financial stability. Therefore, all central banks who have announced CBDC design features have also announced limits on CBDC holdings per individual. In the case of the ECB, for example, a limit of EUR 3000 per citizen has often been mentioned.
- *Access criteria*: while access to banknotes cannot be constrained, central banks can limit access to CBDC. So far, central banks seem to plan to limit holdings of CBDC, at least initially, to domestic natural persons, implying that non-residents and both financial and non-financial corporates would in principle be excluded. This eliminates important categories of banknote holders: for example, Devigne et al. (2023) suggest that 40% of euro banknotes are held abroad. In the phase of low interest rates in the euro area, also banks and corporates hoarded banknotes to escape somewhat from the negative interest rate policies of the ECB.[6]
- *Features that reduce incentives or even eliminate the necessity to hold positive CBDC balances*: many retail payment instruments like credit cards, debit cards or PayPal, do not require the user to hold separate balances but the instrument eventually debits the commercial bank account of the account holder and bridges the time between the payment and that debit through a temporary credit. Some central banks designing CBDC have announced somewhat similar features which also remove the necessity to hold balances in advance. For example, ECB (2023a, p. 14) explains that "Users would not need to prefund a digital euro account before making payments. If there are insufficient funds in the digital euro account, the shortfall could be transferred immediately" and calls this the reverse waterfall functionality.

Within these design features, the amount of circulation of CBDC will be entirely driven by the demand of households, in a similar way as households' demand influences the amount of banknotes in circulation. Both banknotes and CBDC are thus "autonomous factors" in the demand for central bank liquidity that the central bank needs to accommodate, whereas the holdings of commercial banks' reserves with the central bank (minimum reserve requirements and excess reserves) are rather driven by monetary policy considerations.

Beyond impacting on the expected demand for CBDC, the first of the above-mentioned key parameters, the remuneration of CBDC also directly impacts on the seigniorage income. The term seigniorage refers to the revenue from money creation, which is not uniquely defined in the literature. In a broader definition as applied in this paper, seigniorage income is essentially equal to the volume of

[6] Euro area banks' monthly stocks of vault cash roughly doubled from around 50 billion euros to 100 billion euros between 2015 and 2022, before quickly falling to 60 billion euros once the ECB started raising key interest rates in summer 2022 (see Devigne et al., 2023, Chart 3).

monetary liabilities (banknotes, commercial banks' deposits or "reserves" with the central bank, CBDC), which are matched by a corresponding volume of monetary policy assets, times the difference between the average remuneration of these assets and liabilities.[7]

Not remunerating CBDC makes it equivalent to banknotes in terms of contribution to seigniorage. Any positive remuneration of CBDC will ceteris paribus reduce its contribution to seigniorage, and thus to central bank profitability, accordingly. However, the positive remuneration of CBDC might increase the CBDC take-up, which would have a compensating impact on seigniorage that would likely be constrained by CBDC holding limits.

Last but not least, issuing CBDC is not cost free. Similarly to the case of banknotes, the production costs would need to be deducted from the gross seigniorage income to determine its net contribution to central bank profits. The costs of the core settlement layer of CBDC (the back end) are likely to be moderate compared to its expected contribution to central bank seigniorage. Running costs of CBDC including the amortization of investment costs would generally be expected to be lower than seigniorage income from CBDC. Costs of CBDC issuance may go beyond the settlement layer, depending on the distribution arrangement established by the central bank, functionality and public good-related specific services financed by the central bank (see Bindseil et al., 2024b). Even taking these special cost factors into account, the profitability of issuing unremunerated CBDC should normally be solid.

2.2 *Issuance of CBDC and the Central Bank Balance Sheet*

CBDC is a new liability item on the central bank balance sheet. CBDC is created and funded by households exchanging their banknotes or their deposits with commercial banks. For commercial banks, an outflow of household deposits will imply either a reduction of their reserves with the central bank, or additional recourse to central bank credit. Alternatively, the central bank may decide to restore previous levels of reserves through purchases of securities.

The flow chart in Fig. 1 illustrates how the choices of households, banks and the central bank determine the impact of the CBDC issuance on the central bank balance sheet. Figure 1 starts by highlighting that households' holdings of banknotes and deposits will evolve from today also in the absence of CBDC—a reflection of the "endogeneity" of the CBDC issuance decision discussed above, that can thus be separated from the choices during the CBDC issuance process:

[7] Narrower definitions of seigniorage focus on the profit from the creation of banknotes (see, e.g., the ECB explainer "what is seigniorage?", https://www.ecb.europa.eu/ecb/educational/explainers/tell-me/html/seigniorage.en.html, accessed 1 February 2024)

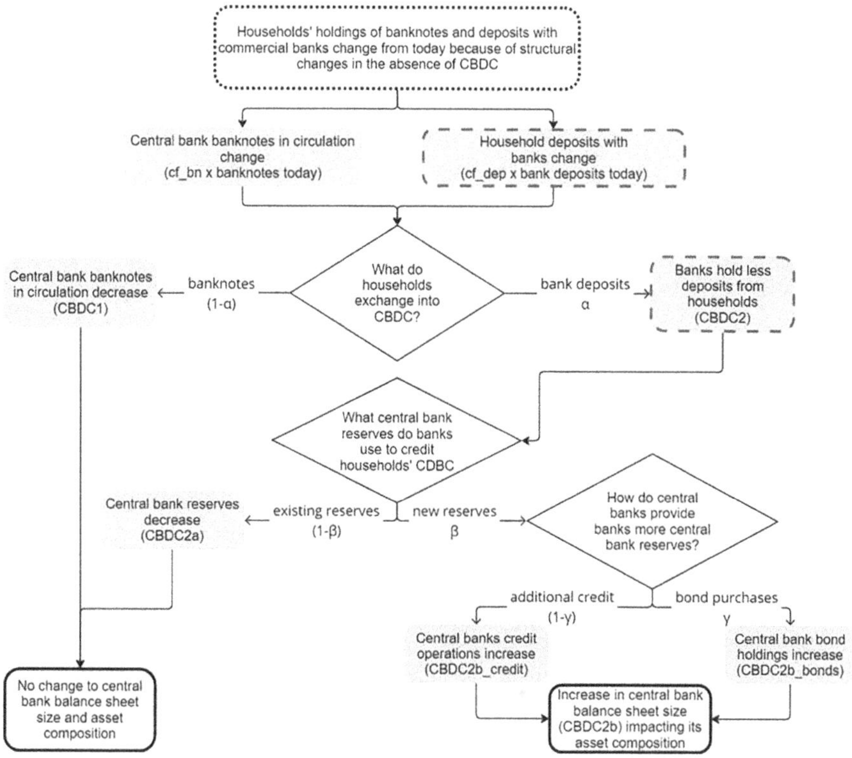

Fig. 1 Flow chart of CBDC issuance process

1. Households choose whether they substitute their banknotes (share $1 - \alpha$ of total created CBDC) or their bank deposits (share α) with CBDC.
2. Commercial banks then choose whether they use their existing reserves with the central bank (share $1 - \beta$ of CBDC2 created from bank deposits) or need new reserves (share β) to credit the households' CBDC accounts. The central bank may constrain this choice of commercial banks via its monetary policy implementation framework and depending on its monetary policy stance. For example, if the central bank wants to treat CBDC fully as an autonomous factor and maintain the level of excess reserves unchanged for monetary policy reasons, the central bank would create additional reserves (i.e. $\beta = 1$).
3. Central banks then choose whether they provide the new reserves via bond purchases from banks (share γ of required new reserves CBDC2b) or additional collateralized lending to commercial banks (share $1 - \gamma$).

The creation of CBDC as presented in Fig. 1 can also be captured in a simplified system of financial accounts (Fig. 2). CBDC is split into two parts: CBDC1 which substitutes banknotes and CBDC2 which substitutes deposits with commercial banks. The effects of CBDC1 on the central bank balance sheet are neutral, but the effects of CBDC2 are not: either banks reduce their (remunerated) "excess"

Households, pension and investment funds, insurance companies			
Real Assets	X		
Sight Deposits with banks	X -CBDC2		
CBDC	0 +CBDC1 +CBDC2		
Banknotes	X -CBDC1		
Bank bonds	X		
Gvt/corp bonds	X		
Commercial Banks			
Loans to Gvt/corp	X	Deposits	X -CBDC2
Gvt/corp bonds	X -CBDC2b_bonds	Bonds issued	X
Central bank deposits	X **-CBDC2a**	Central bank credit	X +CBDC2b_credit
Central Bank			
Credit to banks	X +CBDC2b_credit	Banknotes	X -CBDC1
Bonds (non-banks)	X +CBDC2b_bonds	CBDC	0 +CBDC1 + CBDC2
		Deposits of banks	X **-CBDC2a**

Note: The positions "X" stand for stocks prior to any transactions, whereby X varies across the accounts (i.e. each X in the table is nominally different and could initially be zero).

Fig. 2 Financial accounts representation of CBDC (left: assets; right: liabilities)

reserves (CBDC2a)—which is only possible if the banking system initially operates in a liquidity surplus vis-à-vis the central bank (i.e. holds reserves in excess of its minimum reserve requirements)[8]—or the central bank balance sheet needs to lengthen (CBDC2b). To allow for this lengthening, the central bank has to fill the funding gaps of commercial banks by providing additional collateralized credit (CBDC2b_credit). Alternatively the central bank may decide to purchase government and corporate bonds (CBDC2b_bonds) from the banks, so that the total creation of CBDC is the sum of these components:

$$\begin{aligned} \text{CBDC} &= \text{CBDC1} + \text{CBDC2} \\ &= \text{CBDC1} + \text{CBDC2a} + \text{CBDC2b}_{\text{credit}} + \text{CBDC2b}_{\text{bonds}} \end{aligned} \tag{1}$$

Using the shares α, β, γ as defined above allows rewriting (1) as

$$\text{CBDC} = (1-\alpha)\,\text{CBDC} + \alpha\,(1-\beta)\,\text{CBDC} + \alpha\beta\,(1-\gamma)\,\text{CBDC} + \alpha\beta\gamma\text{CBDC}. \tag{2}$$

[8] We note that the reduction of bank deposits reduces the minimum reserve requirements by the minimum reserve ratio (1% in the euro area, 0% for the Federal Reserve and the Bank of England, for example) and thus can create additional excess reserves (of 1% of CBDC2 in the case of the euro area, nothing in the USA and the UK), which we ignore for simplicity in this paper. There is a theoretical but highly unrealistic possibility that banks would actively further reduce their minimum reserve requirements to create the excess reserves needed for the exchange into CBDC2 by massively restricting bank lending and thus reducing bank deposits. Central banks will usually adopt policies that avoid such interference from CBDC with their monetary policy stance.

Note that CBDC lengthens the central bank balance sheet if and only if CBDC2b > 0. This can be easily shown: CBDC as a new central bank liability can only be created via the substitution of existing central bank liabilities, i.e. banknotes (CBDC1) or commercial banks' excess reserves (CBDC2a), or via the lengthening of the central bank balance sheet by additional central bank credit to banks (CBDC2b_credit) or purchases of assets (CBDC2b_bonds).

In principle, it is possible that the CBDC introduction changes commercial banks' preferences as regards their borrowing from the central bank and their holdings of reserves (in excess of their minimum reserve requirements) beyond the direct needs to credit the household's CBDC account, e.g. as an additional precautionary liquidity demand (see Caccia et al., 2024). It is a choice of the central bank as part of its monetary policy implementation whether such preference changes are reflected in prices on the interbank market or quantities on its balance sheet.[9] The analysis of the effects on the central bank balance sheet, its profitability and risks in the following sections could be easily extended to cover for the latter case, i.e. further changes to the quantities on the balance sheet.

3 CBDC Impact on Central Bank Profitability: Measured by Net Interest Income

3.1 Methodological Approach

Central bank profits are largely driven by their net interest income on their monetary assets and liabilities. Since CBDC is a new monetary liability of the central bank, our profitability analysis focuses on its impact on the central bank's net interest income. The operating cost implications were already discussed in Sect. 2.1.

For the profitability impact analysis we adopt the stylised central bank balance sheet presented in Fig. 3 and the related simplified net interest income as measure of profitability. In a related paper, Gross and Letizia (2023) use an agent-based model to simulate the demand for CBDC and also derive some simulated central bank

[9] For example, the central bank can decide to endogenously accommodate the changing demand for credit operations via standing lending facilities or full allotment operations, or to provide additional reserves via asset purchases. This is similar to the central bank decision whether to allow for the reduction of excess reserves, i.e. $\beta < 1$. The situation is different in the absence of excess reserves: in this case, the households' decision to exchange commercial bank deposits into CBDC (i.e. $\alpha > 0$) strictly requires that the central bank increases the reserves (i.e. $\beta < 1$) because as it has to accommodate this autonomous liquidity demand, whereas the central bank can still choose whether it accommodates a greater preference by banks for reserves via additional reserves or higher money market rates.

Assets			Liabilities		
	Quantity	Remuneration		Quantity	Remuneration
Credit to banks	A_c	r_c	Banknotes	L_{bn}	0
Bonds	A_b	r_b	CBDC	L_{cbdc}	r_{cbdc}
Net Non-Monetary Policy Assets and Liabilities	A_{nmp}	r_{nmp}	Deposits of banks	L_d	r_d
			Equity	E	0

Fig. 3 Stylised central bank balance sheet and related remuneration

profits in this context.[10] In this section, we present the modelling framework while in the following sections we present results based on different scenarios.

The remuneration rate always reflects the average accounting return on the operations included in the sub-indexed balance sheet item. Using the Eurosystem as an example,

- r_c is the average return on all lending to commercial banks, comprising main refinancing operations, (targeted) longer-term refinancing operations and the marginal lending facility.
- r_b is the average accounting return on all bonds purchased outright for monetary policy purposes, comprising public sector bonds, covered bonds, asset-backed securities and corporate bonds and assuming they are accounted at amortized cost (i.e. not mark-to-market).[11]
- r_{nmp} is the average return on the other non-monetary policy assets and liabilities, which are only included to complete the balance sheet.
- Banknotes have no remuneration (almost) by definition.[12]
- r_{cbdc} is the remuneration of CBDC, which the ECB has already announced would be 0.
- r_d is the average return on all deposits of commercial banks ("reserves") with the Eurosystem, comprising minimum reserve requirements and other holdings

[10] Several macroeconomic models considering CBDC also include the associated profits of the central bank. However, central bank profits are not at the core of the authors' attention and usually reflected as lump-sum transfers to the government in order to close the models (see, e.g., Assenmacher et al., 2023 and Abad et al., 2023, as well as Bindseil & Senner, 2024b, for a more comprehensive overview).

[11] Many central banks, like all central banks of the Eurosystem and the Federal Reserve, account their monetary policy securities holdings at amortised cost, while other central banks mark-to-market their monetary policy portfolios. Marking-to-market increases the volatility of profits, because in the case of an interest rate increase (as in recent years) the market prices of bonds immediately decrease and a large unrealised loss would be recorded. Over the entire holding period, total income earned from the holding will be equal under both accounting rules, mark-to-market and amortised cost.

[12] While not applicable for the Eurosystem, a notable exception from this zero remuneration is Silvio Gesell's proposal for "depreciative money" in the early twentieth century.

of banks in the current account (both currently not remunerated), excess reserves in the deposit facility (remunerated at the deposit facility rate).[13]
- Equity has no remuneration.

The usual balance sheet identity of assets and liabilities applies of course also for central banks:

$$A_{\mathrm{c}} + A_{\mathrm{b}} + A_{\mathrm{nmp}} = L_{\mathrm{bn}} + L_{\mathrm{cbdc}} + L_{\mathrm{d}} + E, \tag{3}$$

which can be written in changes as

$$\Delta A_{\mathrm{c}} + \Delta A_{\mathrm{b}} + \Delta A_{\mathrm{nmp}} = \Delta L_{\mathrm{bn}} + \Delta L_{\mathrm{cbdc}} + \Delta L_{\mathrm{d}} + \Delta E. \tag{4}$$

Equation (5) can be rearranged to resemble Fig. 1 and Eq. (1) as described in Sect. 2.2, i.e. any increase in CBDC has to be balanced by an increase in monetary policy assets (credit to banks and bonds), or a decrease in Banknotes or a decrease in Deposits—and vice versa—while leaving Non-Monetary Policy Assets and Liabilities as well as Equity unaffected (i.e. $\Delta A_{\mathrm{nmp}} = \Delta E = 0$):[14]

$$\Delta L_{\mathrm{cbdc}} = \Delta A_{\mathrm{c}} + \Delta A_{\mathrm{b}} - \Delta L_{\mathrm{bn}} - \Delta L_{\mathrm{d}} \tag{5}$$

Note the following relationships between Eqs. (1), (2) and (6):

$$\Delta L_{\mathrm{cbdc}} = \mathrm{CBDC} \tag{6}$$

$$\Delta L_{\mathrm{bn}} = -\mathrm{CBDC1} = -(1-\alpha)\,\Delta L_{\mathrm{cbdc}} \tag{7}$$

$$\Delta L_{\mathrm{d}} = -\mathrm{CBDC2}a = -\alpha\,(1-\beta)\,\Delta L_{\mathrm{cbdc}} \tag{8}$$

$$\Delta A_{\mathrm{c}} = \mathrm{CBDC2}b_{\mathrm{credit}} = \alpha\beta\,(1-\gamma)\,\Delta L_{\mathrm{cbdc}} \tag{9}$$

$$\Delta A_{\mathrm{b}} = \mathrm{CBDC2}b_{\mathrm{bonds}} = \alpha\beta\gamma\,\Delta L_{\mathrm{cbdc}} \tag{10}$$

Combining the quantities with their remuneration rates yields the Net Interest Income equation:

[13] Note that the remuneration for bank deposits can be a controversial issue (see, e.g., De Grauwe & Ji, 2023) and change over time with monetary policy needs. For example, the Eurosystem applied a two-tier remuneration system for banks' current accounts between October 2019 and September 2022, exempting part of the banks' excess reserves from the negative deposit facility rate. The Eurosystem stopped paying interest on minimum required reserves in September 2023 when ECB key interest rates were at or above 4%. The U.S. Federal Reserve did not pay interest on reserves before October 2008 (see https://www.federalreserve.gov/monetarypolicy/20081006a.htm)

[14] Recall from Sect. 2 that access to CBDC is limited to entities that have so far no other access to the central bank balance sheet than holding banknotes.

$$\mathrm{NII} = A_\mathrm{c} * r_\mathrm{c} + A_\mathrm{b} * r_\mathrm{b} + A_\mathrm{nmp} * r_\mathrm{nmp} - L_\mathrm{cbdc} * r_\mathrm{cbdc} - L_\mathrm{d} * r_\mathrm{d} \tag{11}$$

and changes in Net Interest Income equation related to CDBC are:

$$\Delta\mathrm{NII} = \Delta A_\mathrm{c} * r_\mathrm{c} + \Delta A_\mathrm{b} * r_\mathrm{b} - \Delta L_\mathrm{cbdc} * r_\mathrm{cbdc} - \Delta L_\mathrm{d} * r_\mathrm{d} \tag{12}$$

Following a "Δ-(changes)-approach" for NII has the benefit of abstracting from the counterfactual size and composition of the central bank balance sheet in the absence of CBDC at any point in time. In particular, it allows to abstract from the profit implications of changes in banknotes in circulation that are independent of CBDC and of changes triggered by future monetary policy implementation needs.

Assuming CDBC to be unremunerated as in the case of the Eurosystem, we have:

$$r_\mathrm{cbdc} = 0 \tag{13}$$

$$\Delta\mathrm{NII} = \Delta A_\mathrm{c} * r_\mathrm{c} + \Delta A_\mathrm{b} * r_\mathrm{b} - \Delta L_\mathrm{d} * r_\mathrm{d} \tag{14}$$

$$\mathrm{CBDC} = (1 - \alpha)\,\mathrm{CBDC} + \alpha\,(1 - \beta)\,\mathrm{CBDC} + \alpha\beta\,(1 - \gamma)\,\mathrm{CBDC} + \alpha\beta\gamma\mathrm{CBDC}. \tag{15}$$

We can rewrite Eq. (14) using (8), (9) and (10) and obtain:

$$\Delta\mathrm{NII} = \Delta L_\mathrm{cbdc} * \alpha\ \left(\beta\left((1 - \gamma)\,r_\mathrm{c} + \gamma\ r_\mathrm{b}\right) + (1 - \beta)\ r_\mathrm{d}\right) \geq 0 \quad \text{if} \quad r_\mathrm{c}, r_\mathrm{b}, r_\mathrm{d} \geq 0. \tag{16}$$

This means that the impact on the net interest income is equivalent to the size of CBDC not substituted with banknotes by the household times the weighted average rate of the three balance sheet items that are potentially impacted by the introduction of CBDC, namely the central bank's credit to banks and its bond holding, as well as the deposits of commercial banks.

Equation (1) also shows that the introduction of unremunerated CBDC will have a positive impact on central bank income (ΔNII ≥ 0) in a positive interest rate environment (r_c, r_b, $r_\mathrm{d} \geq 0$). Note that this positive income impact is relative to counter-factual profits without CBDC at the respective point in time—which will be influenced by structural developments like the digitalization of payments and the evolution of monetary policy—and not relative to today's situation. We discuss the special case of a negative interest rate environment in Bindseil et al. (2024b).

The two corner cases under this set up are: (1) if the increase in CBDC is fully compensated by a decrease of Banknotes ($\alpha = 0$), there is no impact on profitability given the substitution of two unremunerated liabilities; and (2) if the increase in CBDC is fully compensated by an increase of bond purchases ($\alpha = 1, \beta = 1, \gamma = 1$), the impact on profitability will be the largest in the likely case that the return on purchased assets is greater than the return on lending to banks.

3.2 *Profit Projections with CBDC: Using Euro Area Data as an Example*

The model set-up presented above implies that the impact of CBDC on profitability can be represented as a function of seven variables as formulated in Eq. (16). Intuitively, the impact depends on the size of the new liability, its size impact on other monetary assets and liabilities, and the remuneration of these other monetary assets and liabilities. We use euro area data to present a baseline analysis in this section.

We calibrate the three relevant average *remuneration rates* as follows:[15]

- The remuneration of banks' deposits $r_{\mathrm{d}} = 1.5\%$, reflecting the historical average ECB deposit facility rate from 1999 to 2023.
- The remuneration of monetary policy credit to banks $r_{\mathrm{c}} = 2.0\%$, reflecting the 50 basis points spread between the ECB's main refinancing operations rate and the deposit facility rate since 2019.[16]
- The remuneration of monetary policy bond portfolios $r_{\mathrm{b}} = 2.5\%$, roughly reflecting the average historical term spread between the weighted average maturity of the Eurosystem's net asset purchases and the deposit facility rate.

With the above calibration, we can rewrite (16) as:

$$\Delta \mathrm{NII} = \Delta L_{\mathrm{cbdc}} * \alpha \ (\beta\,((1-\gamma)\,2.0\% + \gamma\ 2.5\%) + (1-\beta)\ 1.5\%) \tag{17}$$

The actual *CBDC take-up* is still rather uncertain. As explained in Sect. 2, the CBDC take-up depends on the design of the CBDC and the central bank is likely to choose key design parameters of CBDC in a way to limit its demand, thereby reducing risks of undesired effects on monetary policy and financial stability. Therefore, we consider in this section three different take-up scenarios: (1) a scenario with low demand, (2) a medium demand scenario and (3) a scenario with very large demand:

- For the *low demand scenario*, we assume the demand for CBDC to be similar to the average holdings of cash by citizens in their wallet. According to ECB (2022, Chart 24), the euro area citizens have on average 83 € cash in their wallet at the beginning of the day. This can be translated into approximately 30 billion euros of demand for CBDC.

---

[15] For details on the underlying data sources and calculations, see the extended version of this paper in Bindseil, Marrazzo and Sauer (2024).

[16] It is noted that on 13 March 2024 the ECB has announced changes to the operational framework for implementing monetary policy which included that the spread between the rate on MROs and DFR will be reduced to 15 basis points as from 18 September 2024, see Changes to the operational framework for implementing monetary policy (europa.eu).

- For the *medium demand scenario*, we consider that (1) only 50% of the euro area residents will adopt the digital euro, (2) 50% of the adopters will prefund their CBDC wallet (therefore generating the need of a CBDC take-up) rather than fully use the reverse waterfall functionality (which in the extreme case of users setting a limit to zero would bring to null the CBDC take-up), (3) these adopters will have digital euro holdings on average over time that are only 50% of the maximum limit allowed, and (4) we start from a hypothetical maximum CBDC take-up around 1 trillion euros because of a hypothetical holding limit of 3000 € per person, in line with, e.g. Bindseil et al. (2021), and a potential user base of 349 million euro area residents. Under these assumptions, we get a take up scenario of around 125 billion euros (i.e. 1 trillion euros * 50%^3).
- For the *high demand scenario*, we follow the same reasoning as for the medium demand scenario, but select a much higher percentage (80%) for each step. We thus obtain approximately 512 billion euros (i.e. 1 trillion euros * 80%^3).

We finally turn to the *substitution and asset composition choices of households, banks and the central bank* that are reflected in the flowchart of Fig. 1 and the parameters α, β and γ. We assume for illustrative purposes and simplicity that (1) the household substitution between banknotes and deposits is split half-half (i.e. $\alpha = 50\%$), (2) the central bank enables banks to react to the reduction in deposits from households by reducing their deposits with central banks and recurring to new liquidity in equal proportions (i.e. $\beta = 50\%$),[17] and (3) that new monetary policy assets are equally split between additional credit to banks and bond purchases (i.e. $\gamma = 50\%$).

With the above calibration assumption for the medium demand scenario, we obtain an increase in CBDC of 125 billion euros balanced by a decrease in banknotes by 62.50 billion euros, a decrease of deposits by 31.25 billion euros and increase in assets by 31.25 billion euros, which is equally split into new credit to banks and bonds holdings. The outlined changes in the balance sheet, together with the assumed interest rates, implies a profitability impact of this scenario equal to an increase in annual net interest income by 1.17 billion euros, as shown in Table 1. The impact for the low and the high demand scenario would be 0.28 billion euros and 4.80 billion euros, respectively. To put these numbers into perspective, the Eurosystem has made on average about 30 billion euros of annual profits between 2012 and 2021.[18] Even the low demand scenario leads to an additional seigniorage income of 0.28 billion euros, i.e. more than double the annual cost of TARGET2 0.11 billion euros,[19] one of the largest Eurosystem market infrastructure projects.

[17] It is likely that the level of β would be either close to 0% or to 100%, depending on the existing level of excess reserves in the system.

[18] See https://www.ecb.europa.eu/ecb/educational/explainers/tell-me-more/html/ecb_profits.en.html [accessed 1 February 2024].

[19] See TARGET Annual Report 2022, https://www.ecb.europa.eu/pub/targetar/html/ecb.targetar2022.en.html

Table 1 Balance sheet and profitability impact for three digital euro demand scenarios (billion euros)

	Low demand		Medium demand		High demand	
	ΔBS	ΔNII	ΔBS	ΔNII	ΔBS	ΔNII
Assets						
Credit to banks	3.75	0.08	15.63	0.31	64.00	1.28
Bonds	3.75	0.09	15.63	0.39	64.00	1.60
Liabilities						
Banknotes	−15.00	–	−62.50	–	−256.00	–
CBDC	30.00	–	125.00	–	512.00	–
Deposits	−7.50	0.11	−31.25	0.47	−128.00	1.92
Total	7.50	0.28	31.25	1.17	128.00	4.80

Note: The delta net interest income reported is already adjusted of sign to allow simple summation of rows entries regardless of if belonging to assets or liabilities, e.g. the entry for deposit in low demand is 0.11 which means a decrease of interest expenses by 0.11 and therefore an increase of net interest income by 0.11

Note again that the net interest income impact of CBDC is always calculated *relative to the situation without CBDC at any point in time*. Hence, positive profitability impacts of CBDC may in reality still be over-compensated by other developments that negatively impact central bank profits. We consider several alternative scenarios in an extended version of this paper (Bindseil et al., 2024b), starting from our medium CBDC demand scenario: first, the absence of CBDC and a redirection of the demand for digital payments to private forms of payments and digital wallets would have a moderate negative impact on net interest income. Second, a major reduction of banknote demand by one third—independent of the issuance of CBDC in parallel—would lead to a significant reduction of net interest income, almost ten times larger than the additional income from CBDC. Third, in a negative interest rate environment like during the COVID19-pandemic, unremunerated CBDC would have a marginal negative net interest income impact.

4 CBDC Impact on Central Bank Financial Risk Taking

Since CBDC represents a new item on the central bank balance sheet, it can also affect its financial risks in multiple ways—none of which is however really new for a central bank. Banknotes and commercial banks' reserves with the central bank have no market, credit or liquidity risk and thus everyone rightly considers them as risk-free assets in the domestic currency. However, their issuance needs to be matched -at least to some extent—by central bank assets, which allow for the implementation of monetary policy. These assets are subject to market and credit risk and central banks thus have well-established frameworks to manage these financial risks (see, e.g.,

ECB, 2015). This section considers the different channels through which CBDC can affect central banks' financial risk taking.

First, the issuance of CBDC does not directly create additional financial risks in the sense that if households exchange only banknotes with unremunerated CBDC (i.e. $\alpha = 0$ and thus CBDC2 = 0), the central bank balance sheet size, composition of assets and financial risks remain completely unchanged. Even if households exchange part of their deposits with commercial banks into CBDC (i.e. $\alpha > 0$ and thus CBDC2 > *0*), CBDC does not in itself create additional financial risks, but only indirectly through the additional assets that are matching the additional issuance.

Second, indirect financial risks occur mainly if the issuance of CBDC leads to an increase of its balance sheet or a changing composition of central bank assets, therefore such changes should be managed in a risk-efficient way. Previous sections have shown that only the creation of additional central bank reserves (i.e. *CBDC2b* > *0*) leads to changes in the size and composition of central bank assets. The central bank should implement such changes in a risk-efficient way, i.e. minimizing the financial risk subject to achieving the policy objective (see ECB, 2015). All else equal, a larger balance sheet size obviously entails larger financial risks. As highlighted in Sect. 2.1, central banks are likely to take measures such as appropriate CBDC remuneration and usage limits to keep the amount of CBDC in circulation contained.

The composition of the asset side is even more important for financial risks than the balance sheet size: additional credit operations can be managed to have small or even minimal residual credit, market and liquidity risks, in particular if the central bank grants credit only to financially sound counterparties against adequate collateral.[20] In contrast, outright purchases of assets can imply high financial risks, such as credit risk for corporate bonds.[21] Purchases of longer-maturity bonds either add to interest rate risk (under amortized cost accounting rules, see below) or create market risk (under mark-to-market accounting rules). Nevertheless, asset purchases may be needed for monetary policy reasons, for example because there may be limits to the extent banks want to borrow from the central bank. Since purchases are under the complete discretion of the central bank to govern and execute, also their risks can be managed in a risk-efficient way via a dedicated framework involving the definition of benchmarks, eligibility criteria, credit risk assessments, due diligence, pricing and limits (see ECB, 2015).

Third, if financial stability implications of CBDC via its effects on commercial banks' balance sheets were not addressed through careful design decisions, these

[20] The Eurosystem has a statutory requirement to conduct credit operations only against adequate collateral. It accepts relatively high-quality assets that are subject to daily valuation (for marketable assets) and haircuts that address the remaining credit, market and liquidity risk of the collateral in the event of a counterparty default. It calibrates its haircuts so that it covers its expected shortfall at a 99% confidence level (see ECB, 2015).

[21] Also domestic government bond holdings can imply financial risks for the central bank: While central banks may consider their domestic sovereign as credit risk free, this is not necessarily the case in a monetary union with multiple sovereigns (see, e.g., ECB, 2021, for the related challenges).

could ultimately lead to further indirect financial risk effects on the central bank. The potential financial stability implications of CBDC have been identified for a while, and it has been argued that absent mitigation measures, CBDC could reduce banks' retail deposit funding and facilitate bank runs, which would imply a need for central banks to be ready to provide additional emergency liquidity assistance (e.g. CPMI-MC, 2018).[22] Such financial stability risks exist in a digitalized financial system also in the absence of CBDC, as evidenced by the speed and magnitude of uninsured deposit outflows from several US banks in March 2023 (see, e.g., Metrick, 2024, Bindseil & Senner, 2024a). Should the conventional banking sector become more fragile, it could translate in, inter alia, the deterioration of the credit risk profile of counterparties for central bank operations. Central banks like the ECB have included safeguards in their CBDC design such that financial stability risks are addressed (Adalid et al., 2022; Bindseil et al., 2024a; Lambert et al., 2024).

Fourth, the issuance of unremunerated CBDC can change the interest rate risk of the central bank. This financial risk type arises from different sensitivities of the remuneration of central bank assets and liabilities to changes in interest rates.[23] Since the interest rate risk depends on the asset-liability sensitivity mismatch of the *whole* balance sheet, the "Δ-(changes)-approach" followed in Sect. 3 for NII needs to be complemented with the interest rate sensitivity of assets and liabilities that are already on the balance sheet. A useful tool is the income-based repricing gap model (see, e.g., Resti & Sironi, 2007, ch. 1), according to which the gap is defined as the difference between the amount of rate-sensitive assets and rate-sensitive liabilities, with "sensitive" implying that the asset or liability matures or is repriced over a given time period. On the liability side, if households exchange part of their bank deposits into CBDC (i.e. CBDC2 > *0*) and reserves are remunerated, the amount of unremunerated and thus non-rate-sensitive central bank liabilities increases. In addition, the amount of rate-sensitive liabilities decreases if banks reduce their excess reserves (i.e. CBDC2a > *0*). On the asset side, central banks' operational frameworks tend to use monetary policy assets to steer short-term interest rates. Before the Great Financial Crisis in 2008, central banks usually held only short-maturity and thus interest rate-sensitive assets. Since 2008, central banks have repeatedly decided to take duration risk from the market onto their balance sheet via purchases of longer-maturity bonds ("quantitative easing") and thus increased

[22] If CBDC was wrongly designed, could create a structural shift away from bank deposits and hamper the funding base in particular of commercial banks relying on retail deposits, as well as increase the frequency and severity of bank runs. In addition to the impact on the funding base, associated liquidity constraints could hamper these institutions' ability to fulfil regulatory obligations, and, as a result, could deteriorate their credit risk profile.

[23] In contrast to the income-based repricing gap model, the equity-based duration gap model focuses on the changes of values of assets and liabilities based on their duration. The duration gap model is less relevant for central banks like the Eurosystem and the Federal Reserve, for which the majority of their long-term assets are accounted for at amortised cost and not mark-to-market. In contrast, for example the Sveriges Riksbank uses mark-to-market accounting rules (see https://www.riksbank.se/en-gb/markets/riksbanks-balance-sheet/qa%2D%2D-the-riksbanks-income-statement-and-balance-sheet/ [accessed on 1 February 2024]).

the share of non-interest rate-sensitive assets under amortized cost accounting rules as for the Eurosystem and the Federal Reserve. The provision of longer-term lending operations ("credit easing") at fixed interest rates has the same effect.[24] The interest rate sensitivity of the asset side is thus mainly an implicit consequence of monetary policy needs.[25] At the moment, many central banks have a large balance sheet with a negative repricing gap because the rate-sensitive liabilities (L_d) exceed rate-sensitive assets (limited share of short-maturity A_c and A_b). In this case, the CBDC issuance tends to reduce the repricing gap and thus the interest rate risk. In contrast, interest rate risk increases if the central bank balance sheet already has a positive repricing gap as common before 2008.[26]

Fifth, from a risk management perspective, it is also important to establish sound risk control measures to duly protect the central bank balance sheet in a scenario where 24/7 access by credit (and payment) institutions could be foreseen. From an implementation standpoint, adaptations may be needed in payments systems and central bank credit operations to ensure 24/7 availability. This implies, from a risk management perspective, the need to actively control, monitor and safeguard the central bank's balance sheet to potential intraday and off-business hours spikes in exposure and would be important to steer risk management practices in such a way that comprehends this non-stop availability.

Finally, CBDC adoption also changes non-financial risks for central banks, for which a detailed assessment would go beyond the scope of this paper. The digital nature of CBDC moves operational risks related to the physical production, distribution and exchange of banknotes (and coins) into the digital sphere. The Bank for International Settlements has set up the "Project Polaris" that supports central banks in designing, implementing and operating secure and resilient CBDC systems to mitigate the operational, legal and reputational risks central banks face from cyber threats or operational failures.[27]

To summarize, the central bank's financial risk implications of CBDC as a new central bank liability are likely mitigated by measures to limit the CBDC take-up and can be managed via well-established frameworks. They depend on the CBDC's impact on the central bank balance sheet size and asset composition. Ceteris paribus, central banks' financial risks would increase most if central banks had to increase the size of their balance sheets via additional outright purchases of long-term assets. If,

[24] The interest rate on most longer-term Eurosystem credit operations has not been fixed but linked to the evolution of the policy rate, so that these operations belong to the interest rate-sensitive assets also under amortised cost accounting.

[25] However, there is some scope for central banks to actively manage their other assets like their foreign reserve portfolio and own funds with an asset-liability management perspective.

[26] If—in contrast to currently discussed CBDC design features (see Sect. 2)—the CBDC remuneration was not set at zero but linked to the (variable) policy rate, the impact on interest rate risk would obviously be reversed, as part of the unremunerated banknotes (*CBDC1*) would be substituted for remunerated CBDC.

[27] See https://www.bis.org/about/bisih/topics/cbdc/polaris.htm [accessed 1 February 2024], and in particular BIS (2023).

however, the digitalization of payments leads to an overall shrinking balance sheet because of a declining use of banknotes and despite CBDC issuance, seigniorage and financial risks could actually decrease.

5 CBDC Impact on Central Bank Capital and Net Equity

Since the introduction of CBDC can affect both central bank profits (Sect. 3) and financial risks (Sect. 4), CBDC can also impact the actual and desired amount of central bank capital and its more broadly defined net equity. This section first explains the general link between net interest income and central bank capital/net equity. It then turns to the CBDC impact on capital/net equity, building on the key drivers for the CBDC impact identified in previous sections.

Due to the diversity of their accounting rules, but also due to different arrangements with their shareholders, central banks do not have harmonized definitions of financial strength, net equity or financial buffers. Definitions usually start from the central bank's capital, and then add accounting reserves (not to be confused with the deposits of commercial banks with the central bank, which we called "reserves" above), general risk provisions, and revaluation accounts. They may also subtract losses carried forward from previous years when relevant and consider the profit/loss for the year. Moving from this accounting-oriented perspective to more economic-oriented measures, the financial strengths of a central bank can also be calculated after valuing all balance sheet items at their market price. The most comprehensive view on the financial strength of a central bank takes into account the present discounted value of future seigniorage income (see, e.g., Buiter, 2020) while the stock of banknotes can also be seen as part of the comprehensive net worth of a central bank (see Archer & Moser-Boehm, 2013).

In principle, a central bank's net interest income combined with its net other operating income yields its annual net income. This net income is either used to increase the central bank's financial buffers or distributed as a dividend to its shareholders (usually the government, sometimes (also) the private sector). The policy implications of considerations around central banks' financial strengths make it useful to distinguish between the stand-alone central bank balance sheet and the consolidated balance sheet of the public sector (see, e.g., Box 2 in ECB, 2021). For example, Bunea et al. (2016) analyse how central banks' financial strength is affected by their profit distribution rules and accounting rules. According to Bunea et al. (2016) profit distribution rules can have a material impact on the financial strength of a central bank, particularly when profits are volatile, and furthermore "[a]n inappropriate profit distribution policy can interfere with the objectives of monetary policy" (p. 34). In this context, the greater net worth from higher average seigniorage could, ceteris paribus, suggest less need for accounting buffers on the balance sheet. At the same time, greater profit volatility (either because of the nature of the underlying operations, the balance sheet structure or because of the accounting rules) can suggest a greater need for financial buffers to smoothen out the profit distributions and avoid negative net equity situations—even if they do not prevent the central bank from operating.

The analysis in the preceding sections has shown that the impact of an unremunerated CBDC on the central bank crucially depends on the three ways how CBDC is created:

First, the exchange of banknotes into CBDC (*CBDC1*) is a simple shift between two unremunerated central bank liabilities with no further implications on central bank net interest income, profits (abstracting from operational costs), and financial risks. It should thus—ceteris paribus—have no implications on central bank capital and net equity.

Second, the exchange of households' bank deposits into CBDC via a reduction of commercial banks' excess reserves (*CBDC2a*) represents an exchange of a remunerated central bank liability (banks' reserves) into an unremunerated central bank liability (CBDC) with no impact on the overall balance sheet size. However, it increases average seigniorage/net interest income in a normal (positive) interest rate environment. Starting from today's balance sheet for many central banks with a large share of non-interest rate sensitive assets and thus a negative repricing gap, *CBDC2a* would reduce the central bank's interest rate risk, i.e. make net interest income less volatile to changes in interest rates. If the asset side is sufficiently interest rate sensitive for a positive repricing gap, however, the higher average profits will also be more volatile. In any case, the central bank can decide to use the additional income generated because of the introduction of CBDC to increase its capital/net equity by increasing its general risk provisions[28] or its accounting reserves. It can alternatively, distribute the profits to the government, in line with the respective local preferences, needs and profit distribution rules (see, e.g., Bunea et al., 2016).

Third, the exchange of households' bank deposits into CBDC resulting into additional central bank credit to banks/purchases of bonds (*CBDC2b*) lengthens the central bank balance sheet. The income from the additional credit/bonds on the asset side, which are "financed" by unremunerated CBDC, increases the average seigniorage/net interest income. The impact on interest rate risk and net interest income volatility is the same as for *CBDC2a* if all additional credit/bonds are fully interest rate sensitive. The less the additional credit/bonds are interest rate sensitive, the less the *CBDC2b* issuance changes the income volatility compared to the initial stage before introducing CBDC. The composition of the additional assets for *CBDC2b* can lead to additional financial risks, in particular credit risk in the case of bond purchases. This is also reflected by the higher expected income compared to *CBDC2a*, and may lead to the need for greater general risk provisions and reserves on the central bank balance sheet. In addition, the selection of the accounting rules

[28] The ECB reviews the level of its general risk provision on a basis of the central bank's overall risk exposure (see Article 8 of the so-called Accounting Guideline ECB/2016/34).

(amortized cost or mark-to-market) for the additional assets can impact the volatility of central bank profits and thus the need for central bank capital/net equity.[29]

Another, potentially even more important, result of our analysis in the preceding sections relates to the quantitative relevance of CBDC versus other factors influencing central bank capital in the future: most central banks, including the Eurosystem, consider the introduction of CBDC with safeguards that would significantly constrain the amount of CBDC in circulation. At least if CBDC is implemented with such safeguards, its impact on profits and thus on central bank capital is less relevant than the impact of the future demand for banknotes and for digital payment solutions in the absence of CBDC. The same applies to the balance sheet size and composition implications of future monetary policy implementation frameworks.

6 Conclusion

This paper has focused on the impact of CBDC, a new central bank liability, on the central bank balance sheet, its profitability, risk taking and capital. The choices of households, commercial banks and the central bank determine the impact of the CBDC issuance on the central bank balance sheet. Central banks have announced that they would issue CBDC with holding limits and without remuneration. The ECB for example has also announced access constraints (e.g. only to domestic natural persons) and sweep facilities that allow users to avoid the excessive use of digital euro as a store of value. All these design features limit the likely demand for CBDC as store of value, and therefore reduce the impact on the central bank balance sheet (and of commercial banks). If one takes into account in addition that the demand for banknotes in circulation will likely increase less than in the past or even decrease because of the digitalization of retail payments, and the limited distinguishability of banknotes and unremunerated CBDC from the balance sheet and profit perspective, then it could appear that the outlook of the central bank balance sheet, profitability and capital needs over the next decades is neither very different, nor more uncertain than it has been in the past. And the contribution of CBDC is more likely to stabilize the outlook as it aims at preserving the (in principle present) use of central bank money relative to commercial bank money.

This perspective differs from the usual narrative that the issuance of CBDC will necessarily imply a much larger central bank balance sheets, and therefore considerably higher financial risks and higher capital needs. This narrative was

[29] Schwarz et al. (2014) show that the Eurosystem accounting rules (hold-to-maturity assets at amortized cost subject to impairment) have been more beneficial in preserving the financial buffers and thus the financial strength of the ECB from 1999–2013 than their counterfactual simulation of IFRS rules (mark-to-market). These results are driven by the lack of a protection from distribution to shareholders of unrealised profits under IFRS because of the symmetrical recognition of unrealised results in the IFRS-based income statements, which is not the case under the Eurosystem accounting rules.

legitimate as long as the design features of CBDCs were not known and the possibility of unlimited and remunerated CBDC was in focus. However, such assumptions are outdated at least for the digital euro with its design features that clearly disincentivize the store of value function (and limit it anyway). In the quantitative parts of the paper, we nevertheless also consider the case that CBDC would increase the central bank balance sheet, as this case may materialize for other CBDC designs.

We develop a model to quantify the change in the central bank's net interest income relative to a balance sheet without CBDC and apply it for the euro area and the potential introduction of a digital euro under different scenarios. While a pure exchange of banknotes into CBDC has no further implications on the central bank balance sheet, the exchange of households' bank deposits into CBDC increases the amount of unremunerated central bank monetary liabilities and may require the creation of additional reserves of banks via corresponding additional central bank assets. The last two points would tend to lead to higher central bank income in a positive interest rate environment. This additional income would be relatively modest for the design features of digital euro because of the expected low take-up and could in principle be distributed as dividend to the government (and possibly other shareholders). However, given that the additional central banks' assets may lead to an increase in financial risks, central banks may prefer to use the additional income to increase their financial buffers, thus supporting their capital and financial independence and reinforcing their credibility.

The central bank's financial risk implications of CBDC arise primarily through the amount and composition of the additional assets that match the additional issuance of central bank liabilities. The risk implications can be managed via well-established frameworks and also likely mitigated by measures to limit the CBDC take-up. Ceteris paribus, a central bank's financial risks would increase most if it had to increase the size of its balance sheets via additional outright purchases of long-term assets, while the effect on the central bank's interest rate risk is ambiguous: interest rate risk decreases if the central bank balance sheet has without CBDC a negative repricing gap between interest rate-sensitive assets and liabilities as common nowadays, and vice versa for the positive repricing gap as common before 2008. Non-financial risks of CBDC deserve a detailed separate analysis.

It is important to note that there is anyway considerable uncertainty regarding the future size and composition of central bank balance sheets. The monetary policy needs will evolve and the currently still sizable balance sheets following the pandemic-related quantitative easing measures may shrink further. And central banks' decisions to issue CBDC will be endogenous to the general transformation of payment habits of society away from banknotes towards more and more digital means of payments. The uncertainty arising from structural changes in payments and monetary policy needs is thus likely to be greater than from a potential CBDC introduction, at least if central banks take robust measures that limit the take-up of CBDC, as the ECB has done with the already agreed safeguards in relation to a potential digital euro.

References

Abad, J., Nuño, G., & Thomas, C. (2023). *CBDC and the operational framework of monetary policy*. BIS Working Paper 1126.

Adalid, R., Álvarez-Blázquez, Á., Assenmacher, K., Burlon, L., Dimou, M., López-Quiles, C., Fuentes, N. M., Meller, B., Muñoz, M. A., Radulova, P., d'Acri, C. R., Shakir, T., Šílová, G., Soons, O., & Veghazy, A. V. (2022). *Central bank digital currency and bank intermediation*. ECB Occasional Paper No. 293.

Archer, D., & Moser-Boehm, P.. (2013). *Central bank finances*. BIS Papers No 71, Bank for International Settlements.

Assenmacher, K., Bitter, L., & Ristiniemi, A. (2023). *CBDC and business cycle dynamics in a New Monetarist New Keynesian model*. ECB Working Paper No. 2811.

Bell, S., Chui, M., Gomes, T., Moser-Boehm, P., & Pierres Tejada, A. (2023). Why are central banks reporting losses? Does it matter? *BIS Bulletin* No. 68.

Bindseil, U. (2020). *Tiered CBDC and the financial system* (Working Paper Series, No 2351). ECB.https://www.ecb.europa.eu/pub/pdf/scpwps/ecb.wp2351~c8c18bbd60.en.pdf

Bindseil, U., & Lanari, E. (2022). Fire sales, the LOLR, and Bank runs with continuous asset liquidity. *Journal of Financial Crises, 4*(4), 77–102.

Bindseil, U., & Senner, R. (2024a). *Destabilisation of bank deposits across destinations: assessment and policy implications*. ECB Working Paper Series No. 2887.

Bindseil, U., & Senner, R. (2024b). *Macroeconomic modelling of CBDC: A critical review*. European Central Bank, mimeo.

Bindseil, U., Manzanares, A., & Weller, B. (2004). *The role of central bank capital revisited*. ECB Working Paper Series No. 392.

Bindseil, U., Panetta, F., & Terol, I. (2021). *Central Bank Digital Currency: Functional scope, pricing and controls*. ECB Occasional Paper Series No 286, December 2021.

Bindseil, U., P. Cipollone, & Schaaf, J. (2024a). *The digital euro after the investigation phase: demystifying fears about bank disintermediation*, VoxEU, 19 February 2024.

Bindseil, U., Marrazzo, M., & Sauer, S. (2024b). *The impact of central bank digital currency on central bank profitability, risk taking and capital*, extended version.

BIS. (2023). *Project Polaris—Part 2: A security and resilience framework for CBDC systems*.https://www.bis.org/publ/othp70.pdf

Buiter, W. (2020). *Central banks as fiscal players: The drivers of fiscal and monetary policy space (Federico Caffè Lectures)*. Cambridge University Press.

Bunea, D., Karakitsos, P., Merriman, N. & Studener, W. (2016). *Profit distribution and loss coverage rules for central banks*. ECB Occasional Paper Series No. 169.

Caccia, E., & Tapking, J., & Vlassopoulos, T. (2024). *Central Bank Digital Currency and Monetary Policy Implementation*, ECB Occasional Paper Series, forthcoming.

CPMI-MC. (2018). *Central bank digital currencies*. Joint report of the Committee on Payments and Market Infrastructure and the Markets Committee, Basel, March.

De Grauwe, P., & Ji, Y. (2023). *Fighting inflation more effectively without transferring Central Banks' profits to banks*. CESifo Working Paper No. 10741, November 2023.

Devigne, L., Michel, V., de Pastor, R., & Tricot, J. (2023). *Despite inflation, Europeans are still holding on to their banknote reserves, Banque de France Eco Notepad*, 18 December 2023.

European Central Bank. (2015). *The financial risk management of the Eurosystem's monetary policy operations*.

European Central Bank. (2021). *Monetary-fiscal policy interactions in the euro area*. ECB Occasional Paper No. 273.

European Central Bank. (2022, December). *Study on the payment attitudes of consumers in the euro area* (SPACE) - 2022. https://www.ecb.europa.eu/stats/ecb_surveys/space/shared/pdf/ecb.spacereport202212~783ffdf46e.en.pdf

European Central Bank. (2023a). *A stocktake on the digital euro*. Summary report on the investigation phase and outlook on the next phase, 18 October 2023.

European Central Bank. (2023b). *Profits and losses of the ECB and the euro area national central banks: where do they come from?* ECB Explainers, updated on 19 May 2023, accessed on 1 February 2024.

Goncharov, I., Ioannidou, V., & Schmalz, M. C. (2023). (Why) do central banks care about their profits? *Journal of Finance, 78*(5), 2991–3045.

Gross, M., & Letizia, E. (2023). *To demand or not to demand: On quantifying the future appetite for CBDC*. IMF Working Paper No. 23/9, International Monetary Fund.

Lambert, C., Meller, B., Pancaro, C., Pellicani, A., Radulova, P., Soons, O., & van der Kraaij, A. (2024). *Safeguards on a digital euro—Protecting financial stability and liquidity in the banking sector*. ECB Occasional Paper, forthcoming.

Metrick, A. (2024). The failure of Silicon Valley Bank and the panic of 2023. *Journal of Economic Perspectives, 38*(1), 133–152.

Resti, A., & Sironi, A. (2007). *Risk management and shareholders' value in banking*. Wiley.

Schwarz, C., Karakitsos, P., Merriman, N., & Studener, W. (2014). *Why accounting matters: a central bank perspective*. ECB Occasional Paper No. 153.

Simmel, G. (1900). *Philosophie des Geldes*. Duncker & Humblot.

Stella, P. (1997). *Do Central Banks need capital?* IMF Working Paper No. 97/83. International Monetary Fund

Wessels, P., & Broeders, D. (2022). *On the capitalisation of central banks*. https://www.dnb.nl/media/5sdmsgld/74393_dnb_os-capitalisation-of-central-banks_web.pdf

Open Access This chapter is licensed under the terms of the Creative Commons Attribution 4.0 International License (http://creativecommons.org/licenses/by/4.0/), which permits use, sharing, adaptation, distribution and reproduction in any medium or format, as long as you give appropriate credit to the original author(s) and the source, provide a link to the Creative Commons license and indicate if changes were made.

The images or other third party material in this chapter are included in the chapter's Creative Commons license, unless indicated otherwise in a credit line to the material. If material is not included in the chapter's Creative Commons license and your intended use is not permitted by statutory regulation or exceeds the permitted use, you will need to obtain permission directly from the copyright holder.

Part III
Central Bank Capital and Changes in the External Environment

Impact of Transitions on the Financial Stability and LOLR Roles of Central Banks

Dirk Schoenmaker

Abstract Meeting net-zero targets poses a major challenge for companies. Some companies are able to adapt to the new low-carbon world, while others may fail to do so and thus risk turning into stranded assets. This chapter argues that central banks should treat transition risk as endogenous. Central banks can set macroprudential limits on carbon exposures to guide a smooth transition to net zero by 2050. Hard limits are needed as banks have been reluctant so far to hive off profitable fossil-fuel-related loans. Strong and effective macroprudential policies help to minimize climate-induced financial instabilities and reduce the need for lender of last resort (LOLR) assistance to carbon-heavy banks. Such LOLR assistance may result in substantial central bank losses, as carbon-heavy banks face permanent losses on their carbon-intensive assets.

Keywords Central bank losses · Financial stability · Lender of last resort · Transition risk

1 Introduction

Society faces multiple challenges on the social and environmental front. Major sustainability transitions are underway to address these social and environmental challenges. Companies are at the heart of these transitions, as social and envi-

The author would like to thank Dirk Bezemer, Dion Bongaerts, Dieuwertje Bosma, Dirk Broeders, Stephen Cecchetti, Nathan de Arriba-Sellier, Casper de Vries, Aerdt Houben, Tjeerd Krumpelman, Hesse McKechnie, Olaf Sleijpen, Hans Stegeman, and participants at the Workshop for useful suggestions and discussions. In this chapter, my earlier research on financial stability and my current research on sustainability transitions converge nicely.

D. Schoenmaker (✉)
Rotterdam School of Management, Erasmus University, Rotterdam, The Netherlands
e-mail: schoenmaker@rsm.nl

© The Author(s) 2025

D. Broeders et al. (eds.), *Central Bank Capital in Turbulent Times*,
Contributions to Finance and Accounting,
https://doi.org/10.1007/978-3-031-73549-3_10

ronmental impacts are not perfectly separable from production decisions (Hart & Zingales, 2017). Only companies that can adapt to these transitions by changing their business model will survive (Kurznack et al., 2024). Sustainability transitions can thus have a major impact on company valuation. Moreover, sustainability transitions are uncertain and happen shock-wise (Loorbach et al., 2017).

The toxic cocktail of large losses and shock-wise transformations is a recipe for financial instability. Focusing on the climate transition, the Paris agreement of 2015 is a legally binding international treaty to limit global warming to well below 2 °C and pursue efforts to limit it to 1.5 °C above pre-industrial levels. Paris introduces instability into the financial system by requiring a transition to a low-carbon world, culminating in net-zero by 2050. It does so because worldwide policymakers have made a judgment that this is a worthwhile price to pay for a reduction in the physical risk of catastrophic climate failure. Bolton et al. (2020) have coined the term 'Green Swan' for climate shocks which may occur if we fail to limit global warming. These climate shocks pose large and non-linear risks to the economy and underlying financial system.

The policy challenge for policymakers, including those at central banks, is to minimize the downside disruptions of the climate transition they are legally committed to. We propose that a straight-line path toward the net zero goals is the least disruptive way to achieve transition and the one that minimizes transition risk. Since 2015, empirical measures of carbon emissions have not followed a straight-line path toward net zero, but, if anything, are still rising globally. Every year that the transition deviates from the straight-line path toward net zero, central banks are faced with a build-up of instability in the financial system. Therefore, to fulfill their core financial stability mandate, central banks must take urgent action to redress the build-up of these instabilities stemming from transition.

Microprudential supervision, which incorrectly treats these transition risks as exogenous, cannot really cope with this policy challenge. By contrast, macroprudential supervision is designed for dealing with system-wide shocks, as macroprudential supervision treats the build-up of risk as endogenous and explicitly recognizes feedback loops and amplification mechanisms within the system (Borio, 2003). Yet there is a disconnect at the policy level: microprudential supervisors have been busy incorporating transition risks into the supervisory toolkit over the last 5 years, while macro supervisors have only very recently started to explore macroprudential policy options to address climate change (ECB/ESRB, 2023). We seem to have forgotten the lessons from the global financial crisis: the lack of macroprudential policies focusing on the financial system as a whole was one of the key regulatory failures that fueled the flames of the global financial crisis (Brunnermeier et al., 2009).

The research question in this chapter is which macroprudential instruments can minimize financial disruptions and thereby minimize losses for the lender of last resort (LOLR), i.e., the central bank. There will no doubt be major shocks impairing financial stability, but the question is how to design the most effective guard rails. We argue that an orderly transition and more-or-less equal-sized annual reductions of carbon emissions toward net zero by 2050 offers a good approach. We also argue that policymakers' and economists' favorite approach of extra systemic risk buffers for banks with concentrated carbon exposures (ECB/ESRB, 2023) will not be enough to enforce the required reduction in carbon emissions. Rather, we propose a hard macroprudential limit on banks' exposures to carbon-intensive companies and projects, which is calibrated on an annually tightened pathway toward net zero by 2050. These macroprudential limits could also be applied to other financial institutions (insurance companies, pensions funds, and investment funds) to avoid leakage to other sectors.

Although central banks are not-for-profit (Goodhart, 1988), such a hard limit would help central banks to manage LOLR losses from depleting their capital. While ordinary LOLR operations are temporary to bring the financial system back to long-term equilibrium, transitions move the financial—and the wider economic—system to a new equilibrium. Any companies not prepared for these transitions may inflict permanent losses on banks and their guarantors (i.e., central banks as lender of last resort). The risk management challenge is to minimize such losses from creative destruction (Schumpeter, 1942) for the public sector; these losses should be borne by the private sector.

This chapter is organized as follows. Section 2 analyzes transitions and their impact on company value. Sections 3 and 4 discuss the micro- and macroprudential perspective on transitions. Section 5 reviews the impact of transitions on the use of LOLR assistance. Section 6 concludes.

2 Transitions[1]

Transition is about radical change rather than incremental change. Figure 1 depicts the dynamics of socio-technical transitions as iterative processes of build-up and breakdown over a period of time (Loorbach et al., 2017). In a changing societal context, incumbent regimes develop path-dependently through optimization, while change agents start to experiment with alternative ideas, technologies, and practices. Over time, pressures build on regimes to transform, leading to destabilization as alternatives start to accelerate and emerge. The actual transition is then chaotic and disruptive and new combinations of emerging alternatives and transformative regime elements grow into a new regime. In this process, elements of an old regime that do not transform are broken down and phased out. This is an example of creative destruction, a process in which new technologies and business models replace the old ones (Schumpeter, 1942).

To guide the transition toward a sustainable and inclusive economy, the United Nations has developed the 2030 Agenda for Sustainable Development (UN, 2015). The 17 UN Sustainable Development Goals (SDGs) encourage action over the 2015–2030 period in areas of critical importance for humanity and the planet.

[1] This section is based on Schoenmaker and Schramade (2022), 'Valuing companies in transition'.

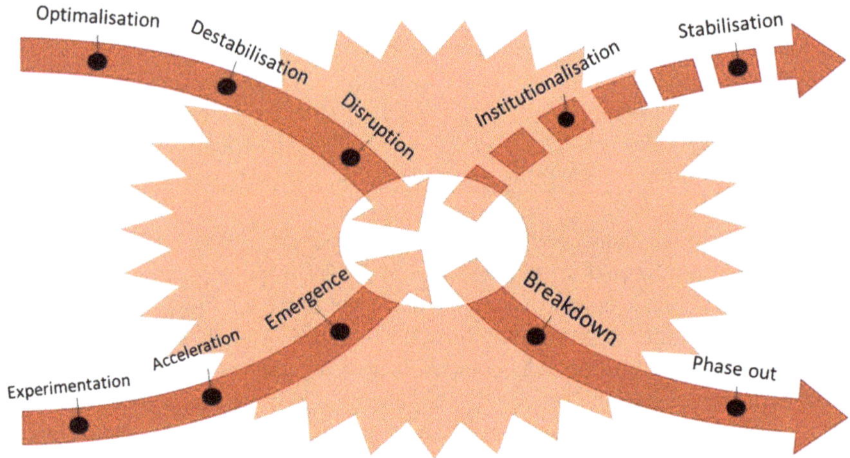

Fig. 1 The x-curve of transition dynamics. Source: Adapted from Loorbach et al. (2017)

Within the larger SDG agenda, we identify four clusters of large sustainability transitions that are important for business (Schoenmaker & Schramade, 2022):

1. *Climate –energy transition*: Moving from the use of fossil fuels to renewable energy. This has not only an impact on energy companies, e.g., oil and gas companies and electricity utilities, but also on other carbon-intensive sectors, such as manufacturing and mobility, that rely on the use of fossil fuels.
2. *Raw materials—circular economy*: Redesign and recycle products leading to less use of raw materials and less carbon emissions (e.g., recycling aluminum saves on carbon emissions in the production of aluminum).
3. *Biodiversity—healthy food and regenerative agri- and aquaculture*: Trend toward healthy food production with respect for land and water. This implies moving from intensive to regenerative farming to preserve the quality of the land without the use of fertilizer and pesticides. Protecting biodiversity also implies no overfishing and preserving ocean health.
4. *Labor practices—social transition*: Trend toward decent labor practices across the value chain of production. Decent labor implies paying a living wage, ensuring safe working conditions and respecting human rights.

Sustainability transitions are imposed by policy goals, while other examples of major transitions, such as digitalization, are innovation transitions, where market developments lead to creative destruction (Schumpeter, 1942). In this chapter, we focus on the climate transition.

2.1 Transition and Company Value

Transitions have a major impact on the viability of companies in certain sectors. Only those companies that can adapt to these transitions by changing their business model will survive. Building on the widely used model for expected credit losses (Hull, 2018), Schoenmaker and Schramade (2022) formalize the expected transition losses ETL_{ij} for company i in sector j as follows:[2]

$$\begin{aligned}\mathrm{ETL}_{ij} &= \mathrm{EAT}_{ij} \bullet \mathrm{PT}_j \bullet \mathrm{LGT}_{ij} \\ &= b_j \bullet V_{ij} \bullet PT_j \bullet (1 - a_{ij}) \qquad (1)\end{aligned}$$

where EAT_{ij} represents the exposure at transition. It measures which part b_j of the value V_{ij} of company i, active in sector j, is exposed to transition: $\mathrm{EAT}_{ij} = b_j \bullet V_{ij}$. Figure 2 shows the extreme case of $b_j = 1$, when the full sector j is in transition from conventional to sustainable products or production processes. Transition exposure ranges from no transition to full transition: $b_j \in [0, 1]$. The assumption is that the sectoral transition b_j is representative of all companies i in that sector. We thus assume full correlation of transition risk between companies in the same sector, culminating in a systemic shock within the sector. Sectors that are characterized by large negative external effects and the availability of substitutes (that address these negative effects) tend to have a high b_j.

The second variable PT_j represents the probability of transition for sector j over a certain time period. The size and timing of transition are uncertain. Scenario analysis

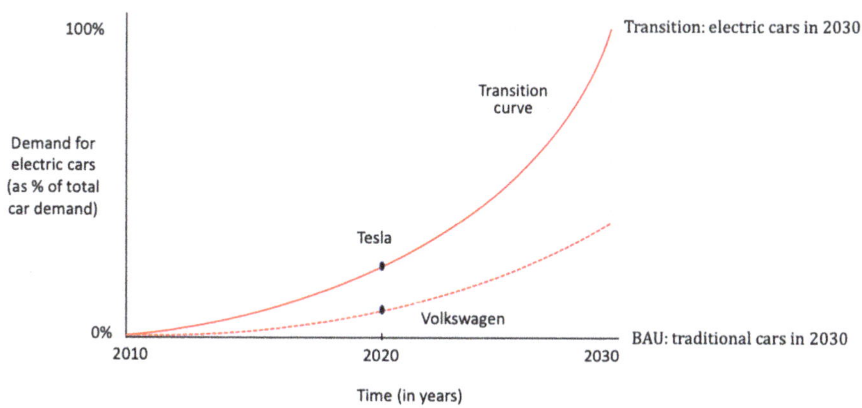

Fig. 2 Transition to electric driving

[2] For ease of exposition, we leave out the subscript t for time. Value is always assessed or computed at some point in time, whereby perceptions (rightly or wrongly) change over time.

can be used to determine the probability of transition of a sector. This analysis contains different scenarios for the degree of transition and the timing of transition. Figure 1 on transition dynamics shows that transitions do not happen smoothly, but shock-wise along a dynamic time-path. However, many companies plan on a business-as-usual scenario. In our model, the probability of the business-as-usual scenario BAU_j is:

$$\mathrm{BAU}_j = \left(1 - \mathrm{PT}_j\right) \tag{2}$$

whereby BAU_j falls over time as transition pressure builds up. The business-as-usual scenario for the energy sector, for example, becomes less likely as global warming increases. Scenario analysis assumes that one can assign probabilities to the various scenarios. But in the case of fundamental uncertainty (including possible tipping points—see Sect. 4) it is impossible to assign probabilities. It is therefore also important to allow for tail events such as Green Swans (Bolton et al., 2020) or Black Swans (Taleb, 2007).

The final variable LGT_{ij} is the loss given transition. This loss depends on company i's adaptability a_{ij} to transition in sector j, whereby $\mathrm{LGT}_{ij} = (1 - a_{ij})$. A company can recover or retain its value by adapting to transition (which may be more difficult in certain sectors than in other sectors). By doing so, it can limit its expected transition loss. A company can anticipate societal trends by building capabilities to learn about and serve these new societal needs as part of its strategy. a_{ij} is non-negative with the following range: $a_{ij} \in [0, 1]$. $a_{ij} = 1$ denotes the case where a company can fully adapt to the new world, allowing it to reach its long-term value potential. As seen from Eq. (1), the expected transition losses are then zero: $\mathrm{ETL}_{ij} = b_j \bullet V_{ij} \bullet \mathrm{PT}_j \bullet (1 - 1) = 0$.

The transition model of Eq. (1) shows that companies should be early in building the capabilities that give them the option to enter the market with new technologies and business models. Schoenmaker and Schramade (2022) illustrate the working of transition valuation with company cases from the photography industry and the car industry. The first example is Kodak, that kept its print-based photography business (business-as-usual) and failed to see the transition to digital photography $a_{\mathrm{Kodak,\,photo}} = 0$. Kodak lost its full value and filed for bankruptcy in 2012: $\mathrm{ETL}_{ij} = b_j \bullet V_{ij} \bullet \mathrm{PT}_j \bullet (1 - a_{ij}) = 1 \bullet V_{\mathrm{Kodak,\,photo}} \bullet 1 \bullet (1 - 0) = V_{\mathrm{Kodak,\,photo}}$.

The second example refers to the transition to electric driving. Tesla, the US electric carmaker, is ahead in its capabilities and can quickly scale up its production capacity to serve increased demand. Traditional German carmakers, such as Volkswagen, are behind and are losing market share. In terms of Eq. (1), Tesla is fully prepared for the electric vehicle market with $a_{\mathrm{Tesla,\,car}} = 1$, while VW is only partly prepared with $a_{\mathrm{VW,\,car}} = 0.4$. Therefore, transition losses may amount to 60% of VW's value: $ETL_{ij} = b_j \bullet V_{ij} \bullet PT_j \bullet (1 - a_{ij}) = 1 \bullet V_{\mathrm{VW,\,car}} \bullet 1 \bullet (1 - 0.4) = 0.6 \bullet V_{\mathrm{VW,\,car}}$.

These examples show the importance of adaptability to transition. A shortfall in adaptability has large value implications. Companies can invest in their capabilities to adapt (Schoenmaker & Schramade, 2022).

3 Microprudential Perspective

We now turn to central banks in their supervisory capacity. Transitions have an impact on company value. The financial sector holds company equity and debt as assets on their balance sheet. The shock-wise pattern of transitions can thus inflict losses on banks.[3] The probability of sectoral transition (denoted by PT_j) and the value and adaptability of companies in this sector (denoted by V_{ij} and a_{ij}) determine the scope of losses. The question arises how these variables are treated in microprudential and macroprudential supervision.

Microprudential supervision has traditionally been the key focus of supervisory authorities. The intermediate objective of microprudential supervision is to promote the safety and soundness (i.e., limit the distress) of individual banks, with the ultimate objective of protecting the bank's depositors. It does not focus on the financial system as a whole. Still, by preventing the failure of individual banks, microprudential supervision of course helps maintain confidence in the stability of the banking (and wider financial) system.

Borio (2003) shows the key differences between macroprudential and microprudential supervision (see Table 1). The intermediate objective of macroprudential supervision is to limit financial-system-wide distress, with the ultimate objective of protecting the overall economy from significant losses in real output and well-being. While risks to the financial system can in theory arise from the failure of one bank, common exposures of many banks to the same risk factors are more important.

Macroprudential analysis pays particular attention to common or correlated shocks. Moreover, macroprudential supervision should take account of the interactions between banks and their environment (i.e., other financial institutions, financial

Table 1 Micro versus macro perspective

Topic	Macroprudential	Microprudential
Intermediate objective	Limit financial-system-wide distress	Limit distress of individual banks
Ultimate objective	Avoid wellbeing losses	Depositor protection
Correlations and common exposures across banks	Important	Irrelevant
Characterization of risk	Seen as dependent on collective behavior ('endogenous')	Seen as independent of individual agents' behavior ('exogenous')
Calibration of prudential controls	In terms of system-wide risks; top-down	In terms of risks of individual banks; bottom-up

Source: Adapted from Borio (2003)

[3] The focus is on banks. There are lessons that apply more broadly to other financial institutions, as we explain toward the end of Sect. 4.

markets, infrastructure, and the real economy) as well as the dynamics with which imbalances may build up over time. As such, the macroprudential perspective assumes that the risk of a shock is (partly) generated and amplified within the system (i.e., the risk is *endogenous*), while the microprudential approach focuses on individual banks' vulnerability to threats emanating from their environment (i.e., the risk is *exogenous*).

To avoid financial-system-wide distress, the macro-perspective takes a top-down approach to calibrating prudential controls by identifying risks in the system as a whole and then applying the relevant macroprudential tools (see the next section). By contrast, the microprudential approach is bottom-up, setting the prudential controls in relation to the risk of each individual bank.

Before discussing climate risks in the microprudential and macroprudential supervisory framework, it is useful to examine how banks currently behave in today's supervisory framework. As explained in the Introduction, the Paris agreement of 2015 is a legally binding agreement to reduce carbon emissions in order to limit global warming. However, a further $2 trillion of fossil fuel loans have been issued since 2015.[4] The cost of increased financial instability, from transitioning to net zero (see Fig. 3), has so far not been internalized by banks.

3.1 *Financial Supervision Policy (the Microprudential Perspective)*

The ECB is among the frontrunners in addressing climate risks in its financial supervision (Grunewald et al., 2024). It takes climate risks into account in its Supervisory Review and Evaluation Process (SREP), which is part of the Pillar 2 supervisory review process of the Basel Capital Adequacy Framework. In its 2022 SREP cycle, the ECB reviewed these risks on a qualitative basis, resulting in qualitative measures and feedback to individual institutions. Based on the 2022 SREP, the ECB imposed qualitative measures for climate risk, but no capital add-ons as yet (ECB, 2022). Pending higher Pillar 1 requirements (see below), the ECB can impose Pillar 2 add-ons for banks that are exposed to carbon-intensive companies, which is possible under existing law (De Arriba-Sellier, 2021).

A next step is the introduction of higher capital charges for climate risks in the Pillar 1 capital adequacy rules. These Pillar 1 capital rules are part of the wider Basel Capital Adequacy Framework. Climate risks relate not only to transition risks, but also to physical and liability risks (see Box 1). Capital adequacy rules are modeled on the assumption that risks are exogenous. In terms of our model of expected transmission losses, the probability of transition PT_j, company value V_{ij}, and adaptability a_{ij} are taken as given.

---

[4] See Bloomberg (27 March 2024), 'UBS Banker's Frustration Exposes Cracks in World of Climate Finance': ESG Backlash in Climate Finance Exposed by UBS Banker's Concerns - Bloomberg.

Box 1 Breaking Down Climate Risks

Environmental risks, such as climate risk or biodiversity loss, are well established in international agreements (e.g., the 2015 Paris agreement on climate change and the 2022 Kumming-Montreal Global Biodiversity Framework) and anchored in various regulations across the world. These environmental risks can be broken down in several components:

- *Physical risks* are environmental events like floods or storms due to climate change or workplace injuries due to unsafe factories. Physical risks can affect companies directly through damage/loss of assets and injuries/deaths of employees, and indirectly through its effects on value chains and customers.
- *Transition risks* arise from changes in policy and new technologies. A carbon tax can affect the profitability of a company's business model, potentially rendering it a stranded asset (see Sect. 2). The limitation of this definition, which looks at the impact on individual companies, is that the wider system dimension of climate transition is ignored. The Paris agreement poses a system-wide obligation to reduce carbon emissions.
- *Liability risk* is the risk that a company faces legal action. Examples are big litigation cases against oil companies for not adhering to the Paris climate agreement (e.g., *Milieudefensie v Shell* in 2021). These lawsuits are also brought against banks (e.g., *Notre Affaire à Tous v BNP Paribas* in 2023) and countries (e.g., *Urgenda v the Netherlands* at the Dutch Supreme court in 2019; *Neuenbauer* et al. *v Germany*, where the Germany's Federal Constitutional Court found the then nationally applicable Climate Protection Act to be partially unconstitutional because, among other things, it significantly impaired the freedoms of young people and future generations (2021); and *KlimaSeniorinnen v Switzerland* at the European Court for Human Rights (2024)). More than 100 climate lawsuits have been filed per year globally since 2015 (Wetzer et al., 2024).

Climate-related capital requirements may help to shift the balance toward low-carbon assets. However, Oehmke and Opp (2023) show that 'green' capital requirements do not necessarily reduce carbon emissions. A carbon capital surcharge for carbon-intensive assets will only be effective in reducing the amount of carbon-intensive (dirty) loans in proportion to low-carbon (clean) loans when the extra cost of carbon capital rules—in comparison to green capital rules—exceeds the profit difference on the activities financed by dirty and clean loans. Otherwise, the overall higher capital requirement may crowd out clean loans, assuming that banks have a fixed amount of capital available for lending.

A recent microprudential instrument is bank transition plans, as required by the latest revision CRD VI of the Capital Requirements Directive (CRD/2013/36/EU). Banks should assess and embed forward-looking climate (and other ESG) risk considerations in their strategies, policies, and risk management processes through transition planning for short-, medium-, and long-term time horizons (the new Article 76 of the CRD). Banks should demonstrate their overall resilience to climate risks. Smoleńska and Van't Klooster (2022) argue that bank transition plans are a hybrid instrument halfway between risk management (internal to banks) and transition guided by supervisors.

4 Macroprudential Perspective

The macroprudential perspective looks at the system-wide dimension of climate risk. This dimension has a transition and physical component. The first component refers to transitions as a result of the Paris agreement. Climate change mitigation to achieve net zero by 2050 as mandated by the Paris agreement is a joint effort involving many players. The government is an important player in setting overall policies, with clear carbon reduction targets, carbon taxes to reduce the use of fossil fuels (stick) and climate subsidies to adapt production processes and products (carrot). Next, there is the demand side with the users of fossil fuels, such as (heavy) manufacturing, utilities and transport, and the supply side with the oil, gas, and coal companies. Finally, the financial system finances the users and suppliers of carbon-intensive products and technologies.

The focus of this chapter is on the role of the financial system to reduce financed carbon emissions (i.e., ceasing financing of companies on the supply and demand side that are not adapting to the net zero world). If central banks, as guardians of the stability of the financial system, take as given the need to achieve net zero in 2050, what is the least disruptive way to achieve this?

Moving to the second component, Bolton et al. (2020) show in their seminal publication *The Green Swan* that climate shocks are subject to uncertainty, whereby "climate tipping points could lead to catastrophic and irreversible impacts that would make quantifying financial damages impossible. Avoiding this requires immediate and ambitious action toward a structural transformation of our economies, involving technological innovations that can be scaled but also major changes in regulations and social norms" (Bolton et al., 2020, p. 1). Importantly, some potential tipping cascades (e.g., melting ice sheets) are more likely to occur if there is global warming between 1 and 3 °C, while other more severe tipping cascades (e.g., affecting rainforests, changing the jet stream, melting permafrost) are more likely to occur if global warming exceeds 3 °C. Bolton et al. (2020) highlight the endogenous nature of the impact of climate risk on financial stability. If we manage to reduce carbon emissions in a timely fashion, we may face less severe climate shocks and thereby less financial instability. The time dimension in our transition model in Sect. 2 is thus important. If you delay action, it comes at a non-linearly increasing cost. Adaptation to transition can thus be profitable at the macro level when it avoids increasing cost.

4.1 Financial Stability Policy

Following from their financial stability mandate, the policy question for central banks is which macroprudential instruments addressing climate risks would minimize financial stability disruptions from climate transitions and climate shocks. Of course, government regulation and taxation, such as carbon taxes, is first best. Tirole (2023) is in favor of appropriate government policies (subject to the democratic process) and argues that "the central bank can act as a 'climate-change fighter of last resort'" (Tirole, 2023, p. 172).[5] The question at hand is, given the stance of government policy (as policymaker), what could central banks (as policytaker) do to minimize financial stability disruptions?

The main macroprudential instrument to date has been climate risk stress tests. While climate risk stress tests are a very useful tool to make potential financial losses in the financial system transparent, they do not reduce carbon emissions by themselves.[6] Moreover, current climate stress tests give a false sense of security, because these tests underestimate the size of climate shocks and the impact of climate shocks on the financial system (ignoring feedback loops) (Reinders et al., 2023).

It is time to develop and implement macroprudential policy tools that force banks (and other financial institutions) to reduce financing activities that lead to carbon emissions. The favorite instrument of macroprudential policymakers is imposing systemic risk buffers. The ECB/ESRB report (2023) proposes a systemic risk buffer (called concentration charges) for climate-related concentration risk. If and when carbon-intensive exposures exceed a concentration threshold, the systemic risk buffer kicks in, as higher concentrations are associated with higher bank losses. Setting the appropriate level of the systemic risk buffer is the main challenge. First, estimates from the impact of 1 percentage point increase in capital requirements on aggregate credit growth vary from a 1 to 10 percentage points decrease in credit growth (ECB/ESRB, 2023). This large variance in expected impact makes it difficult to calibrate the exact level of the systemic risk buffer. Second, policymakers tend to set capital buffers at the lower level,[7] making them less effective. A case in point is the countercyclical capital buffer, implemented after the global financial crisis, which is not regarded as sufficiently sizeable to be able to counter the credit cycle when activated. Third, the buffer has to be large enough to tilt the balance from carbon-intensive to low-carbon loans (Oehmke & Opp, 2023). In the current outlook with energy shortages and high interest rates, fossil-related loans are more profitable

[5] A major concern of Tirole (2023) is that multiple agencies in charge of a given policy (too many cooks in the kitchen) may imply that no-one is accountable. That is a real concern. Our answer would be that the government keeps primary responsibility and accountability on climate policies.

[6] Unlike classic stress-tests, no capital add-ons addressing climate risks have been imposed following climate stress tests in major developed countries to date.

[7] Even if a higher limit is advisable. Broeders and Schlooz (2021) argue that the large uncertainty about climate change would be in favor of setting a high limit based on the precautionary principle.

than loans for renewable energy projects, which need high upfront investment at the currently high interest rates. So, just like the countercyclical capital buffer, a systemic risk buffer for climate concentrations is likely to have limited effect, unless it is set at a variable and sufficiently high level (which is unlikely to happen for political economy reasons, such as bank lobbying, as suggested earlier).

An alternative to buffers (which are basically pricing tools) is to cap financed carbon emissions via a large exposure rule limit (Schoenmaker & Van Tilburg, 2016; Schoenmaker & Stegeman, 2023). This would directly 'limit' the amount of financed carbon emissions in an effective way. A design feature is to apply a general concentration limit for all banks, or design bank-specific limits for carbon exposures. From an individual bank risk perspective, a concentration limit helps to 'limit' bank-specific losses. But from a macro perspective, high-carbon loans may be reshuffled within the sector (just as banks finance each other by issuing bank bonds which are bought by other banks). The intended reduction of carbon emissions only kicks in after all banks are fully loaded with carbon-intensive loans up to the limit, leading to more severe financial stability disruptions later. Moreover, it discourages banks from concentrating in certain transition-sensitive sectors that are building sector-specific knowledge and capabilities. A concentration limit still allows the entire sector to be financed, only by more banks. We thus argue for a bank-specific macro limit for carbon exposures. Bank-specific means a limit based on a bank's actual carbon exposures. And macro means that the aim of the limit is to reduce carbon exposures in the banking system (and in the wider financial system). As banks have to report detailed carbon emissions under the ECB guideline on climate-related risks (ECB, 2020) and the Corporate Sustainability Reporting Directive (CSRD), the central bank—as the macroprudential authority—can easily determine and apply bank-specific macro limits on carbon exposures. The central bank can also apply similar institution-specific macro limits on carbon exposures to other financial institutions that fall under the CSRD.

To calibrate the height of the macro limit, the intended aim of the instrument should be crystal clear. As argued above, the aim is to limit financial stability disruptions from climate risks. Currently, the main risk is transition risk. Taking net zero by 2050 as the ultimate goal of the energy transition, we need to reduce absolute carbon emissions to net zero over the next 25 years. Figure 3 shows three possible pathways: (1) a fast pathway, with steep declines in the first years; (2) a straight pathway, with equally sized declines over the full period; and (3) a late pathway, with steep declines over the last years. The steeper the reduction, the more loans banks will need to foreclose on, potentially causing companies to fail. The straight line leads ceteris paribus to minimal disruption.

Factors such as technical innovation, discount rates for future losses, and duration of (stranded) assets play a role in setting carbon emissions pathways. But we can no longer place all our bets on technical solutions in the future and apply high financial discount rates culminating in the 'too late, too sudden' scenario (ASC, 2016). Stern (2006) suggests using the relatively low social discount rate for climate investments, so that future benefits of today's low-carbon investment are properly taken into account. If anything, we should err on the side of caution, slightly bending

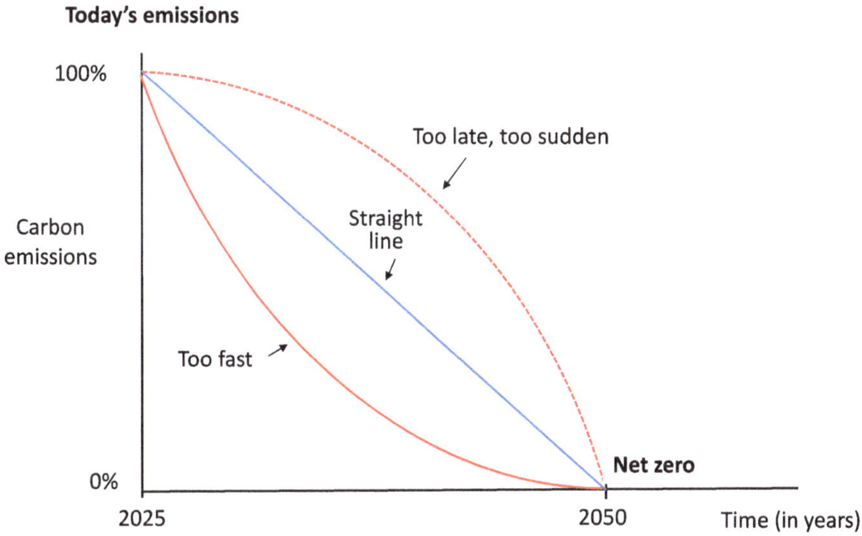

Fig. 3 Carbon emissions pathways and financial stability

to the fast pathway. First, we could apply the precautionary principle: scientists urge remaining within the safe operating limits of system earth, as climate effects are accompanied by many uncertainties (Steffen et al., 2015). Second, at a later stage (beyond 2025) physical risks with tipping points (Bolton et al., 2020) must be added to Fig. 3, which is modeled on transition risks. These tipping points will prompt policymakers to accelerate the reduction further. Third, the ECB's second economy-wide climate stress test indicates that the overall costs and risks are lower when the green transition takes place more rapidly (ECB/ESRB, 2023). Finally, UNEP (2020) shows that absolute emission reduction percentages of about 7% to 8% per year are needed globally for mitigation pathways consistent with limiting warming to 1.5 °C, with steeper pathways in some countries.

4.2 Calibrating a Macroprudential Limit

In the remainder of this section, we calibrate our macroprudential limit on the straight reduction pathway (we fully acknowledge that further research is needed to model the appropriate reduction pathway in a more sophisticated way, taking into account inter alia non-linear effects of transition and physical risk). As indicated in Table 1, such macroprudential controls are designed top-down from a system perspective. The starting point is the amount of today's financed emissions as a percentage of bank capital. The starting macroprudential limit should be tightened to achieve an absolute emission reduction of 4 percentage points per year in comparison to the base year (100% divided by 25 annual steps). Thus, we get a macroprudential limit of 100% (of 2025 emissions) in 2025, 96% (of 2025 emissions) in 2026, 92% (of 2025 emissions) in 2027 down to 0% in 2050. The annual 4% reduction of the starting limit should be adjusted for increases in aggregate bank capital. So, in case bank capital grows with 10% (in comparison to the bank capital in the starting year), the limit should decline by 4.4% (4% × 1.1).

The aim of the macroprudential limit should be to steer the energy transition in an even-handed way to net zero by 2050, across time and across banks. All banks (with high or low carbon exposures at the start in 2025) have to set annual steps toward net zero. It is important to encourage companies to adapt to the new low-carbon world. Companies with a high level of adaptability a_{ij} in our transition model (laid down in credible and testable transition plans) should be kept in banks' loan portfolios as much as possible. Given the tightened macro limit over time, banks have an incentive to stop lending to non-adaptable companies first, as these companies will never contribute to reduced carbon exposures. Adaptable companies will contribute, but with some delay. The aim is to achieve timely reductions, not to punish high-carbon companies that are on a credible and timely path to reduce their carbon emissions.[8] The proposed macro limit is thus an incentive compatible with accelerating the transition. Banks should thus only finance companies that are willing to adapt.

Another question is whether a general limit (with an annual 4% reduction) or more granular, sector-differentiated limits are more suitable, as some sectors are more transition-resistant than others (ECB/ESRB, 2023). The design of such a granular approach (including accompanying sectoral transition paths) is challenging and should be sound to avoid gaming (e.g., banks reporting carbon-intensive loans under sector headings with a more favorable treatment). A final question relates to leakage to other financial sectors and to foreign financial institutions. This is a serious threat. The good news is that Europe is bank-based (Langfield & Pagano, 2016), meaning that macroprudential limits for banks are relatively effective there. The European Systemic Risk Board can advise to apply the macroprudential limit to all regulated financial entities (pension funds, insurance companies, and investment funds next to banks) across the European Union (EU). Moreover, the macroprudential limit could be location-based, just like the countercyclical capital buffer. Non-EU institutions operating in the EU would then also fall under the macroprudential limit. To prevent international leakage, these macroprudential limits could also be implemented at the global level through the Financial Stability Board and the G20.

[8] We could consider allowing a very temporary exclusion of transition-prepared companies from the limit, but within strict bounds otherwise we do not achieve the reduced carbon budget.

4.3 Legal Considerations

Exposure limits as a macroprudential measure are defined in Article 458 of the Capital Requirements Regulation (EU/575/2013). Article 458 states that national authorities may use this article where they identify "changes in the intensity of macroprudential or systemic risk in the financial system with the potential to have serious negative consequences to the financial system and the real economy in a specific Member State ...". Pending the adoption of national macroprudential limits, the ECB, as the supervisory authority for the euro-area banks, could start to require banks to include annual reductions of financed carbon emissions in their prospective transition plans, as supervisors (including the ECB) will be entitled to assess the robustness of banks' transition plans under the new Article 87a(4) of the CRD, as revised by CRD VI (see Sect. 3).[9]

A legal challenge is how to prevent company boards—under pressure from their shareholders—from splitting companies into high-carbon and low-carbon entities. That would undermine the effectiveness of the macroprudential limits. First, this reinforces the need to expand the macroprudential limits to all financing sectors (banking, insurance, pension funds, and investment funds) and apply the limits at a global scale. Second, corporate governance may need to be reformed from a shareholder approach toward a stakeholder approach to include ecological considerations (Schoenmaker et al., 2023).

5 Lender of Last Resort and Central Bank Capital

The role of the lender of last resort (LOLR) is to stabilize the financial system (Goodhart, 1988). LOLR support concerns emergency liquidity assistance to individual banks in difficulties. Central bank losses on their LOLR function are typically limited, as LOLR assistance is provided on a temporary basis to stabilize the financial system in order to return to 'normality'. When asset prices recover, banks can repay their LOLR borrowing. There is an implicit assumption of some form of mean reversion, aided by the LOLR intervention. Of course, central bank losses can and do occur, and therefore central bank capital plays an important role in absorbing such losses. Goodhart (1988) stresses the not-for-profit nature of central banks. They should operate for the greater good of monetary and financial stability. The intended function of LOLR operations is to restore financial markets to normality, preventing banks from hiving off assets in a fire sale at the trough of the cycle. The central

[9] Moreover, Article 104(1)(e) CRD, as revised by CRD VI, will grant supervisors the power to "restrict or limit the business, including with regard to the acceptance of deposits, operations or network of institutions or to request the divestment of activities that pose excessive risks to the soundness of an institution".

bank's role is to counter the inherent instability of the financial system, as argued by Minsky and Kindleberger (Mehrling, 2023).

But climate-induced financial instabilities may follow a different pattern. Our transition model in Sect. 2 highlights that potential transition losses can be high (up to the full value of a company) when a company's transition preparedness is low. When a company is not prepared for transition and subsequently fails when the transition sets in, the losses are permanent for its financiers. The popular term for this phenomenon in the transition literature is stranded assets (Caldecott et al., 2014). The implicit assumption of mean reversion no longer holds, as transition entails by definition a move from an old to a new equilibrium (see Sect. 2 and in particular Fig. 1).

5.1 Permanent Losses

Banks with high exposures to carbon-intensive companies that are not prepared for the transition can thus be confronted with high losses that cannot be recovered (i.e., permanent losses). Temporary repayment relief from its lending banks (and the central bank behind the banks) cannot undo a company's unpreparedness for transition. LOLR assistance to banks financing such companies is very risky, even with collateral, posing potentially substantial and permanent losses to the central bank's capital. When banks get into severe difficulties, they may need to pledge their entire balance sheet to the central bank in return for LOLR assistance. The high emissions portfolio on the balance sheet of banks will become worthless when the underlying collateral of loans turns into stranded assets.

Bolton et al. (2020) show that climate-induced financial instabilities are unpredictable. Both the intensity and the shock-wise pattern of climate shocks can lead to large financial damages, as climate tipping points can result in catastrophic and irreversible impacts. To reduce their own exposure (through LOLR activities) to these financial damages, central banks have themselves the right mandate (as well as incentive) to reduce climate impacts by monetary and financial stability policies that accelerate the energy transition. On the monetary policy side, central banks could tilt the collateral requirements for monetary policy operations toward low-carbon assets (Schoenmaker, 2021). Higher haircuts for carbon-intensive assets would raise the cost of capital for carbon-intensive companies, incentivizing them to switch to low-carbon technologies and products. On the financial stability side, central banks could pose hard macroprudential limits on carbon exposures, as argued in Sect. 4. This would incentivize banks to phase out high-carbon lending and switch to low-carbon lending. Again, this will in turn raise the cost of capital for carbon-intensive companies.

Central banks employ risk management procedures to safeguard their capital. The adjustments outlined above in monetary and financial stability policies serve as preventative measures aimed at protecting their capital. Central banks could also tighten the LOLR and resolution regimes in case a bank with large carbon exposures is likely to fail or is failing. LOLR support to carbon-heavy banks could be done at a higher (penalty) interest rate and/or at a (far) higher haircut on carbon-intensive collateral. The resolution regime could be tightened by allocating a larger part of losses of failing carbon-heavy banks to debtholders (private sector bail-in). Moreover, there is less reason to preserve the credit capacity of carbon-heavy banks. These measures should be pre-announced in order to be effective in maintaining bank discipline. Notwithstanding these measures to reduce LOLR losses from climate-induced financial instabilities, central banks may also want to increase their capital as they will not be able to eliminate these losses fully. It should be noted that, technically, there is no need for higher capital as central banks are typically recapitalized by the government if and when needed (depending on the political willingness and capacity of public finances).

Central banks are usually owned by the government (see Goodhart (1988) and Bonetti et al. (2024)). LOLR losses are thus ultimately government losses. This gives governments an incentive to set a sufficiently high carbon tax to encourage companies to decarbonize.[10]

6 Conclusions

The Paris agreement compels companies to adapt to the new net zero world. Failing to accomplish this transition puts a company's survival at risk. The key point of this chapter is that a company's transition preparedness or adaptivity is endogenous and should not be treated as exogenous, as typically done in microprudential supervision. By contrast, macroprudential regulations, which treat risks as endogenous, can help to accelerate a company's transition.

The research question in this chapter is which macroprudential instruments can central banks adopt to reduce climate-induced financial disruptions. We thus argue from a central bank's financial stability mandate. We find that the proposed systemic risk buffers (ECB/ESRB, 2023) are less effective in reducing climate-related transition risks. Hard macroprudential limits on carbon-intensive lending are more effective, accelerating the green transition. Companies are incentivized to adapt if they want to retain access to (bank) finance. Hard macroprudential limits are also important to speed up the transition of banks. While banks finance new renewable projects, they have to date been reluctant to hive off profitable loans to the fossil-fuel sector and other carbon-intensive sectors. The proposed annual reduction of carbon-intensive lending can be embedded in bank transition plans.

[10] This would counter the argument of Tirole (2023) that central banks' new duties may give an additional excuse to the government not to act when it is precisely its failure to act that creates the impetus for central bank mission enlargement.

Failing to apply effective macroprudential tools to reduce carbon emissions in a timely manner will lead to increased financial stability disruptions in the future. Banks will then want to make more use of the central bank's lender of last resort function. This will in turn entail central bank losses, as banks cannot recover money from stranded companies. Although central banks are not-for-profit, their lender of last resort function is in principle only meant to help banks through the temporary downturn of the financial cycle. However, climate-induced financial instability may well lead to permanent losses for banks and central banks.

References

Advisory Scientific Committee. (2016). *Too late, too sudden: Transition to a low-carbon economy and systemic risk*. Reports of the Advisory Scientific Committee, No. 6, European Systemic Risk Board.

Bolton, P., Despres, M., Da Silva, L., Samama, F., & Svartzman, R. (2020). *The green swan: Central banking and financial stability in the age of climate change*. Bank for International Settlements, Books.

Bonetti, M. Broeders, D., Chen, D., & Dimitrov, D. (2024). *Central bank capital and shareholder relationship* (in this volume).

Borio, C. (2003). Towards a macroprudential framework for financial supervision and regulation? *CESifo Economic Studies, 49*(2), 181–216.

Broeders, D., & Schlooz, M. (2021). Climate change uncertainty and central bank risk management. *Journal of Risk Management in Financial Institutions, 14*(2), 121–130.

Brunnermeier, M., Crockett, A., Goodhart, C., Persaud, A., & Shin, H. (2009). The fundamental principles of financial regulation. Geneva report on the world economy 11, ICBM, Geneva, and CEPR.

Caldecott, B., Tilbury, J., & Carey, C. (2014). *Stranded assets and scenarios*. Discussion Paper, Smith School of Enterprise and the Environment, University of Oxford, Oxford.

De Arriba-Sellier, N. (2021). Turning gold into green: Green finance in the mandate of European financial supervision. *Common Market Law Review, 58*(4), 1097–1140.

European Central Bank. (2020). *Guide on climate-related and environmental risks: Supervisory expectations relating to risk management and disclosure*. Frankfurt.

European Central Bank. (2022). *Aggregated results of SREP 2022*. ECB Banking Supervision, February 8.

European Central Bank and European Systemic Risk Board. (2023). *Towards macroprudential frameworks for managing climate risk*.

Goodhart, C. (1988). *The evolution of central banks*. MIT press.

Grunewald, S., Knijp, G., Schoenmaker, D., & van Tilburg, R. (2024). Embracing the brave new world: A response to Demekas and Grippa. *Journal of Financial Regulation, 10*(1), 127–134.

Hart, O., & Zingales, L. (2017). Companies should maximize shareholder welfare not market value. *Journal of Law, Finance, and Accounting, 2*(2), 247–274.

Hull, J. (2018). *Risk management and financial institutions* (5th ed.). Wiley.

Kurznack, L., Schoenmaker, D., & Schramade, W. (2024). A model of long-term value creation. *Journal of Sustainable Finance & Investment, 14*, 1–19.

Langfield, S., & Pagano, M. (2016). Bank bias in Europe: Effects on systemic risk and growth. *Economic Policy, 31*(85), 51–106.

Loorbach, D., Frantzeskaki, N., & Avelino, F. (2017). Sustainability transitions research: Transforming science and practice for societal change. *Annual Review of Environment and Resources, 42*(1), 599–626.

Mehrling, P. (2023). The Minsky-Kindleberger connection and the making of *manias, panics, and crashes*. *Œconomia, 13*(4), 1029–1053.
Oehmke, M., & Opp, M. (2023). Green capital requirements. *Financial Markets Group*, Discussion Paper No. 865.
Reinders, H., Schoenmaker, D., & van Dijk, M. (2023). *Climate risk stress testing: A conceptual review*. Erasmus Platform for Sustainable Value Creation, Working Paper.
Schoenmaker, D. (2021). Greening monetary policy. *Climate Policy, 21*(4), 581–592.
Schoenmaker, D., & Schramade, W. (2022). Valuing companies in transition. *Sustainability Letters, 1*(1), 1–12.
Schoenmaker, D., & Stegeman, H. (2023). From market to green economics: Impact on monetary and financial policies. In D. Adamski, F. Amtenbrink, & J. de Haan (Eds.), *Cambridge handbook on European Monetary, Economic and Financial Integration* (pp. 215–236). Cambridge University Press.
Schoenmaker, D., & van Tilburg, R. (2016). What role for financial supervisors in addressing environmental risks? *Comparative Economic Studies, 58*(3), 317–334.
Schoenmaker, D., Schramade, W., & Winter, J. (2023). Corporate governance beyond the shareholder and stakeholder model. *Erasmus Law Review, 16*(1), 27–35.
Schumpeter, J. (1942). *Capitalism, Socialism and Democracy*. Harper Perennial.
Smoleńska, A., & Van 't Klooster, J. (2022). A risky bet: Climate change and the EU's microprudential framework for banks. *Journal of Financial Regulation, 8*(1), 51–74.
Steffen, W., et al. (2015). Planetary boundaries: Guiding human development on a changing planet. *Science, 347*(6223), 736–747.
Stern, N. (2006). *The economics of climate change: The Stern review*. Cambridge University Press.
Taleb, N. (2007). *The black swan: The impact of the highly improbable*. Random House.
Tirole, J. (2023). Socially responsible agencies. *Competition Law & Policy Debate, 7*(4), 171–177.
UNEP. (2020). *Emission gap report 2020*. UN Environment Programme.
United Nations. (2015). *UN sustainable development goals (UN SDGs) - Transforming our world: The 2030 agenda for sustainable development*. A/RES/70/1, New York.
Wetzer, T., Stuart-Smith, R., & Dibley, A. (2024). Climate risk assessments must engage with the law. *Science, 383*(6679), 152–154.

Open Access This chapter is licensed under the terms of the Creative Commons Attribution 4.0 International License (http://creativecommons.org/licenses/by/4.0/), which permits use, sharing, adaptation, distribution and reproduction in any medium or format, as long as you give appropriate credit to the original author(s) and the source, provide a link to the Creative Commons license and indicate if changes were made.

The images or other third party material in this chapter are included in the chapter's Creative Commons license, unless indicated otherwise in a credit line to the material. If material is not included in the chapter's Creative Commons license and your intended use is not permitted by statutory regulation or exceeds the permitted use, you will need to obtain permission directly from the copyright holder.

Through the Lens of Legal Mandate: Central Bank Capital in a Time of Climate Crisis

Megan Bowman and Anat Keller

Abstract Motivated by the sentiment of the Central Bank of Ireland's Governor in 2022 that 'social capital is essential to what central banks do every day and why we do it', this chapter explores how central banks, driven by their legal mandates and acting within them, can harness forms of 'soft' capital to advance their efforts in legitimately addressing climate and nature-related risks. It analyses the legal mandates of central banks in the European Union and the United Kingdom to evidence the foundational argument that climate and sustainability imperatives fit squarely within their mandates to support a *protective approach* to mitigating climate risk by these central banks. It then explores the concepts of inward-looking 'organizational cultural capital' and outward-looking 'engagement capital' as manifestations of soft capital that are not only relevant to a protective approach but also to a proactive or *legitimate promotional approach* by central banks to work coordinatively with governments and other stakeholders to facilitate a net zero transition. In so doing we put forward two novel arguments. First, that central banks must be sustainable and resilient from the inside if they are to meet the challenges presented by climate change imperatives when pursuing their respective mandates. Secondly, that 'regulator ecosystems for sustainable finance' are emerging that encourage cooperation and collaboration domestically and also internationally, and help to nudge government leadership of an economy-wide transition.

Keywords Central bank legal mandate · Climate change · Social capital · Soft capital

Bowman's research underpinning this chapter was funded by a Leverhulme Fellowship (RF-2020-441\8); Keller's research underpinning this chapter was funded by a British Academy/Leverhulme Small Grant (SG2122\210367).

M. Bowman (✉) · A. Keller
King's College, London, UK
e-mail: megan.bowman@kcl.ac.uk

© The Author(s) 2025

D. Broeders et al. (eds.), *Central Bank Capital in Turbulent Times*,
Contributions to Finance and Accounting,
https://doi.org/10.1007/978-3-031-73549-3_11

1 Introduction

The final report of the Intergovernmental Panel on Climate Change in March 2022 left no doubt that climate change poses a clear and present danger for markets and the global economy (IPCC, 2022). It presented stark evidence of a world on track for 3 degrees Celsius above pre-industrial levels; an unlivable world, absent urgent and systemic action. In such a world, stable inflation rates, financial stability, and fair and functioning markets would cease to exist. Therefore, a stable temperature is a precondition to price stability and also financial stability. As such, this puts climate change (and other sustainability risks) squarely on the plates of central banks, supervisors, and financial market regulators whose legal mandates are to guard price stability and financial stability.

Broadly speaking, the legal mandate for central banks comprises attention to price stability, maintained through monetary policy that seeks to stabilize (low) inflation rates; and also a more recent mandate of financial stability through macroprudential supervision that seeks to prevent or mitigate systemic risk and ensure resilience of the financial system. To this end, central banks may also be responsible for microprudential supervision that protects the safety and soundness of individual financial institutions. Climate change has been described as 'the ultimate systemic risk' because central banks and the financial firms they supervise cannot reduce exposure by hedging it at an individual level; they cannot 'diversify away from their exposure to the planet' (Hurley, 2022; Bolton et al., 2020). Indeed, the European Central Bank (ECB) recently made a commitment in its *Climate and Nature Plan 2024–2025* to 'consider climate change in the preparation of monetary policy decisions' (ECB, 2024). Therefore, the very nature of climate risk and sustainability imperatives creates implications, opportunities, and tensions regarding the core responsibilities and *raison d'être* of central banks as encapsulated in their legal mandate.

As Wessels and Broeders (2022) make clear, central banks run significant financial risks because they implement monetary policy and financial stability policy using their own balance sheets. Those risks are low in stable economic times, limited mostly to credit and market risks. Yet in turbulent times, through measures to reduce economic shock and market dysfunction such as large-scale asset purchases, a central bank will expand its balance sheet to absorb additional risks (Hauser, 2021).

Earlier chapters in this volume have posited that these risks can and ought to be mitigated through buffers that take the form of capital and reserves. Our chapter approaches the topic of capital in turbulent times from a slightly different perspective. By building on prior research in economics and behavioural science, we argue that the concept of capital as a risk mitigant refers not just to hard currency but also to non-financial resources known as 'soft capital'.

We argue that soft forms of capital, most notably organizational 'cultural' capital and also 'engagement' capital are as important as other, more tangible, forms of capital. While they are not recorded on the balance sheet, they can, nevertheless, generate a significant impact in terms of legitimacy and managing trade-offs in an increasingly complex policymaking environment for central banks. Going forward, we encourage central banks to utilize a more encompassing and inclusive view of capital to support their respective prudential and/or promotional approaches to climate change. In short, to ensure the role of central banks as the guardians of price stability and financial stability in a time of climate and ecological crises, attention must be given to the sufficiency of central bank capital, which we argue includes not just the quantitative measure of such capital but also its *qualitative nature* as well.

What is soft capital and how can it promote risk mitigation? Economists think of capital as a factor of production 'used to create goods or services that are not themselves significantly consumed in the production process' (Boldizzoni, 2008). Originally, the conventional notion of capital was understood to be a stock of tangible often durable things such as buildings, machinery, and inventories. Capital, therefore, broadly stood for 'a stock of produced or natural factors of production that can be expected to yield productive services for some time' (Solow, 1999). In its physical conception, capital could be readily measured and presented with three delineated characteristics: 'extension in time, deliberate sacrifice for future benefit, and alienability' (Arrow, 1999). Despite economists' initial reluctance, this narrow conception of capital was soon reassessed and broadened to encompass a plethora of capital (Baron & Hannan, 1994) such as human capital (Goldin, 2016), social capital (Adler & Kwon, 2002), and organizational cultural capital (Barrett, 1998).

Whilst soft capital may seem less concrete, efficacious, or *masculine* than hard capital, we argue that it is a necessary part of a central bank's risk mitigative logic and toolkit. Indeed, all capital can be perceived as abstract and intangible to some degree; the rise of digital currencies provides a clear example. Moreover, the inchoate and human dimensions of markets are revealed in various circumstances: the cognitive-psychological nature of financial markets has been well-documented in post-crisis literature (e.g., Tooze, 2018); the capital sufficiency of a bank balance is similarly conceptual, being reliant on agreed accounting standards and heuristics (Wessels & Broeders, 2022); and it can certainly be argued that central bank mandates are constructed (and thus can be reconstructed or at least adjusted) based on shared understandings or perceptions of key participants, often in response to exogenous events and existential threats. This last point is well-illustrated by the addition of financial stability to many central bank mandates post-2009 global financial crisis; and can also be discerned by the inclusion—and subsequent exclusion—of climate risk as a priority in the Bank of England annual remit by the UK Government (as discussed in Sect. 2).

With this in mind, this chapter takes the words of Gabriel Makhlouf (2022), Governor of the Central Bank of Ireland, as its departure point: 'social capital is essential to what central banks do every day and why we do it'. This chapter explores how central banks, driven by their mandates and acting within them, can harness forms of soft capital to advance their efforts in addressing climate and nature-related risks. In so doing, we first start by analyzing the legal mandates of central banks in the European Union (EU) and United Kingdom (UK) (Sect. 2) to evidence the foundational argument that climate and sustainability fit squarely within their mandates and thus legitimate a 'protective approach' to climate risk by these central banks. We then explore the concept of inward-looking cultural capital (Sect. 3) and outward-looking engagement capital (Sect. 4) as manifestations of soft capital that are relevant to both a protective approach and also a more proactive or 'legitimate promotional' approach by central banks to facilitate the net zero transition, prior to concluding in Sect. 5.

2 Legal Mandate and Sustainability: Analysis Through Case Studies

We limit our analysis to the European and UK jurisdictions with a specific focus, where relevant, on the ECB, De Nederlandsche Bank (DNB), Banque de France (BdF), and Bank of England (BoE) as case studies in this space. These central banks have been providing leadership in the climate risk space since at least 2015 (e.g., Carney, 2015) and, together, facilitated the creation of the global Central Banks and Supervisors Network for Greening the Financial System (NGFS) in 2017 with the aims of: assisting the development of climate risk mitigation and management (in central banks and also financial firms and markets), mainstreaming finance to support the low-carbon transition, and defining and promoting best practices (NGFS, n.d.). The BdF continues to provide the NGFS Secretariat, the BoE chairs the Monetary Policy workstream, and the BdF and DNB co-chair the Nature-Related Risks workstream. Those three national central banks are also implementing initiatives domestically.

2.1 The European System of Central Banks

2.1.1 The ECB

As a response to the 2009 global financial crisis, in addition to conducting monetary policy for the eurozone, the ECB also became responsible for banking supervision in participating Member States under the Single Supervisory Mechanism (SSM) (per *1024/2013 SSM Regulation*). Nonetheless, those responsibilities are shared with national central banks via joint supervisory teams, which together comprise the European System of Central Banks (ESCB) as governed by the 2007 *Treaty on the Functioning of the European Union* (TFEU) and the 1998 *Statute of the European System of Central Banks and of the European Central Bank*.

Under Art 127(1) of the TFEU, the primary objective of the ECB and ESCB national banks is to maintain price stability through monetary policy that can achieve low and stable inflation rates. Moreover, through the ESCB system, the ECB must also contribute 'to the smooth conduct of policies pursued by [national] competent authorities relating to ... the stability of the financial system' (Art 127(5) TFEU). Further, the combination of Art 127(1) with 119(2) and 282(2) of the TFEU provides the secondary objective to support EU general economic policies (without prejudice to the primary objective). Finally, as an institution of the EU, the ECB is bound by the objectives of the EU in accordance with Art 3(3) of the 1992 *Treaty on European Union* (TEU), which includes an obligation to 'work for the sustainable development of Europe based on balanced economic growth and price stability, a highly competitive social market economy, aiming at full employment and social progress, and a high level of protection and improvement of the quality of the environment'.

Importantly, there is much room for manoeuvre in how the ECB and ESCB banks achieve mandate objectives. This is due to, first, central bank independence as guaranteed by Art 130 TFEU and that, secondly, objectives and tasks outlined in the TFEU are not a definitive catalogue of measures (per Art 119(2) and (3), 127(1) and (2), Art 282(2) TFEU). The ECB is thus entitled to select the most suitable instruments for the fulfilment of its mandate. This is important for ensuring dynamism and responsiveness in a world that has changed much over the decades since ESCB inception to now include existential threat from sustainability risks and the imperative to transition to net zero. Certainly, when the ECB was given its mandate of price stability in 1992, there was little thought for its involvement in addressing climate risk. Nonetheless, for that very reason, some ECB climate-related measures (such as green quantitative easing), have raised questions regarding compatibility with its mandate and the efficacy of monetary policy instruments (e.g., Deyris, 2023; Aloui et al., 2023; van 't Klooster & de Boer, 2023).

Nonetheless, it is clear that climate risk implicates both primary and secondary objectives of the ECB mandate in two ways: directly by influencing price stability (as seen from concerns about energy scarcity due to the Ukraine War); and indirectly because national central banks are compelled by the TFEU to support secondary objectives of the EU. Specifically, prior legal scholarship contends that the ECB and other EU supervisory authorities have extant legal duties to account for climate and environmental impacts such that their mandates are *already green* due to a 'principle of environmental integration' that results from analysis of Art 3(3) TEU in combination with Art 11 TFEU which provides that 'environmental protection requirements must be integrated into the definition and implementation of the Union's policies and activities, in particular with a view to promoting sustainable development' (see e.g. Solana, 2019; de Arriba-Sellier, 2021).

2.1.2 Relevance of National Context

On this point, the role of national central banks becomes quite relevant. As members of the ESCB, national central banks in the EU obtain their primary and secondary mandates straight from the TFEU. Nonetheless, as can be gleaned from above, national circumstances remain relevant within the SSM system. In practice, national central banks take the lead in supervisory teams as they have specialist knowledge of their local banks. Moreover, supervision of financial institutions other than banks (such as insurers or pension funds) sits outside the SSM and is therefore undertaken solely by national authorities such as financial market regulators. Moreover, national circumstances differ regarding national legislative provisions and policy discretions given to a central bank as well as their institutional culture. As such, some national central banks institutionally do more than others in the climate and sustainability space even though they all come under the same TFEU.

By way of example, the mandates of BdF are found in the French Monetary and Financial Code (*Code monétaire et financier*) in the *Statutes of the Banque de France* (the Statutes) which conform with TFEU objectives via the phrase 'shall perform the tasks and comply with the objectives assigned to it by the Treaty' (Art L. 141-1 of the Statutes). Furthermore, the Statutes require BdF to 'monitor... the stability of the financial system' (Article L. 141-5-1). Thus the BdF has the primary objectives of upholding price stability and financial stability, and the secondary objective of supporting the economic policies of the EU as per Art 127 TFEU. The Statutes also confer an additional secondary objective to BdF to, without prejudice to the primary objective, 'contribute to the [French] government's general economic policy' (Art L. 141-1 of the Statutes). Indeed, prompted by the French *Energy and Climate Law 2019* (LEC), the mandate of the Autorité de contrôle prudentiel et de résolution (ACPR), which is the arm of the BdF that is responsible for prudential supervision, was legislatively amended. This amendment upgraded its supervisory power to enable direct supervision and sanction of transition planning and climate/sustainability reporting pursuant to Art 29 of the LEC.

Similarly, the DNB mandate is found in the *Bankwet* 1998 (*Bank Act 1998*), which came into force on 1 June 1998, the same day that the ESCB was created and which The Netherlands joined. Reflecting Article 127 of the TFEU, the DNB has an 'objective to maintain price stability' (s 2(1) Bank Act 1998) and, subject to this, a secondary objective that 'supports the general economic policies in the European Union with a view to contributing to the achievement of the objectives of the Union [in Art 3(3) TEU]' (s 2(2) Bank Act 1998). Additionally, the Bank Act 1998 confers further tasks to DNB that are beyond the scope of the TFEU, including 'to promote the stability of the financial system' (s4(1)(c) Bank Act 1998). Therefore, the DNB has primary objectives to uphold price stability and financial stability; and a secondary objective to support European economic policies. Interestingly, there is no legislated secondary objective regarding the policies of the Dutch national government. However, in 2011 the DNB Board updated its mission statement (and thus its operational framework) to 'safeguard financial stability and thus contribute to sustainable prosperity in the Netherlands' (DNB, n.d.). This has been described as a response to the 2008 financial crisis to publicly 'differentiate the new approach from the pre-crisis one' (Dikau & Volz, 2021). However, it has become clear over time that the DNB interprets the meaning of 'sustainable' to include not just financial longevity but also ecological sustainability in the face of climate change (Elderson, 2018). Whilst this amendment was made to the mission statement and not the Bank Act 1998, it is an important statement of intent and willingness by DNB itself (Bowman, 2022).

Due to this complex multi-jurisdictional layering of legislative mandate, there has been additional legal debate surrounding the monetary policy mandate of EU national central banks, such as BdF and DNB, due to the distinction between primary and secondary objectives that they pursue (Bovenschen & Lieshout, 2020;

Dikau & Volz, 2021). A problem may occur if climate-related measures by a central bank will increase inflation. At that point it becomes difficult to fulfil the secondary objective of supporting EU policy without prejudicing the primary objective of maintaining price stability. However, it can be argued that the main difference between the two objectives is the latitude for national central bank proactivity. That is, given the nature of the secondary objective, national central banks must wait for the EU to provide relevant policy (such as the 2020 *EU Green Taxonomy* and disclosure rules under the 2022 *Corporate Sustainability Reporting Directive* (*CSRD*) and 2019 *Sustainable Finance Disclosure Regulation* (*SFDR*)) after which it can then take actions to support that policy. By contrast, when a risk falls under the primary objectives then it becomes part of a national central bank's daily work; and they can be proactive in addressing it and have much more leeway to consider and act on it. Arguably then, and given the 2024 policy position of the ECB towards climate change and the net zero transition, it makes perfect sense for a national central bank to view climate risk as falling within its primary objectives, and indeed this is the preferred approach by some (Bowman, 2022).

2.2 *The Bank of England*

The 'mission' of the BoE is 'promoting the good of the people of the United Kingdom by maintaining monetary and financial stability' (Bank of England, 2023). This mission reflects the mandate of the BoE which is enshrined in the *Bank of England Act 1998* (the 1998 Act) and various subsequent amendments.

The 1998 Act ordained the BoE as an independent institution from HM Treasury, granting it a primary mandate of monetary policy to maintain price stability (per s11(a)). Subsequently in 2013 in the wake of the global financial crisis, the 1998 Act was amended by the *Financial Services Act 2012* to add an additional primary objective titled the 'Financial Stability Objective' to 'protect and enhance the stability of the financial system of the United Kingdom' (s2A(1) 1998 Act as amended). In so doing, the 2012 amendment also brought structural change to the BoE. It created separate divisions and committees for monetary policy (overseen by a new Monetary Policy Committee) and financial stability (overseen by a new Financial Policy Committee) and established the Prudential Regulation Authority (PRA) with the objective of 'promoting the safety and soundness of PRA-authorized persons' (now governed by Part 3A of the 1998 Act together with s2B of the *Financial Services and Markets Act 2000* as amended by the 2012 Act). Moreover, in 2016, the PRA Board was replaced with the Prudential Regulation Committee (s30A 1998 Act as amended), thus positioning it on the same legal footing as the Monetary Policy Committee and the Financial Policy Committee to become the three BoE policy committees. Thus, financial stability falls under the purview of the Financial Policy Committee (s9C(1) 1998 Act as amended) which is tasked to contribute to its achievement by taking action to identify, monitor and mitigate 'systemic risks with a view to protecting and enhancing the resilience of the UK financial System' (s 9C(2) 1998 Act as amended).

Although the BoE was originally part of the ESCB system, the new post-Brexit *Financial Services and Markets Act 2023* (FSMA 2023) has revoked a long list of retained EU law regarding financial services, including regulations for market abuse and capital requirements (s1 FSMA 2023). Nonetheless, any retained EU law as incorporated into the rulebooks of UK financial regulators (being the PRA and the Financial Conduct Authority (FCA)) has not been revoked by FSMA 2023. The understanding is that those rules can be updated by the regulators themselves via processes set out in the *Financial Services and Markets Act 2000* (as amended by FSMA 2023).

Thus, like the DNB and BdF, maintaining financial stability is an additional primary objective for the BoE. Subject to these primary objectives, the BoE has a secondary objective 'to support the economic policy of Her Majesty's Government, including its objectives for growth and employment' (per ss11(b) and 9C(1)(b) 1998 Act). Moreover, in acquitting both its primary and secondary objectives, the BoE must 'have regard' to 'recommendations' made by HM Treasury about matters, including potential risks, to which the BoE ought to attend in the coming year (ss 9E and 12 1998 Act). This is done by the UK Chancellor providing an 'annual remit letter' to the three BoE policy committees, which set out new influences on price stability and financial stability, and the current priorities of government economic policy. It is understood that the word 'remit' is broadly synonymous with 'mandate' (UK Parliament, 2023a).

Thus, in the UK, the government has power to fine-tune central bank mandate by re-focusing BoE priorities to explicitly include climate and sustainability, outside of legislative reform. Indeed, in March 2021, the BoE annual remit was adjusted exactly in this way to reflect the government's economic policy objective for achieving 'strong, sustainable and balanced growth that is also environmentally sustainable and consistent with the transition to a net zero economy' (HM Treasury, 2021). In so doing, the Treasury acknowledged that pursuing price and financial stability is essential to achieving that economic policy objective and will include 'structural reform ... to transition to an environmentally sustainable and resilient net zero economy, including through regulation' (HM Treasury, 2021). Therefore, the BoE's operations were updated to align with the government's net zero strategy. This move was applauded by the UK Environmental Audit Select Committee which had noted repeatedly that the BoE was 'at risk of creating a moral hazard by purchasing high-carbon bonds and providing finance to companies in high-carbon sectors' (UK Environmental Audit Committee, 2021).

As such, from 2021, the BoE added climate and sustainability criteria to its financial stability and monetary policy operations, including corporate bond purchases, Biennial Exploratory Scenario exercises, and 'the Financial Policy Committee's work [s9C] to support sustainable investment in areas such as renewable energy infrastructure and green technologies' (Bank of England, 2021).

In November 2023, the UK parliamentary House of Lords published results of an Inquiry titled Bank of England: How is Independence Working? in which it found that the BoE's continued attention to climate change could jeopardize both its independence and ability to fulfil its price stability objective (UK Parliament, 2023b). In December 2023, the Chancellor's annual remit letter removed climate change from the list of BoE priorities (HM Treasury, 2023); and by February 2024 the BoE had reduced its climate-related resources by way of response, although certainly not without external criticism for increasing its own risk exposures (as documented in Costa, 2024). All of this occurred even though it is clear that climate risk remains a core part of the BoE's financial stability objective due to the well-evidenced relevance of climate change to systemic risk which thus triggers s9C(2) of the 1998 Act (as amended). Importantly, after a national Labor government was elected into power in 2024, the new UK Chancellor issued her annual Remit Letter on 14 November 2024 in which she explicitly identified climate change as the 'greatest long-term global challenge that we face' (HM Treasury, 2024). This Remit Letter re-established the BoE's obligation to have regard to climate risk and introduced a new obligation to have regard to nature-related risks when executing its dual primary objectives; and reinstated sustainable finance 'as one of the government's priorities which the FPC should support as part of its secondary objective' (ibid).

Interestingly, this story of political vicissitude in the UK occurred even despite the legal clarity of the BoE mandate as contained in the amended 1998 Act, FSMA 2000, and FSMA 2023. Indeed, if further ammunition were needed to support the argument that climate and sustainability risks sit squarely on the plate of the BoE, the recent FSMA 2023 has inserted new 'regulatory principles' into s3B of FSMA 2000 that require the PRA (and also the FCA) to 'contribute towards achieving compliance by the Secretary of the State' of UK net zero emissions targets and environmental targets 'where each regulator considers the exercise of its functions to be relevant to the making of such a contribution' (added by s27 FSMA 2023). Although the regulatory principles regarding climate and environmental targets do not directly apply to the Financial Policy Committee (and thus its remit of financial stability), it can be cogently argued that those regulatory principles do apply indirectly. This is because the regulatory principles apply to the BoE as Financial Market Infrastructure (FMI) supervisor by virtue of s30E of the 1998 Act (as amended by FSMA 2023); and s30D of the 1998 Act states that the BoE must have regard to the regulatory principles in s30E when exercising its FMI functions in a way that advances the Financial Stability Objective. As such, our argument is that the legal mandate of the BoE for addressing climate risk and, even more importantly, proactively facilitating the net zero transition (as discussed in Sect. 4) remains very much intact in the UK.

3 Organizational Cultural Capital: Inward-Looking Perspectives on Central Banks in the Context of Sustainability

A legal mandate that refocuses the attention of central banks, to varying degrees, on climate change and sustainability requires a holistic view of capital. In this section, we argue that organizational 'cultural' capital is as important as other, more tangible, forms of capital since it plays a key role in enhancing the legitimacy of central banks and their capacity to navigate trade-offs in an ever more complex policymaking landscape. What constitutes 'good culture' is, by its nature, open to interpretation. However, in this section, we offer an initial sketch of essential elements and characteristics that should form part of a healthy culture within central banks.

3.1 What Is 'Culture' and 'Organizational Cultural Capital'?

There is little agreement across management scholarship about the meaning of 'culture' in the context of organizational management (Keller & Kokkinis, 2022). The often-cited definition of Schein refers to the culture of a group as 'the accumulated shared learning of that group as it solves its problems of external adaptation and internal integration, which has worked well enough to be considered valid and, therefore, to be taught to new members as the correct way to perceive, think, feel, and behave in relation to those problems . . . ' (Schein, 2016). Schein identifies three distinct layers of culture that differ in their observability and susceptibility to transformation: a (deepest) layer of basic underlying assumptions; a middle layer of espoused values and ideology; and a surface layer of more observable factors such as artefacts and behaviours of members of the organization that reflect those assumptions and shared meanings (ibid). In other words, we can define culture as the 'social or normative glue that holds an organization together . . . ' (Siehl & Martin, 1982).

Central banks, similar to other organizations or institutions, exhibit organizational culture or more accurately, cultures of 'deeply embedded patterns of organizational behaviour and the shared values, assumptions, beliefs, or ideologies that members have about their organization or its work' (Peterson & Spencer, 1990). Since organizational culture is recognized as a potential source of sustainable competitive advantage, it can also be viewed as a type of soft capital (Ellson, 2004). This 'organizational cultural capital' is, accordingly, defined as the 'value attached to the collective mental programming (values, beliefs, and behaviours) of the organization that supports its relationship with its employees, customers and society' (Barrett, 1998). Nevertheless, striving for a good, healthy culture in central banks presents unique challenges. To begin with, as publicly owned or publicly controlled corporations, central banks are exposed to problems that are typical for public organizations including 'diluted monitoring incentives due to multiple layers of delegation, weak incentives to reduce costs and innovate, and political distortions' (Frisell, 2008). In contrast to private corporations, central banks are also insulated from powerful disciplining mechanisms such as product market competition and the market for corporate control and they are often susceptible to the risks of both industry and political pressure, which has implications when pursuing mandate objectives.

3.2 *The Importance of Organizational Cultural Capital to Central Banks in Addressing Climate and Nature-Related Risks*

As can be seen from Sect. 2, when legal mandate encompasses sustainability it can result in an even more complex and layered policymaking and supervisory environment (NGFS, 2021). Increasingly, central banks face trade-offs and potential conflicts across their tasks in fulfilling their mandates and legal objectives. Scholarly literature and policy debate focus on the role that good governance plays in managing trade-offs by central banks when pursuing mandate objectives (BIS, 2009; Keller, 2020). Yet, analysis of organizational culture as a key driver of good governance in central banks is scarce (Momani & Manad, 2015). As we shall see, this can be partly attributed to the perception that central banks are experts and therefore 'unbiased' and 'detached' (Riles, 2018: 22). As such, a more robust understanding of culture in central banks is needed, especially to highlight the important role of good culture in managing and meeting the challenges that flow from pursuing their mandates.

In simple words, central banks must be sustainable and resilient *from the inside* if they are to meet the challenges that climate change presents when pursuing their respective mandates. In practical terms, this means that central banks should aim to foster a culture that promotes good governance through diversity of thought and encouraging challenge. In addition, central banks can be encouraged to move beyond a culture of expertise to one that also includes a dynamic dialogue with the public and ordinary laypeople. A culture that embraces deliberative public engagement is instrumental to the trust and credibility of central banks and legitimating their policy decisions (Hunt et al., 2003). This is particularly the case when it comes to climate change objectives, where the reported loss of credibility and trust in experts and democratic deficit are thorny issues (Fiorino, 1990).

In this environment, culture has two important functions for central banks. First, culture can drive good governance (FCA, 2023) and assist central banks in managing potential trade-offs and conflicts, particularly when integrating climate-related risks into their operations. Indeed, maintaining a healthy purposeful culture recently became a central theme in UK financial supervision (FCA, 2020). Central banks can seize this opportunity to 'lead by example' (Rowland, 2023). Second, central banks' attention to climate change and sustainability can be politically sensitive and may have large distributional effects 'by increasing the price for or by supporting technologies to reduce carbon emissions' (Eurofound, 2021; Beckmann et al., 2023; DiLeo, 2023). For example, maintaining high interest rates to meet the inflation target may hamper green investments, which are sensitive to financing conditions (Schoenmaker, 2023). The political and distributional nature of climate-related policy decisions may result in political and industry pressures, jeopardizing the independence of central banks. A healthy organizational culture can alleviate these concerns by strengthening a central bank's legitimacy, inter alia, by promoting open dialogue between central bank experts and the public as well as external experts, as discussed below.

3.3 What Does a 'Good' or 'Healthy' Central Bank Culture Look Like?

Naturally, there is considerable diversity among central banks and, in turn, a corresponding diversity in their governance and culture. But can we identify a best practice or a benchmark against which a good or healthy culture could be calibrated? Much can be learnt from the notion of organizational culture as developed in social sciences. Key elements include tone from the top, psychological safety to speak up, and effective governance at the board and senior management levels, in addition to a broader set of processes, systems and controls (Keller & Kokkinis, 2022), all of which could be implemented in central banking operations.

Specifically, an acknowledged element of a healthy culture is the diversity of thought and inclusion. Diversity is conducive to building trust to deliver the central bank remit, leading to more creative thinking and to reducing the risks of groupthink and bias (New Financial, 2020). The BoE may provide here a useful case study. For over a century, it had been criticized for being the 'bank man' with a noticeable unbroken line of white men as its governors (ibid). Recognizing this, increased attention to inclusion and diversity of thought was introduced into the BoE's agenda and priorities via the One Bank initiative, launched in 2014, which aimed to cultivate 'a strong common culture... which brings together the whole of the organization to better support each policymaker and every policy decision' (BoE, 2023). This initiative is centred around building a culture that values diverse ideas, encourages open debate, and empowers people at all levels to take the initiative (Carney, 2019). Similarly, the *Bank Underground* blog was introduced to enable staff to share views that challenge (or support) prevailing policy orthodoxies. Gradually, the BoE also enhanced its dialogue (as opposed to merely explaining what the Bank does) with the general public and external experts. For instance, it introduced an outreach program, an ongoing series of engagement panels including a citizens' forum, a community forum, and a youth forum that provide a way for members of the public to share their experiences of the economy with the Bank. This dialogue enabled staff to understand how policy decisions are viewed 'outside the "bubble" of Threadneedle Street' in which they work on a day-to-day basis (BoE, 2023). The BoE has also been seeking input from climate scientists and other industry experts on the design, coverage and nature of stress testing scenarios of the financial system's resilience to the physical and transition risks of climate change (BoE, 2022).

Still, while these initiatives were welcomed as a step forward in operationalizing healthy culture at the BoE, the risk of slipping back 'into being an opaque institution blighted by group think' remains real (Spicer et al., 2016). Acknowledged by both the Bank (Bailey, 2021) and the UK Parliament, there is still 'perceived to be a lack of intellectual diversity in many central banks, including the Bank of England' (House of Lords, 2023). In the 2020 Bank of England's *Court Review of Ethnic Diversity and Inclusion*, findings revealed that minority ethnic colleagues, in particular Black colleagues, felt 'less included at the Bank', reporting lower levels of psychological safety and feeling less comfortable expressing controversial opinions or disagreement compared to White colleagues (Bank of England, 2020). The recommendations emphasized the key role of managers in challenging 'a culture that can perpetuate inequalities in the allocation of opportunities and career advancement' and improving recruitment practices including increasing efforts to attract a diverse pool of external candidates for all roles and reducing internal preference in screening (ibid). In its recent 2023 report *Making an Independent Bank of England Work Better*, the Economic Affairs Committee concluded that the BoE must 'do more to foster a diversity of views and strengthen a culture that encourages challenge' (House of Lords, 2023).

However, a healthy organizational culture does not begin and end with diversity. It also includes attention to innovation and experimentation of new ideas; features that are particularly needed when seeking to facilitate a net zero and sustainable finance transition. There is growing evidence that central banks are adopting a flatter management structure (BIS, 2009). This can result in staff interacting more directly with senior members of policymaking committees and assist in the development of a corporate mentality of experimentation (Sanchez-Canizares et al., 2007).

These findings give food for thought about ways to enhance the internal resilience of central banks in times of climate crisis. The pursuit of multiple objectives under the same roof can generate conflicts and trade-offs and may result in diluted accountability and institutional overburdening. These issues become particularly pertinent in the context of politically sensitive topics like climate change. Enhanced internal diversity of staff to ensure diversity of thought together with outward-facing processes that seek to listen to the public and also experts, can reinforce both the credibility and legitimacy of central banks whether they adopt a protective or a promotional approach to climate change, as discussed in the next section.

4 'Engagement Capital': Moving Outwards from a Protective Approach to a Proactive Approach

Taking a 'protective' approach to climate risk treats climate change as a conventional risk management issue that sits well within mandate. It requires a central bank to measure, manage, and mitigate climate risks (physical, transition and increasingly liability and litigation) to its balance sheet, and to encourage supervised firms to do likewise (Campiglio et al., 2018; Broeders & Schlooz, 2021). Thus, taking a protective approach to climate risks, as outlined above in Sects. 2 and 3, is both legal and legitimate because central banks need a strong balance sheet to credibly implement monetary policy and the requisite trust to acquit supervisory remit.

Nonetheless, there is increasing acceptance that a more ambitious approach by central banks 'is the only approach in line with the climate emergency' (Dafermos, 2021). Such an approach is described variously as 'promotional' or 'proactive' because it promotes a starring role for central banks to facilitate the transition to a low-carbon, climate resilient, and net zero economy by *proactively assisting the greening of the financial system.* At its heart, this approach is predicated on the fact that climate risks will always remain largely unhedgable unless systemic and structural transformation takes place (Bolton et al., 2020). In other words, financial stability and price stability are ongoingly threatened and will only get worse in a status quo system. Indeed, the ECB has recently acknowledged that 'financial stability is a precondition for price stability, and vice versa' and thus risks to financial stability need to be regarded when ensuring the proportionality of monetary policy decisions 'even if those risks may materialize only in future' (Schnabel, 2023). These realizations have prompted 'a second epistemological break' regarding the conceptualization of central banking as evolving from a protective position to an active approach that seeks to build the resilience of complex adaptive systems in order to fulfil mandate (Bolton et al., 2020).

At this point, it is critical to make two points clear. First, a promotional/proactive approach does not replace a protective one but rather subsumes it. Indeed, for reasons outlined in Sect. 1, both approaches are needed; and what this chapter proposes can be conceived in terms of concentric circles of central banking activity. Secondly, a promotional approach provides a starring role but does not assume a solo role for central banks. Rather, it acknowledges the coordinative role and convening power of central banks, termed alliteratively by Bolton et al. as 'contributing to coordination to combat climate change' (2020: 63) so as to fulfil their legal mandate over longer time horizons (Baer et al., 2021). Indeed, for reasons of independence and accountability, it is quite clear that it is the responsibility of elected national governments to centrally draw up and coordinate a national net zero strategy, which includes feasible milestones and how to reach them, and hard decisions about real economy reforms via fiscal and economic policy that is in line with the Paris Agreement goals (Bowman, 2022; Manning et al., 2024; also Barmes & Dikau, 2024).

Importantly, there is recent evidence that an emerging *legitimate promotional approach* is being taken by early-moving central banks in the UK and EU whereby they are promoting and actively participating in coordination and cooperation with government and other agencies and stakeholders for net zero goals. A recent empirical study by Bowman (2022) has revealed that case-study central banks and financial regulators see themselves as part of a broader political response in which: (a) government fiscal policies are key to mitigating climate change and eliminating dependence on carbon-intensive activities/sources for a net zero transition; and (b) prudential, monetary and market regulatory tools act complementarily to actively facilitate that transition in line with central banks' legal mandate and government policy. Respondents did not see these arrangements as an affront to independence but rather a statement of reality that navigating and addressing such a complex landscape requires working together. In other words, 'the principle of independence does not imply a total isolation from, or a complete absence of cooperation' between relevant institutions and bodies within a jurisdiction (de Boer & van 't Klooster, 2021: 13).

More specifically, Bowman's study evidenced that case-study central banks are embracing experimentalism and cooperation, evidenced by the emergence of *regulator ecosystems for sustainable finance* that comprise central banks, financial market regulators, Treasury, and government ministries. These 'regulator ecosystems' encourage cooperation and collaboration domestically and also internationally, and help to nudge government leadership of an economy-wide transition. Moreover, in addition to enhanced cooperation and collaboration amongst peers, case-study central banks also demonstrated heightened *convening powers amongst stakeholders* to help initiate and implement new climate-related financial regulation and corporate law.

These 'regulator ecosystems' can be perceived as another form of soft capital, namely engagement or relational capital. Indeed, the Central Bank of Ireland has emphasized the importance of this type of soft capital to central bank legitimacy and efficacy, describing it as 'the social connections, attitudes and norms that contribute to societal wellbeing by promoting coordination and collaboration between people and groups in society' (Makhlouf, 2022). In a time of climate crisis, it is clear that central banks comprise a symbiotic component of a larger interconnected regulatory matrix. Such 'regulator ecosystems for sustainable finance' will be key to countering the complexity of systems change and ensuring timely action along the full value chain to achieve regulatory goals for a successful net-zero transition.

5 Conclusion

This chapter has called attention to the importance of soft capital in the operation of central banks, particularly in a time of climate crisis, and what this could entail in practical terms. We have recommended that, alongside utilizing tangible forms of

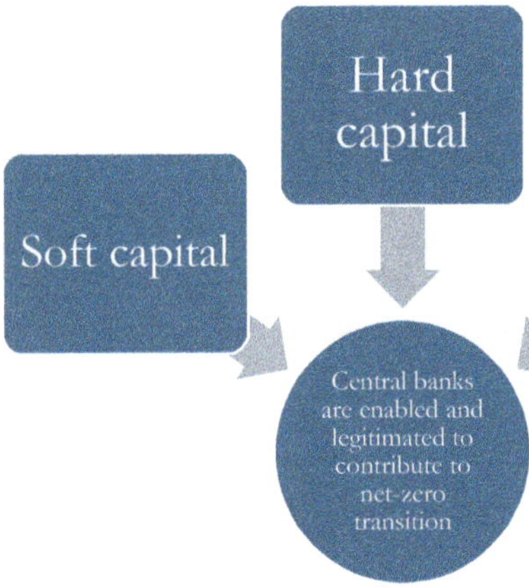

Fig. 1 Diagram of central bank's powers and legitimacy

capital, central banks should harness soft forms of capital to advance their efforts in facilitating a net-zero and sustainable finance transition.

Central banks' powers and legitimacy can be conceived as the diagram in Fig. 1. The legal mandate provides the source of a central bank's delegated authority and legitimizes its activities. In a time of climate crisis, the legal mandate provides the foundation of both a protective approach to mitigate internal risks and a legitimate promotional approach that facilitates the transition to a low-carbon, climate-resilient and net-zero economy. In addition, the hard capital on a central bank's balance sheet can enable mandate objectives and reputational credibility, particularly in times of turbulence. But most importantly, soft forms of capital, including inward-looking organizational cultural capital and outward-looking engagement capital, are crucial for strengthening legitimacy, enhancing accountability, and assisting central banks in managing trade-offs across objectives and policy areas (especially in politically sensitive realms) when acquitting their mandates. Thus, a legal mandate combined with both forms of capital establishes the essential pre-conditions for central banks to support the net-zero transition effectively and legitimately through their monetary and financial stability operations.

References

Adler, P., & Kwon, S. (2002). Social capital: Prospects for a new concept. *The Academy of Management Review, 27*(1), 17–40.

Aloui, D., Benkraiem, R., Guesmi, K., & Vigne, S. (2023). The European Central Bank and green finance: How would the green quantitative easing affect the investors' behaviour during times of crisis? *IRFA*.

Arrow, K. (1999). Observations on social capital. In P. Dasgupta & I. Serageldin (Eds.), *Social capital: A multifaceted perspective* (pp. 3–5). The World Bank.

Baer, M., Campiglio, E., & Deyris, J. (2021). It takes two to dance: Institutional dynamics and climate-related financial policies. *Grantham Research Institute on Climate Change and the Environment Working Paper No. 356* (April).

Bailey, A. (2021). *I am Going to Make the Bank of England Better: By Improving Racial Diversity* (Letter to the Guardian, 21 July). Available at https://www.theguardian.com/commentisfree/2021/jul/21/i-am-going-to-make-the-bank-of-england-better-by-improving-racial-diversity

Bank of England. (2020). *Court Review of Ethnic Diversity and Inclusion* available at https://www.bankofengland.co.uk/report/2021/court-review-of-ethnic-diversity-and-inclusion#:~:text=Our%20findings,minority%20ethnic%20and%20White%20colleagues

Bank of England. (2021). *Response to the remit for the Financial Policy Committee—July 2021* (13 July 2021) at https://www.bankofengland.co.uk/letter/2021/july/remit-for-the-fpc-2021

Bank of England. (2022). *Results of the 2021 Biennial Exploratory Scenario (CBES)*. Available at https://www.bankofengland.co.uk/stress-testing/2022/results-of-the-2021-climate-biennial-exploratory-scenario

Bank of England. (2023). *Working at the Bank an Introduction One Bank*. Available at https://www.bankofengland.co.uk/-/media/boe/files/careers/workingatthebank.pdf

Bank of International Settlement. (2009). *Issues in the Governance of Central Banks: A report from the Central Bank Governance Group* available at https://www.bis.org/publ/othp04.pdf

Barmes, D., & Dikau, S. (2024). Rethinking inflation in times of environmental instability. *LSE-GRI Commentary* (14 February, 2024), at https://www.lse.ac.uk/granthaminstitute/news/rethinking-inflation-in-times-of-environmental-instability/?mc_cid=ff6afa2fda&mc_eid=c44a763982

Baron, J., & Hannan, M. (1994). The impact of economics on contemporary sociology. *Journal of Economic Literature, 32*(3), 1111–1146.

Barrett, R. (1998). *Cultural capital: The new frontier of competitive advantage*. Butterworth-Heinemann.

Beckmann, J., Gern, K.-J., Jannsen, N., & Sonnenberg, N. (2023). Climate change and monetary policy in the Euro Area. *Monetary Policy Dialogues* at https://www.europarl.europa.eu/RegData/etudes/STUD/2023/747833/IPOL_STU(2023)747833_EN.pdf

Boldizzoni, F. (2008). *Means and ends: The idea of Capital in the West, 1500–1970*. Palgrave Macmillan.

Bolton, P., Despres, M., Pereira Da Silva, L. A., Samama, F., & Svartzman, R. (2020). *The green swan: Central banking and financial stability in the age of climate change*. Bank for International Settlements.

Bovenschen, W., & Lieshout, R. (2020). EU taxonomy, Action Plan & Supervisory Developments on sustainable finance: What uses may these have for the E(S)CB? *2020 ESCB Legal Conference.*

Bowman, M. (2022). *Regulatory leadership for a net zero transition: Central banks and Financial regulators: Levers and limits* (King's College London, September), 60 pp.

Broeders, D., & Schlooz, M. (2021). Climate change uncertainty and Central Bank risk management. *Journal of Risk Management in Financial Institutions, 14*(2), 121–130.

Campiglio, E., Dafermos, Y., Monnin, P., RyanCollins, J., Schotten, G., & Tanaka, M. (2018). Finance and climate change: What role for central banks and financial regulators? *Nature Climate Change, 8*, 462–468.

Carney, M. (2015). *Breaking the tragedy of the horizon—Climate change and Financial stability*, Speech given at Lloyd's of London (Bank of England, 29 September 2015).

Carney, M. (2019). Governor of the Bank of England In conversation with... Mark Carney, Governor of the Bank of England. *Civil Service Quarterly*. 13 February 2019.

Costa, M. (2024). BoE trims back work on climate change. *Green Central Banking* (26 February 2024). https://greencentralbanking.com/2024/02/26/bank-of-england-trims-back-climate-change/?utm_source=linkedin&utm_medium=social&utm_campaign=news

Dafermos, Y. (2021). How Should Central Banks respond to the climate crisis? *SOAS* online (10 May).

de Arriba-Sellier, N. (2021). Turning gold into green: Green finance in the mandate of European Financial supervision. *Common Market Law Review, 58*(4), 1097–1140.

de Boer, N., & van 't Klooster, J. (2021). The ECB's neglected secondary mandate: An inter-institutional solution. *Positive Money Europe* (October).

Deyris, J. (2023). Too green to be true? Forging a climate consensus at the European Central Bank. *New Political Economy, 713*, 713.

Dikau, S., & Volz, U. (2021). Analysis: Central Bank mandates, sustainability objectives and the promotion of green finance. *Ecological Economics, 184*(2021), 107022.

DiLeo, M. (2023). Climate policy at the Bank of England: The possibilities and limits of green central banking. *Climate Policy, 23*(6), 671.

DNB. (n.d.). 'Mission and Tasks' at https://www.dnb.nl/en/about-us/mission-and-tasks/

ECB. (2024). *Climate and Nature Plan 2024–2025—Annex: Our Roadmap*, at https://www.ecb.europa.eu/press/pr/date/2024/html/ecb.pr240130_annex~b239ad1c2e.en.pdf

Elderson, F. (2018). Commentary: From Mission to Supervision: Putting sustainable prosperity on the agenda of the Dutch Central Bank (4 July) *LSE Grantham Research Institute* at https://www.lse.ac.uk/granthaminstitute/news/from-mission-to-supervision-putting-sustainable-prosperity-on-the-agenda-of-the-dutch-central-bank/

Ellson, T. (2004). *Culture and positioning as determinants of strategy personality and the business organization*. Palgrave Macmillan.

Eurofound. (2021). *Distributional impacts of climate policies in Europe* (Publications Office of the European Union, Luxembourg) at https://www.eurofound.europa.eu/en/publications/2021/distributional-impacts-climate-policies-europe

FCA. (2020). *Transforming culture in financial services—Driving purposeful cultures DP 20/1*. https://www.fca.org.uk/publications/discussion-papers/dp20-1-transforming-culture-financial-services-driving-purposeful-cultures

FCA. (2023). *Culture and Governance*. https://www.fca.org.uk/firms/culture-and-governance

Fiorino, D. (1990). Citizen participation and Environmental risk: A survey of institutional mechanisms. *Science, Technology and Human Values, 15*(2), 226.

Frisell, L. (2008). Governing the Governor: A clinical study of Central Banks. *Sveriges Riksbank Working Paper Series 22* at https://www.econstor.eu/bitstream/10419/81899/1/559756674.pdf

Goldin, C. (2016). Human Capital. In *Handbook of cliometrics* (pp. 55–86). Springer.

Hauser, A. (2021). *Speech: From Lender of Last Resort to Market Maker of Last Resort via the dash for cash: why central banks need new tools for dealing with market dysfunction* (Bank of England, 7 January 2021). https://www.bankofengland.co.uk/-/media/boe/files/speech/2021/january/why-central-banks-need-new-tools-for-dealing-with-market-dysfunction-speech-by-andrew-hauser.pdf

HM Treasury. (2021). *Remit for the Monetary Policy Committee (MPC)* (3 March).

HM Treasury. (2023). *Remit and Recommendations for the Financial Policy Committee.*https://assets.publishing.service.gov.uk/media/655cad7d544aea000dfb31c2/Financial_Policy_Committee_Remit_and_Recommendations_-_Autumn_Statement_2023.pdf

HM Treasury. (2024). *Remit and Recommendations for the Financial Policy Committee (FPC)* (14 November 2024), https://assets.publishing.service.gov.uk/media/6737146da1972150bf3e5d3e/FPC_Remit_2024_-_FINAL.pdf

House of Lords. (2023). *Making an independent Bank of England work better* 1st Report of Session 2022/23 HL Paper 10.

Hunt, J., Littlewood, D., & Thompson, B. (2003). *Developing participatory consultation – a review from four experimental dialogue processes* (Centre for the Study of Environmental Change, Lancaster University, England).

Hurley, M. (2022). Climate change the ultimate systemic risk says BOE. *Environmental Finance* (online) (3 May).

Intergovernmental Panel on Climate Change (IPCC). (2022). IPCC sixth assessment report: Climate change 2022: Impacts, adaptation and vulnerability (IPCC).

Keller, A. (2020). *Legal foundations of macroprudential policy: An interdisciplinary approach*. Intersentia.

Keller, A., & Kokkinis, A. (2022). The senior managers and certification regime in financial firms: An organisational culture analysis. *Journal of Corporate Law Studies, 22*(1), 299–334.

Makhlouf, G. (2022). Social Capital and Central Banks (13 April), *Central Bank of Ireland*, at https://www.centralbank.ie/news-media/press-releases/blog-social-capital-and-central-banks

Manning, M., Sachs, L., Smolenska, A., Bowman, M., Stewart, F., Knaack, P., & Toledano, P. (2024). Towards an integrated transition planning ecosystem (T20 Policy Brief: TF02, Subtopic 1 *Fostering Sustainable, Inclusive, and Just Energy Transitions*, 2.1.7). https://t20brasil.org/media/filemanager/T20%20Brasil_%20TF02%20Accepted%20Policy%20Briefs.pdf

Momani, B., & Manad, S. (2015). Best practices in central Bank organizational culture, learning and structure: The case of the Moroccan central Bank. *Economic Notes by Banca Monte dei Paschi di Siena SpA, 44*(3), 449–481.

New Financial. (2020). *Diversity from a Central Bank perspective: A case study of the Bank of England* at https://newfinancial.org/wp-content/uploads/2020/01/A-case-study-The-Bank-of-Englands-approach-to-Diversity.pdf

NGFS. (2021). *Adapting Central Bank Operations to a Hotter World Reviewing some options.* https://www.ngfs.net/sites/default/files/media/2021/06/17/ngfs_monetary_policy_operations_final.pdf

NGFS. (n.d.). 'Governance', at https://www.ngfs.net/en/page-sommaire/governance

Peterson, M., & Spencer, M. (1990). Understanding academic culture and climate. In B. Miller (Ed.), *The evolution of diversity, equity and inclusion new directions for institutional research 68* (pp. 3–18). Wiley.

Riles, A. (2018). The culture of central banking financial citizenship: Experts, publics, and the politics of Central Banking. In: Riles A (d) *Financial citizenship* (pp. 22–34). Cornell University Press.

Rowland, D. (2023). Speech: The Importance of Enhanced Diversity and Inclusion within the Financial Services Sector (Central Bank of Ireland, 10 March), at https://www.centralbank.ie/news/article/diversity-and-inclusion-within-the-financial-services-sector-remarks-by-deputy-governor-derville-rowland-at-walkers-ireland

Sanchez, S., Munoz, M., & Lupez-Guzman, T. (2007). Organizational culture and intellectual capital: A new model. *Journal of Intellectual Capital, 8*(3), 409–430.

Schein, E. (2016). *Organizational culture and leadership* (5th ed.). Wiley.

Schnabel, I. (2023). Speech: Monetary and Financial Stability—Can they be separated? (19 May), *European Central Bank,* at https://www.ecb.europa.eu/press/key/date/2023/html/ecb.sp230519~de2f790b1c.en.html

Schoenmaker, D. (2023). Low-Carbon Allocation in the Implementation of Monetary Policy. *Monetary Papers Dialogue* at https://www.europarl.europa.eu/RegData/etudes/STUD/2023/747833/IPOL_STU(2023)747833_EN.pdf

Siehl, C., & Martin, J. (1982). *Learning organizational culture.* School of Business Stanford University Research Paper: 654.

Solana, J. (2019). The power of the Eurosystem to promote Environmental protection. *European Business Law Review, 30*(4), 547–575.

Solow, R. (1999). Notes on social capital and economic performance. In P. Dasgupta & I. Serageldin (Eds.), *Social capital: A multifaceted perspective* (pp. 6–12). The World Bank.

Spicer, A., Lindley, D., Gond, J.-P., et al. (2016). *Cultural change in the FCA, PRA Bank of England: Practising what they preach?* New City Agenda/Cass Business School. https://openaccess.city.ac.uk/id/eprint/18758/

Tooze, A. (2018). *Crashed: How a decade of financial crises changed the world* (Viking).

UK Environmental Audit Committee. (2021). 'Appendix: Correspondence with the Bank of England' in *Growing Back Better: Putting nature and net zero at the heart of the economic recovery* (17 February), at https://publications.parliament.uk/pa/cm5801/cmselect/cmenvaud/347/34709.htm#_idTextAnchor153

UK Parliament. (2023a). *Appendix 3: Overview of the Bank of England's remit*, at https://publications.parliament.uk/pa/ld5804/ldselect/ldeconaf/10/1012.htm

UK Parliament. (2023b). *Inquiry: Bank of England: How is independence working?* Available at https://committees.parliament.uk/work/7356/bank-of-england-how-is-independence-working/publications/

van 't Klooster, J., & de Boer, N. (2023). What to do with the ECB's secondary mandate? *Journal of Common Market Studies, 61*(3), 730–746.
Wessels, P., & Broeders, D. (2022). *On the capitalisation of central banks* (De Nederlandsche Bank N.V., Occasional Studies Volume 20 – 4).

Open Access This chapter is licensed under the terms of the Creative Commons Attribution 4.0 International License (http://creativecommons.org/licenses/by/4.0/), which permits use, sharing, adaptation, distribution and reproduction in any medium or format, as long as you give appropriate credit to the original author(s) and the source, provide a link to the Creative Commons license and indicate if changes were made.

The images or other third party material in this chapter are included in the chapter's Creative Commons license, unless indicated otherwise in a credit line to the material. If material is not included in the chapter's Creative Commons license and your intended use is not permitted by statutory regulation or exceeds the permitted use, you will need to obtain permission directly from the copyright holder.

Index

A
Accounting policies, 61–92
Asset purchase programs, 36, 48, 96, 115, 116, 119, 121, 128, 130–132, 134, 150, 158, 169, 171, 174, 175, 177, 194

B
Bank of England (BoE), 4, 5, 8–10, 12, 23, 28–29, 33, 65, 77, 87, 97–101, 104, 108, 110–114, 116, 122, 154–157, 169, 174, 177, 178, 181–183, 192, 193, 216, 253, 256, 297, 298, 301–303, 306, 307

C
Capital adequacy, x, ix, 3–42, 126, 282
Capital policy, 123, 127, 129, 132–134, 137–142, 150–159, 187–212
Central bank, 3, 45, 62, 96, 126, 167, 188, 216, 250, 276, 296
Central bank accounting, 61–92, 181
Central bank balance sheet, xi, ix, 5, 49, 58, 74, 98–100, 102, 109, 119, 121, 130–132, 167–184, 188, 192, 196, 204, 236, 251, 252, 254–260, 263, 264, 266–270
Central bank capital, ix–xiv, 3–42, 45–58, 62, 65, 71, 97, 98, 125–162, 187–212, 215–270, 289–291, 295–310
Central bank digital currencies (CBDCs), ix, xii, xiii, 11, 58, 249–270
Central bank independence, xi, 40–41, 64, 68, 78, 85, 87, 129, 152, 208, 215–246, 251
Central banking, 126, 158, 306, 308
Central bank legal mandate, 295–310
Central bank losses, x–xii, 5, 7, 22, 24–41, 48, 65, 68, 72, 77, 78, 86, 95–122, 128, 180–183, 189, 190, 202, 208, 289, 292
Central bank profitability, xi, xii, 67–73, 77, 249–270
Central bank recapitalization, 219, 233–245
Central bank solvency, 5, 6, 8, 22, 23, 41, 50, 98, 251
Climate change, ix, xiv, xii, 40, 276, 283–285, 296, 297, 300–309
Consolidated balance sheet, 38, 39, 99, 103, 104, 106, 108, 111, 128, 218, 267
Contingent claim analysis, 138, 158

D
Deferred asset, 7, 9, 31–37, 81, 86, 89, 114, 115, 122, 133, 155, 157, 182
Dividend, 29, 61, 126, 180, 234, 267
DSGE model, xii, 189, 197

E
European Central Bank (ECB), x, 5, 7–10, 12, 22, 25–27, 29, 33, 35–40, 66, 68, 87, 88, 96, 114, 119, 126, 131, 132, 171, 180–182, 193, 195, 205, 216,

© The Author(s) 2025

D. Broeders et al. (eds.), *Central Bank Capital in Turbulent Times*, Contributions to Finance and Accounting,
https://doi.org/10.1007/978-3-031-73549-3

218, 224, 250–254, 258, 259, 261, 264, 265, 267–269, 282, 286, 287, 289, 296, 298–301, 308

F

Fair value, xi, 5, 8, 9, 12, 24, 34, 36, 38, 39, 41, 49, 63, 64, 66, 67, 70, 72–74, 78, 80, 88, 90, 99, 106, 108, 122, 180, 181, 183
Federal Reserve, 32, 66, 82, 86, 96, 97, 99, 100, 104, 108–110, 114–116, 120, 122, 133, 157, 169–171, 182, 183, 188, 193, 256, 258, 259, 265, 266
Fiat money, 5, 6, 41, 46, 52, 54, 55, 57, 58
Financial stability, ix–xiv, 7, 8, 22, 23, 28, 32–35, 40–42, 155, 158, 184, 189, 202, 204, 205, 209, 216, 227, 228, 230, 246, 251, 253, 261, 264, 265, 275–292, 296, 297, 300–303, 308, 310
Fiscal sustainability, 55

G

Gold, 6, 9, 11, 25, 27, 36, 37, 53, 225, 228, 234, 236, 237
Governing council, 36, 38, 220–224, 229, 230, 232, 250

I

Inflation target, 25, 26, 28, 98, 188, 200, 218, 220, 223, 237
Insolvency, x, 5–7, 10, 22, 27–30, 32, 34, 37, 39–42, 50, 98, 99, 127, 128, 140, 173, 207, 250

L

Large-scale asset purchases, xi, ix, 48, 96, 100, 105, 116, 120, 131, 195, 197, 219, 296
Lender of last resort (LOLR), xii, 4, 40, 130, 168, 172–174, 177, 224, 275–292

M

Market maker of last resort (MMLR), 4, 40, 168, 170, 174, 177
Monetary policy, xi, ix, xiv, xiii, 9, 10, 22, 28, 32, 33, 36, 38, 40, 42, 48, 62, 64, 85–88, 90, 99, 111, 114, 118, 126–130, 132, 133, 138, 150, 155, 157–159, 181, 184, 188, 190, 193, 198, 208, 216, 222, 228, 230, 236, 237, 250, 251, 253, 255–265, 267, 269, 270, 290, 296, 298–302, 308
Monetary stability, 47, 58
Money, x, ix, xii, 5, 6, 11, 14, 15, 20, 22, 23, 25, 27–30, 32, 34, 38, 39, 41, 45–58, 77, 78, 96, 97, 109, 129, 134, 141, 148, 149, 156, 175, 192, 223, 250–253, 257, 258, 269, 292

N

Negative carry, 106, 107, 111, 113

O

Open market operations, 130

P

Pandemic-era last-resort policy interventions, 168
Provisions, 30, 33, 35, 36, 38, 39, 50, 58, 62–64, 66–68, 70, 72, 73, 77, 78, 80, 81, 85–90, 173, 181, 191, 206, 207, 209, 229, 235, 266–268, 299

Q

Quantitative easing (QE), ix, xi, xii, 4, 10, 28, 33, 74, 77, 78, 87, 99, 115, 121, 126, 128, 131, 168, 169, 177–180, 183, 187–212, 236, 237, 240, 241, 265, 270, 299

R

Radical uncertainty, xiv
Recapitalization, 7, 50, 68, 98, 126, 191, 217, 291
Revaluation accounts, 10, 27, 36–38, 49, 156, 220, 223, 228, 231, 233, 235, 237, 240, 244, 267
Risk management, ix–xii, 150, 158, 249, 266, 277, 284, 290, 307
Risk provision, 50, 62–64, 66–68, 70, 72, 73, 77, 78, 80, 81, 85, 87–90, 207, 267, 268

S

Seigniorage, x, 4, 7, 8, 11, 14–16, 21–24, 32–34, 37, 40–42, 49, 50, 58, 62, 77,

102, 104, 108–110, 120, 128, 131, 141, 142, 155, 159, 206, 210, 217, 219, 224, 226, 228, 231, 232, 246, 252–254, 262, 267, 268
Sequential games, 144
Shareholders, xi, 27, 32, 35, 37, 40, 81, 85, 125–162, 208, 267, 269, 270, 289
Social capital, 297
Soft capital, xiv, xiii, 296–298, 304, 309, 310
Swiss National Bank (SNB), 4, 5, 8, 9, 26–27, 66, 67, 77, 82, 85, 90, 98, 101, 117, 118, 122, 181, 184, 205, 218

T
Transition risk, xiv, 276, 279, 283, 286, 287, 291, 306
Trust, xiv, xiii, 45–58, 86, 134, 140, 305, 306, 308

U
Uncertainty, xiv, 129, 169, 174, 195, 232–234, 242, 243, 246, 270, 280, 284, 285, 287
Unrealised losses, 258

V
Vega, 148, 149

GPSR Compliance
The European Union's (EU) General Product Safety Regulation (GPSR) is a set of rules that requires consumer products to be safe and our obligations to ensure this.

If you have any concerns about our products, you can contact us on

ProductSafety@springernature.com

In case Publisher is established outside the EU, the EU authorized representative is:

Springer Nature Customer Service Center GmbH
Europaplatz 3
69115 Heidelberg, Germany

www.ingramcontent.com/pod-product-compliance
Lightning Source LLC
Chambersburg PA
CBHW071912040825
30594CB00003B/52
* 9 7 8 3 0 3 1 7 3 5 4 8 6 *